Longman Criminology Series

Series Editor: Tim Newburn

Titles in the series:

Victims and Victimology: Research, Policy and Practice

Jo Goodey

PEARSON
Longman

Harlow, England • London • New York • Boston • San Francisco • Toronto
Sydney • Tokyo • Singapore • Hong Kong • Seoul • Taipei • New Delhi
Cape Town • Madrid • Mexico City • Amsterdam • Munich • Paris • Milan

For Ernsto and Polly, with love

Pearson Education Limited
Edinburgh Gate
Harlow
Essex CM20 2JE
England

and Associated Companies throughout the world

Visit us on the World Wide Web at:
www.pearsoned.co.uk

First published 2005

ISBN 0582 43779 2

British Library Cataloguing-in-Publication Data
A catalogue record for this book is available from the British Library

Library of Congress Cataloging-in-Publication Data
A catalog record for this book is available from the Library of Congress

10 9 8 7 6 5 4 3 2 1
09 08 07 06 05

Typeset in 10/12pt New Baskerville by 35
Printed in Great Britain by Henry Ling Ltd., at the Dorset Press,
Dorchester, Dorset

The publisher's policy is to use paper manufactured from sustainable forests.

Contents

Series editor's preface

Our society appears to be increasingly preoccupied with crime and with criminal justice. Despite increasing affluence in the postwar period, crime has generally continued to rise – often at an alarming rate. Moreover, the rate of general social change at the beginning of the twenty first century is extraordinary, leaving many feeling insecure. High rates of crime, high levels of fear of crime, and no simple solutions in sight, have helped to keep criminal justice high on the political agenda.

Partly reflecting this state of affairs, the study of crime and criminal justice is burgeoning. There are now a large number of well-established postgraduate courses, new ones starting all the time, and undergraduate criminology and criminal justice degrees are also now appearing regularly. Though increasing numbers of individual textbooks are being written and published, the breadth of criminology makes the subject difficult to encompass in a satisfactory manner within a single text.

The aim of this series is, as a whole, to provide a broad and thorough introduction to criminology. Each book covers a particular area of the subject, takes the reader through the key debates, considers both policy and politics and, where appropriate, also looks at likely future developments in the area. The aim is that each text should be theoretically informed, accessibly written, attractively produced, competitively priced, with a full guide to further reading for students wishing to pursue the subject. Whilst each book in the series is designed to be read as an introduction to one particular area, the Longman Criminology Series has also been designed with overall coherence in mind.

As Jo Goodey notes, in recent times 'victims' have come increasingly to play a central role in debates about crime and its control. In part this, as she argues, is undoubtedly because of the success that victimisation surveys such as the British Crime Survey have had in increasing our knowledge and understanding of the extent and impact of crime. Undoubtedly, it is also a consequence of the highly politicised context in which debates about 'law and order' now take place. There are many dangers here –

not least the increasing punitive populism associated with single-issue victims' movements in other countries (though not quite yet, the UK) in which justice is presented as a 'zero sum' game in which, for example, supporting defendants' rights is presented as being 'anti-victim'.

Jo Goodey steers the reader through theoretical, empirical and political debates, providing a rich, comparative guide to victimology, and to current trends and developments in criminal justice and penal policy. Notably in this regard she focuses her critical attention on arguably the most powerful of recent developments in this field: restorative justice. The impetus behind the spread of restorative justice has been incredibly strong. Critics are few and far between and there is a danger that what often borders on uncritical acceptance will eventually turn to cynicism if the empirical evidence is anything less than hugely positive. Jo Goodey's sympathetic but critical treatment of restorative justice initiatives, and in particular their claim to provide for victims' needs, is especially welcome.

Until relatively recently students of criminology could easily have survived without reading about, or making much reference to, victims and victimology. Happily, this is no longer the case. There is now a rich and growing literature in this area, and policy developments are legion. Jo Goodey provides a thorough guide to what is fast becoming one of the most prominent areas of debate and discussion in criminal justice and penal policy. It will be an indispensable volume for students, teachers and researchers in this field.

Tim Newburn
London, September 2004

Acknowledgements

I would like to thank Jim Dignan, Jan van Dijk and Brian Williams for their helpful comments on draft chapters. Their willingness to devote time, often at short notice, to read material and provide useful inputs is greatly appreciated. I would also like to thank the Max Planck Institute for Foreign and International Criminal Law in Freiburg for having provided me with both the opportunity and the funding to undertake research using the Institute's excellent library facilities. Elizabeth Joyce of the United Nations (UN) Global Programme Against Money Laundering provided me with some useful material on white-collar crime/money laundering that otherwise I would not have easily come by – my thanks to her for this, and for her encouragement and support as a friend. Adam Crawford also deserves a mention for having suggested that I write this book in the first place, and for having put me in contact with the publishers. My thanks too to Michelle Gallagher at Pearson Education for her patient work as I approached completion of the manuscript.

My attendance at different World Society of Victimology symposia, since Adelaide in 1994, stirred my interest in the subject of 'victims and victimology', and my period as a Research Fellow at the UN Office on Drugs and Crime, in Vienna, gave me the chance to attend meetings and approach victim-related work that would have eluded me from the confines of academia. For this I must thank the European Commission for having funded my fellowship and the UN for having hosted me.

Much of this book was written as I commuted between Vienna and Brussels every other week. Under these circumstances, and without proper childcare, I was only able to complete the work thanks to my parents, Richard and Patricia Goodey, and their Austrian counterparts, Ernst and Johanna Gesslbauer, who were able and all too willing to look after their grandchild – many thanks! And last but not least, I would like to thank Ernsto for his support and understanding, and for much more besides – thank you.

Author details

Jo Goodey works for the European Commission (EC) at the Vienna-based European Monitoring Centre on Racism and Xenophobia.[1] From 2000 to 2003 she worked as an EC-funded Marie Curie Research Fellow at the United Nations in Vienna. Before that she was lecturer in criminology at the University of Leeds, and prior to that at the University of Sheffield. She has also worked as a consultant for the UN's International Narcotics Control Board. Her publications include a co-edited book with Adam Crawford on *Integrating a Victim Perspective within Criminal Justice* (2000), and many journal articles and book chapters on a range of victim-related research.

Note

1. The opinions of the author expressed in this book do not represent those of the European Monitoring Centre on Racism and Xenophobia.

Introduction

Most of us do not experience crime as criminals but as victims, and more generally as something that affects our lives as a sense of unease, and as part of a range of insecurities. Yet although criminal victimisation and 'fear of crime' are a pervasive part of many people's lives, the study of victims, through the criminological sub-discipline of victimology, has not enjoyed the same status as criminological research, policy and practice on crime and criminals.

This book documents and critiques selected themes in victim-centred research, policy and practice, and in the process explores some of the reasons for the neglect and recent upsurge in victim-centred criminal justice. But before outlining the book's central themes, this introduction briefly maps where victims have emerged from to become the group that, today, is enjoying extensive attention from criminal justice policy and practice.

Understanding the 'place' of victims

If a timeline were drawn to mark the arrival of significant criminal justice developments over the last few decades, in Britain and other developed countries there would be few victim-centred initiatives until the last quarter of the twentieth century. In the decades following the Second World War, early research on the aetiology and characteristics of victimisation was in the hands of a few scholars (von Hentig, 1948; Mendelsohn, 1956; Rock, 1994; Wolfgang, 1957, 1958), and practical and policy initiatives for victims were few and far between; 1964 marking the arrival of Britain's State compensation scheme for victims of violent crime.

It was with the unabated increase in the crime rate in the latter half of the twentieth century that academics, policy makers and practitioners began to take more notice of victims' plight as the forgotten actors in criminal justice. At the same time, and echoing developments on a broader canvas in relation to feminism and the civil rights movement, the politicisation of victim issues emerged in recognition of the abuse encountered by vulnerable social groups such as women, children and, latterly, ethnic minorities. But these social movements were quite different from the single-issue victims' groups that developed in the 1980s/1990s, particularly in North America. While the former looked at the causes of abuse and injustice, the latter concentrated on criminal justice reform and political lobbying with respect to particular victim groups and their families, such as victims of murder and manslaughter. In the increasing climate of retributive justice since the 1970s, victims were often misused as the emotive tool for meting out severe sentences as governments appealed to populist demands for tough action against criminals (Sarat, 1997). But Britain largely sidestepped the influence of single-issue victims' groups as a less politicised response to victims emerged in the form of the nationwide charity Victim Support.

Arguably it was in the 1980s, with the British government's adoption of the crime/victim survey, that victims entered centre-stage on the criminological scene. These surveys, as a means of quantifying crimes other than through official police statistics, revealed the extent and nature of hitherto unrecorded crime, and also introduced intriguing revelations about people's 'fear of crime'. Yet the crime/victim survey did not emerge as a victim-centred initiative. Rather, it came about as a reaction to rising crime rates and the need for a politically astute response, in North America and also in Britain, to be seen to be 'doing something' about crime. Without actually reducing victimisation, but with its recognition of victims, the crime/victim survey, at least in the hands of governments, was heralded as part of a tough law and order response to offending and social disorder. At the same time, feminist calls for recognition of violence against women, in both the public and private domain (the 'street' and the 'home'), and often as part of a lifetime of abuse, challenged central government's focus on crime as single events, committed by unknown offenders, against property and person.

The victim survey also reflected the growth in 'administrative' criminology during the 1980s, with its remit to audit crime and the performance of individual criminal justice agencies. In an age where increasing importance was given to meeting 'service standards' for 'consumers' of public services – be these victims or hospital patients – customer satisfaction became a driving force in both the rhetoric and practical action adopted by public and private organisations. Outputs (such as the number of victims assisted) and, to a lesser extent, outcomes (the satisfaction of victims with service delivery) became commonplace barometers of victim services. These ideas have been carried over to the present day, with other measures of criminal justice initiatives introduced through reference to the private sector's 'managerialist' tenets of efficiency, economy and effectiveness.

As adversarial criminal justice increasingly came under fire for its insensitive treatment of victims, that frequently served as the cause of their 'secondary victimisation', so established criminal justice standards were critiqued for their failure to meet victims' needs (Ash, 1972; Christie, 1977). In Britain, the development of victim-centred justice has focused on meeting victims' needs through service provision. But increased calls for victim-centred justice came up against objections from the criminal justice establishment that promotion of victims' needs, let alone rights, would be at the expense of defendants' rights. A debate sprang up which unhelpfully constructed criminal justice responses to victims as a dichotomised choice between, on the one hand, service standards versus legal provisions, and, on the other, defendants' rights versus victims' rights. In reality, British developments in victim-centred justice have melded service standards with recognition of victims' rights, in an effort to provide equitable justice for victims and offenders.

As this brief and selective 'history' of victim-centred developments in criminal justice shows, a combination of factors coalesced in the 1980s and 1990s to promote so-called victim-centred justice, including: rising crime rates and means of measuring them; the need for government to be seen to be responsive to victims; the emergence of criminal justice as service provider; accountability of individual agencies to their 'users'; and the rise of an audit culture to measure agencies' outputs. At the same time as policy makers and practitioners were beginning to acknowledge victims as central players in criminal justice, academics were reacting to these developments by researching and publishing work on victims. The extent to which research informed policy or was itself informed by policy during this period is difficult to gauge. But key publications testify to the parallel development of research, policy and practice on victims in the 1980s/1990s (Lurigio et al., 1990; van Dijk, 1985; Viano, 1989) and the advances made in empirical academic research on victims both in Britain (Maguire and Pointing, 1988; Shapland et al., 1985) and abroad (Kaiser et al., 1991; Singh Makkar and Friday, 1995).

Critical commentators, largely from academia, have come to question the extent to which many so-called victim-centred initiatives can be considered 'victim-centred'. Many criminal justice initiatives that supposedly have victims in mind do not often ask victims directly about their satisfaction with the services provided: an accusation that has been levelled at restorative justice as the most recent manifestation of a criminal justice 'movement' that supposedly has victims at its heart (Daly, 2002). In turn, any suggestion that justice has swung too far in favour of victims, at the expense of defendants/offenders, can be rejected for its narrow and negative reading of 'victim-centred' as 'anti-offender'. Improvements in criminal justice responses to victims should not be assessed on the basis of either/or models of justice as offender-centred or victim-centred, as retributive versus restorative, or as 'traditional' versus 'new'. As van Dijk suggested (1985: 20): 'The ideal package of victim services seems to be a mixture of community-based care provision and a less bureaucratic criminal justice system' – in other words, a system that can incorporate aspects of a refined traditional justice with elements of service-based and/ or restorative justice principles. What we currently have is a traditional retributive justice model that is on the cusp of adopting aspects of a hybrid model in recognition of victims' 'place' in criminal justice.

Themes for discussion

Although victims used to be described as the 'forgotten actors' in criminal justice, they are now at the heart of criminal justice considerations for policy reform. The content of this book reflects the broad sweep that is encompassed by contemporary research on, and political and practical responses to, crime victims. Drawing on significant developments in recent years, the book takes established and emergent themes in the field of victim-centred research, policy and practice, and moulds them into eight chapters. Each chapter focuses on a particular theme and employs in-depth case studies to illustrate some of the arguments in connection with its chosen theme. While the book looks mainly at examples from England and Wales, developments in other countries illustrate the 'place' of crime victims, and the sub-discipline of victimology, as part of a global push towards recognition of, and improved criminal justice responses to, crime victims. The chapters also point to important national and international legal instruments and practice 'gold standards' that have put victims increasingly at the centre of criminal justice developments.

To this end, Chapter 1 introduces some of the dynamics behind the current focus on crime victims by criminal justice agencies. The increasing significance given over to crime and victimisation is briefly contextualised with respect to ideas about risk, insecurity and globalisation, which in turn are set against the particular British experience of new modes of governance. Turning to recent examples of well-publicised sex crimes against, most notably, children, the chapter explores popular calls for retributive justice, and sets these against dominant criminal justice models that are frequently played off against each other as victim-centred or offender-centred.

Having set the scene with respect to some of the debates and reasons behind the current growth in victim-centred justice, the next two chapters focus on the extent and nature of victimisation, and its related components of fear and vulnerability. Chapter 2 explains what we know about victimisation, the methods employed in gaining this information, and the limitations of what we know and how we come to know about it. Sources of information on victimisation are addressed from the crime/victim survey and police recorded crime statistics, through to contributions from feminism and geography. The chapter focuses on repeat victimisation as an innovative and under-utilised tool for understanding the extent, nature and causes of victimisation. Chapter 3 charts what was a dominant theme in 1980s'/early 1990s' victim-centred research, policy and practice – namely, 'fear of crime'. The term is explored and critiqued for what it does and does not tell us about 'fear' as an expression of vulnerability. In turn, the idea of 'vulnerability' is approached and critically assessed with respect to some of the theoretical propositions that set out to explain an individual's likelihood of becoming a victim. Focusing on male fear of crime and vulnerability, the chapter turns some of the long-held assumptions about appropriate fear and fearlessness on their head.

Chapter 4 revisits some of the themes addressed in Chapter 1 to analyse the frequently contrasting paths adopted by academic victimology and victim advocacy in their response to 'victimhood'. Dominant influences in academic victimology and victim advocacy are mapped out as a prelude to understanding the links and, in particular, unexplored synergies between academic victimology, victim advocacy and social policy in the promotion of victim-centred justice. In response to this critique, the chapter tentatively proposes a means for improving social policy responses to crime victims through application of 'good practice' principles. The term 'good practice' is itself evaluated as the chapter suggests how practice standards can be transferred between contexts, and how, importantly, victims can play a more central role in the assessment of practice initiatives that purport to be 'victim-centred'.

Chapters 5 and 6 move the discussion on to the subject of victims' concrete 'needs' with respect to service provision, and the appropriate circumstances and means under which these can become substantive rights. In Chapter 5, examples of recent government initiatives are set alongside international standard-bearers for victims to illustrate the gap between the theory and practice of law. The discussion is grounded in policy developments that encompass broader considerations regarding 'rights and responsibilities', citizenship, and the victim as 'consumer' of services. A detailed case study of State compensation to victims of violent crime is inserted at the end of the chapter to probe how and why compensation emerged as a key government response to victims' apparent needs. The limitations of State compensation are assessed and set against examples from other countries, including the specific example of compensating victims' families in the aftermath of the terrorist attacks of 11 September 2001 in the USA.

Chapter 6 continues the theme of victims' rights by centring its discussion on the need to balance victims' and offenders' rights. Taking on the accusation that 'victim-centred' justice is to the detriment of 'due process' in law for defendants, the chapter examines how justice can be balanced for victims and defendants/offenders. The adversarial nature of British justice forms the backdrop to the chapter's account of recent developments in criminal justice that seek to serve victims. Particular attention is paid to the influence of the European Convention on Human

Rights on developments in British criminal justice with respect to victim and offender rights. The chapter employs two cases studies – on 'victim statements' and 'victim contact work' – to sketch out some of the problems encountered, for both victims and offenders, when attempts are made to enhance victims' rights.

From here, Chapter 7 offers an introduction to and critique of 'restorative justice' as an alternative to traditional justice, and for its claims to balance the needs and rights of victims and offenders. The chapter outlines what is meant by restorative justice and its resonance with earlier periods of justice. Early mediation initiatives in North America and Britain are outlined and evaluated as 'restorative' practices. In turn, examples from New Zealand and Britain of 'conferencing', as another take on restorative justice, are outlined and set alongside ideas about 'reintegrative shaming' as the theory behind some core restorative ideals. The chapter concludes with a discussion of the promises and limitations offered by restorative justice as a possible paradigm shift in criminal justice, and of the suggestion that restorative justice meets victims' needs as central players in the resolution of their own conflicts.

Finally, the book ends with an insight into some areas of victim-centred research, policy and practice that can be described as neglected or emergent. Chapter 8 recalls arguments developed in Chapters 2 and 3 with respect to 'who' and 'what' can be considered legitimate areas for victimological research and policy intervention. The chapter also echoes ideas expressed in Chapter 1 with respect to the place and time of victimisation, and the need to contextualise certain experiences of victimisation as local realities that are usefully interpreted as part of a globalised criminal phenomenon. Herein, the chapter also engages with globalised constructions of a transnational criminal threat, and the criminalisation of 'outsiders', which neglect to address its counterpart in the form of marginalised and vulnerable 'outsiders' who are often victims of transnational crime and internal criminal markets. The chapter turns to the example of trafficking in women for sexual exploitation, and explores recent research, policy interventions and practices that have brought this crime to prominence at a global level, and that set out to combat trafficking and intervene on behalf of victims. Finally, the chapter explores various streams of white-collar crime, as the ultimate 'victimless' crime, through an analysis of policy responses to fraud, money laundering, capital flight and corruption.

Established and emergent themes

From established to emergent themes in victim-centred research, policy and practice, the book sketches a varied picture of some of the most important developments in recent decades and in the last few years. Yet, like any publication, the book is a product of its time, and so, in its discussion of academic debates and policy responses, reflects the dominant thrust of current critiques in the first decade of the twenty-first century. In this respect, Chapter 7 is given over to one of the most hotly promoted and contested areas in current victim-centred research, policy and practice – restorative justice – and Chapter 8 explores 'new' victim avenues that have recently come to prominence on a global stage, while Chapter 3 focuses on what was arguably the 'hot topic' of 1980s' and early 1990s' victim-centred research – fear of crime.

Although the book endeavours to cover, in the space of eight chapters, a range of subjects on the broad theme that is 'victims of crime', it undoubtedly neglects areas that individual readers will consider important. At the same time as the book undertakes to present a range of viewpoints with respect to the themes presented in each of the eight chapters, it necessarily reflects my own standpoint as the writer. In presenting 'the facts' of victimological research, policy and practice, these very 'facts' are open to interpretation and debate about their accuracy and underlying agendas. Hence, the book sets out a number of points in the context of wider policy and political debates that shape victim-centred criminal justice practice. Otherwise, to present legal developments and practice initiatives that are supposedly 'for' victims without illustrating the context of their political setting is to leave out vital information that helps us understand the 'place' of victims at the beginning of the twenty-first century.

The term 'victim-centred' is used throughout the book to mean research, policy and practice initiatives that have victims of crime in mind. The term should not be misconstrued as meaning initiatives that are 'anti-offender' (unless otherwise stated). Instead, 'victim-centred' is a catch-all phrase that is employed here in reference to research, policy and practice that is sensitive to victims, and works 'for' and sometimes 'with' victims, as important actors in criminal and social justice. To have reached the point where we can begin to refer to practice initiatives as 'victim-centred' is an indication of how far criminal justice has developed, both 'at home' and 'abroad', towards a conscious recognition of victims as actors with service demands (or needs), and in some instances legal provisions (or rights), that rank alongside those of defendants/offenders and the State.

Finally, the book was written with a British graduate audience largely in mind. To this end most of its examples are drawn from developments in England and Wales. Other continents and other countries also provide examples that pepper the book; but here I have relied on English-language accounts or, at times, German texts as sources of information. Because of this, the book is necessarily limited in its comparative account of different victim-centred initiatives. This says more about my own language limitations than it does about the true extent and nature of victim-centred research, policy and practice. This is a cautionary note that needs to be borne in mind given that other examples of victim-centred initiatives exist in other continents where English is not the language of communication; here one thinks of Latin America, and, closer to 'home', some recently arrived members of the European Union. As an antidote to this, the book often turns to examples of international instruments, from the United Nations (UN), the Council of Europe and other inter-governmental bodies, for their influence on 'home-grown' victim-centred initiatives. And, rather than view the local context of victimisation as separate from wider regional and international crime trends, the book begins and ends, in Chapters 1 and 8, with a description and discussion of some of the influences that make the experience of victimisation part of a global 'whole'. Other chapters, which focus on the particulars of selected criminal justice developments for victims, can also be read with these themes in mind. In sum, victim-centred research, policy and practice currently form a dynamic development that sees 'victim' issues increasingly at the heart of criminal and social justice.

Chapter 1

Contextualising victims and victimology

Introducing themes for discussion

This chapter sets out some key themes that help us to contextualise the place of crime victims with respect to criminal justice developments at the beginning of the twenty-first century. The circumstances under which crime victims came to prominence and continue to enjoy attention are explored through the lens of increasing crime rates, wider developments in consideration of risk, insecurity and globalisation, and political responses to these trends.

While later chapters outline positive criminal justice developments for victims that stem from government administrations, this chapter explores the politician's need to do and be seen to be doing something for victims. The chapter highlights how so-called victim-centred criminal justice needs careful interpretation with respect to seductive calls for retributive justice that appeal to penal populism.

In its second half, the chapter identifies particularly heinous and high-profile crimes that have fanned the flames of retributive justice, which governments and criminal justice agencies have had to temper. Appeals to penal populism, which come with the need to govern through crime, are critiqued alongside efforts to fit crime victims within criminal justice models that have traditionally been constructed with offenders in mind. But before launching into a contextual critique of the 'place' of victims in the new world order, as it impacts on Britain, the next paragraphs briefly outline why victims came to prominence, and what is meant and encompassed by the terms 'victims' and 'victimology'.

The increasing importance of victims and victimology

Defining 'victims' and 'victimology'

The 1985 United Nations Declaration of Basic Principles of Justice for Victims of Crime and Abuse of Power provides a broad definition of 'victims':

> 'Victims' means persons who, individually or collectively, have suffered harm, including physical or mental injury, emotional suffering, economic loss or substantial impairment of their fundamental rights, through acts or omissions that are in violation of criminal laws operative within Member States, including those laws proscribing criminal abuse of power . . . A person may be considered a victim, under this Declaration, regardless of whether the perpetrator is identified, apprehended, prosecuted or convicted and regardless of the familial relationship between the perpetrator and the victim. The term 'victim' also includes, where appropriate, the immediate family or dependants of the direct victim and persons who have suffered harm in intervening to assist victims in distress or to prevent victimization.[1]

This definition encompasses anyone who is victimised as a result of a violation of the criminal law, and captures a range of abuses relating to criminal abuse of power. In turn, both direct and indirect victims are brought under the wing of the Declaration. In this regard, the Declaration surpasses the criminal law in many countries, particularly in its identification of 'abuse of power' as victimisation.

In turn, according to the World Society of Victimology (WSV), the academic study of victimology can be defined as:

> The scientific study of the extent, nature and causes of criminal victimization, its consequences for the persons involved and the reactions thereto by society, in particular the police and the criminal justice system as well as voluntary workers and professional helpers.[2]

Other definitions of 'victims' and 'victimology' exist that are both broader and narrower in scope than the above (Karmen, 1990), but the UN and the WSV's definitions, emanating as they do from international arenas, provide the weight of shared consensus. In contrast to these 'neat' definitions, Rock, a British academic, supplies an in-depth critique of what is meant by and what it means to become a 'victim' (2002: 14):

> 'Victim', in other words, is an identity, a social artefact dependent, at the outset, on an alleged transgression and transgressor and then, directly or indirectly, on an array of witnesses, police, prosecutors, defence counsel, jurors, the mass media and others who may not always deal with the individual case but who will nevertheless shape the larger interpretive environment in which it is lodged.

Rock calls for a dynamic understanding of the 'victim' identity that looks to the experience and construction of 'victim' by different actors in different contexts. Rock's interpretation of 'victim' may not be helpful to students of criminal law, but he offers readings of 'victimhood' that allow us to understand and critically navigate how and why it is that 'victims', and the subject of victimology, were neglected before coming to prominence in recent years. He goes on to quote an unpublished Ph.D. thesis, on 'Criminal Theories of Causation and Victims', which says that victimology was dismissed in its early days as 'the lunatic fringe of criminology' (2002: 3),[3] to which he later adds that, in reference to debates about use of the term 'survivor' in preference to 'victim', ' "Victim" itself is not then necessarily considered an appealing term' (2002: 14). In other words, not only has the 'science' of victimology suffered because of its inauspicious origins as the wayward sub-discipline of criminology, but its very subjects, 'victims', have been weighed down by negative imagery that connotes their status with that of the 'weak' underdog.

Victimology, as the study of victims and victimisation, does not carry the academic weight of theory and critique that is the domain of criminology. The term 'victimology' can be attributed to a paper presented by Mendelsohn at a congress meeting held in Rumania in 1947.[4] In the years following the Second World War, a handful of scholars approached the subject of victims: von Hentig (1948), Mendelsohn (1956), Wolfgang (1957, 1959), and Nagel (1963). Von Hentig's text, *The Criminal and His Victim*, was reflected in Schafer's book two decades later, *The Victim and His Criminal* (Schafer, 1968). What these various authors have in common is their exploration of the part played by victims in precipitating crimes of violence – what came to be known as 'victim precipitation', or, latterly, 'victim blaming'. For example, von Hentig identified different victim 'types', one of which was the 'tormentor', who, as the victim of attack from 'his' target of abuse, provoked 'his' own victimisation – typically, the 'nagging' wife who is beaten by her husband. This early work on victims variously talked about victims' conscious and unconscious role in their own victimisation, and focused on victims' responsibility in the escalation and manifestation of a situation into a criminal incident.

Rock says of these 'proto-victimologists' (2002: 3), as he calls them, that they were 'often not much more than abstracted empiricists searching for a theory, a language and academic legitimacy'. Much of this early work is now discredited for its limited and damaging interpretation of victimisation minus the social context in which crime is committed. For example, this is the case for Amir's controversial publication on rape (1971). Feminist criminologists, from the 1970s on, were quick to condemn ideas that blamed victims for their own victimisation, particularly in the case of physical and sexual violence against women (Edwards, 1981; Griffin, 1971). And clinicians, later with feminist criminologists, also alerted the public and practitioners to the extent and nature of child abuse that could not readily be explained away by 'victim precipitation' (Griffiths and Moynihan, 1963).

Much like the work of early 'scientific' criminologists, such as Lombroso, we can readily fault the proto-victimologists for their sexist readings of crime/victimisation. But what this work usefully reflects is the cultural climate in which victims were regarded, at least by influential males who were writing about them. Looking at these interpretations of victim/ offender encounters, where social norms of behaviour were narrowly constructed, we are able to see the legalistic culture from where victims were marginalised and, in turn, often blamed for their own victimisation. At the same time, ideas about victim precipitation have resurfaced in other guises in recent periods, principally under the banner of situational crime prevention and repeat victimisation (see Chapter 2), and have, through these channels, gained a degree of respectability.

With this early work in mind, we are able to appreciate just how far victim-centred research, policy and practice have evolved in the last few decades. Van Dijk suggests that victimology, as 'scientific endeavor', only took off as a separate discipline 'around 1970' (1999: 1). He is pointing to the significant social and political developments around this period that together gave birth to victimology as a discipline and saw victims and victims' 'causes' gain recognition, services and rights in the criminal justice system. But since the 1970s, academic victimology, government policy, and criminal justice practice have taken often contrasting and conflictual approaches to the problem of victimisation (crime) and its aftermath. Chapter 4 addresses these developments in more detail, but the remainder of this chapter focuses on 'how' and 'why' victims came to prominence in criminal justice and politics from the 1970s on.

Victims in the spotlight

Victims urge international trials for terror suspects.

(*The Guardian*, 27/1/04)

Police target homophobic crimes: victims of homophobic crimes are being encouraged to come forward in a new initiative by Strathclyde Police.

(BBC News Online, 28/1/04)

At the beginning of 2004, as the above headlines illustrate, a diverse range of victim-centred issues were considered under the spotlight of the British media. The attention given to these issues reflects the sea-change in criminal justice and public responses to victims of crime that has occurred in Britain, and globally, since the latter half of the twentieth century. For example, in 1974, at the beginning of this international sea-change in victim-centred research and criminal justice, Drapkin and Viano wrote (1974: x): 'Students and professionals in the criminal justice system have become increasingly aware that a victim of a criminal becomes – more often than not – also the victim of the criminal justice system'. 'Victims', as a generic group, are now both 'newsworthy' and deserving of public and criminal justice support. But while victims are increasingly important to law and criminal justice reform in England and Wales, their new-found status is relatively recent in the country's common law history. Where once victims were simply viewed as potential witnesses for the prosecution, and their experiences of victimisation were responded to primarily as harms against the State, now their needs, and to some extent their rights, are recognised and acted upon. Whether we can talk of the victim's central role in criminal justice is, however, dependent on the standpoint of those interpreting the victim's place at the beginning of the twenty-first century. Prosecutors and probation officers might consider victims as having considerable new 'rights' with the potential to undermine defendants' rights. On the other hand, the main organisation offering victim assistance in Britain, Victim Support, suggests that much needs to be done by criminal justice and non-criminal justice agencies to help neglected victims. Individual victims, depending on their particular experience or experiences of victimisation, can feel at times either satisfied or acutely dissatisfied with 'the system' as they have encountered it. Whatever the positive or negative critique levelled at so-called victim-centred developments in England and Wales over the past three decades, there can be only one conclusion – victims of crime now enjoy a status that is unprecedented since the advent of the modern State.

Why did victims (and victimology) become important?

In exploring victims' new-found status in criminal justice in England and Wales certain questions need to be asked: What were and are the circumstances under which victims now play an increasingly important role in law and criminal justice? Why have victims come to prominence? In answer to these questions, a number of key factors have to be taken into account that encompass developments in the second half of the twentieth century through to the present period. These include:

- an increase in official crime rates;
- revelation of extensive hidden crime by crime surveys;
- heightened fear of crime among the public;
- public intolerance towards increasing crime and social disorder;
- failure of the offender treatment model, and its replacement with retributive justice linked to victims;
- media reports of crime against vulnerable victims and victims' maltreatment by the criminal justice system;
- recognition, and politicisation by feminists, of the problem of violence against women/child abuse;
- recognition, and politicisation by civil action groups, of the problem of racist violence;
- politicisation of rising crime rates by politicians focusing variously on 'law and order', 'crime reduction', and victims as 'vote winners';

- a movement towards citizens' charters/patients' rights that also encompasses victims.

These factors, in combination, have enhanced the standing of crime victims in criminal and social justice. Other factors can be added to this list that help explain the growth of victim-centred justice, factors that are both specific and general in their explanatory qualities. For example, at the level of the specific, localised initiatives, often attributable to the work of key individuals, were important to the development of victim-centred justice; here one thinks of the Bristol forerunner to Victim Support that was established in the early 1970s with the assistance of local probation officers. At the level of the general, central government's recognition of victims was a necessary response to the problem of rising crime rates, and a belated response to deep underlying social problems connected with crime and victimisation such as unemployment and other indicators of social deprivation.

And importantly, as crime rates soared, one justice model declined and another rose in its place that allowed for ideas about victim-centred justice to be aired. The offender treatment model, when criminal justice briefly experimented with the idea of offender rehabilitation, was declared a 'failure' by the political Right, though much of this was attributable to inadequate application of the model, rather than simply the failure of its underlying principles. A new ideological space was created to be filled by a retributive law and order politics with its focus, and political rhetoric, on victims. In this atmosphere, victimology, as the study of victims, was able to gain a foothold.

At the same time, the 1960s/1970s, challenges to the establishment through a combination of influences such as the civil rights movement in the USA, the rise of the women's movement, and the emergence of alternative youth cultures, have seen demands for justice – *and substantive rights* – from a variety of hitherto neglected groups. With this, not only were new victims put on the agenda – victims of racism and violence against women, and victims of State oppression – but new offenders, ranging from individuals to the State, were also recognised. The descriptors of 'who' or 'what' could be considered victims opened up in the latter part of the twentieth century to consider new victim categories. Under the banner of 'radical' or 'critical' victimology, critiques emerged of narrow interpretations of and responses to 'victimhood' offered by a 'conservative' or 'traditional' victimology that limited itself to the criminal law and established criminal justice policy.

The landmark 1985 United Nations Declaration on Victims of Crime and Abuse of Power is testimony to the importance and global reach of a comprehensive victimology that has come to recognise 'abuse of power' as part of its remit, and which has also made demands on governments to recognise victims' rights. However, while the UN Declaration is wide-ranging in its definition of 'victims', the field of victimology is not a 'catch-all' dumping ground for all research on human suffering.

In 1989, following the remit of a radical victimology and commenting on recent efforts to recognise crime victims and witnesses, Viano wrote (1989: xviii): 'While victims and witnesses of crime have received the most attention, victimology can and should also be concerned with other types of victims as well, for example, victims of earthquakes, natural disasters, occupational accidents and hazards, dislocation and famine.' But Viano's call for a wide-ranging victimology can be readily critiqued as 'catch-all' and as undermining victimology's strengths as the 'science' or 'discipline' to address the flipside of crime and criminality – that is, victims of man-made crime rather than natural disasters. It was because of the dramatic increase in *crime* in the second half of the twentieth century (rather than any dramatic increase in natural disasters) that victimisation and fear of crime emerged as key barometers of public well-being. But to understand fully why and how victims of crime came to prominence in recent decades, we need to understand the influence of political parties on victim policy.

The politician's response

In Britain, the *rising crime rate* in the last decades of the twentieth century, in combination with a *'law and order'* response to this under the Conservative administration of the Thatcher and post-Thatcher period (1979–97), saw a corresponding emphasis on *victims of crime*. Where once crime and victims played a marginal role in party politics and political manifestos, from the 1970s on they have occupied centre-stage.

Here it is important to distinguish between recognition of 'victims of crime' and 'victimisation' as they are variously employed by governments and victim interest groups. Where the term 'victims of crime' serves to individualise the problem of crime by reducing it to a personal experience of victimisation, 'victimisation' digs deeper to explore the underlying causes behind people's experiences of victimisation. These distinctions are also encountered with reference to 'criminals' and 'criminality', with the first focusing on the actions of individual criminals and the second emphasising social-structural factors influencing crime trends and patterns. In response to what was portrayed as Labour's 'soft' and failed approach to crime and criminality against a rising crime wave, successive Conservative governments took up the cause of 'victims' from the late 1970s with a call for tougher law and order policies against offenders. Retributive justice was promoted as victim-centred justice. And with this, in its most ardent form, there was no corresponding need to address underlying causes of victimisation. In this atmosphere, Michael Howard, as Home Secretary under John Major's Conservative administration, was able to utter the words 'prison works' as if incarceration was a comprehensive response to crime and victimisation.

The Labour Party, during its period in opposition to the Conservatives, could not afford to repeat its previous incarnation as the 'soft' party on crime as law and order became central to party politics. To this end, Tony Blair, as Shadow Home Secretary, introduced the mantra 'tough on crime, tough on the causes of crime'. This neatly implied a law and order response to crime that was worthy of the Conservatives with the addition of a tough exploration of crime's origins that refused to let offenders off lightly. This stance has been carried over by 'New Labour' since it came to power in 1997 (J. Young, 2000). Victims and potential victims, as the voting public, are the audience that Labour seeks to satisfy with its crime policies.

Since the Conservatives put law and order at the heart of British politics, the manifestos of political parties have not been in a position to ignore the issue of crime and victimisation – as long as crime rates remain high (Downes and Morgan, 2002). At the same time, political policy is responsive to external influences such as crime trends, and reflects the ascendancy, in various periods, of different victim-centred issues – be this violence against women or restorative justice (see Chapter 7). Later in the chapter government responses to the problem of crime and victimisation are explored; let it suffice to say here that any interpretation of so-called victim-centred policy responses by government has now to consider the parts played by 'the public' (as victims and communities) *and* the private sector (businesses) in shaping victim-centred policy responses.

'Risk' and 'insecurity': recent buzzwords that resonate with victims

In the last twenty years or so risk has moved from the periphery to the core of criminological theorizing and crime control practice.

As Loader and Sparks indicate (above, 2002: 92), the idea of 'risk', its manifestation and responses to it, is increasingly important in criminology, and this reflects wider considerations of 'risk' that encompass politics at a national and international level.

In recent years, theoretical and practical responses to crime and other threats to social order have been constructed in the language of 'risk'. Early criminological references to risk were limited to ideas about youth who were 'at risk' of offending, or, in the field of victimology, to one's risk of becoming a victim of crime. Risks have traditionally been interpreted as being particular to the individual or the group. Responses to questions about 'who you are' (gender, age, socio-economic status, race/ethnicity), 'where you live' (type of housing, neighbourhood), and 'how you live' (your lifestyle) have traditionally been collected as variables that help to determine risk of offending and/or victimisation. From the 1970s, interpretation of risk went hand in hand with the rise of positivist methods of data collection and analysis that relied heavily on collecting these variables in consideration of different populations. In this period, risk was narrowly delimited to the realm of statistical analysis and considerations of probability.

Recent criminological incarnations of 'risk' have moved beyond their earlier limited references to the likelihood of something occurring either as crime or victimisation. Instead, risk has been adopted as a term that refers to a wide range of social insecurities. The obvious overlap between ideas of risk and fear of crime, or insecurity, has not been taken up by victimology to the same extent as risk has been utilised as a concept by criminologists and sociologists (Hollway and Jefferson, 1997; Hope, 2001). This is largely because risk has been elaborated as a range of influences that induce insecurity in people in advanced industrialised societies; such explanations tend not to examine people's direct experiences of victimisation. Ideas about risk are often framed in theoretical terms that implicitly, rather than explicitly, touch on victimisation (Hope and Sparks, 2000; Stenson and Sullivan, 2001).

In Britain, at the beginning of the twenty-first century, the idea of risk is often described in relation to any or all of the following 'big' social issues:

- the diminished power of the nation-state;
- the expansion of the European Union (EU);
- mass migration of economic migrants, refugees and asylum seekers;
- unemployment and job insecurity;
- organised crime by 'outsiders';
- terrorism, war and weapons of mass destruction;
- environmental pollution and disease.

This list can be added to, and if written with respect to a different country, or at a different time, it might prioritise and include other issues such as civil war, democracy, rule of law, and famine, in the construction of risk. For example, Łoś (2002), writing about Poland, looks at changes in the construction of 'fear' between communist and post-communist societies. Exploring the 'risk/security' implications stemming from the collapse of the police-state and the subsequent rise of private security, along with the media's switch from State-censored reports of 'good' news to open reports about crime and other 'bad' stories, Łoś explores the ideological and practical influences on people's changing experiences of risk and insecurity as 'fear of crime'.[5]

Understanding 'risk' and 'insecurity' through 'globalisation'

From developed countries to countries in transition, the idea of risk has been defined as a comprehensive experience that affects us all – so much so that we are all now part of what Ulrich Beck has described as the 'risk society' (Beck, 1992).

If risks are myriad and different in time and place, then the phenomenon of 'globalisation' is the cement that binds them together. According to Beck (2000: 11), globalisation equates to 'the processes through which sovereign national states are criss-crossed and undermined by transnational actors with varying prospects of power, orientations, identities and networks'. What this definition tells us is that we can no longer live and comprehend life under the cosy confines of the nation-state. In other words, no 'man' is an island. Rather, we are deeply connected to each other by a range of influences that encompass international organisations and international law, trade, travel, and communications technology (Bauman, 1998).

For centuries exploration and international trade have brought the peoples of the world together, but globalisation distinguishes itself from these earlier periods on four key counts. First, the nation-state has devolved much of its decision-making capabilities to supra-national organisations that are involved in the politics of diplomacy and trade (such as the European Commission, the United Nations, the International Monetary Fund, the World Bank). Second, decisions about the production, consumption and trade in goods and services are in the hands of multinational companies whose main concern is profit rather than the impact of the globalised economy on specific localities and populations (think Indian call centres, IKEA, supermarket fruit and vegetables from developing countries). Third, travel has been made easy, cheap and relatively fast, and has been opened up to a mass public (think Boeing's creation of the 'Airbus', Ryanair). Fourth, communication technology, from computing to satellites, has made information available across the globe almost instantaneously (think internet banking, BBC World/CNN).

Globalisation has brought with it both promise and pitfalls. More of us, at least in Britain, enjoy cheap holidays abroad, buy cheap clothes and a diverse range of supermarket products, and can watch satellite television coverage of war from the safety of our living rooms. At the same time, these recent 'benefits' to our lifestyle and purchasing power come at a cost. What we like to think of as new-found consumer choice is more correctly the end product of a series of global business decisions, taken by an elite few, that determine what we purchase, how we purchase it, and where it is made. The drive for cheaper products and services means that global competition in the marketplace is tough and is therefore controlled by big multinational corporations that increasingly operate without restrictions imposed by nation-states. What this means for 'us' at the level of our localised experiences – our neighbourhood, town and country – is that decisions about whether a factory opens or closes or how goods are distributed are often beyond the control of local business interests and government. Essentially, globalisation evokes risk because it brings with it loss of control, and with this uncertainty.

Risk affects all of us, and is deeply felt by those at the margins of society who are less able to insure themselves against the whims of the new global economy. Unemployment or inflationary prices for goods impact most on those at the lower end of the income scale. At the same time, the middle classes also suffer from enhanced levels of job insecurity and the stress related to this from the demands of keeping up a high-earning two-income lifestyle. Where we previously enjoyed security in employment coupled with large-scale adherence to institutions of social control – 'God, Queen and Country' – at least for a few decades after the Second World War, there is now insecure employment and scepticism, or outright distrust, concerning these once formidable institutions. People's insecurities are also exacerbated by a range of developments to established social-familial structures. These include: challenges to men's and women's roles in society; increases in divorced and single-parent families; an ageing population and a youthful immigrant population; and an increase in single-person households. In addition, the increase in the crime rate in the last decades of the twentieth century has also raised people's personal risk of victimisation and their fear of crime, and, at the same time, has served to question the authority of the State to control crime.

Through a combination of increased insecurities about economic and social stability – including crime – people's sense of risk is now experienced at the level of (1) the personal and the local (Will I have a job next month? Will my home be burgled when I'm out?) and (2) the general and the global (Will increased immigration threaten jobs? Does terrorism threaten social stability?). These insecurities are both real and perceived, and can culminate in fears about crime/victimisation and civil incivility that are easily targeted at 'outsiders' as the cause of problems related to insecurity.

In the locality of the home and the neighbourhood people are no longer able to insulate themselves from change as they previously were. Television news reports and factory closures ordained from distant head offices bring globalisation to reality at the level of the local, and with this serve to threaten people's identities about their place in a globalised world. Under conditions of globalisation people's sense of 'place' is experienced and reinforced by distinguishing their experiences, and who they are, from 'outsiders' who appear to threaten their sense of identity. 'Outsiders' can be any group that appears to threaten social order. Dominant social groups determine who is constructed as a social threat and 'outsider'. Whereas in the past local youths (essentially young men) provided a ready scapegoat to blame for crime and public disorder, the spotlight has turned in recent years to other 'outsiders' (such as asylum seekers) who are perceived as a new threat to the local social order. These new 'outsiders' can be blamed for anything from unemployment, through to disease and crime. In the case of refugees and asylum seekers, their status as potential victims of oppressive regimes is sidelined by populist references to their essential 'otherness' which is deemed to harm the local social order. Tabloid newspapers, and sometimes broad-sheets, inflate people's sense of insecurity by depicting unwanted immi-gration – be this legitimate refugees or economic migrants – as a threat to our very 'culture'.

In sum, people's sense of risk and insecurity is experienced at the level of the local but reflects global shifts concerning change and threats to the established social order (Girling et al., 2000). When crime surveys ask people to express their 'fear of crime' in relation to their locality, not only are they describing fear in relation to actual and perceived victimisation, but they also evoke a range of underlying insecurities. More recently these insecurities have been aligned with the supposed global criminal threat posed by undesirable 'outsiders'. Here, concerns about crime/victimisation, fear of crime, and globalisation merge as part of a continuum of insecurities.

The crime survey, which reached its explosive zenith in the 1980s, encapsulates the mood and methods employed by a society that has become increasingly concerned with risk, insecurity, and, latterly, globalisa-tion. Employing data analysis that allows the probability of risk to be measured against a set of variables, the crime survey, in its first incarna-tion, was an alternative means of measuring the crime rate. At the same time it revealed as much about people's fear of crime and anxieties as it did about their actual experiences of victimisation. The crime survey was made possible by the following factors: first, the growth in methods of large-scale data collection for purposes of statistical analysis; second, the rising crime rate that demanded that something be done about crime, if only simply to 'count it' accurately; third, enhanced public concern about crime as a manifestation of more general social insecurities.

Our understanding of the growth in research on and political responses to victims, at the end of the twentieth century, needs to be contextualised with respect to these developments surrounding risk, insecurity and globalisation.

From government to governance

As crime rates increased along with the public's fear of crime and general sense of anxiety concerning the new social order related to globalisation, successive British governments, from the late 1970s on, have responded to this apparent crisis in three ways: first, with an increased emphasis on the rule of law and retributive justice that could not be accused of being 'soft' on offenders; second, by devolving criminal and social justice duties that were previously the sole control of the State to public–private partnerships; and third, by emphasising individual responsibility in com-bating crime. These developments can be characterised with respect to: (1) a shift from 'government' to 'governance' of crime control, wherein tasks that were formerly the sole province of the State are devolved to other agencies and individual citizens; and, at the same time, (2) a shift from the traditional view that criminal justice simply 'administers justice', regardless of the social effects, to the idea that the State has some responsibility, in partnership with other agencies/individuals, towards 'crime reduction'. These developments have had significant repercussions on the management of crime, the treatment of offenders, and, hence, victims.

Characterising governance

Different criminological and political commentators have identified central and overlapping manifestations of the new governance of crime and risk (including Barry et al., 1996; Clarke and Newman, 1997; Crawford, 1997; Garland, 2001: 119–120; Loader and Sparks, 2002: 87–88; Shearing and Wood, 2003). These can be summarised as follows:

1. *Shifting expectations of the State*: In the decades after the Second World War, before the escalation of the crime rate, the State's ability to govern went unquestioned except by a radical few. Civil servants and selected academics were able to shape crime control policy without much interference from politicians and little consideration for public opinion. More recently, recognising the limited ability of the police and other criminal justice agencies to control crime, in the face of its growth, 'realistic' expectations of criminal justice have been stressed to dampen public expectations of the State's ability to reduce crime or, more modestly, control it.

2. *Public–private partnerships*: As a practical response to the above, local public–private crime prevention partnerships have been established between the traditional agencies of social control (police; probation) and local government, schools and businesses (for example). The emergence of these partnerships is in recognition of the fact that the police cannot manage crime alone, and brings the public on board in an active effort to encourage responsible citizenship against crime. These partnerships were encouraged by the politics of the New Right which set out to break people's dependence on the State (through their reliance on social-welfare institutions established after the Second World War) by fostering private enterprise and individual responsibility.

3. *Managerialism*: The private sector mantras of efficiency, economy and effectiveness are injected into the criminal justice system from the police through to prisons. The language and methods of the private sector are brought to bear on public sector agencies in an effort to identify and realise performance targets. The public, and in particular victims, are constructed as consumers of the criminal justice system.

The onus is on public satisfaction with services, which is coupled
with efforts at reducing the crime rate. In other words, 'outputs' (such
as victim take-up of a service) are prioritised alongside 'outcomes' (such
as a reduction in victimisation).

Focusing on the first two characteristics of 'governance', the following
key points should be noted that particularly resonate with victims.

First, decisions about criminal justice are no longer the sole realm
of law makers and criminal justice agencies. As crime has moved from
the margins to the centre of politics, the public and public–private
partnerships have become central players in shaping criminal justice
policy. Politicians can no longer afford to make decisions about policy
without consulting victim interest groups, and without being aware of the
media's interpretation of events. In other words, criminal justice policy
is now highly responsive to the electorate; or at least it gives the appearance of being so. Whether government policy actually puts public opinion
on criminal justice into action is, in most cases, doubtful, particularly
as opinion is diverse and at times goes against the human rights responsibilities of government. But politicians do not introduce criminal justice
policies that might seem too liberal for fear of alienating a public who
they believe want a tough law and order response to crime. In some
respects the government, in its efforts to be re-elected, is too cautious in
its interpretation of what the public wants – note the furore over the
recent liberalisation of the cannabis laws in England and Wales. Because
of politicians deciding to err on the side of caution, some criminal
justice commentators (Ashworth, 2002) have aired concerns that policy
is targeted too much at appeasing victim-interest groups while ignoring
due process for offenders.

Second, as the public has been asked to play an ever more active
role in crime prevention, so responsibility for crime has been devolved,
in part, from the State and its agencies of social control (the police) to
the public. Whereas the 1960s/early 1970s were characterised by a brief
period of liberal criminal justice reform that allowed for 'social crime
prevention' initiatives, from the late 1970s the emphasis was placed on
'situational crime prevention'. The marketplace responded to increased
levels of crime and fear of crime by promoting the need for situational
crime prevention at the level of the person and property. In practical
terms this means that people are encouraged to buy a range of crime
prevention devices: locks and bolts, car alarms, and personal alarms. The
mobile phone is itself promoted as a tool for use in threatening and
dangerous situations. Converting your home into a fortress against
crime by 'target hardening' is now the norm in Britain, the USA, and
large parts of both the developed and developing world (Felson, 1994).
Businesses also have to invest in security measures that would have been
unthinkable in previous decades. All this is, of course, a sensible response
to a real threat. But it is also a response to an astute marketing campaign

by security firms, and, at the same time, is an obligatory response to insurance industry requirements. In other words, you will not receive an insurance payout against any theft or damage against your property if you fail to make the requisite security adjustments to your home or business. At the personal level, much of this emphasis on 'being safe' is targeted at women, the elderly and children (or at least their parents). And, in this respect, calls to secure your home or person appeal to fears about crime as a threat from outsiders. Given that violence against women, the elderly and children is disproportionately committed by family, acquaintances or care employees, target hardening will do little to dispel this real threat.

Third, as the limits of the nation-state to control crime are recognised, and as the neo-liberal politics of the marketplace encourage personal responsibility for crime control rather than reliance on the State, so alternatives to State-run crime control and crime prevention are promoted: for example, public–private partnerships involving the police, representing the State, working with businesses, schools, shops, and transport services in an effort to tackle crime. Crime prevention partnerships tend to be locally based and involve members of the 'community'. But, in reference to 'community', partnerships can easily fall foul of stereo-typical ideas about what community is and who can speak on behalf of 'the community'. In this regard, established local figures, and the most vocal, tend to be represented in partnerships. Those who are perceived as causing trouble or crime – particularly young people – are often left out of partnerships (Brown, 1998). In addition, interpretation of 'community' is often left open and can be narrowly framed according to who decides what and which groups comprise the local community; again, undesirable 'outsiders' are often left out of this process.

Fourth, with responsibility for one's own safety resting with the individual, and local crime prevention partnerships, those of us who fail to take responsibility for our own safety are constructed as irresponsible. The socially marginalised – young people, immigrants, the poor and the unemployed/unemployable – are often unrepresented in community partnerships, and yet these are the groups that are particularly vulnerable to victimisation. Whether this makes them irresponsible in the face of crime is a moot point given that they tend to be ill-equipped, both financially and practically, to respond to calls for community involvement against crime.

In turn, in the language of governance, people have been constructed as citizens with 'rights and responsibilities'. In other words, 'rights' have to be earned with the adoption of 'responsibilities'. This is the doctrine of active citizenship which means that you have a 'right' to State protection and assistance, should you be a victim of crime, and a 'right' to due process in law, should you be an offender, but these rights come with responsibilities to the State and your 'community'. In this respect, the public should make every effort to ensure their own safety and cooperate with the criminal justice authorities in the administration of justice. But, as the example of marginalised citizens illustrates, some groups are not in a position to engage actively in crime prevention and personal safety initiatives.

New modes of governance

Managerialism, as the third central tenet of 'governance', demands that a new set of objectives and outputs is brought into play in the management of criminal justice agencies and other agencies working with them. The tenets of efficiency, economy and effectiveness are moulded around the need to 'manage' the agency. Outputs can be formulated around customer satisfaction with service delivery or examples of 'best practice'. In this regard, outputs do not *have* to indicate measurable decreases in crime or victimisation, which in the past might have been the barometer of an agency's 'success rate', though of course crime reduction remains a desirable goal. Measures of customer satisfaction become equally important to police clear-up rates or the number of victims who recover stolen property.[6]

These developments can be easily dismissed as having only a cosmetic impact on crime and victimisation. Yet research with victims repeatedly indicates that they want to receive respect and regular information about the progress of their case from criminal justice authorities *rather* than be on the receiving end of erratic and impersonal information letting them know that an offender has been apprehended and charged (Maguire and Pointing, 1988; Moody, 2003; Shapland et al., 1985; Wemmers, 1996). In this sense, 'customer care', along with 'results' (finding a criminal and sentencing 'him'), is now a key element for policing and other criminal justice agencies, such as the probation service, when dealing with victims of crime. Crime reduction is obviously good for victims (and potential victims), but correct treatment of victims by criminal justice agencies has emerged as a value in its own right.

These developments, emphasising outputs alongside outcomes, are fortuitous at a time when crime rates have been increasing, as they shift attention to the management of justice and treatment of victims, or criminal justice 'outputs', rather than 'outcomes' relating to crime reduction. They also correspond to a culture of 'actuarial justice' – as a form of crime auditing and risk assessment – that came to prominence in the 1980s/1990s and is most closely associated with the 'new penology' of crime control from this period (Feeley and Simon, 1992, 1994; Simon, 1988). Using data collection and statistical analysis, actuarial justice identifies probable and persistent crime problems (and offenders) and suggests ways of managing them (by locking them up in the case of persistent offenders).

The 1998 Crime and Disorder Act for England and Wales places particular emphasis on the need to manage crime through data collection

(Hough and Tilley, 1998). Working squarely within the framework of new governance, the Act requires local councils, police and other agencies, in partnership, to undertake the following:

- conduct and publish an audit of local crime and disorder problems;
- consult locally on the basis of the audit;
- set and publish objectives and targets for the reduction of crime and disorder;
- monitor progress;
- repeat the process every three years.

Interestingly, no direct requirement is made actually to reduce crime; rather, the requirement is to set targets and monitor them. In turn, the Home Office's crime reduction homepage outlines a number of 'toolkits' for the implementation of crime reduction programmes against a range of crimes and social disorders, from 'vehicle crime' through to 'dysfunctional families'. Each toolkit draws from research evidence, such as the British Crime Survey, to present a 'risk profile' or 'victim profile' that identifies 'who' is most often victimised, and most likely to be victimised, by the crime in question. And, in a Kafkaesque play on crime management, there is even a toolkit about how to set up 'audits and strategies'.

Actuarial justice is made popular because it utilises 'scientific' methods to approach the problem of crime. But while actuarial justice might employ so-called scientific techniques for the management of crime and persistent offenders, it is debatable whether it actually reduces crime and reoffending – rather it 'manages' them. A case in point here is the development of 'Compstat' by the New York Police Department (NYPD) in the early to mid 1990s.

Case study: NYPD and Compstat

'Compstat' (or 'computer comparison statistics' or 'computerised statistics' as it is variously referred to) is a computer-based crime incident mapping exercise that was developed by NYPD in 1994. Compstat requires police personnel at the level of the individual precinct, of which there are over 70 in New York City, to collect summary statistical data, on a weekly basis, about crime and social disorder, along with a written record of significant cases, crime patterns and police activities. This information is compiled in a weekly Compstat report which is discussed and compared with other precinct reports at weekly Crime Strategy Meetings.[7]

Compstat emerged under Police Commissioner William Bratton and the city administration of Mayor Rudolph Giuliani, which brought

(Box continued)

in a philosophy of 'zero tolerance' policing that, borrowing from Wilson and Kelling's 'Broken Windows' thesis (Wilson and Kelling, 1982), mounted an aggressive police campaign against crime and social incivilities that were considered as part of the crime problem. Compstat reflected a new culture that demanded information about the extent and nature of crime and incivilities. The NYPD's Compstat Unit also prepares weekly 'Commander Profile Reports' as performance indicators (such as number of arrests made, and response time to emergencies) that are able to compare the work outputs of commanders at precinct level.

As New York City's crime rate fell dramatically throughout the 1990s, Commissioner Bratton attributed the decline to 'zero tolerance' policing, and the Compstat reports were able to support his assertions. However, with pressure to meet NYPD's new performance indicators, and direct comparison of results between precincts, there have been ready accusations thrown at this 'success story' that commanders were willing to 'massage' their Compstat figures in an effort to produce 'results'. Other factors can also be noted when assessing the decline in New York City's crime rate (Dixon, 1998): there is evidence to show that the crime rate was in decline before the introduction of zero tolerance policing; the crime rate declined in other major US cities that were not employing 'zero tolerance' policing methods, at the same time as it declined in New York City; changes to the city's drug market, with the decline in crack cocaine use in the late 1980s/1990s, meant that the influence of violent drug gangs on the city's crime profile was lessening; the demographic profile of the population changed in this period with a decline in the number of young men – the main perpetrators of crime; there was also an economic upturn and a decrease in unemployment in New York City which also had repercussions for the city's crime rate. Critiques of the city-wide zero tolerance campaign also pointed to the overuse of 'heavy-handed' policing targeted at poor ethnic minority communities (Cunneen, 1999).

In sum, while Compstat, as the tool of actuarial zero tolerance policing, was heralded as a breakthrough in the management of crime, its findings are not as clear-cut as they might appear. Arguably, police 'outputs' (such as management performance indicators) became as important as police 'outcomes' (declining levels of crime). And the actual reduction in the city's crime levels – which did take place – can be attributed to a range of factors alongside the introduction of zero tolerance policing. But in light of these criticisms, aspects of zero tolerance policing were taken up by police forces in Britain (Palmer, 1997), in an effort to both reduce *and* manage crime, to varying degrees of success.

Outside of specific examples of application of actuarial 'methods' to policing and other aspects of crime control and management, such as prisons, actuarial justice reflects wider developments about the management of risk and insecurity.

We have developed a culture that seeks to reduce risk through its management and control in an effective 'audit' of crime. Just as the thalidomide scandal[8] of the 1960s and 1970s cannot be countenanced today by a society that demands a high degree of risk avoidance, so we are no longer prepared to become victims of crime by leaving its control to chance. Yet in our efforts to control our environments and avoid risk, increased power is given over to insurance companies that offer the promise of risk management but do this with the exclusion of those who do not fit the profile of the ideal consumer (Johnathan, 1987). New methods of governance, in drawing up their tables of crime-prone communities and crime-prone individuals, based on actual and predicted experiences of victimisation, result in the exclusion of the most vulnerable groups in society from insurance against risk. As a result, the vulnerable are left more vulnerable to victimisation. With insurance companies' efforts to increase profit margins, high-risk individuals and communities are not an attractive market to capture. In this regard the 'risk society' emerges as a two-tiered response to risk with the rich able to buy in to crime prevention and insurance, and the poor left out of this process (Burchell et al., 1991). Herein, the role of government in managing the most vulnerable communities who are at risk of victimisation needs to be reinforced. Rather than leave the management of crime to the private sector – private security firms and gated communities – government also needs to recognise its responsibilities to 'at risk' citizens.

Responses to victimisation: appeals to populism

In the last ten years a number of high-profile crimes, most notably with children as victims, have resulted in a groundswell of populist public condemnation. Responses to these crimes, by public and politicians alike, can be understood with regard to 'risk', 'insecurity' and 'governance' in relation to two key concepts – 'penal populism' (Clarkson and Morgan, 1995) and 'governing through crime' (Simon, 1997):

1. *Penal populism*: In response to moral panics about crime, and particular high-profile cases, the government promotes tough penal policies which it believes the public wants. This approach is not the same as developing policies based on sound research into public opinion. In a crude characterisation, British criminal justice reform, in the wake of certain crimes, can be identified as government-led while appealing to populist calls for justice. In comparison, US criminal justice reform

displays a greater willingness to change in response to public opinion (see focus on Sarah Payne/Megan's Law below). Since the introduction of tough 'law and order' campaigns from the late 1970s, governments can ill afford to ignore penal populism as it shapes election fodder and government policy.

2. *Governing through crime*: In the 1980s, crime came to represent a defining political problem that successive British governments have had to address. At the same time as governments have increasingly adopted a 'hands off' approach to governing the people, at least as far as expenditure on public services is concerned, so calls for 'law and order' demand government intervention. This presents something of a dilemma for politicians who, on the one hand, want to reduce government expenditure and make citizens responsible for their own safety, while, on the other hand, they need to increase expenditure to cover policing and prison costs. However, in responding to calls for 'law and order' the government succeeds in legitimising itself as the people's 'policeman' and therefore in its ability to govern safely. Crime becomes pivotal to the ability to govern.

Bearing in mind the above, two cases are briefly referred to (below) involving recent high-profile child murders that have provoked popular demands for tougher action against paedophiles. The media's coverage of these cases has been central to calls for tough political intervention in the mould of retributive justice. But by focusing on the individual victim(s) and offender(s) involved, the populist media has sidelined underlying causes of child abuse and the ever-present problem of abuse in the home.

Set against overwhelming evidence that the majority of interpersonal violence is between victims and offenders who are known to each other, the populist focus of crime remains with sex crimes and other violent crimes committed by strangers in the public domain. These crimes are considered newsworthy as they appeal to deeply held fears about crime and risk that centre on 'stranger danger'. Although domestic violence and child abuse by family members are now widely acknowledged as significant social problems, the public and the media continue to focus their concerns and their moral outrage on crimes committed by 'outsiders' who are deemed to be 'not like us'. The process of distancing yourself and your own experiences from heinous crimes, such as child sexual abuse and murder, can be viewed as a coping strategy that separates the criminal world from the one we live in – in effect separating 'us' (as non criminal) from 'them' (as criminals). It also serves to distance the threat of crime, so reducing our sense of insecurity.

More careful analysis of the problem of child abuse has been undertaken by charities such as Barnardos and the NSPCC (National Society for the Prevention of Cruelty to Children) whose campaigns have done much to balance populist and narrow interpretations of child abuse with more rounded public information about its nature and origins. These long-established charities, respectively founded in 1870 and 1884, together with more recent additions such as Kidscape and Childline, help to focus public attention on child abuse as a common phenomenon in the environment of the home, school and care institutions. Countering the worst excesses of tabloid campaigns to 'name and shame' known paedophiles, the established children's charities have focused in recent years on hard-hitting public campaigns that highlight child abuse as a problem that predominantly involves abusers who are known to their victims. The NSPCC's 'Full Stop' campaign, launched in 1999, has aired a series of television and poster advertisements focusing on child abuse as a problem that manifests itself in the home and in other settings. Importantly, the charity also offers advice to abusers in an effort to get them to stop abusing and seek help. Herein the charity achieves a rare balance between advertisements highlighting the pervasive problem of child abuse, and campaigns recognising that abusers can be 'one of us' – messages which governments, in appealing to 'penal populism', are loath to stress.

Case study: Sarah Payne

In July 2000, Sarah Payne, aged eight, was abducted and murdered while playing in fields near her family home. Her killer, Roy Whiting, who was living in the area, was sentenced to life imprisonment for her murder in December 2001. After Whiting's conviction it emerged that he was sentenced for a similar offence in 1995, but, in that instance, he had allowed his victim to live.

The Sarah Payne case caught the public's attention as *News of the World* editor Rebekah Wade initiated a campaign to 'name and shame' paedophiles by publishing their names and addresses. Calls for a 'Sarah's Law' to identify known paedophiles were based on the USA's 'Megan's Law', which was enacted in all fifty states after the rape and murder of seven-year-old Megan Kanka by a known paedophile who was living across the road from her family home. The idea for a 'Sarah's Law' gained popular appeal, with some charities, such as Kidscape, backing its introduction for the most dangerous paedophiles. Sarah's parents were supportive of a law to identify known paedophiles, and campaigned to raise the profile of murdered children and their families. However, public support for the law gained an unhealthy edge when some residents of the Paulsgrove estate in Portsmouth, after Sarah's killer was convicted and the *News of World* renewed its campaign to 'name and shame' child sex offenders, drove from the estate a paedophile who was identified in the newspaper.

(Box continued)

In other instances men were wrongly identified as paedophiles and suffered at the hands of mob vigilante 'justice'.

Against this background, a 'Sarah's Law' has not materialised in Britain. Instead, the case raised a number of dilemmas for the criminal justice system and government as it showed the need to temper populist calls against paedophiles with reasoned argument that, at the same time, did not portray the government as distanced from the public's demands for tough justice. In response, the government, leading charities (such as Victim Support), defence lawyers, and police and probation officers argued against the introduction of a 'Sarah's Law'. They claimed that such a law is fundamentally flawed at a number of levels. For example, known paedophiles can go 'underground' instead of reporting their whereabouts to the authorities, and offenders can travel to commit crimes in places where they are not registered as living. In turn, evidence from the USA has not indicated that Megan's Law has reduced offences by strangers against children.

However, in the aftermath of the Sarah Payne case, and in an effort to govern through penal populism, David Blunkett, as Home Secretary, indicated that serious sex offenders should receive life sentences on their first offence. In addition, the Criminal Justice and Court Services Act 2001 introduced tough restraining orders restricting the activities of sex offenders on release.

Case study: Holly Wells and Jessica Chapman

In August 2002, Holly Wells and Jessica Chapman, aged ten, were murdered by Ian Huntley in the house he lived in as 'caretaker' (janitor) of the school the girls attended. In December 2003 Huntley was sentenced to life imprisonment for murder. It emerged after the trial that Huntley had a string of previous allegations against him for rape of and sex with under-age girls. However, these cases were dropped either because the victims and their families decided not to press charges or the Crown Prosecution Service decided there was insufficient evidence to pursue each case.

Renewed calls for a 'Sarah's Law' to be introduced were aired after Huntley's conviction, but in this case such a law would have had little effect as Huntley escaped the net of police and social service vetting procedures which should have identified him as a danger to young girls and women. Instead, and mirroring calls in the aftermath of the Sarah Payne case, the Huntley case has opened up

(Box continued)

renewed criticism of current limitations on the prosecution's right to disclose previous convictions or related allegations that closely resemble the case being tried. At present, disclosure of 'similar fact evidence' is severely restricted as it is seen to prejudice cases against defendants. Campaign groups such as Liberty point to the fact that the principles of a 'fair trial' are jeopardised when juries are told about a suspect's prior criminal history. However, the groundswell of public opinion, in light of the Sarah Payne case and that of Holly Wells and Jessica Chapman, is encouraging a review of current procedure. The authorities are also coming under strong criticism for their failure to effectively administer a vetting system for applicant employees that is supposed to identify people with histories of child abuse and/or sex-related crimes. What has strongly emerged from the Huntley case is the absence of accurate record-keeping within authorities and between authorities, such as the police service, that are supposed to share and pass on relevant information about suspected or known paedophiles to potential employers.

Damning criticism of justice: popular dissent

Other high-profile cases have also served to identify problems in the administration of justice for victims for a variety of reasons. Miscarriages of justice against identifiably innocent victims, be these children or ethnic minority victims of racism, can serve to rally people against the administration's failure to see that justice is done on behalf of the innocent against the guilty. Reform of the justice system can occur when particular cases, or a series of cases, generate strength of public opinion (and, sometimes, official condemnation) that threatens to discredit the credibility of the establishment and its institutions. In other words, when the establishment's ability to govern effectively is under question, so posing a potential problem for re-election, then government needs to respond. And with concern about crime high on the agenda of both the British government and electorate, the government cannot afford to neglect victims.

A pivotal example of damning criticism of the justice system – which had huge repercussions for the police – relates to the murder of Afro-Caribbean teenager Stephen Lawrence, who was stabbed to death by a gang of men in 1993 while waiting at a London bus-stop. The MacPherson Report (MacPherson, 1999) into the police investigation of the murder identified 'institutional racism' in London's Metropolitan Police as the central factor behind the mismanagement of the case. To date, both a criminal case and civil cases against the five suspects accused of the murder have not resulted in a conviction for murder (Bowling and Phillips, 2002). At the time these cases were being brought against the suspects, and the police's failings became public knowledge, a media campaign to 'out' the suspects emerged. In some respects this campaign resembled the *News of the World's* efforts to 'name and shame' paedophiles. Given that the driving force behind the campaign was the politically right-of-centre newspaper the *Daily Mail,* accompanied in its efforts by the conservative *Sunday Telegraph,* the media's backing of the Lawrence family's efforts to convict the suspects gave the case mass and diverse popular support.

In turn, the case of Harold Shipman, the north of England family doctor who was convicted in 2000 of murdering fifteen of his patients by lethal injection, resulted in a public inquiry headed by Dame Janet Smith. The inquiry concluded that as many as 236 patients might have been murdered by Shipman, which, if correct, would make him the world's most prolific serial killer. Shipman was able to carry out his murders over a number of years because he singled out elderly and vulnerable patients whose deaths were unlikely to be questioned as suspicious. The inquiry criticised the police, the coroner's office and the General Medical Council for their failure to notice patterns in Shipman's behaviour that should have raised suspicion. With this critique, the establishment, in the form of the police and the medical profession, came under attack for its inability to save scores of vulnerable victims.

Many more cases, both in Britain and abroad, have resulted in populist media and public outcries against the criminal justice system's mismanagement of investigations. But the most infamous case in recent years – which combines the victims' innocence with the offender's guilt and gross misconduct by the authorities – is the Dutroux case in Belgium. In 1996 Marc Dutroux led the Belgian police to the remains of four young girls who were buried underground in the grounds of his house. Two of the girls, aged eight, had starved to death. Unlike the British case of Fred and Rosemary West, who were separately convicted of murdering over a dozen young women and girls between them and of burying their remains in various locations, the Dutroux case has attracted international media attention not only for its gruesomeness but also because of the gross ineptness and possible corruption of the Belgian authorities managing the case. In 1996, hundreds of thousands of Belgians marched through Brussels, in what became known as 'The White March', to protest at police incompetence and corruption surrounding the case. Allegations were also made, as yet neither proved nor disproved, that a paedophile ring containing high-ranking Belgian officials was involved in the case, and that this has resulted in a cover-up and delays.

In the aftermath of 'The White March', representing Europe's single biggest public display of dissent against a criminal justice system's mismanagement of justice, some changes have been made to the Belgian criminal justice system. Principal among these is the restructuring of the police – from two separate services to one service – in an effort to promote greater cooperation and exchange of information. Yet, writing at the beginning of 2004 from Belgium, where Dutroux has finally been brought to trial, it is notable that eight years have been allowed to elapse since the discovery of the girls' bodies and the opening of the trial against Dutroux. Reports from the Belgian media (television channels La Deux and Canvas) indicate a weariness and deep-seated scepticism about the Belgian system's ability to 'do justice' with any modicum of efficiency, economy and effectiveness, and without the taint of corruption.

Finally, mention should also be given to another case of a different nature that saw a similar mob-style response against the offenders as the Sarah Payne case – the 1993 murder of two-year-old James Bulger. But what makes this case markedly different from the others noted already is that the offenders, Jon Venables and Robert Thompson, were also children, aged ten, at the time they committed the murder. Perhaps more than any other recent British case, this one has resulted in mixed responses from different camps. On the one hand the parents of the murdered boy, and in particular the mother, have adopted a retributive response to the offenders and have been backed in this by the populist press. On the other hand, liberal campaigners and the liberal press have been outraged that two children, the offenders, should have been tried in an adult court and subsequently subjected to attempts to 'out' them in much the same way as adult paedophiles.

What this case clearly illustrates is the deep conflicts and anxieties that are raised in society when 'innocents' – young children – murder other children. This crime, as with an earlier case from the 1960s involving child murderer Mary Bell, can only be made sense of by many people by constructing the offenders as 'demons' who are anything but 'like us'. Governments, in their need to appeal to 'penal populism' and to 'govern through crime', cannot afford to lose sight of their electorate when responding to these cases. But the trial of Jon Venables and Robert Thompson, in an adult court under the full glare of the media, has subsequently faced condemnation in the European Court of Human Rights for its treatment of the ten-year-old defendants. In this case, the government's ability to govern, by apparently appealing to penal populism, served the interests of the populist press and members of a bloodthirsty public, but arguably did little in the long term to respond effectively to the problem of violence, in particular by children, as stranger or acquaintance-based.

Set against the media's continued focus on horrendous crimes that usually involve victims and offenders as strangers, charities such as the NSPCC and Victim Support highlight the fact that a large proportion of offenders and victims in cases involving violence and abuse know each other, and that this is particularly the case with respect to violence against women and child abuse. But against this overwhelming evidence on the nature of violent offender–victim relationships, successive governments too often play into the hands of populist interpretations of offending and appeals to 'justice' that reduce the administration of crime to retributive principles and polarised stereotypes about victims and offenders. Although the government has funded research and practical initiatives to combat violence against women and child abuse where offender and victim are known to each other,[9] the focus of the government's public position on law and order continues to rest with appeals to populism in an effort to be seen to be 'tough' on crime. At the same time, as Victim Support's report '30:30 Vision' indicates, justice fails many victims who either never engage with the criminal justice system in the first place, often because they fear reprisal from a known offender, or whose cases are dropped by the criminal justice system for a variety of reasons.

In responding to the problem of crime and victimisation, other justice models and alternatives to justice can be evoked that look beyond 'penal populism' and the idea of 'governing through crime', but which, at the same time, do not lose sight of the need to make justice responsive and responsible to the public.

The following section sketches some competing justice models that recognise the increasing importance of victims to contemporary concerns centring on crime, risk, insecurity and new modes of governance.

Responses to victimisation: competing criminal justice models

Pressure groups emerge when social groups feel unrepresented by mainstream government. Britain has a long history of pressure groups working on behalf of defendants, offenders and prisoners. The oldest of these is the Howard League for Penal Reform, which was established in 1866, and more recent additions include NACRO (the National Association for the Care and Resettlement of Offenders) in 1966. In comparison, aside from organisations that have worked on behalf of vulnerable social groups such as the NSPCC, pressure groups working specifically for victims of crime are a relatively recent invention. Margery Fry can be singled out as one of the earliest British campaigners for victims, whose work in the 1950s and 1960s led to the establishment of a criminal injuries compensation fund in 1964. A decade later, in 1974, Victim Support emerged and has since become the leading UK charity offering support to victims. The 1970s also saw the beginnings of feminist-led campaigns highlighting the problem of violence against women which also offered practical support and accommodation to victims of rape and domestic violence.

Offender-based and victim-based criminal justice reform groups have traditionally existed separately. The separation of victim and offender interests, particularly between the more narrowly framed single-issue groups such as Support After Murder and Manslaughter (SAMM) and the Prison Reform Trust, reflects a number of factors: the zeal with which founders of interest groups tend to follow their particular cause to the exclusion of others; the need to control often limited funds and resources to essential expenditure on the cause in question; and the need to maximise media coverage by focusing on core interests.

But overlap between victim and offender interests has recently emerged in the area of human rights, with groups such as Liberty and JUSTICE calling for balanced approaches to criminal justice reform that respect the rights of both victims and offenders. This new development marks an interesting shift that reflects the increasing importance given over to victims by the criminal justice system that human rights groups cannot afford to overlook. At the same time, recent developments, such as Britain's adoption of the Human Rights Act, have meant that 'rights' – which have traditionally been constructed with the defendant's right to a fair trial in mind – are gaining increasing importance in British criminal justice as 'human rights' that encompass both offenders *and* victims. And, with the apparent 'mainstreaming' of victim-centred rights in Britain, radical victim interest groups, such as Justice for Victims, are increasingly sidelined by government in favour of more apolitical groups, like Victim Support, that enjoy government support and funding. Single-issue victim groups that appear to promote victims' rights at the expense of defendants' rights cannot be supported by a government that needs to be responsive to victim and offender rights. For single-issue victims' groups to gain ground, and more importantly government money, their initial radical tones have to be tempered.

What these developments amount to is a set of apparently conflicting interests – coming variously from single-issue victim groups, human rights groups, international criminal law/courts, the media, and the public – that present government with a range of appropriate victim-centred responses. Traditionally, these various appeals to victim-centred justice have been boxed into two opposing camps: (1) retributive justice, as victim-centred (single-issue victims' groups; the populist media); or (2) due process, as offender-based (human rights; international law). Today, these polarised camps are not reflected by British criminal justice as it is currently practised. Appeals to 'penal populism', in an effort to 'govern through crime', belie the reality of 'mixed' criminal justice practice.

The mainstreaming of victim-centred justice in Britain not only reflects recognition of victims as important players in the criminal justice process, but more significantly shows the extent to which victim-centred justice can be disassociated from right-wing calls for retributive justice. In contrast, many offender-centred penal reform groups were and continue to be characterised as left-wing and radical as they challenge the establishment and the government's ability to govern fairly. In the same vein, it would have been easy for victim support groups to have adopted a radical right-of-centre approach to law and order in the late 1970s when the new Conservative administration, and in turn its opposition, developed a tough law and order response to offending. Yet, to the credit of Victim Support, victim-centred justice in Britain has not been allowed to fall into the hands of groups that promote victim-centred justice seemingly at the expense of offender-centred justice (as is the case in parts of the USA with its death penalty and adaptations of Megan's Law). Britain's Victim

Support promotes victim-centred justice through consensus with government, criminal justice organisations, and offender-centred penal reform groups, and does this by being, in the main, non-partisan.

Modelling justice: increasingly less tenable?

Traditionally, models of criminal justice have presented contrasting standpoints about the underlying principles that characterise each justice system over time. Different models are usually compared to one another, and different researchers emphasise the advantages of some models over others. For example, King (1981) outlines six contrasting criminal justice models (due process model; crime control model; medical model; bureaucratic model; status passage model; and power model), to which Davies et al. (1995) add a seventh model (just deserts model). When describing the particular features of different models, most researchers explore each model's impact on defendants/offenders, and ignore or briefly refer to their impact on victims/witnesses. But some researchers, most notably in victimology, have drawn tables that characterise the victim's role in different justice models at different periods (Dignan and Cavadino, 1996; Sebba, 1982; van Dijk, 1988). These models, like their offender/defendant-focused counterparts, typically present an 'ideal type' and tend to exaggerate differences between models. In some instances models bear little resemblance to criminal justice practice either past or present, though they may resonate with practice in other jurisdictions. For example, for the sake of crude comparison, three contrasting criminal justice models that resonate with victims can be identified as follows:

1. *Retributive justice*: Retributive justice has formed the backbone of criminal justice in England and Wales for centuries. It is based on the principle of punishing offenders for their crimes, or 'just deserts', and is said to be in the public interest. Cases are brought to trial in a court of law. The State 'owns' cases and victims are essentially witnesses for the prosecution who can only take part in the trial when questioned by the defence, prosecution, or trial judge. Recent initiatives in some jurisdictions, notably in the USA, can be characterised as 'retributive justice' that includes the possibility of active victim participation. For example, 'victim impact statements' allow victims to inform the court, prior to sentencing, about the impact the crime has had on them. These developments have been characterised by some victim-interest groups as giving victims 'a voice'.

2. *Civilian justice*: Civilian justice 'exists only as a set of principles' (Dignan and Cavadino, 1996: 165). It is based on the idea of treating offenders humanely – of both 'civilising' criminal justice responses to offenders, and of employing 'civil' remedies away from the adversarial setting of

a criminal court. Ideally, cases should be convened in civilian courts or through mediation panels. The model also acknowledges the personal interests of victims in the justice process; victims can expect to play an active part in proceedings and in the negotiation and resolution of outcomes with offenders. The process seeks to promote restitution from offender to victim, and, where appropriate, compensation.

3. *Restorative justice*: Restorative justice is an ancient form of justice that has gained renewed interest and practical application in recent years in different jurisdictions, and in different forms ranging from mediation through to family group conferencing (see Chapter 7). It is based on the principle of restoring or reintegrating offenders back into their communities and, as far as possible, undoing the harm suffered by victims and communities as a result of crime. Restorative justice variously demands an apology from offender to victim (and community), and some form of reparative work/compensation. Some manifestations of restorative justice employ the process of 'reintegrative shaming' whereby offenders are first shamed for their offence and then, after an apology and reparation to the victim, are reintegrated back into society.

Essentially, retributive justice, in its purest incarnation, places the public interest – for justice to be served and offenders to be punished – before the personal interest of the victim to have their case resolved with their interests taken into account. Conversely, civilian justice accommodates the victim's personal interests, alongside those of State and public, but does this while prioritising the need to redeem offenders humanely. The restorative justice model adapts some of the ideas forwarded in the civilian model, but introduces wider considerations about community into the process. But reintegrative shaming, as a variation of restorative justice, can be assigned the label of retributive justice if offender shaming occurs without effective reintegration taking place.

The above models, and variations on them, are variously described as pitching the interests of victim, offender, State and public (or community) against each other. In turn, each model can be assigned a political label. In this regard, retributive justice is characterised as right-of-centre, civilian justice as left-of-centre, and restorative justice as a mixture of the two (though its proponents prefer to think of it as leaning as far as possible from established forms of adversarial and traditionally retributive justice). Van Dijk (1988) identifies three different models, reflected in the above list, and characterises their approach to victims, to which he then assigns a 'political' label: (1) the retributive model: gives victims a 'voice'/politically 'Right'; (2) the welfare model: focusing on victim support and compensation/politically 'Left'; and (3) the critical model: focusing on restorative ideals/politically 'Green'. Yet since the advent of 'law and order' politics in the late 1970s, and the efforts by both Conservative *and* Labour British party politics to jump on the justice bandwagon, it has become increasingly difficult to distinguish some aspects of party politics concerning crime and anti-social behaviour.

In turn, present-day criminal justice practice is anything but a clear-cut example of our long history of adversarial and largely retributive justice, as recent criminal justice initiatives can take the form of mediation and family conferencing. Today's criminal justice system is required to balance the needs and rights of victims, offenders and, at times, communities, in a process that remains State governed but which is increasingly influenced by public–private crime prevention partnerships and other new modes of governance. One might argue that to assign a 'retributive' or 'restorative' label to a system of justice that is both diverse and in transition is neither easy nor helpful. But the experience of justice in England and Wales, as it is currently encountered by the majority of victims and offenders who enter the criminal justice process, is tied to an adversarial and traditionally retributive system. We are not, as restorative justice proponents would like to believe (see Chapter 7), moving towards a hybrid justice model; however, we are in a process of transition that is partly thanks to victim-centred developments that have, over the last three decades, brought significant challenges and changes to the criminal justice system.

At the same time, a range of victim-centred services have been developed for victims outside the setting of criminal justice. These services can encompass anything from temporary accommodation and repair to damaged property through to counselling. They provide support to those victims, the majority, who experience crime without intervention from the criminal justice system. These are the victims who do not report crime or whose cases are not followed through by the police and the Crown Prosecution Service. And, in this regard, according to Victim Support in its report '30:30 Vision',[10] many services – with the exception of the Criminal Injuries Compensation Scheme – are underfunded and cannot meet the needs of around seven million crime victims in England and Wales. Victim Support suggests that only three out of fifty victims who report their crimes to the police see their case go to court. Furthermore, of these three, and depending on the crime in question, conviction rates can be low. The report identifies victims of racist, sexual and domestic violence as particularly unlikely to report crimes to the police. In other words, some of the most vulnerable victims in society are currently outside the criminal justice system. The mainstreaming of victim-centred justice, as I have ventured to suggest in this chapter, is as yet a long way off for the majority of victims who either don't engage with the justice system or, when they do, often find their cases dropped.

The focus on victim-centred developments in the *criminal justice system*, by academic victimology, victim practitioners and politicians, often means that equally important 'social justice' or 'welfare' developments for victims (like specialist counselling and healthcare) are not given the attention they deserve. Instead, other academic disciplines and professions (such as social workers and the medical profession) address victims' needs that fall outside the criminal justice system. There is considerable room for 'joined up' research and practical intervention by victimologists/criminal justice practitioners and other disciplines/welfare practitioners in consideration of crime victims who fall outside traditional criminal justice but who fall within models of social justice/welfare assistance (for example, emergency room intervention with victims of violent crime).

And, as government recognises its limitations in managing crime, people are increasingly required to take responsibility for the management of their own risks against crime (Clarke, 1980; Felson and Cohen, 1981). Public–private crime prevention partnerships are an extension of this idea. In tandem with these developments, actuarial justice, as the measurement and mapping of crime patterns and trends, allows us to concentrate on the management of risk and how to avoid becoming a victim, but does this without dwelling on underlying causes of crime and victimisation. To this end, actuarial justice supports the insurance industry and private security as they encroach on areas of public safety that were previously the domain of government. These trends – like victims' experiences of social institutions outside criminal justice – cannot be adequately accounted for by models that concentrate on criminal justice interventions with victims.

In conclusion, the majority of models that describe different types of criminal justice are not ideal templates from which to examine the 'place' of victims in criminal and social justice. This is because:

- most models are designed to explain the place of a variety of actors in the criminal justice system, but descriptions and critiques of these models tend to concentrate on the impact of each model on defendants/offenders;
- as most victims do not engage with the criminal justice system, the majority of models cannot address victims' experiences outside the narrow framework of criminal justice;
- the public is increasingly asked to take responsibility for the management of its own risks (against crime) through private initiatives; these new developments can also be understood without resorting to traditional critiques of models that are formulated around opposing criminal justice processes.

Concluding comments

In England and Wales, victims and victim-centred justice have become increasingly important since the last decades of the twentieth century. This situation is primarily the result of an increasing crime rate in this period, which in turn has been married with an astute political response to the problem of crime and victimisation.

Using the experience of England and Wales as a template, the 'place' of victims in contemporary society can be contextualised against recent concerns focusing on risk, insecurity and globalisation. New approaches to 'governance', which reflect appeals to 'penal populism', have placed the need for victim-centred criminal justice responses centre-stage in Britain. Certain high-profile cases have highlighted the need to balance penal populism with due process in law for both offenders and victims.

Whether descriptions of criminal justice that are based on polarised models of victims' and offenders' 'place' in this system can adequately explain the current transitional status of victim-centred justice is, however, debatable. Given that people's experiences of crime and victimisation take place, in the main, outside the confines of the criminal justice system, it is apposite to interpret these experiences as more than an encounter with criminal justice. The contextualisation of victims and victimology – as the 'science' that studies victims – demands that we consider victims within and beyond the narrow confines of criminal justice. To this end, the next chapter explores 'who' are the victims, while Chapter 3 looks at the manifestation of fear and vulnerability (as victimology has traditionally referred to insecurities), and does this with reference to examples both within and outside criminal justice.

Suggested reading

The 1985 United Nations Declaration on Victims of Crime and Abuse of Power is a good starting point from which to comprehend the political importance and global significance of victims since the last decades of the twentieth century (www.victimology.nl or www.unodc.org). The particularly British response to crime victims is best interpreted through a political lens that examines the growth of law and order politics, and subsequent responses to it, from the late 1970s; here, the chapter by Downes and Morgan (2002), in the third edition of *The Oxford Handbook of Criminology*, is a well-rounded introduction to the politics of crime control that, by default, describes the circumstances under which victim-centred justice could come to prominence. Other texts, particularly from the 1980s, outline the ascendancy and divergent strands of victim-centred research and criminal justice developments at the end of the twentieth century; see, for example, Maguire and Pointing's edited book (1988), and Walklate's text (1989). Recognising the important place that victims now occupy in criminal justice, both in the UK and other jurisdictions, Dignan and Cavadino's (1996) paper neatly critiques the promise and pitfalls of attempting to 'place' victims in different criminal justice models that are, in the main, constructed with offenders in mind. Finally, the growth in public and political concern about crime and victims needs to be interpreted against the backdrop of wider concerns centred on risk, insecurity and globalisation; herein, Bauman (1998) and Beck (1992, 2000) provide ground-breaking texts that help to contextualise the place of victims at the beginning of the twenty-first century; see also Hope and Sparks's edited collection (2000).

Notes

1. www.unhchr.ch/html/menu3/b/h_comp49.htm.
2. www.victimology.nl.
3. Becker (1981), quoted in Rock (2002: 3, fn 17).
4. Van Dijk (1991: 1).
5. Beck and Robertson (2003) provide a less sophisticated reading of post-communist Russian experiences of victimisation and concern about crime based on a victimisation survey.
6. The description of new modes of governance, outlined here, is particular to Britain. While other countries, particularly the USA, have developed responses to crime and victimisation that resonate with the British experience, there are many other countries that promote crime reduction but which give insufficient attention to victim satisfaction with criminal justice services and correct treatment. In time, it might be the case that British criminal justice pays less attention to victim satisfaction and correct treatment of victims as newer and different modes of governance, with different priorities, come in to play. Also, criminal justice agencies, and victim agencies, can become complacent to the ongoing need to review and update victim services having been focused on these issues in the past.
7. www.nyc.gov/html/nypd.
8. Pregnant mothers took the thalidomide drug to reduce symptoms of morning sickness and so, unknowingly, damaged their unborn foetuses; many were born without limbs. The drug had undergone insufficient pre-trial tests by the company promoting it.
9. See www.homeoffice.gov.uk/rds/violencewomen.html. In June 2000 the British government assigned £6.3 million from its £250 million Crime Reduction Programme to local agencies and multi-agency partnerships to develop and implement strategies to reduce violence against women, focusing on domestic violence and rape and sexual assault by known perpetrators.
10. See Guardian Unlimited website, 'Millions of crime victims go without help' (26/2/04) on Victim Support's report '30:30 Vision'; also Victim Support's website www.victimsupport.org.uk.

Chapter 2

Counting victimisation: who are the victims?

Introducing themes for discussion

The survey showed that the statistically average person age 16 or over can expect: a robbery once every 5 centuries (not attempts), an assault resulting in injury (even if slight) once every century, the family car to be stolen or taken for a joy ride once every 60 years, a burglary every 40 years . . . and a very low rate for rape and other sexual offences.

(Hough and Mayhew, 1983: 15)

Anyone can be a victim of crime. The likelihood of becoming a victim of crime is dependent on a number of factors which, contrary to the above quote taken from Hough and Mayhew's report on the first British Crime Survey, impact differentially on individuals. What this quote serves to illustrate is the limited meaning of averages and the seductive quality of statistics for victimology (Pease, 1999). Crime and victimisation statistics can both support and refute our worst fears about the likelihood of our own victimisation, while providing governments with the necessary evidence, selectively interpreted, for their agendas in the areas of crime and victim assistance.

This chapter proceeds to critique how we come to know about the extent and nature of victimisation by asking the questions 'how do we know about crime?' and 'who are the victims?' The chapter is divided into two broad themes, the first of which borrows from the title of a chapter in Sparks et al.'s (1977) seminal work on crime victimisation, 'Counting Crimes and Counting Victims'. The first part looks at the 'counting' of victimisation in England and Wales. A brief summary of major sources of victimisation information is presented, from officially recorded crime data through to national surveys of victimisation which sidestep criminal justice agencies. The second part acknowledges innovations in crime counting with examples from the contributions of left realist victimisation surveys, feminism, geography and the International Crime Victims Survey. From here, 'repeat victimisation' is introduced as one of the most revealing, yet grossly under-utilised, research innovations to have emerged in the victimological field in recent years with respect to patterns of victimisation.

Rather than attempt a definitive account of the myriad extent and nature of victimisation, the chapter presents an introduction to, and critical overview of, various sources of information on victimisation. Explanation of 'why' victimisation occurs is tentatively introduced, with fuller interpretations of the origins of victimisation, its risks and consequences, left to subsequent chapters.

Counting victimisation

When is a crime a crime?

> Social groups create deviance by making the rules whose infraction constitutes deviance.
>
> (Becker, 1963: 9)

Becker's observation, that crime is in the eye of the beholder, also rings true with respect to victimisation. Before we are able to 'count' acts of criminal victimisation, against the person, a business, or property, we need to recognise that something has happened that might constitute a breach of the law. While the law may proscribe what it deems to be criminal acts, which society can selectively agree with, it remains with victims and witnesses to perceive these acts as instances of victimisation which might come under the criminal law. In turn, having decided that something is an instance of victimisation, it rests with the victim or witness, or another interested party, to report to the police. People decide to report or not report a crime for various reasons. Increasingly, the desire to claim insurance explains, to a large extent, people's willingness to report property crime (at least in the developed world). Alongside this, belief in the police's ability to 'do something' about crime – that is, to apprehend a criminal or recover stolen property – is another factor influencing reporting behaviour. These series of decisions constitute the first stage towards recognition and recording of victimisation as 'crime'.

What is essential in this process is the public's role in 'detecting' the bulk of instances of victimisation and defining them as potentially criminal acts. The police generally react to information from the public in their day-to-day work. The image of the police officer who stumbles on a criminal 'red-handed', or the cunning detective who pieces together criminal evidence to unearth other crimes, is largely just an 'image' that serves the needs of television police dramas. While it is the police's responsibility to apprehend criminals and investigate possible crimes, they can only do this after an offence has come to their attention; and for this they rely disproportionately on the public. In turn, once something has been brought to the police's attention, the second stage of crime recognition comes into play as the police must decide whether, based on the evidence before them, something should be noted in the official statistics as a 'crime', or whether to 'no crime' it. Just as the public may weigh up the pros and cons in their decision to report or not report something to the police, so the police go through a similar series of decisions in their consideration of whether to record something as a criminal act; instrumental to this are factors such as the police's willingness to believe a victim's account, or the seriousness or triviality of an event in the eyes of the police. Having decided to record something as a criminal act, the next stage of the criminal justice process steps in. The police investigate a case and members of the Crown Prosecution Service (CPS) review the evidence before them when deciding whether there is a case to be pursued in the courts – if, that is, a suspect is apprehended by the police. In turn, once a case is successfully brought to court, everyone concerned, from victims and defendants through to police officers and victim support workers, awaits the outcome.

One could go on to document the subsequent stages of the criminal justice process and the impact that these have on those remaining victims whose experiences of victimisation are recognised in the criminal courts. However, the message to be taken from the above is that each instance of criminal victimisation can easily be waylaid once the criminal justice process takes possession of it; that is, the police and the CPS can decide not to pursue the case, victims can become non-cooperative, and suspects can go missing. The 'counting' of victimisation produces an entirely new set of figures dependent on where and when the count takes place. Of particular concern to this chapter are the first stages in the decision-making process, and the amount and nature of victimisation revealed at each stage with respect to: (1) the victim's recognition of their 'victim' status, which might identify a criminal act; and (2) the police's decision to record public reports of victimisation.

Sources of information on victimisation

In England and Wales there are two major sources of information about the extent of criminal victimisation: police recorded crime statistics, which are published in the annual Criminal Statistics, and the British Crime Survey. While police recorded crime produces data on the extent of crime as reported to and recorded by the police, the British Crime Survey also identifies instances of victimisation which go unreported. 'Crime surveys' or 'victim surveys', as they are variously referred to, have been championed as the tools for unmasking the 'dark figure' of crime, or crime that does not come to the police's attention. Comparisons of police recorded crime statistics with victim surveys reveals that both have their advantages and disadvantages when 'counting' victimisation.

Police recorded crime for England and Wales

In England and Wales, police recorded crime data has been collected since 1857. Longitudinal interpretations of recorded crime, over anything more than a few years, are, however, relatively meaningless as indicators of changing victimisation patterns given the fluctuating definition and application of the criminal law and the emergence of new recording practices. Today, the recorded crime figures provide an account of 'notifiable' offences – that is, offences which the police are required to notify to the Home Office, and which are arrived at through an operational definition of crime that considers those incidents which meet the following criteria: (1) demands of 'reasonable evidence'; (2) warranting the attention of the criminal justice system; and (3) punishable in a court of law (Aye Maung, 1995). Recorded crime figures are gathered on a monthly basis for all 43 police force areas in England and Wales, and are published at regular quarterly intervals and in the annual Criminal Statistics. They provide a limited measure of crime and victimisation.

Looking to the recorded crime figures for England and Wales for the twelve months to September 2000, one is able to extract a few interesting points. First, notifiable offences recorded by the police over this twelve-month period totalled 5.2 million; this represents a fall of 0.2 per cent over the previous twelve months to September 1999. Of these 5.2 million offences, 83 per cent were against property and 14 per cent were violent crimes. In contrast with the overall fall in recorded crime, violent crime rose by 8 per cent. But, as the Home Office was keen to point out, the rate of increase in violent crime slowed down in the twelve months to September 2000. However, breaking down the violent crime figures, the startling picture emerges that not only did violence against the person increase by 7 per cent, but robbery increased by a staggering 21 per cent. The violent crime figures to September 2000 may, as the government suggested, be enhanced by an increase in teenager-on-teenager muggings, primarily of desirable goods like mobile phones. Other explanations for the increase lie with changes in the law and the application of rules concerning the 'counting' of violent crime. For example, the 1998 Crime and Disorder Act amended the offences of wounding and common assault to introduce 'racially aggravated offences' with higher maximum penalties, which arguably encouraged victims of racism to report these crimes.

Throughout the 1990s in England and Wales, violent crime, as recorded by the police, increased. While 'burglary' and 'theft of and from vehicles', two crimes that impact on significant numbers of the public, have decreased since the early 1990s, this is small comfort to a population which has learnt to read 'violent crime' as a barometer of the 'state of the nation'. The *Guardian* newspaper headlined the publication of the police recorded crime figures to September 2000: 'Sharp rise in violence mars figures' (17/1/01). Although Britain's Labour government may feel able to praise its policy on crime, with evidence that notifiable offences, overall, have decreased since Labour came to power in 1997, the facts on violent crime serve to harm that image. Politicians have long used crime statistics as social indicators that can be used to shape policy and, when favourably interpreted, assist election campaigns. As Sparks et al. note in the opening sentence to their book *Surveying Victims* (1977: 1): 'The first motive for collection and publishing official statistics of crime and criminals was a political one' – and the same is true with respect to publishing data on the flipside of criminal events, that is, victimisation. Violent crime figures, more than any other measure of crime, capture the media's attention and stir public and political fears alike, but for very different reasons. In the search for explanations of 'how' and 'why' violent crime is increasingly reported to the police, and 'how' the police go on to record these reports, the impact of violent crime on 'real' victims, be these teenagers or victims of racism, must not be overlooked.

The British Crime Survey

In Britain, the first major survey of victims was the above-mentioned study by Sparks, Genn and Dodd in the early 1970s. The survey applied a questionnaire, asking about respondents' experiences of victimisation, to samples of the population in three London boroughs. Unlike police recorded crime statistics, Sparks et al.'s survey, as with all victim surveys, differs in its methodology and results because of one fundamental reason – it asks the public directly about their experiences of victimisation rather than wait for them to report to the police. The victim survey removes the police from their job as 'gatekeepers' in the counting of crime. This technique results in the unmasking of what has come to be known as the 'dark figure' of crime: that is, those crimes, or victimisations, which are not reported to the police.

In comparison with the long history of police recorded criminal statistics, the first national British Crime Survey (BCS) was carried out in 1981, and the results published in 1982. There have been subsequent surveys, or 'sweeps', every few years, with surveys now conducted once every two years. The latest survey results, at the time of writing, were published in the 2000 BCS. The British survey owes its origins to the US National Crime Survey (NCS), which was established in 1972. As Block notes (1993: 183): 'Many countries have followed the US lead, using methodologies and questions that derived from the NCS model.' For better or worse, the content and format of the NCS have shaped subsequent victim surveys, so much so that the old mould of victimisation investigation was for a long time in need of reform. But while the methodology of the NCS was a model for the BCS, the two surveys emerged in different periods, in different countries, and with different political agendas. Whereas the NCS was primarily promoted in the United States as a tool for mapping and controlling crime, the BCS was introduced in England and Wales as a means for more accurately counting the 'dark figure' of crime beyond the limitations of police statistics. To put it crudely, the NCS can be characterised as 'control' focused, while, arguably, the BCS in its early manifestations could be characterised as 'victim' focused.

Traditionally, the BCS has randomly sampled, in each sweep of the survey, up to 18,000 people from private households across England and Wales.[1] More recently, its sample size has doubled, and for the first time will provide data at the level of individual police force areas – so enabling BCS data to be directly compared with police statistics on crime. The usual format of the BCS, since its origins in 1982, has been as follows: one person, aged 16 and above,[2] is selected from each household and questioned about his or her experiences of property and personal crime, including sexual assault, over the past twelve months. A detailed questionnaire, administered by an interviewer, documents respondents' victimisation experiences, and asks them about household crimes against other residents. Respondents are also asked about their attitudes to, and concerns about, crime and criminal justice. As a random household survey, the BCS accommodates for gender, age, income distribution and ethnicity across different regions. However, recognising that this sampling method can fail to pick up enough ethnic minority households for the purpose of a statistically significant analysis, the BCS has boosted its sample of 'Asian'[3] and Afro-Caribbean households since the 1988 survey. The BCS also records 'series incidents', or similar experiences of victimisation against the same respondent, over the twelve-month period of the survey. While the 'dark figure' of unrecorded crime has been enthusiastically adopted as a comparative tool against police recorded crime, the BCS's findings on 'series incidents', as a version of repeat victimisation, are under-utilised as an invaluable source of information about the nature of crime patterns and victimisation proneness.

The 2000 BCS estimates that there were just over 14,700,000 crimes against adults living in private households in 1999. Since the first BCS, reports of crime steadily increased in the 1980s, and more so in the early 1990s. However, this trend has been reversed in the latter half of the 1990s. Comparison of the 2000 survey results with the previous survey's results for 1998 (with data collected for 1997) reveals a 10 per cent decrease in crime. Breaking down the 2000 BCS according to crime type, a decrease in nearly all types of crime is revealed when we compare the results with the previous survey; for example, burglary reports decreased by 21 per cent and vehicle-related theft by 15 per cent. With respect to violent crime, common assault fell by 3 per cent and wounding by 11 per cent; however, robbery increased by 14 per cent. Here we are reminded of the police recorded crime statistics for the twelve months to September 2000, which revealed strikingly similar trends with respect to different crime types.

Looking at the example of violent crime, the 2000 BCS confidently states that the average chance of experiencing violence in 1999 was

4.2 per cent. In other words, the 'average' citizen in England and Wales had less than a 1 in 20 chance of being the victim of violent crime in 1999. However, young men aged 16 to 24 were most at risk of being victims of violence, at 20.1 per cent, or a 1 in 5 chance. Young women aged 16 to 24 were also found to be at high risk of violence, as were single parents, the unemployed and private renters. In turn, while victims of violent incidents were predominantly male, at 57 per cent, it must not be over-looked that the remainder were female. Similarly, if we take the 'average' chance of being a victim of domestic violence, at 0.8 per cent, the figure is not only low but misleading. In 74 per cent of domestic violence incidents the victim was female, and the most common location for violence reported in the survey was in or around the home (26 per cent), followed by the street (23 per cent), pub or club (19 per cent) and around the workplace (17 per cent). What this summary overview reveals is that certain groups are more vulnerable to certain types of violence, in certain locations, and these patterns are consistent with each sweep of the BCS. The next chapter explores 'why' certain characteristics make people more vulnerable to certain types of crime; let it suffice to say here that crime 'counting' is only meaningful to explanations of victimisation when we move away from bland averages.

While the overall drop in victimisation reported by the 2000 BCS appears encouraging, particularly as this trend seems to marry with official statistics on recorded crime, these figures have to be cautiously interpreted. The number of crimes reported in the 2000 BCS is still one-third higher than the total number of crimes reported in the first survey. Likewise, one has to ask 'what' is being compared when attempting to draw on the findings of official crime statistics in an effort to support the results of the BCS.

Comparing police recorded crime with the BCS

Looking at the 2000 results for police recorded crime and the BCS, it would appear that the BCS reveals nearly three times the number of experiences of victimisation when compared with officially recorded data. While the totals may differ dramatically between the two data sets, the overall reduction in all crime types, in comparison with data from earlier years, set against an upward trend for certain crime types, is shared between both sets. Armed with evidence from both recorded crime and the BCS one could conclude, with some confidence, that the public are experiencing less property and vehicle-related crime, while they are experi-encing more violent crime of a particular nature – namely robbery/ mugging. However, only a sub-set of BCS crimes can be coded into crime types that match the criminal law; which, since 2001/2, have been com-bined in an annual Home Office report on police recorded crime and BCS results. Looking to this comparable sub-set of crimes[4], it would appear, according to the BCS, that there are four and a half times as many crimes against the general public than the police statistics indicate. As this sub-set of comparable crimes shows, the extent of hidden victimisation is truly a 'dark blot' which the official criminal statistics do not reveal.

Having stated the case that the victim survey is able to reveal the 'dark figure' of crime, it has to be acknowledged that police recorded crime includes those crimes which tend not to be counted by victim surveys: namely, so-called 'victimless' crimes such as drug abuse and consensual, but illegal, sexual acts; murder and manslaughter; and fraud. Likewise, police recorded statistics 'count' crimes against members of society, businesses and institutions which tend not to be covered by victim surveys: namely, the under 16s; commercial businesses and public sector establishments; and people not living in private households. In comparison, the BCS is limited in its scope to crimes committed against people living in private households. In acknowledgement of their sampling and methodological limitations, some localised victim surveys have tried to unearth the extent and nature of commercial and other white-collar crimes (Pearce, 1990), though research in this area has not been taken up to the extent that it could have been (see Chapter 8).

Much of the variation in information provided by police statistics and victim surveys is explicable with respect to their different reference periods for and methods of counting crime. Whereas the police are the recipients of all information about crime that comes to their notice, be this from the public, the police themselves, or criminal informants, which they subsequently sift according to the criteria of the law, victim surveys source their information directly from the public. The BCS counts incidents which could be punishable under law but which the police, in practice, might decide not to pursue. Likewise, the BCS codes incidents into crime types which respondents might not perceive as crime. The BCS is solely reliant on what victims are able and willing to recall with respect to their experiences of victimisation, or the experiences of other household members, over a twelve-month period. In this respect, it is hardly surprising that the BCS reveals very low rates of sexual assault and 'domestic' violence, when compared with estimates from feminist research, given the sensitivity of the subject matter. On the other hand, one has to consider whether the BCS fares any worse than the police when 'counting' crimes that the public are less likely to reveal to either the police, an interviewer, a friend, or a family member.

Whereas police recorded crime statistics tend to deal with incidents that the public recall and are willing to report, victim surveys suffer from the problem of 'backward' or 'external telescoping'. In other words, surveys, because of their bounded timeframe, are at risk of including incidents prior to the survey period. Similarly, 'forward telescoping', or memory decay, can occur with respect to forgetting earlier incidents in favour of later incidents. Block (1993), in his overview of victim surveys in twelve countries, has argued that the NCS reduces the problem of 'telescoping' by returning to the same address over several cycles of the survey in order to separate incidents into clearly bounded time slots; in turn, each sweep of the NCS is limited to a recall period of six months.

Looking for broad comparisons between police data and the BCS can only reveal so much about the nature of victimisation. It is more interesting and practically useful to know 'who' is being victimised, what crimes they are experiencing, where, and how often. In other words, knowing the gender, age, socio-economic background and ethnicity of victims, and in some cases their offenders, tells us that victimisation is anything but a succession of random events where we are all equally at risk. In this respect, the BCS produces data about the risks of victimisation which vary between different groups in the population. In comparison, police recorded crime data does not have this information to hand, but is able to produce a breakdown of victimisation risks according to each police force area in England and Wales. However, as Farrington and Dowd's (1984) research on recorded crime statistics revealed, striking variations between police force areas can, to a large extent, be explained by each force's different method of 'counting' crime. To take either officially recorded crime statistics or victim survey data at face value is, if not carefully interpreted, a highly misleading exercise when attempting to understand the layered realities of victimisation experiences.

Developments and innovations in crime counting

Alongside the BCS, we can look to other research and other surveys, which emerged from various political and non-political agendas, to discover some interesting 'counts' of divergent experiences of victimisation.

Political will

In the UK, since Sparks et al.'s (1977) ground-breaking survey of Londoners' experiences of victimisation, there have been a number of locally based surveys, for example in Islington (Jones et al., 1986), Merseyside (Kinsey, 1984, 1985) and Sheffield (Bottoms et al., 1987). These surveys, like their national counterpart, came to prominence in the 1980s through a combination of political will and academic interest, and in response to the problem of rising crime rates (see Chapter 1).

First, there was the political will to be seen to be doing something about the country's rising crime rate and the underlying problem of 'fear of crime', fanned by the media's flames, which the public had taken on board. Local government authorities promoted victimisation surveys, often funded by central government initiatives such as 'Safer Cities' projects (Ekblom et al., 1996), with the aim of highlighting crime and victimisation in certain localities. Victimisation surveys were often the precursor to community-based situational crime prevention initiatives (Crawford, 1998). 'Target hardening' is one such crime prevention initiative that came to the fore in the 1980s, its primary objective being to make property, from the individual's private home through to entire government housing schemes, a less attractive target for criminals (Allatt, 1984). At the same time in the 1980s, the police were encouraging neighbourhoods to organise themselves into 'Neighbourhood Watch' schemes (Bennett, 1988). These schemes emphasised burglary prevention and community cohesion in their effort to make local residents 'look out' for each other's property and report suspicious incidents or individuals to the police.

Victimisation surveys and situational crime prevention initiatives were variously developed in the 1980s as part of the political drive for crime prevention through 'community' involvement and personal responsibility for one's own safety. These developments purported to place equal emphasis on crime *and* the public – as victims or potential victims of crime. The public, as citizens, were encouraged to become active participants in their own crime prevention initiatives. However, the idea of 'active' citizenship, in the field of crime prevention and victimisation reduction, has its limitations. For example, those with money can afford to install security devices in their homes, while poorer households, those most often at risk of victimisation, cannot afford to do so. Likewise, the idea of 'community' or 'neighbourhood', as part of 'active citizenship', was inadequately developed with respect to early crime prevention initiatives. For example, local areas suffering from high crime rates and high degrees of social incivility also tend to suffer an absence of the kind of 'community' cohesion which might facilitate the organisation and upkeep of various crime prevention initiatives over the long term (Hope and Shaw, 1988). While target hardening and Neighbourhood Watch have had varying degrees of success in their attempt to reduce crime, victimisation surveys have benefited from their lack of a 'results' based remit. In particular, locally based victimisation surveys flourished in an era when administrative criminology and actuarial justice, as the criminology of government, set out to 'count' crime – the age of the audit had emerged.

But in 'counting' victimisation and fear of crime, victimisation surveys succeeded in revealing particular crime problems, for certain groups, in localised settings. Enthusiasm for these surveys spilled over into the 1990s, with many towns and cities replicating the format to produce their own survey on victimisation and fear of crime. Replicating the survey format also resulted in the replication of a number of survey findings. Regularised patterns emerged, regardless of where each survey was conducted, showing that, for example, young men were more at risk of public place violence while displaying low levels of 'fear' of crime, while the elderly were at low risk of public place violence while showing high levels of 'fear'. But whether much beyond data reproduction emerged from the bulk of this research is debatable. Given the general remit of local government to use research money for practical outcomes, it appears that there was much duplication of research on victimisation and fear in the 1980s and 1990s, with inconsistent evidence of practical results 'for' victims. Practical initiatives to reduce and prevent crime, employing variations on the victim survey, have centred around the particular problem of repeat victimisation on high-crime public housing estates (see focus on repeat victimisation at end of this chapter), but these initiatives have often been hampered by a simplistic interpretation of what transferable 'best practice' can be expected to achieve when looking to reduce crime in different places and with different populations (see Chapter 4).

More recently, the installation of town-centre CCTV (closed circuit television) cameras has surpassed the victim survey as the favourite tool of local authorities in their endeavours to undermine crime and social disorder (Honess and Charman, 1992). But whether CCTV, as part of the crime prevention industry, can be viewed as anything but offender-focused, rather than victim-oriented, is questionable. From asking the public about their experiences of crime, victimisation, and fear of crime, the victim industry has, with the support of local British government and commercial business interests, moved on to other initiatives which are part of the crime as 'control' industry that has its echoes in Neighbourhood Watch.

Left realism and feminism

Alongside the influence of political will, the 'counting' of victimisation flourished in the 1980s as British academic criminology, in the guise of left realism and feminist criminology, adopted the victim survey as a form of 'action research'.

In the hands of the left realists, the victim survey set out to highlight victimisation as a 'real' and everyday problem for, in particular, some of the most deprived segments of the population. Academia and left-wing local government authorities often collaborated to undertake victimisation surveys of localised populations in, typically, inner-city areas with diverse crime problems.[5] Left realism endeavoured to take victimisation and the victim 'seriously' through the incorporation of four central elements in an active response to crime: (1) formal social control, by the police and other agencies; (2) informal social control, by members of the public; (3) the offender; (4) the victim. This fourfold response to crime and victims, at a theoretical and practical level, is referred to as the 'square of crime' (Taylor et al., 1973). The square has been variously developed over the years to include more 'variables' in the consideration of victimisation. For example, Anderson et al. (1994) added a fifth element, 'the city', which they intersected with the 'variables' of gender, age, class and race; while DeKeserdy (1996) focuses on the introduction of race/ethnicity, class and gender into the square's reading of victimisation.

The Islington Crime Survey (Crawford et al., 1990; Jones et al., 1986) typifies left realist academic criminology. The survey set out to address a number of topics that had hitherto remained untouched by the BCS. Alongside accounts of victimisation which could be variously coded as 'criminal' events, the Islington Crime Survey (ICS) asked about the following: non-criminal experiences of harassment and incivilities in the street, particularly against women and minority ethnic groups; inter-racial incidents; drug use; membership of political groups and victimisa-tion; and local policing. The survey, based as it was on a left-wing political ideology, was also 'challenging' because its central remit endeavoured to unearth the crime problem for some of the most deprived groups in inner-city London at a time when a Conservative government was in power. However, the ICS suffered something of a crisis of legitimation in its wholesale adoption of a methodology, the questionnaire survey, that has its roots in positivist criminology, from the NCS through to the BCS, designed with mainstream political goals in mind (Smart, 1990). Having said that, the questionnaire format of the ICS lent its results, which could be statistically tested, some legitimacy in the eyes of sceptical 'mainstream' agencies. In turn, the transferability of the ICS's questionnaire format must have served to encourage subsequent British Crime Surveys in their development of questions on previously neglected subjects, such as sub-legal harassment and inter-racial victimisation.

Arguably, feminist research on violence against women superseded some of the 'innovations' of left realism with respect to the theory, the content and often the methodology applied in their research (Dobash and Dobash, 1979). Two years before the ICS, feminist academics Hanmer and Saunders (1984) undertook a community-based study of violence against women in northern England. Their research showed the 'everyday' reality of many women's experiences of violence at the hands of men, which surveys like the BCS, and even the ICS, were not designed to reveal. Feminist research, from the 1970s on, was (and is) instrumental in the development of victimology in the UK and elsewhere. Most significantly, feminist research noted women's experiences of harassment and violence over a lifetime, a timeframe which the bounded quantitative victim survey is unable to capture, and in the home as well as public space (Kelly, 1987; Stanko, 1988). Rather than ask about experiences over the last twelve months, feminist research enquired and theorised about women's victim-isation as part of a 'continuum' of experience, from a young age, from low-level harassment through to sexual and physical abuse. One can posit that feminist victimology, having revealed women's ongoing experiences of harassment and violence, paved the way for research developments in the field of repeat victimisation. However, these observations were not employed beyond a limited feminist reading grounded in patriarchal theorising about the causes of men's violence against women.

To some extent the localism, targeted sampling, and grass-roots political activism of feminist research on violence against women makes it similar, in many respects, to the political idealism of left realist surveys. Also, feminist research and left realism were often as 'guilty' as each other in their uncritical application of the survey method in their attempt to 'count' crime. However, left realism, coming at the same time as the height of 1980s' academic feminist victimology, has been critiqued for its failure to take on the lessons of feminist researchers with regard to women's lifetime experiences of harassment and victimisation at the hands of men (Walklate, 1989). Left realism was politicised, but its politics has been accused of remaining, at least in its early work, strangely 'genderless' in its effort to explain victimisation through a class analysis of crime. In the same vein, early left realism did not engage with racism and homophobic crimes to the extent that it should have.[6] In its drive to explain crime through a class analysis, while revealing high levels of harassment and victimisation against women and ethnic minority groups, the ICS underplayed the fact that crime tends to be experienced within social groups. In other words, 'real' people experience 'real crime' often from their social and economic peers.

Geographical contributions

Outside academic criminology and victimology, brief mention should be given to geography's active participation in the field of crime and victimisation 'counting'. Given the resonance of the Chicago School's early urban sociology to both criminology and human geography, it is hardly surprising that academic geographers have revisited the 'geography of crime' on a number of occasions (Evans and Shaw, 1989). More recently, geographic information systems (GIS) (Goldsmith et al., 2000) have given crime mapping a new lease of life, and have been utilised by the police for advanced practical applications.

Geographers have enthusiastically resurrected Oscar Newman's ideas on 'defensible space' and the 'community of interest' (Newman, 1972). Through its focus on designing the built environment to reduce opportunities for criminals to commit crime, while enhancing informal social control, defensible space resonates with criminological concerns in the area of crime prevention and the active participation of communities. Like their criminology counterparts, British geographers responded to the funding demands of administrative criminology in the 1980s and early 1990s with practical research applications of defensible space ideas.

A good example of focused defensible space applications, which Hale somewhat dismissively refers to as 'mundane' (1996: 127), can be found in the street lighting projects which geographers (Herbert and Moore, 1991) and criminologists (Ditton et al., 1991) have worked on in partnership with local authorities, police, local communities and private business. These projects typically employ a 'before' and 'after' victimisation survey of local residents, often in a few streets, to map any changes in their experiences of victimisation and fear of crime as a result of improved street lighting. Though seemingly 'mundane' in their remit, innovative research can be pulled from various lighting studies. For example, Painter (1989) examines the 'place' and 'time' of crime for women and the elderly in a couple of streets in inner-city London; and Davidson and Goodey's (1991) research, based in a geography department, includes a rare insight into children's views on crime and fear of crime in a 'before' and 'after' study of street lighting in a small neighbourhood of Hull, northern England. However, while these studies may demonstrate some reduction in crime for the period in which research was undertaken, commentators have critiqued their potential for 'crime displacement' – that is, crime can move on to neighbouring areas which do not enjoy the benefits of crime prevention initiatives, and in time crime may rise to its former level in the targeted area once the initial impact of crime prevention initiatives has worn off (Cornish and Clarke, 1987).

While geography has applied itself to the demands of administrative criminology, by mapping victimisation, it is feminist geography which has been better placed to theorise the spatial resonance of victimisation and fear of crime for certain populations, namely women (Pain, 1991), the elderly (Pain, 1995), children (Valentine, 1997a, 1997b), and to a lesser extent ethnic minorities (Pain, 2001). Feminist geographers have mirrored the concerns of their victimological counterparts to address the experiences of victimisation for some of the most vulnerable groups in society. In this tradition, Valentine (1989a, 1989b, 1990) examines the 'place' of victimisation and fear of crime in heterosexual and homosexual women's everyday management of public space; while Pain explores the elderly's experiences of victimisation in public space and private care. Feminist geography has been particularly active in analysing women's gendered experiences of crime, everyday incivility, and fear, with respect to the 'place' of these experiences as posed dichotomously around the notion of 'public' and 'private' space. By deploying the specifics of 'place' to interpretations of victimisation of weaker social groups by stronger groups, feminist geography has given a new spatial spin to work by feminist criminologists on violence against women and women's fear of crime.

Through a combined interest in 'mapping' patterns and looking at space as a unit of study, geographers have engaged with crime and victimisation at a number of levels that differ from the mainstream focus of criminologists and victimologists. While victim surveys have tended to employ the town or city as a site for sampling, with some degree of comparison of victimisation in districts with different socio-economic and ethnic backgrounds, geography has taken 'place' and 'time' as central reference points for understanding crime and victimisation. Taylor et al.'s (1996) broad sociology/criminology-based study of two cities, Manchester and Sheffield, goes some way towards marrying the interests of criminological and geographical audiences. The research examines aspects of victimisation and fear of crime in the context of two diverse urban cultures. Using extracts from qualitative interviews with a range of social groups (gays; minority ethnic groups; women; the elderly; teenagers), Taylor et al. begin to offer an in-depth spatial reading of unsafety. Such insights are generally absent from mainstream victimological studies that, even when employing interesting references to urbanisation (Wikström and Dolmén, 2001), tend to remain with positivistic interpretations of victimisation and fear that reflect, to some extent, the funding remit of an era (the 1980s/1990s) which set out to 'count' crime.

The International Crime Victims Survey

At the other geographical extreme to the local small-scale study of victimisation is the International Crime Victims Survey (ICVS). This is a survey of victimisation, fear of crime, and attitudes to crime and criminal justice in different countries throughout the world, and is administered by the Dutch Ministry of Justice with the cooperation of UNICRI (the United Nations Institute for Criminal Research in Italy) and various government administrations. The survey uses a standardised questionnaire and asks respondents about their experience of victimisation over the previous twelve months. Respondents are mainly interviewed over the telephone using computer assisted telephone interviewing (CATI), with respondents sampled through random digit dialling. At the time of writing, there have been four sweeps of the survey: 1989, 1992, 1996 and 2000. Fourteen countries from 'western' Europe, plus Australia, Canada and the USA, took part in the first survey. Since then, developing countries and countries in transition have been included. Seventy countries have taken part in the survey over the course of all four sweeps, with England and Wales included in every sweep. The latest ICVS is a survey of criminal victimisation in seventeen industrialised countries (Van Kesteren et al., 2000).

Overall, looking at crime trends across all four sweeps, the survey suggests that victimisation increased in the period from 1988 to 1991 (the years in which data was collected), and fell or stabilised in 1995, with a further fall in 1999. However, for England and Wales, Finland and the Netherlands, which have taken part in all four sweeps, victimisation levels in 1999 were higher than in 1988. In comparison, North America (Canada and the USA) has experienced a steady decline in victimisation, with the latest victimisation levels lower than in 1988.

Examining the combined results for all seventeen industrialised countries which took part in the 2000 ICVS, it appears that car-related crime is the biggest problem for victims. The 2000 survey indicates that car vandalism, together with thefts of and from cars, accounts for over 40 per cent of victimisation as experienced by ICVS respondents. In comparison, contact crimes (robbery, assaults with force, and sexual assaults (women only)) account for around 25 per cent of victimisation, while burglary, theft of personal property, and motorcycle and bicycle theft each amount to just over 10 per cent of victimisation reported in the survey. Looking at the example of contact crime in detail, the 1996 ICVS revealed that 3.5 per cent of respondents in the USA experienced contact crime once or more in 1995; in 1999 this figure had dropped to under 2 per cent. However, in the case of England and Wales, contact crime has remained at nearly 4 per cent for the two latest sweeps of the survey. As *The Economist* (24/2/02–2/3/02: 40) noted, reporting on the 2000 ICVS:

> Britain may have slipped down many world league tables over the past few decades, but it beats all other rich countries except Australia in one activity: crime . . . people in England and Wales are at greater risk than anywhere else of having a car stolen. And apart from Australia, people who live in England and Wales are at greater risk of being assaulted, robbed, sexually attacked and having their homes burgled . . .

As *The Economist* article goes on to point out, these findings are 'deeply embarrassing to a government which has promised to be "tough on crime and the causes of crime"'. One can add that the 2000 ICVS findings are doubly embarrassing as they are in line with the recorded criminal justice statistics for England and Wales.

While the ICVS cannot, by any means, be described as the definitive 'count' of victimisation in any of the countries it surveys, it does provide the only large-scale cross-national comparative measure of victimisation, as opposed to 'crime', around the world. Comparing police recorded crime data with the ICVS reveals a degree of symmetry between these two sources of information on victimisation. The survey, as applied to countries in transition, has also captured the experiences and moods of respondents as they enter periods of political, economic and social upheaval which are reflected in their anxieties about crime, policing and governance. While there are now any number of victim surveys produced in different countries throughout the world, the ICVS is exceptional with regard to its standardised application of a questionnaire survey in different countries.

Since its launch in 1989, the ICVS has proved to be an innovative development in the field of victimisation 'counting'. Taking the lead from various victim survey initiatives in different countries, the survey captured the mood of administrative criminology in the 1980s and 1990s. In his comparison of victimisation surveys in twelve different countries, Block concludes (1993: 202): 'The best comparison of victimization experience is between identical surveys with identical methodologies.' However, in reference to the ICVS, he adds (1993: 202): 'the relatively small number of respondents to each survey and the differential response rates of the surveys limit comparison'. The ICVS coordinators have aimed at around 2,000 respondents per country, the main objective being to keep costs down. However, there has been great variation in the number of respondents in each country, with, in the first survey, 1,000 respondents for

Switzerland and over 5,000 for West Germany. Likewise, as Block notes, response rates in the case of the first survey ranged from in excess of 60 per cent in four countries to under 45 per cent in the case of seven countries (Van Dijk et al., 1990: 8). The statistical significance of the research findings is reduced by low and differential respondent numbers between countries. However, there are other concerns which can be aired with respect to the ICVS's cross-national comparability.

Given the ICVS's spread of countries with very different political, economic, social and criminal pasts and presents, one has to ask 'what' is being compared when standardised tables of victimisation 'counts' are produced for the reader's consumption. The ICVS does provide, in its fuller versions, an account of the situation in each country that attempts to contextualise the survey's findings culturally. However, this is largely lost in the production of a broad overview of differences in victimisation experiences. What the ICVS does usefully highlight, given its range of countries and the replication of the surveys over time, is any rough trends in victimisation experience and attitudes to criminal justice across regions of the world. As officially recorded crime statistics are the only real altern- ative to the ICVS when attempting to compare victimisation in different countries, it has to be acknowledged that the ICVS offers an alternative source of information on the extent of 'hidden' victimisation. Given that cross-national comparisons of official criminal statistics suffer from the problem of different legislation, criminal justice practice, and reporting and recording norms (Barclay and Tavares, 2000; Kangaspunta et al., 1998), the ICVS, though small with respect to its respondent numbers, is not to be lightly dismissed.

One can go on to critique the ICVS for its reliance, like many other surveys,[7] on computer assisted telephone interviewing (CATI) as a means of obtaining answers to sensitive questions, including sexual assault (Woltman et al., 1980). One can also critique the ICVS for concentrating on respondents in urban areas, or for applying standardised concepts of 'crime' in different cultures. The list of criticisms could go on; however, the standardised cross-national survey has, as Block notes (1993), its advantages over attempts at comparison of national victim surveys which use different questionnaires, different sampling frames, and different timeframes.

Setting the ready criticisms of the survey method to one side, the most important contribution of the ICVS has been its revelations regarding the shared experience of victimisation for many sub-populations of citizens across the world. In addition, the ICVS has been instrumental in highlighting victim satisfaction with policing and the problem of corruption. In particular, corruption has surfaced as a priority concern for survey respondents in developing countries and countries in trans- ition. This reflects the climate of everyday abuse which citizens in these countries suffer at the hands of government officials and private business (see Chapter 8). In this respect, the ICVS has highlighted crimes which traditional victim surveys, pioneered in developed industrialised nations, have not engaged with. As corruption leads to mistrust in the police, as the agency to which people are supposed to report crime, so we can begin to reflect on the reliability of officially recorded crime statistics in developing countries and countries in transition. People are less likely to report crimes they believe the police are unable or unwilling to solve; and, where large segments of the population are uninsured and must rely on an agency they do not respect to recover their assets, so we are left with an indefensible situation for victims. If anything, international comparisons allow us to reconsider the position of victims with respect to 'how well' we are, or are not, responding to their needs in comparison with countries with similar development profiles.

Focus: repeat victimisation

Recognition of repeat victimisation is arguably the most important development in recent years with respect to the 'counting' of crime, as it allows us to see with more accuracy 'who' is victimised. Repeat victimisation, or multiple victimisation as it is often referred to, tells us that a small proportion of the population experience a great deal of crime. As Farrell comments (1992: 85): 'In the British Crime Survey [for 1982], 70% of all incidents were reported by the 14% of respondents who are multiple victims (a conservative estimate).'

Repeat victimisation has only recently received the recognition it deserves. However, as Farrell observes in his overview of the literature on repeat victimisation, there is a long but neglected history of publications that directly or indirectly address the subject. For example, in the 1970s, Johnson et al. (1973) and Ziegenhagen (1976), as Farrell notes, borrowed from established references to the recidivist offender to publish their research findings on the relationship between violence and the 'recidivist' victim (an unfortunate application of the term as it implies the victim's culpability in their own re-victimisation).

In Britain, Sparks et al.'s pioneering victim survey (1977) explored the distribution of reported victimisation; as they noted (1977: 88): 'it will be seen that in all three of our sample areas a minority of respondents reported that they had been victims on more than one occasion during the preceding year'. Sparks et al. went on to test statistically whether the repeat pattern they observed was occurring by chance; it wasn't. Importantly, given the survey's timing, prior to the height of 1980s' feminist victimological concerns in the area of violence against women, Sparks et al. began to explore repeat violence against women. They noted that in the 26–30 and 31–35 age groups, female respondents accounted for almost all of the excessive variance in violence reported in their survey. However, they went on to note (1977: 94):

this is due almost entirely to the extremely high numbers of incidents (in one case, 18) reported by a few West Indian [Afro-Caribbean] female respondents; if these cases are excluded from the analysis on the ground that they are atypical, the amount of multiple victimization observed in the sample in different categories of age, sex, and race is not much greater than would be expected purely by chance.

The above reflects Sparks et al.'s goal to test their data statistically for patterns of multiple victimisation which may or may not be occurring by chance. However, while their statistical model was thrown into question, Sparks et al. noted the importance of the pattern which they observed (1977: 94):

Nonetheless, this approach can be of considerable heuristic value, since it may make it possible to identify particular sub-groups defined by attributes associated with relatively high rates of multiple victimization . . . which may be obscured by an overall comparison of victims and non-victims . . .

Sparks et al. proceeded to distinguish between counts of victimisation that focus on the *rate*, or *incidence*, of victimisation, and the more accurate use of *prevalence* when attempting to understand repeat victimisation. Their distinction has been variously adopted by victim surveys, and can be summarised as follows:

- The *victimisation rate*, or *incidence of victimisation*, is the number of victimisations per 100, 1,000 or 10,000 people, or households, sampled. It reports on the average likelihood of becoming a victim and obscures the reality of repeat victimisation for certain sub-groups within a population, while raising the 'average' risks for the population as a whole.
- The *prevalence rate* is the percentage of the population victimised on one or more occasions in a given time: for example, the previous twelve months.

In highlighting the importance of counting the prevalence rate, rather than the victimisation rate, Sparks et al. recognised victimisation's multiple reality for certain sub-groups in a population. They proceeded to ask the question 'why do some people become victims of crime?' Unfortunately, in their reference to 'the wife who continues to live with a drunkard who beats her' (Sparks et al., 1977: 97), as a typical 'commonsense' situation where multiple victimisation is likely to occur, they implicitly appear to 'blame' the victim. However, Genn, one of the co-authors of Sparks et al.'s study, later published research on multiple victimisation (1988) which, in the case of 'domestic' violence, clarified the normality of violence in many households. Genn's research benefited from her insights gleaned from participant observation which revealed the extent of multiple victimisation in particular households. In her successful application of a qualitative research method, Genn was able to question the victim survey as a credible tool for unearthing the reality of multiple victimisation regarding sensitive subjects.

Since the 1970s, surveys of victimisation have variously proceeded to note, or ignore, the importance of repeat victimisation to our understanding of victimisation. While the first Islington Crime Survey briefly comments on the phenomenon (Jones et al., 1986: 84), research on violence against women and in particular feminist contributions to this field (Stanko, 1988) have been central to the development of knowledge on repeat victimisation. Significantly, feminist research has emphasised the continuation of violence against women over time, and over a lifetime, which is often obscured in victimisation surveys limited to questions about experiences of violence over the last twelve months. However, it is through the BCS, and subsequent analysis of its various sweeps, that recognition of repeat victimisation has been brought to a potentially wider British audience. The first BCS published an appendix on the subject (Gottfredson, 1984), while subsequent surveys have collected information on victimisation prior to the twelve months covered by the survey (Ellingworth et al., 1997). There have also been detailed Home Office publications on specific aspects of repeat victimisation, including, for example, experiences of domestic violence in the twelve months prior to the BCS and over the respondent's lifetime (Mirrlees-Black, 1998), and experiences of racial attacks on problem housing estates (Sampson and Phillips, 1992). But it is with respect to property crime, and in particular burglary, that repeat victimisation has gained its widest audience in Britain.

The work of Ken Pease and his various research collaborators, most notably Graham Farrell, has in the late 1980s and 1990s exercised the interest of the British government and local authorities in the 'counting' of crime for the practical purpose of crime prevention (for example: Forrester et al., 1988; Forrester et al., 1990; Pease, 1991; Pease, 1998; Trickett et al., 1992). In repeat victimisation, administrative criminology's goal, to 'count' and respond to crime, was met. Most notably, the Kirkholt Burglary Prevention Project was an innovative local initiative which applied the principles of repeat victimisation and crime prevention to practical ends on a council estate in Rochdale, in the north of England (Forrester et al., 1988; Forrester et al., 1990). Through a combination of evidence from interviews with burglary victims, victims' neighbours, detained burglars, and police data on burglary, the project established that burgled households were four times as likely as non-burgled households to experience another burglary. The project's practical response, which also reflected its limited budget (Pease and Laycock, 1999), was to target scarce resources for situational crime prevention and opportunity reduction on those houses which had been burgled. The research concluded that burglary was reduced by 75 per cent in the three-year period of the project (Forrester et al., 1990). In targeting houses where people had already been victimised, rather than the entire estate, the Kirkholt project succeeded in preventing the bulk of further victimisation on the estate. As a result, there have been numerous attempts to replicate the Kirkholt model, but with varying degrees of success (Robinson, 1998).

Repeat victimisation's focus on the place of victimisation and the individual who is victimised has been neatly expressed in the following way: (1) the 'hot dot' is a term for the victim-prone individual; and (2) the 'hot spot' is a term for the place, or neighbourhood, prone to victimisation. As Pease and Laycock note (1999: 2): 'The hot spot is usually a hot smudge, with crimes occurring within a block or two of each other. The ultimate hot spot, the hot dot, is the victim who repeatedly suffers crime.' Having offered this definition, Pease and Laycock proceed to highlight questions with respect to the practical application of responses to the 'hot spot' or 'hot dot'. They refer to the blurred distinction between the 'hot spot' and the 'hot dot' in cases of repeat burglary and domestic violence. In other words, is the focus on the place or the victim? They also remind us that some individuals may be repeatedly victimised in different locations, by different people, and at different times. Explanation of 'why' repeat victimisation occurs, to particular individuals in a particular time and place, can inadvertently focus on the victim's actions, or inaction, as putting him or her at risk of victimisation. Various victimological theories, which attempt to explain the likelihood of victimisation in broader socio-structural terms, can be applied to repeat victimisation, most notably Hindelang et al.'s (1978) 'lifestyle' approach to victimisation, and Cohen and Felson's (1979) 'routine activities' theory. Both interpret the individual's routine daily activities, as mediated by their adaptation to social structural constraints such as access to work and leisure, with respect to individual risk of victimisation. A number of studies have applied these theories to explanations of repeat victimisation. The next chapter will explore some of these ideas in more detail, in terms of 'vulnerability' to and 'risk' of victimisation.

Cohen and Felson's (1979) 'routine activities' theory has been widely adapted to research on repeat victimisation. The theory considers the individual's experience of victimisation with regard to their routine daily activities (for example, where you go, how you get there, who you interact with) which converge with the following three factors in time and place: (1) a likely offender; (2) a suitable target (the 'hot spot' or 'hot dot'); and (3) the absence of guardians, or witnesses, against crime. Taking all three aspects of routine activities theory into account, there are a number of studies which have variously explored aspects of repeat victimisation with respect to the routine activities of victims, offenders, and the place and time of victimisation. For example, Wittebrood and Nieuwbeerta (2000) examine the relative influence of routine activities and previous victimisation on experiences of victimisation during one's lifetime. The routine activities of offenders, as rational choice actors, have been used to interpret 'why' offenders decide to target the same place repeatedly (Ashton et al., 1998). And Sherman et al. (1989), in a seminal

article, examine routine activities with respect to the occurrence of predatory crime in certain places. Similarly, repeat victimisation has been
used as a form of performance indicator when measuring police responses
to domestic violence (Farrell and Buckley, 1999) and the effectiveness of
victim support when offered to repeat victims (Farrell and Pease, 1997).

To conclude this focus on repeat victimisation: victimology, like its
criminology cousin, continues to dwell on interpretations of victimisation
which remain grounded in the criminal law and its concern with the
single instance or act of victimisation. Repeat victimisation offers a means
of 'counting' crime that can more accurately reveal and predict 'who' is
experiencing the bulk of victimising incidents and 'where'. In alerting
policy makers and criminal justice agencies to the significance of victimisation for certain populations and certain properties, over a period or a
lifetime, repeat victimisation can assist in the development of crime prevention initiatives that target those who are most vulnerable to victimisation. Through the insights of feminist victimology, repeat victimisation
has lent itself most readily to research and crime prevention initiatives
in the field of violence against women. In contrast, given the British government's recent focus on racism and the need for improved policing of
ethnic minority groups (see MacPherson, 1999), it is surprising that more
research on racism and repeat victimisation has not been carried out (see
Bowling and Phillips, 2002; Fitzgerald and Hale, 1996; London Borough
of Newham, 1987; MacLeod et al., 1996; Phillips and Sampson, 1998;
Sampson and Phillips, 1992). Any research on ethnic minorities should
address the interplay of various factors when attempting to explain repeat
patterns of victimisation: namely, the low socio-economic status of certain
ethnic minorities which makes them vulnerable to victimisation when
living and working in high crime areas; the younger age profile of
particular groups which increases their likelihood of victimisation; and
the racist motivation of offenders who see ethnic minority people, and
their homes and businesses, as suitable targets. In turn, more research
and practical responses need to be promoted with respect to repeat
victimisation as it affects other vulnerable social groups, such as children,
the mentally and physically disabled, the elderly, gays and lesbians.

Concluding comments

This chapter set out to document how we come to know about the extent
and nature of victimisation. In describing methods that are employed
to 'count' crime, from the victim survey through to the innovations of
repeat victimisation, the chapter has begun to answer the question 'who
are the victims' by critiquing the methods employed to count them. Later
chapters will present more detailed case studies of victims' experiences
with respect to the criminal justice system and alternative means of

victim assistance. In this respect, the chapter does not provide an overview of the range of victims, and of victims' experiences, in time and place. Such detail is best left to individual studies which the reader is alerted to in the chapter. What the chapter has illustrated is the difficult task of 'counting' victimisation, and the centrality of accurate accounts of the extent and nature of victimisation if criminal justice policy is to target victims effectively and prevent future victimisation.

Suggested reading

Summarised versions of the police's recorded crime figures and the British Crime Survey provide a good starting point from which to gauge the extent and nature of criminal victimisation in England and Wales; both are available through the government's Home Office site (see www.homeoffice.gov.uk), which also provides critiques of the victim survey method. To appreciate the various roads that research on criminal victimisation has taken, some notable work can be picked out from left realism (Crawford, 1998); feminist criminology (Kelly, 1987; Stanko, 1988); and feminist geography (Pain, 1991, 1995; Valentine, 1989a, 1989b, 1990, 1997b). Pease (1991), Farrell (1992) and Pease and Laycock (1999) provide the best introduction to the problem of and responses to repeat victimisation.

Notes

1. The 1982 and 1988 British Crime Survey included Scotland in its sample. Since 1993 Scotland has introduced its own crime survey.
2. There are exceptions to the '16 and above' sampling frame of the British Crime Survey; for example, the 1992 BCS included a separate self-completion questionnaire for children aged 12–15 (Aye Maung, 1995); see also Finkelhor (1997) for an overview of the victimisation of young people in the USA.
3. 'Asian' includes UK residents of Indian, Pakistani and Bangladeshi origin.
4. Comparable sub-set of crimes: (since 1982) vandalism (criminal damage); burglary (attempts and entry); vehicle-related theft (theft of and from, and attempted); bicycle theft; theft from person; wounding; robbery; (since 1998) common assault; vehicle interference.
5. See, for example, the Merseyside Crime Survey and the Edinburgh Crime Survey.
6. Bowling (1993) provides an insight into how 'racial harassment' can be included as a measure in local crime surveys; and research by Mason and Palmer (1996) and Truman et al. (1994) provides an overview of the extent and nature of homophobic violence and crime in major UK cities.
7. Since 1987 the US National Crime Survey has used CATI.

Chapter 3

Understanding 'fear of crime' and 'vulnerability'

Introducing themes for discussion

Having outlined in the previous chapter how we come to count and know about conventional experiences of victimisation, this chapter proceeds to elaborate on the subject of victimisation. Discussion focuses on two established and broad themes in victimology: (1) 'fear of crime', and (2) 'vulnerability'. Victimisation's wide reach is examined to include the influence of crime beyond the actual act of victimisation and the stereotypes of 'who' can be victimised. Rather than 'list' all the factors that contribute to the individual's 'fear of crime' and 'vulnerability', the chapter sets out to highlight a few salient points, from theoretical discussions and empirical research, that have characterised these central concerns of victimological discourse over the last decades.

A number of themes are explored with respect to their interconnections. First, 'fear of crime' is introduced as a revealing but limited concept that helps us to understand the impact of victimisation beyond the 'counting' of crimes against individuals. From here, 'vulnerability' is outlined as a generic term encapsulating factors that influence risk assessment and consideration of victimisation's consequences. The interplay between 'fear', risk of crime, and the assessment of crime's consequences is considered with evidence from the 2000 BCS. Following this, the chapter returns to interpret critically 'fear of crime' and 'vulnerability' as social barometers of crime and other public concerns that are not readily revealed through conventional measurements of crime and victimisation.

Finally, the chapter focuses on the subject of 'male fear of crime and vulnerability' as a case study in its own right. Male victimisation and vulnerability are explored as neglected subjects in general discourse concerning victimisation and fear, and are included here as illustrative of the limitations of established victimological theory.

Introducing 'fear of crime'

A concept with a wide reach

> The only thing we have to fear is fear itself.
>
> (Franklin D. Roosevelt, inaugural address to US Congress)

Roosevelt may have uttered these words in the context of the Great Depression, as a reassurance to the American economy and the American people, but they resonate with respect to criminology's recognition that, as Chris Hale states (1996: 131), 'Fear of crime is a problem in its own right.' In the last twenty-five years 'fear of crime' has blossomed, and subsequently wilted, as a much used and abused term that has attempted to encapsulate a set of ideas and research findings with respect to people's vulnerabilities and experiences of victimisation. 'Fear of crime' is now an unfashionable term that has been swallowed up by more generic theories about risk and insecurity that encompass ideas beyond narrow references to crime (see Chapter 1). With crime surveys having 'discovered' that 'fear of crime' is just as important in people's lives, if not more so, than actual experience of victimisation, the measurement of 'fear' was prominent in victimology for some years. In contrast, while various noted authors have attempted to conceptualise 'fear' (Fattah and Sacco, 1989; Ferraro and LaGrange, 1987; Killias, 1990), and some victim surveys have incorporated new readings of fear into their research (Hough, 1995; Mirrlees-Black and Allen, 1998), there remains a limited concept, more broadly in victimology, of 'who' can be 'fearful'. Much of this problem lies with the history of counting fear. In this respect, tried and inadequately tested measurements of 'fear' have persisted to this day which negate 'other' experiences of fear that do not conform with accepted wisdom concerning 'who' can be fearful.

More holistic interpretations of 'fear of crime', which look to and beyond crime and victimisation, can reveal a great deal concerning the 'state of the nation', with echoes in Roosevelt's words, in the complexity of people's 'fears'. When people are asked to respond to questions about crime and victimisation in the language of fear, they may, more accurately, be displaying a sense of 'concern', 'anxiety' and 'anger' regarding their vulnerabilities, which incorporates and reaches beyond limited interpretations of 'fear of crime'. Measures of crime and victimisation, be these through official statistics or victim surveys, are one part of how people experience and perceive their relative safety. Insecurities, as variants of 'fear', are measures which reveal a great deal beyond the counting of crime and victimisation. Here, research can stray into areas that have traditionally been on the margins of mainstream victimology, which remains with positivism in its efforts to 'count' crime.

However one defines, measures and interprets 'fear of crime', research indicates that people consciously and subconsciously alter their behaviour as a result of 'fear', concern and insecurities about crime. From crossing the street to avoid certain groups of people, to locking the car and installing home security, we variously employ crime avoidance and prevention measures which may or may not be attributable to 'fear of crime'. As insurance policies demand that 'target hardening' be installed in our homes, and as we police each other's movements with warnings not to visit certain areas of a city, so we are encouraged to be proactive in our own risk avoidance. These measures have become normalised in British society. Where once people reminisced about a 'golden age' when 'communities' could leave their doors unlocked, we have become acclimatised to the perceived risks of everyday life which are partly a reflection of criminal threat and partly an indication of increased social insecurity. While Mirrlees-Black and Allen (1998: 5), in their research for the Home Office, are able to conclude that the British Crime Survey 'provides strong evidence that fear of crime is related to actual levels of crime', the causes of 'fear' are complex and may be attributed to more than fluctuating crime levels. What we are measuring in our attempts to document 'fear of crime', and what we find in our results, is as yet unclear.

Measuring 'fear of crime': what are we measuring?

The majority of us experience crime not as offenders or victims, but as people who are sometimes aware of crime and who may feel ill at ease, vulnerable and potentially fearful in consideration of crime and the likelihood of our own victimisation. As the 2000 BCS reports, 6 per cent of respondents consider that fear of crime greatly affects their quality of life, whereas 4 per cent consider that crime itself has the same impact.

The image of an iceberg representing 'known' and 'hidden' crime, with police recorded crime revealed above the water's edge and the mass of crimes 'hidden' beneath the water's surface, can be transferred to our understanding of victimisation and 'fear of crime'. Here, 'fear of crime' (or, more accurately, vulnerabilities and insecurities), which the majority of us experience, lies beneath the water. In comparison, victimisation, and in turn offending, lie nearer the top of the iceberg, as fewer can claim these experiences as their own. Acknowledging that vulnerability and insecurity are pervasive, and tend to reflect experiences beyond victimisation and offending, demands an accurate interpretation and measurement of 'fear' as it narrowly relates to crime and victimisation.

The standard question

Crime surveys typically attempt to record, as a minimum, the following: experiences of victimisation; experiences of and attitudes towards criminal justice; and concerns about crime which, at their core, focus on 'fear'. Often, enquiries about 'fear of crime' are embedded in standard questions about feelings of personal safety and unease in the area in which the respondent lives, such as 'How safe do you feel being out alone in your neighbourhood after dark?' The 2000 BCS, as with its predecessors, employed such a question,[1] its results indicating that 11 per cent of respondents said they felt 'very unsafe' walking alone in their area after dark, with a further 21 per cent feeling a 'bit unsafe'. In turn, the 2000 BCS reported that 8 per cent of respondents said they 'never' or 'rarely' walk in their local area after dark, at least in part because of fear of crime, with 19 per cent of women aged 60 and over responding in this way.

The basic problem with the above question, if it is used to measure 'fear of crime', is that it fails to mention crime. Breaking the question down into its component parts we can critique it on a number of other levels. First, it assumes that people do the following: (1) go out; (2) go out alone; (3) go out in their neighbourhood; and (4) go out after dark. It is difficult to gauge what is actually being measured here, particularly as many respondents will not engage in the described activity, or at least the specifics of it. More recently, victim surveys have tried to rectify this problem by excluding respondents from their analysis who do not engage in a question's specified activity, such as being out alone at night, for reasons other than fear of crime (Killias and Clerici, 2000).

Second, in critiquing this question, 'safe' is utilised for the concrete measurement, on a sliding scale of possible responses, of abstract feelings. Abstract responses, given in answer to abstract concepts of 'safety', will be elicited from the question as it fails to relate its attempt at measuring 'fear of crime' to people's lived realities. Therefore, it is not only difficult for some people to answer such a question, as the scene and its circumstances are outside their general experience, but it may also lead people to imagine the scene and consequently respond as 'if' they found themselves in it. Some crime surveys go so far as to ask respondents 'How safe *would* you feel?' In this respect the question and its response are in the realms of make-believe. Similarly, respondents may be asked to consider how 'safe' they consider stereotypically vulnerable groups to be, such as women and the elderly. Here, respondents are required to speculate on crime 'risk' and feelings of 'unsafety' for groups whose experiences they are often unfamiliar with. The response to such a question tells us far more about the respondent's conceptions of unsafety than particular groups' actual risks of victimisation or feelings of unsafety. As Killias and Clerici (2000: 442) comment: 'one's own sense of vulnerability tends to increase more slowly with age than the judgement of an observer, especially before the age of 65'. And in support of this, Chadee and Ditton's research with 728 adults concludes that (2003: 417): 'This study offers no evidence for the proposition that the fear of crime increases, in a simple linear way, with age.'

As already noted, there are variations on a theme with respect to the above question. However, there is a general tendency to locate questions in place. Surveys often ask about people's feelings of 'safety' in relation to 'the local'. References to 'your area', 'your neighbourhood' and 'your local streets' are commonly incorporated in the attempt to measure fear. There are a number of problems with this. First, people define their locality differently. If asked to describe what they understand as their 'local neighbourhood', different people incorporate any number of different streets. Second, as people are more mobile in their day-to-day lives, with work, leisure and transport taking them further afield, so there may be little affinity with their immediate locality. And if reference to 'community' is inserted in questions which try to gauge 'fear', then we shift into more ill-defined territory with respect to interpretations of what 'community' means in the context of 'the local' and 'the social' (Crawford, 1998).

One can also critique generic questions on 'fear', such as the above, as they negate the fluidity of people's experiences. While questions may ask respondents to differentiate between their feelings of unsafety during daylight hours and 'after dark', this does not capture the fluctuating nature of people's fear, which can shift from one day to the next depending on personal circumstances. In other words, people respond to questions depending on their experiential and emotional status at the time of questioning. So, a recent bereavement or a redundancy can influence people to answer with, apparently, more 'fear', whereas good news can result in a more positive response and, apparently, less fear. The 2000 BCS included a new question which asked those respondents who indicated they were 'very' or 'fairly' worried about burglary how often they felt this way. In this respect, the BCS is moving some way towards recognition that 'worry' about crime, like 'fear' of crime, is anything but a constant emotion.

Questions on 'fear' or 'worry', as posed in a victim survey, are necessarily constrained by the nature of the survey tool. Responses need to be codified into pre-existing 'boxes' in order to satisfy the demands of the positivist methodology that is searching for concrete responses for the purpose of statistical analysis. While interesting patterns are revealed by responses to standard questions on 'fear', there is also a danger of stereotyping certain groups – women, the elderly – as 'fearful'. As research by Baker et al. (1983: 319) revealed, on responses to a crime wave in Phoenix (Arizona), stereotypes can be overthrown: 'Demographic groups thought to be most fearful (e.g., women and the elderly) were least affected while groups thought to be least fearful (e.g., well-educated whites) were affected most.'

In turn, not only is there great variation between groups in the population with respect to the level of 'fear' encountered, there is also great variation within groups; that is, for example, not all women, or men, respond to crime and 'fear' in the same way. Research on 'fear of crime' which concludes that 'women are more fearful of crime than men' must be cautiously interpreted. 'Fear' is anything but a simple reaction to crime, which standard victimisation survey questions, in their attempt to measure fear, may lead us to believe.

Conceptualising 'vulnerability'

Academic victimology has variously attempted to explain people's risk or likelihood of victimisation with respect to 'who' the potential victims are, where they are in time and place, and the influence of socio-structural variables that shape who they are and what they do. This section focuses on the idea of 'vulnerability' as it relates to the risk and consequences of crime, which in turn help us to understand the experience and expression of 'fear'.

Theories of victimisation proneness

Just as criminological research looks to degrees of culpability when assessing offending behaviour, so early victimological theory concentrated on victim culpability in the enactment of a crime and its associated victimisation. The central focus of these early ideas, emanating as they did from the culture of the criminal law, was on the individual criminal act and the role of its actors (offender and victim) with respect to their relative degrees of 'innocence' or 'blame' for the events that took place. Von Hentig (1948) and Mendelsohn (1956) were pioneering proponents of theories which set out to document victims' personal characteristics and actions that might explain degrees of individual victimisation proneness. Mendelsohn created a typology of victim proneness, from the 'completely innocent' victim through to the 'most guilty' victim, which attributed degrees of 'blame' for victimisation with the victim.

Most controversially, these ideas were taken up in Wolfgang's (1957, 1958) research on 'victim precipitation'. Here, one's risk of and vulnerability to crime, and ultimately the consequences one must face as a victim, are subsumed under a theory measuring victim culpability. Based on his research into police records of homicide cases, Wolfgang concluded that 26 per cent were precipitated by the victim; that is, the victim had a direct role to play in the instigation of violence which led to their homicide. While Wolfgang's theory was narrowly based on the interpretation of events leading to homicide cases, as recorded by the police, his ideas have subsequently been adapted by other researchers to illustrate the role of victim precipitation. Notoriously, Amir (1971), in his study of rape, utilised the idea of victim precipitation in 19 per cent of the cases he studied. While victim precipitation has lost most of its credibility as a victimological theory of cause and effect, the criminal justice system continues to work with ideas of victim 'blaming' in its attempts to prove the defendant innocent by discrediting the victim, again most controversially with respect to rape and sexual assault cases (Lees, 1997). Here, the utilisation of victim precipitation as an explanation for victimisation proneness in cases of interpersonal violence, both of a sexual and non-sexual nature, reduces interpretation to limiting ideas of 'innocence' and 'blame' which focus on the instance of the criminal act and overlook the wider relationship between victim and offender over time.

From the example of 'victim precipitation', and the narrow framework of evidence on which much of it was developed, we can turn to other victimological theories which offer broader explanations of victimisation proneness. 'Lifestyle' or 'routine activities' theory (Cohen and Felson, 1979; Hindelang et al., 1978), as introduced in the previous chapter, surpasses the narrower applications of victim precipitation. While victim precipitation dwells on the act of victimisation when explaining victim proneness, other theories look towards aspects of the individual's lifestyle with respect to the likelihood of victimisation. Here, the individual's daily adaptation to the worlds of work and leisure, and their social structural constraints, as mediated by demographic variables such as gender and age, is directly linked to risk of victimisation. In other words, where you go, what you do and who you are, as determined by the limited choices in your routine daily activities, determines your victimisation proneness. Therefore, some groups are more prone to certain types of victimisation than others.

Borrowing from the inferences of the standard 'fear of crime' question, lifestyle or routine activities theory suggests the following: to go out at night, to go out alone, to go out on a regular basis, to go out in high crime areas – in other words, a regular trip to the pub – increases the individual's risk of victimisation. Hence, young males are at greater risk of assault, in public places at night, than the elderly or women. In turn, women are at great risk of becoming victims of violent crime in private space from known offenders. Having said this, early lifestyle theory disregarded the degree to which particular groups, such as women and children, are exposed to potentially victimising situations in private places as a reflection of their social-structural 'place' in society. Hence, lifestyle theories of victimisation proneness need to be re-interpreted to incorporate the private sphere and the role of gendered power relations which sustain violence, predominantly by men, against women and other vulnerable groups in society. We can only begin to appreciate the impact of gender, age, class, ethnicity and sexuality on the individual's victimisation proneness if due recognition is given to the differential impact of power on social-structural relationships and settings.

Having examined 'variables', such as demographic factors and routine patterns of lifestyle activities, which are instrumental in explaining, to some extent, victimisation proneness, these theories do not assign 'blame' for victimisation with the victim. Instead, they focus on the intersection of a series of circumstances, in time and place, which may manifest in a likely offender and a likely victim. In itself, this represents something of a tautological explanation of victim proneness; that is, you have to go out in order to encounter a likely mugger and in order to become a victim of public place crime. But beyond stating the obvious, these theories help us to understand the relative likelihood of certain groups becoming victimised. Unlike victim precipitation, which focuses on the circumstances of an individual event, lifestyle-based theories engage with victimisation as part of people's lived realities. As theories they encourage consideration of social-structural opportunities and constraints which impact on differential experiences of routine daily activities. However, as already noted, their remit needs to be extended to consider the relative impact of power and powerlessness on social-structural opportunities and constraints which affect social groups differently. So, for example, if you encounter racist violence in a public place as a young Afro-Caribbean male, this needs to be interpreted with respect to your demographic characteristics, your encounter with an offender in time and place, and the social-structural impact of racism. In other words, not only is your victimisation proneness exacerbated by your youth, by you being male, and by you being out in a public place, but fundamentally it reflects your 'place' in white British society.

Walklate (1989: 13–18), in her critique of lifestyle theories, turns to the six-part characterisation of victimisation proneness which Sparks (1982) develops. This includes:

1. precipitation: you precipitate, or encourage, your own victimisation;
2. facilitation: you put yourself consciously or subconsciously at risk, for example by forgetting to lock your car door;
3. vulnerability: the attributes you possess, such as physical weakness, that increase your risk;
4. opportunity: that is, you must have a car to have it stolen, but you can manage the likelihood of its theft by parking it in a secure place;
5. attractiveness: for example, wearing a lot of jewellery makes you an attractive target;
6. impunity: you are victimised as a suspected 'easy target' who is unlikely to report to the police, for example if you live in a low income household without insurance cover.

Sparks's six-point typology neatly encapsulates a number of explanatory factors of victimisation proneness from lifestyle theories, or routine activities theories, alongside the much berated theory of victimisation precipitation. However, Walklate characterises Sparks's work as 'conventional victimology' because it places too much emphasis on victimisation proneness in relation to the individual event and conventional experiences of victimisation. In turn, the typology emphasises the victim's role, or the target's role, in their own victimisation. And, once again, the importance of relative power and powerlessness in shaping the experience of victimisation through social-structural 'variables' is neglected. Herein, Sparks's typology is no different from the majority of theories on victimisation proneness. But what Sparks does offer is an effective checklist, in the form of a typology, which can be neatly employed for a rounded understanding of the circumstances leading to victimisation proneness.

While early theoretical explanations of victimisation proneness were either developed without the benefit of empirical research or based on findings taken from police data, later studies have turned to victim surveys which ask people, grouped according to their demographic characteristics, to relate their routine activities alongside their experiences of victimisation. These same surveys ask about respondents' assessment of victimisation risk. It is here, in the fusion of evidence concerning 'who' you are, what you do, experiences of victimisation, and your own judgement of personal risk, that research can enhance its understanding of victimisation causation, first with respect to the correlation of variables based on 'facts' sourced from respondents, and second with respect to emotive accounts of vulnerability.

Weighing up risk and consequence

Beyond standard questions that are repeatedly employed, somewhat inadequately, as measurements of 'fear', victim surveys examine respondents' judgement of their personal 'risk' of becoming a victim, in relation to specific crimes. For example, the 2000 BCS asked respondents about the likelihood of the following crimes happening to them in the course of the next year: being burgled; having their car stolen; having something stolen from their car; being mugged or robbed; or being attacked by a stranger. It reported that 29 per cent of respondents thought it likely that their car would be stolen, 32 per cent thought something would be stolen from their car, and 20 per cent thought their home would be burgled. In comparison with actual average risks, people's assessment of their risk tended to be higher; for example, for 1999, 1.8 per cent of households had a vehicle stolen and 4.3 per cent of homes were burgled. In turn, the BCS asked respondents how 'worried' they were about specific crimes occurring, a measurement which is linked to perceptions of risk and actual risk. The survey showed that around one in five respondents were 'very worried' about burglary, car crime, mugging, physical attack by a stranger, and rape.

Assessment of crime risk, together with measurement of concerns and/ or worries about crime, are central to any understanding of differential expressions of fear. However, each is measuring something quite distinct. As Hale, in his overview of the 'fear of crime' literature, notes (1996: 92):

> fear of crime refers to the (negative) emotional reaction generated by crime or associated symbols. It is conceptually distinct from either risks (judgements) or concerns (values). Of course fear is both an effect of, and caused by, judgements of risk but to confound the two is to confuse this relationship.

Bearing in mind Hale's warning, which is replicated in the work of Ferraro and LaGrange (1987), one can employ the term 'vulnerability' in an attempt to understand better the interconnected meaning of risk/ concern/worry as it relates to 'fear of crime'. However, 'vulnerability' is a problematic term in itself as it tends to be employed somewhat narrowly in the 'fear of crime' literature to refer to interpretations of people's physical vulnerability. Applied more broadly, vulnerability is, like the term 'victim', also not ideal because of its vagueness and emphasis on notions of weakness and disempowerment. But 'vulnerability' as a generic term can capture a number of factors – demographic, economic, experiential, environmental, physical and psychological – which serve to illustrate and explain different levels of victimisation, assessment of risk, concern/worry and, in turn, 'fear', among the population. While Hale is right to draw our attention to the distinctions between 'fear', 'risk' and 'concern', which are often confused in the 'fear of crime' literature, it must be remembered that people, as the respondents to victim surveys, tend to merge their emotions, judgements and values when referring to crime.

Your personal demographic characteristics, such as your age and sex, together with the environment in which you live, work and spend any leisure time, *and your exposure to and experience of crime,* are among the myriad factors which can shape your sense and experience of vulnerability. 'Fear' and insecurity about crime are one such expression of your vulnerability. For example, you can feel vulnerable to crime because of physical weakness, or low self-esteem, or a marginal socio-economic position that exposes you to fear-inducing circumstances. In this respect, certain groups are 'vulnerable' to crime and the emotive reaction it produces. As the 2000 BCS reports, in response to the question 'how much is your own quality of life affected by fear of crime?', the following groups were most likely to report that fear of crime greatly affected their quality of life: women aged 60 or over; Asians; those in poor health or with a limiting illness or disability; people in low income households; people living in public housing or housing association accommodation; and people living in areas with high levels of physical disorder. In combination, these factors work together to enhance people's sense of vulnerability.

As the above indicates, the environment, or the context in which you find yourself, also plays a large part in determining levels of vulnerability. Here, your sense of vulnerability is moulded by a sense of crime levels and degrees of social incivility in the area where you live and where you find yourself at any particular moment, be this a well-lit crowded shopping centre or a dimly lit deserted subway. Vulnerability is also shaped by direct and indirect experience of victimisation. In other words, personal experience of victimisation, or knowing someone who was victimised, or being a witness to victimisation, has the potential to exacerbate a sense of vulnerability. To some extent, with respect to the crime in question, people's assessment of their risk of further victimisation parallels, at an exaggerated level, their actual risk. As the 2000 BCS indicates, almost half of those who were burgled in the previous year thought it likely that they would be burgled again. While recent victims of burglary are obviously over-estimating their risk of further victimisation, the evidence from research on repeat victimisation, as outlined in the previous chapter, would appear to uphold their concerns.

When assessing their own risk of victimisation, people also consider the practical and emotional consequences should crime actually occur. Looking at the interconnections between risk and consequence assessment helps us to understand and rationalise people's expression of concern and, in turn, fear. Early victim surveys found that while women had apparently a low risk of being victimised in public space, they displayed high levels of fear. The 'rationality' of women's fear was questioned. However, if one takes into account women's vulnerability to sexual assault and rape, as particularly brutal and potentially life-threatening crimes, and the extremely debilitating consequences of these crimes should they occur, then women's apparently irrational expression of fear becomes rational. In a similar vein, many victim surveys show that elderly people tend to express high levels of fear of crime against their low risk of victimisation in public space. However, the elderly, when compared with younger people, have a reduced capacity to cope with crime. Given their physical vulnerability, which can be combined with psychological frailty, economic poverty and social isolation, their heightened fear of crime becomes readily explicable in consideration of the impact crime would have on their lives. Also, one has to consider that levels of crime risk for women and the elderly might be considerably reduced because they avoid situations where they might be victimised; that is, their avoidance of going out alone at night is a precautionary measure that serves them well against victimisation.

Taken together, these factors, as indicators of vulnerability, can help to explain differential experiences and expressions of 'fear', and have been variously constructed into a taxonomy of 'fear' in order to clarify the influence of one over the other (Killias, 1990; Killias and Clerici, 2000). For example, Killias and Clerici's research, based on a sample of 726 Swiss nationals, focused on 'physical vulnerability' as a central determinant of respondents' 'fear of crime', in comparison with demographic and contextual (neighbourhood) factors. Other research has focused on 'fear of crime' as it relates to vulnerability and poverty (Pantazis, 2000). There are any number of combinations of factors, or influential variables, which can be employed in the measurement of vulnerability and 'fear of crime'. But certain factors consistently resurface in the research to illustrate and explain heightened vulnerability. As Ditton and Farrall, in the introduction to their collected volume on 'fear of crime', comment (2000: xvi): 'gender has emerged as probably the biggest single demographic factor related positively to fear of crime'. Age comes in a close second, after gender, as a positive correlate of fear. While there is a great deal of debate concerning the elderly's expression of heightened 'fear' of crime, which according to some studies (Ferraro and LaGrange, 1992; Tulloch, 2000) reflects their general concerns and worries, there is ample evidence to match women's heightened fear with specific crimes that appear to 'target' women – namely, rape, sexual assault, and routine encounters with harassment (Kelly, 1987). In this respect, elderly women's heightened fear might be explicable with regard to a lifetime of targeted victimisation, threat and fear (Pain, 1995). Conversely, men's apparent 'fearlessness', which is consistently lower than women's at different ages, is under-researched as an irrational response to a real threat, or as emotional denial. Research does exist that questions gendered stereotypes about appropriate male and female expressions of 'fear of crime' (Gilchrist et al., 1998); but, given men's high risk of victimisation from certain crimes, such as assault by strangers and known assailants, which cannot always be dismissed as part of male 'horseplay', there is an obvious need for victimology to investigate more thoroughly fear as a gendered phenomenon. With this in mind, the final part of the chapter focuses on 'male victimisation and fear of crime' as a convenient route for revealing the complexity of 'fear' beyond standardised interpretations of 'who' can be fearful.

Having introduced the themes of 'fear of crime' and 'vulnerability', the next section critically examines their limitations with respect to broader considerations of their meaning and application.

Rethinking 'fear of crime' and 'vulnerability'

There is no neat correlation between high levels of victimisation 'risk' and 'fear of crime'. Those at great risk of victimisation can reveal apparently low levels of fear, and conversely those with low levels of risk can reveal high levels of fear.

As the previous sections indicated, people do not simply assess their likelihood of victimisation and respond accordingly with low or high levels of 'fear'. Likewise, people do not always react to victimisation as one might predict given the nature of the crime in question; that is, a victim of an assault might appear less affected than a victim of burglary. A differential sense of 'vulnerability' is developed for a number of reasons. People respond to victimisation and/or the threat of victimisation in different ways according to the nature of the crime in question, who they are, and the particular circumstances in which they find themselves. To reiterate, the following factors are central to any interpretation of emotional reactions to victimisation and/or its threat:

1. previous experience of victimisation;
2. perceived risk of victimisation;
3. vulnerability.

In turn, these factors need to be embedded in understandings of the role that socialisation, from one's childhood upbringing through to the kind of television one watches, has on differential emotional responses to victimisation – its threat and reality.

So, for example, a woman's apparent low risk of public place victimisation and high fear of public place crime can be more readily understood once we acknowledge the particular risks and consequences associated with sexual crimes that predominantly impact on women, and the routine sexualised intimidation and threats that women encounter (Stanko, 1990). In turn, women are socialised into legitimate expressions of fear that the media encourages by exaggerating the threat of public place sexual assault against women (Soothill and Walby, 1991) and downplaying the extent of violence against women in the 'domestic' sphere. A sense of 'vulnerability' and appropriate displays of 'fear' are positively encouraged in women from a young age (Goodey, 1994). Likewise, vulnerability and fear are socially legitimated for the elderly (Pain, 1995).

The apparent paradox that often lies with victimology's search for corresponding levels of risk and emotional response is partially explained by the problematic use of the term 'fear of crime'. Given the range of responses that people can have to the same crime, it would appear that employment of the term 'fear' has been highly detrimental for the advancement of the 'science' of victimological enquiry. Other terms might serve us better in providing a range of responses to crime and experiences of victimisation. But researchers seem loath to abandon the term 'fear of crime'.

In their attempt to construct a 'psychology' of 'fear of crime', Gabriel and Greve narrowly define their field of enquiry by stating (2003: 601): 'the term "fear of crime" is used throughout this paper to mean the individual's fear of personally becoming a victim of crime (in contrast to a general concern about crime . . . or the perceived extent of crime)'. They proceed to mention the 'extensive debate' in the field of psychology concerning the relationship between feelings and emotions, and fear and anxiety, but add (2003: 601): 'For our purposes, it is not necessary to try to resolve these issues, because we focus on reactions to a definite and recognizable external threat, although this threat ("crime") may be something quite vague' – quite so! In their psychology-based exploration of 'fear of crime', Gabriel and Greve contrast the individual's cognitive perception of being threatened ('How likely do you *think* it is that you will become a victim of physical assault?'), a corresponding affective experience ('How often *are you* afraid of becoming a victim of physical assault?') and an appropriate motive or action tendency ('Do you *carry anything* to defend yourself against physical assault?'). These states are briefly compared with established approaches in the 'fear of crime' literature that explore risk perception, vulnerability, and fear of crime. Yet Gabriel and Greve's enquiry lacks a broader recognition and understanding of risk and insecurity, as a range of social vulnerabilities, as they influence and are influenced by 'fear of crime' (see Chapter 1). Their analysis, like much of psychology's reduction of circumstances to the individual (Winkel, 1998), negates wider social influences on, and the politics of, fear.

Politicising victimisation and fear of crime: the neutral victim

In 1988 the British Crime Survey included reference to 'anger' as an alternative emotional response to victimisation other than 'fear'. Kinsey and Anderson (1992) produced a comprehensive review of the survey's results with respect to Scotland, and indicated that 'anger' was more predominant than 'fear' as a reaction to crime by both genders and across different ages and different income groups. While, for example, women expressed more 'fear' than men, both genders were consistently found to be more angry than fearful about victimisation. Given the weight of this evidence, which is supported by earlier (Maguire, 1980) and subsequent research into emotional responses to crime (Mawby and Walklate, 1994; Mirrlees-Black et al., 1996), it has to be asked why 'fear of crime' has come to dominate research on emotional responses to crime. The reason behind the ascendancy of 'fear', over and above alternative measures of emotional responses to crime and victimisation, needs interpretation with reference to the politics of victim-centred research and action.

As referred to in Chapter 1, 1980s' Britain witnessed an unprecedented focus on 'fear of crime' by public, politicians and the media, in correspondence with the rising crime wave which hit Britain during this period. 'Fear' became directly linked with crime. While undoubtedly people could be described as 'fearful' of crime, much of the research from this period, including important research findings from the 1988 BCS, did not emphasise the wide range of other emotional reactions to increasing levels of crime, such as concern and anger. Arguably, 'fear' dominated discourse and reaction to crime as a convenient political scapegoat to hide the deeper malaise of a society experiencing economic uncertainty and social unrest (J. Young, 1999). The British Crime Survey, from 1982 onwards, filled a gap in research knowledge by unearthing the extent and nature of hitherto 'hidden' victimisation, but it also served as the primary means through which the government could display its sensitivity to victims. Although heightened public fear of crime is not something to which any government would willingly draw attention, the 'fear of crime' debate allows for a tangible response to crime and victimisation through the development of victim-centred government initiatives.[2] Crime, or actual victimisation, is a much harder problem for governments to resolve. By measuring and highlighting 'fear' the government could promote its victim-centred stance at the same time as actual crime levels remained stable or increased.

The 1980s' enthusiastic focus on 'fear' can also be explained at another political level with respect to the remit and onus of the dominant government-funded victim agency in Britain – Victim Support (VS). VS, which was established in Bristol in the early 1970s, experienced a significant period of growth during the 1980s as a result of government sponsorship. When compared with alternative agencies for victim support which were set up during the same period, such as women's refuges and rape crisis centres, VS has outstripped them with respect to government funding, police cooperation, publicity, and the number of victims assisted. Although the service is primarily 'for' victims and has defined its own remit to complement the mainstream attentions of criminal justice that lie with the offender, it performs its duty in a strangely apolitical void. Given that VS is reliant on government funding for its continued existence, it is perhaps not so strange that the service should remain with a 'neutral' political stance. However, the service's stance becomes less tenable when one considers the impact that its service has on defining and responding to 'the' victim.

The continued focus on 'fear', as being the appropriate and supposedly the main response of victims to victimisation, corresponds to Victim Support's traditional approach to victims as being in 'need' of assistance and therefore as vulnerable. Undoubtedly, as evidenced by previous sections in this chapter, many victims are vulnerable in the face of crime and their own experiences of victimisation. But this characterisation of victims does not allow for alternative expressions in response to victimisation, while playing to the needs of agencies, rather than victims, in the interpretation of the victim as nothing other than a 'victim'. In other words, although individuals might have been victimised, they might not see themselves as 'victims' of crime, and even less so as 'fearful'. As Ditton et al. (1999b) comment, a 'passive' victim is a more convenient victim for agencies and governments alike to manage.

Victims who express outrage at being victimised, and even go so far as to allude to their desire to harm those who have offended against them, are not politically neutral. The frustrated and vocal victim can 'rock the boat' by demanding 'justice' beyond Victim Support's remit to provide a 'listening ear' and, in some cases, assistance with attending court and applying for restitution under the state compensation scheme. Having said this, Victim Support has, since the 1990s, played a progressively important role in highlighting victims' rights (see Chapter 4). Invited to work alongside the government and, in particular, the Justice and Victims Unit of the Home Office, VS has been instrumental in championing victim-centred criminal justice legislation and policy which to some extent exceeds limiting interpretations of the victim as 'passive'. However, this work is undertaken from a central role alongside government. As a result, Victim Support, unlike its more radical counterparts such as Rape Crisis, can go only so far in its promotion of victims' rights.

The continued focus on the 'fearful' victim can also be understood as reflecting the limited understandings of researchers who set out to document the experience of and emotional response to victimisation. As the first US National Crime Survey reported on the public's 'fear' of crime, so subsequent surveys have uncritically adopted and adapted questions which set out to measure 'fear'. 'Fear' has served as an umbrella term for researchers through which they can capture a range of emotions and responses to crime and victimisation by survey victims. In turn, the media responded to 'fear of crime' as an appropriately titillating research finding worthy of countless pages of newsprint. As 'fear of crime', and crime in general, reportedly decreased in England and Wales during the 1990s (Mirrlees-Black et al., 1996), so other terms have come to interest researchers who continue to plough the 'fear of crime' field as an area of victimological enquiry. Since the 1980s and early 1990s 'fear of crime' might have lost its star status as a central concern of government rhetoric, only to be replaced by alternative measures of public vulnerabilities.

'Anger' as the new fear

As noted earlier, there is ample research evidence to indicate that, alongside expressions of fear, people have always been 'angry' about crime and victimisation. Ditton et al. (1999a, 1999b) have recently explored the need to revisit 'anger' as the forgotten emotional response to victimisation, and have posited the idea that anger surpasses fear as the main component of people's reactions to victimisation. Their research is based on their 1996 quantitative survey of 1,629 adult Scottish residents, alongside a number of qualitative research interviews undertaken with an initial research sub-sample. Given the highly insightful but rare quality of their findings, their research is worth reporting here at some length.

Ditton et al. examine respondents' reactions to experiences of imagined (1999a) and actual victimisation (1999b). For both sets of information, and across different demographic groups with varying degrees of victimisation experience, respondents were found to be, on average, more angry than fearful. Focusing here on Ditton et al.'s research with victims of crime (1999b), one can note a number of interesting points. First, offered a list of possible emotive responses to their experience of victimisation,[3] respondents consistently opted to reply that they were 'angry'; given this, the research compared the response 'angry' with other emotive reactions under the category 'other'. From here, the research was able to compare the response 'angry' with the response 'other' in consideration of age, gender and crime type,[4] and with respect to initial and later responses to victimisation. The research clearly demonstrated that 'anger' dominated other feelings across age–gender categories, crime type and the period after victimisation. There are, however, a number of exceptions to this generalisation. For example, with respect to initial emotive responses to victimisation: (1) women aged 35–59 were found to be more 'other' than 'angry' in response to housebreaking; (2) women aged 60+ were more 'other' than angry for housebreaking and assault, but more 'angry' than 'other' for vehicle crime and vandalism; and (3) the majority of respondents were slightly more 'other' than 'angry' with respect to assault, with the exception of men and women aged 35–59 who were more 'angry' than 'other'.

Ditton et al. proceed to regroup responses into three main types: anger, fear (upset, fearful, shocked, invaded) and other (none, disappointed, other, don't know). Examination of these three response categories over time indicates the continued prevalence of 'anger' as an emotive response, with Ditton et al. able to state (1999b: 44) that 'fear as a consequence of actual victimisation diminishes considerably [with time] as other reactions increase'. Also, gender was found to be more predictive of changing emotions than age, with women more likely to change their feelings than men, and offence type was statistically related to changing feelings, with victims of vehicle crime changing their emotive responses less than victims of housebreaking, vandalism and assault.

Having presented much-needed information with respect to the importance of 'anger' as a response to victimisation, Ditton et al. go on to critique their research findings. First, just as the term 'fear' has been under-researched for its emotive meaning, but over-utilised as a research tool, so Ditton et al. question their use and interpretation of the term 'anger'. They recognise that 'anger', as an initial and delayed response to victimisation, can be measuring very different things. In this respect, one can refer to the importance of their qualitative research that investigates the differential meanings people have when employing the word 'anger' as a descriptive term. Second, they refer to the limiting consequences of asking respondents to identify one emotive response to victimisation from a prescribed list. However, with respect to the methodological demands of a quantitative victim survey, a list is a 'necessary evil' if the research findings are to avoid open-ended responses which can result in a longer list of respondent replies.

Aside from the above, Ditton et al. offer some intriguing questions, which they partially answer, in consideration of their research findings with respect to the neglect of 'anger' as an emotive response to victimisation. As they tentatively suggest (1999b: 51): 'One possibility is that anger may not always have been so dominant, and/or may be more dominant for Scottish victims than for those of other nationalities.' Comparing their evidence with measurements of 'anger' and 'fear' taken from the 1988, 1992 and 1994 British Crime Survey, alongside direct comparison between the 1993 Scottish Crime Survey and the 1996 BCS, they provide some indication that these speculative ideas may have some grounding in reality. However, their evidence, unsurprisingly given the limited extent of comparable research in this field, is not so convincing.

First, to refer to the Scottish as more 'angry' in response to victimisation than, for example, the English is to be guilty of crude reductionism.
Further research is needed to establish whether this finding is consistently proven over time and with respect to different samples. Second,
having referred to different displays of anger according to nationality,
so ethnicity is strikingly absent from their research results and ensuing
discussion. Finally, if 'anger' has indeed surpassed 'fear' as an emotive
response to victimisation, then politicians should be concerned as the
'passive' victim gives way to the dissatisfied victim who is less likely to be
content with renewed references to well-established accounts of 'fear
of crime' in the daily tabloid press. But, given that the 1988 BCS also
indicated significant levels of respondent 'anger' to victimisation, one
must remember that 'anger' is not a new phenomenon; rather, it is the
acknowledgement of anger by researchers that is new. As noted earlier,
the political convenience of remaining with an image of the passive and
therefore compliant victim is undoubtedly of greatest benefit to those
government and non-government institutions with a remit to serve a
certain 'image' of the victim (and to serve, thereby, their own ends).

With this final criticism in mind, and recognising that Ditton et al.'s
research indicated that males, with some exceptions, consistently displayed
higher levels of anger than women, the next section focuses on what has
until recently been the most neglected area of research with respect to
'fear of crime' and 'vulnerability'.

Focus: male 'fear of crime' and 'vulnerability'

While the reader can be referred to any number of studies on women's
fear of crime and experiences of victimisation, research on 'gender and
crime' has only recently focused on the other side of male criminality –
that is, male victimisation and fear of crime. Some early victimological
research inadvertently touched on the subject of male fear (Maguire
and Corbett, 1987; Shapland et al., 1985), but it is only since the 1990s
that criminology has embraced sociological and feminist-led discourse
on the subject of masculinities and crime, and in turn masculinities
and victimisation (Newburn and Stanko, 1995; Stanko, 1990; Stanko and
Hobdell, 1993; Walklate, 1995). Much of this discussion is theoretically
based, and dwells on reworkings of masculinities theory as inspired,
primarily, by the work of Robert Connell (1987; 1995), and to a lesser
extent by others such as Mac an Ghaill (1994) and Messerschmidt (1993).

Criminology has, for obvious reasons, concentrated on male criminality
as the mainstay of its theoretical and empirical research. Given that the
majority of crime is committed by males, this is readily understandable.
However, victimology's neglect of the other side of male criminality –
male vulnerability, fear of crime and victimisation – is less tenable given

the extent of male victimisation. Having said this, victimology's gendered focus on women's vulnerabilities can be understood with regard to two central points. First, academic victimologists, like the rest of society, operate under the influence of gender stereotypes which tend to label women as passive, vulnerable and 'fearful', while men are labelled as active, aggressive and 'fearless'. Second, while feminist researchers have succeeded in highlighting women's experiences of violence at the hands of men, this has indirectly been to the detriment of enlightened discussion on male victimisation. At the same time, feminist research has done much to recast women outside the stereotype of passive victims of male aggression. More recently, with regard to the development of research on male vulnerabilities, the work of feminists in the fields of criminology and victimology (Stanko, 1990; Walklate, 1995) has been instrumental in bringing debates on masculinities, crime and victimisation into the arena of victim-centred research.

The victimological focus on women's experiences of victimisation and fear of crime is a laudable enterprise. But the neglect of equivalent male experiences displays researchers' lack of vision with regard to what is said, and what remains unsaid, in the bulk of conventional victimological research. In this respect, exploration of this largely neglected field can incorporate understandings of childhood gendered socialisation, and adult limitations on emotive expression of fear, to map the contours of 'hidden' male vulnerabilities. Established interpretations of 'who' can be vulnerable – women, children and the elderly – can be readdressed in light of research which questions apparent male 'fearlessness'. With examples from research on domestic violence and childhood vulnerabilities, this section briefly explores the boundaries of established victimological interpretations of 'fear' and 'vulnerability'.

The example of domestic violence

The 1996 British Crime Survey reveals that, of respondents aged 16–59, 4.2 per cent of women and 4.2 per cent of men said they had been physically assaulted by a current or former partner in the course of the previous year. In turn, 2 per cent of women and 1.5 per cent of men indicated that they had experienced 'domestic' assault three or more times during the previous year; while 23 per cent of women, and 15 per cent of men, had been assaulted by a current or former partner during the course of their lifetime (Mirrlees-Black and Byron, 1999).

There are a number of striking points with regard to these research results. First, 'domestic' violence is widespread, and for some it is characterised by repeat victimisation over the course of a lifetime, or at least for the duration of a relationship with an intimate partner, parent or carer. Second, and most remarkably, it is experienced to a similar degree by both sexes. However, the weight of evidence to date, particularly from feminist-based research, points to the gendered nature of domestic violence as characterised by female 'victims' and male offenders (Cretney and Davis, 1997; Dobash and Dobash, 1998; Hoyle and Sanders, 2000). The subject of male-on-male domestic violence and, more pointedly, the taboo arena of female-on-male domestic violence remain under-researched as real phenomena that impact on male lives; though some authors have made notable inroads in this area, pointing out, among other things, the sampling bias inherent in many surveys on domestic violence – that is, surveys tend only to research *women's* experiences (Grady, 2002).

It would appear that the methodological tool employed by the 1996 BCS to uncover domestic violence, computer-assisted self-interviewing (CASI),[5] afforded men the opportunity to admit their experiences as victims of domestic violence. But the Home Office report on the above findings plays down the fact that men are apparently almost equal victims to women (Mirrlees-Black and Byron, 1999: 4):

> This survey uncovered relatively similar levels of recent domestic assault for men and women within the past year. Are men, then, equal victims? The findings suggest not. On average, men were: less upset by their experience; considerably less frightened; less often injured; less likely to seek medical help.

While the 1996 BCS indicates that the risk of domestic violence is similar between the sexes, it would appear from the information supplied by respondents that the consequences of domestic victimisation are considerably less for men when compared with women. Explanations of why this might be the case can focus on differential levels of 'vulnerability' between women and men. At a basic level, women are physically weaker than men, and therefore are likely to suffer more severely from assault. Or, the degree of violence meted out in domestic assaults is greater against women when compared with men. Either way, the greater use and/or impact of violence in domestic cases against women would seem to offer a partial explanation for their heightened reports of emotional distress and medical assistance in the aftermath of domestic violence. This is not to deny the 1996 BCS findings on male victimisation, but rather it helps to contextualise men's risk of domestic violence, and its consequences, as part of a broader gendered experience of crime and victimisation. However, to interpret men's accounts of the impact of domestic violence on their lives at face value is to deny the researcher's role when it comes to the interpretation of information, and the complexity of men's expression of vulnerability.

A basic premise of social science research is to interpret respondent-based results with the following in mind:

1. there is what people say they do/feel;
2. there is what people do/feel;
3. there is what people say about what they do/feel.

As evidenced by the previous chapter's critique of victim surveys, respondents experience general problems of forward and backward 'telescoping' when reporting their experiences of victimisation. Added to this, with respect to requests to provide information about interpersonal violence, respondents may be less able or willing to reveal their experiences. Having done so, they may not reveal the full impact these crimes have had on them. Typically, men and women are socialised to express themselves differently (Goodey, 1994). While late twentieth-century feminism did a great deal to enhance women's personal and socio-economic confidence, so much so that the so-called 'de-feminisation' of women has variously been accused of encouraging female offending (Adler, 1975; Chesney-Lind, 1997), this has not been matched to the same degree by men's ability to express vulnerability. While men might not be as physically harmed by domestic violence as women, researchers should consider that men, because of their socialisation, are less able than women to reveal the emotional impact that domestic violence has on their lives. There may be more to men's experiences of victimisation, particularly interpersonal victimisation, than victimology is currently able to reveal given the subject's limited interpretations of appropriate gendered behaviour, either as offender or victim, and appropriate emotional responses to this behaviour through varying displays of vulnerability and 'fear'.

Learning to be 'fearless'

Broadly speaking, as evidenced by the bulk of research findings to date, women appear to be more fearful of crime than men. To some extent, this gendered expression of 'fear' has been explained by women's physical vulnerability, their vulnerability to particular crimes, and their marginal socio-economic status, relative to men, which enhances vulnerability. However, the blanket assumption that 'women are fearful' and 'men are fearless' negates differences between women, and between men, and the distribution of factors, such as income, age, ethnicity and sexuality, which shape the individual's sense of vulnerability and fear. To illustrate the point quite crudely: a white, affluent, middle-aged woman, living in rural England, might feel less vulnerable and less fearful of crime than a young British-Pakistani male, living in a predominantly 'white', high crime area in the inner city. In other words, people's experience of and emotional reaction to victimisation is mediated by the specifics of 'who' they are and their experiences of victimisation and fear-inducing circumstances to date.

To understand the complexities of how we come to experience and emotionally respond to crime, as victims or potential victims, demands that victimology reinterpret a number of its key research findings. This is not to disbelieve what respondents reveal with respect to accounts of victimisation and fear, but rather it is to consider what is not revealed through the traditional avenues of victimology research. To this end, childhood and adolescent accounts of victimisation, vulnerability and concerns about crime can tell us a great deal about how adults experience victimisation and come to articulate those experiences. My own work has taken up these themes to explore the construction of gendered expressions of fear and vulnerability. Based on questionnaire results from 663 girls and boys aged 11 to 16, alongside a series of in-depth group interviews, my research was able to reveal some interesting patterns in respondents' expression of 'fear' and 'vulnerabilities' (Goodey, 1994, 1996, 1997) – see box below. As the research was conducted in a white, working-class, edge-of-town public housing estate, the 'variables' of class and ethnicity were held constant. The absence of class variation and ethnic difference might be a failing of the research, but it allowed for an insightful account of difference based on gender and age.

Case study: gender, age and 'fear of crime'

Having asked a version of a classic victimisation survey question, 'Have you been worried or has something made you feel "on edge" when outside?', the questionnaire results revealed that more girls (72 per cent) than boys (46 per cent) were worried when outside in public places.[6] This finding, replicating as it does the results of numerous victim surveys, confirms established assumptions about gendered fear. However, reinterpreting this result beyond face value brings with it the acknowledgement that nearly half of the boys surveyed expressed 'fear'. And, breaking down these generic findings with respect to age, one is able to see that at age 11 more boys (72 per cent) than girls (57 per cent) are worried when outside. But, from age 12 on, girls resume their dominant display of 'fear'. Other evidence from the questionnaire, which asked respondents to identify groups they are fearful of, revealed that equal numbers of girls and boys, three-quarters, were worried about drunks and drug addicts when outside. This result may come as no surprise given the 'folk devil' qualities of these groups. Of more interest is the fact that 'older boys' presented boys of all ages with a tangible threat that far exceeded girls' concerns regarding this group, with 48 per cent of boys and 28 per cent of girls specifying this category. With increasing age both girls and boys expressed less concern about specific threats and generic 'fears'. But, overall, the gendered nature of responses remained constant with age; that is, girls tended to express more 'fear' than their male peers at different ages, while boys, in comparison with girls, expressed more concern about 'older boys' at every age.

(Box continued)

Interpreted alongside the findings of the research interviews, these results reveal that boys are not simply a 'fearless' group, but they are 'fearful' of certain categories of people and in certain situations. The single-sex setting of the group interviews also revealed the increasing importance of peer pressure for boys as they went from ages 11 to 16. In the group setting, the desire to be seen to talk 'like a man', or rather like a certain exaggerated interpretation of what a tough man should be, was apparent throughout interview sessions. This observation needs contextualising with respect to the constraints and limited opportunities for boys to be anything other than 'tough men' on a crime-ridden public housing estate. Here, the relevance of considering masculinities theory emerges in the interpretation of apparent male 'fearlessness'.

Appropriate displays of masculinity to one's peers and a female researcher, as an essentially 'fearless' masculinity, surface amongst groups of males and have to be interpreted with respect to the group setting and the mediating social factors of age, ethnicity, class and sexuality which shape these responses. Young working-class males may only have recourse to exaggerated displays of masculinity in a group setting as a means of asserting their limited 'power', in the guise of 'tough' men, when otherwise they are powerless – as boys from poor socio-economic backgrounds. In comparison, young middle-class males may be better placed to express their fears in a group setting as their masculinity may be channelled through other areas, such as academic success, which do not demand their display of an aggressive and 'fearless' masculinity (Willis, 1977). In turn, some groups of ethnic minority males may express heightened levels of masculine bravado as a reaction to their relative powerlessness in white-dominated society, and as a direct result of their experiences of racism (Goodey, 1998). But, as the above questionnaire results revealed, and in line with the BCS findings on domestic violence, males, both young and old, can reveal their vulnerabilities through the medium of the anonymous survey questionnaire if it is carefully constructed to elicit more than the standard gendered response.

What these abbreviated research results should indicate is the need for sensitive research which is able to measure gendered fear as something other than female vulnerabilities. Elsewhere, I have explored the theme of racism and masculine expressions of 'fear', which in the case of some marginalised ethnic minority young men can result in 'defensive-aggressive' displays of exaggerated masculinity (Goodey, 1998). And, as a development from this work, I have examined the potential for in-depth biographical interpretations of male criminality and victimisation (Goodey, 2000a). These are research themes through which academic victimology might be better placed to understand male experiences and expressions of 'fear', vulnerabilities, and of course criminality and exaggerated displays of masculinity. Looking at the social processes of what it means to become male, and reflecting these processes through in-depth accounts of individual men's lives, can help academic victimology to interpret and critique accepted wisdom regarding appropriate displays of male 'fearlessness' and female 'fear'.

My own work on the development of the 'hegemonic masculine biography' (Goodey, 2000a) attempts to interpret significant criminal and victimising moments in men's lives, as identified by male subjects, and interpreted by the researcher. These significant life moments, or epiphanies, are contextualised with respect to broad social influences, of formal and informal social control, and the mediating factors of demographic differences. In 'mapping' men's hegemonic masculine biographies, the research points to a theoretically grounded methodology that can take account of the fluctuating and transitory nature of a life of crime/ victimisation/fear for individual men in the context of the social. Hollway and Jefferson (2000) have also promoted biographical accounts of 'fear of crime', which they develop using a 'psychosocial' approach to explore what they identify as 'two persistent issues in the sets of assumptions that are made about people who are fearful of crime' (2000: 14): (1) to what extent are people's fears realistic or rational?; and (2) are people's fears explicable through shared social characteristics, such as gender and age, rather than the uniqueness of the individual? Hollway and Jefferson interpret their in-depth qualitative interviews with a range of men and women with respect to what people's accounts mean to them, and the researchers, in the context of their lives to date. Expressed and unconscious meanings are interpreted as the reflection of a lived reality that is mediated by place and time, and the adoption of and adaptation to various demographic constraints. Their research examines appropriations of masculinity and femininity among interviewees that result in different accounts of fear and fearlessness that are not gender (or age) bound. In this respect, the rationality or irrationality of gendered fear is exposed as a limiting research issue which reflects, primarily, the interests of conventional victimological methods that seek to understand accounts of 'fear' based on aggregate distinctions between different demographic variables: gender, age, etc. The convenience, to the researcher, of being able to 'box' people's responses into predetermined categories that are reliant on established ideas about difference, according to such categories as gender, is obvious in many mainstream accounts of 'fear' and 'fearlessness'.

In conclusion

The above focus on male 'fear of crime' and 'vulnerability' has alerted us to a number of points. First, contrary to mainstream victimological readings of 'fear' and 'vulnerability', men are both victimised and vulnerable, and, as revealed through childhood accounts, they can also be 'fearful'. Second, men's apparent 'fearlessness' cannot be taken at face value but should be read as reflecting the constraints of their gendered expression of vulnerability. Third, victimological methods can more accurately portray the reality and the diversity of men's 'fear' and 'fearlessness' if they move away from established methodologies that dwell on broad generalisations based on demographic differences. To this end, in-depth qualitative methods offer much for victimological research with respect to more insightful interpretations of male 'fear' and 'vulnerability'.

On understanding 'fear of crime' and 'vulnerability'

Perhaps 'fear of crime' has 'had its day'. As a concept it peaked in British criminological and victimological accounts of crime and victimisation, and almost transcended the focus on crime, during the 1980s and early 1990s. 'Fear of crime' was and remains a tangible reality for some people, but more importantly its ascendancy must also be understood as a reflection of political circumstances. In the last years of the 1990s and the first decade of the twenty-first century, as crime rates reduce and stabilise, so 'fear of crime' has been eclipsed by other public and political concerns such as job insecurity and globalisation. In comparison to the emotive expression of 'fear', exploration of people's 'vulnerabilities' tells us more about people's risk of crime and their consideration of its consequences. In turn, 'vulnerability' needs reading as more than a reflection of physical prowess. Vulnerability reflects 'who' the individual is in the context of different social settings, and can be understood as a reflection of the social dynamics of relative power and powerlessness as they play themselves out on individuals who form part of social groups. In this respect, research on male 'fear of crime' and 'vulnerability' opens victimological enquiry to new understandings of 'who' can be fearful and vulnerable.

Alternatively, as research on 'anger' illustrates, 'fear' has perhaps never surpassed other emotional responses to crime and vulnerabilities. It would appear that 'fear' has in reality reflected the limited preferences of re-searchers and research funding bodies to remain with under-developed conceptions of 'fear' which have only recently been challenged. In other words, assumptions about what 'fear' is, how it can be measured, and who can experience it, has reduced the bulk of victimological enquiry to gendered stereotyping on 'fear'; the same is true with respect to age.

Having provided an overview and criticism of 'fear' and 'vulnerability' as frequently limiting concepts, the next chapter proceeds to examine calls for a wider notion of 'victimhood' from the polarised camps of radical victimology and single-issue victims' groups. Just as this chapter has questioned established constructions of 'who' can be fearful and vulnerable, so the next chapter will ask how far the ascription of 'victim' can stretch.

Suggested reading

The scope and nature of research on 'fear of crime' is comprehensively covered by Hale's (1996) review of the literature and Ditton and Farrall's (2000) edited collection; the latter includes developments in the field from the early 1970s through to the end of the twentieth century. Maguire's 1980 article on the emotional impact of burglary on victims is also worth looking at as an early exploration of the range of feelings that victims can experience in the aftermath of crime. Critiques of and developments on limited references to 'fear of crime', particularly from the 1990s, are addressed in a number of key papers, such as Kinsey and Anderson (1992); Ditton et al. (1999a, 1999b); and Killias and Clerici (2000). These papers bring in references to vulnerability and anger as new ways of exploring people's insecurities in relation to crime alongside a host of other social insecurities. In this regard, the British Crime Survey's questions about safety can be revisited as an insight into how questions on 'fear' have evolved and what surveys are actually measuring in relation to crime and fear/safety/insecurity. New ways of looking at vulnerabilities in relation to crime have been explored, particularly from the 1990s, through the lens of gender/age. Research on gendered interpretations of 'fear' has drawn on masculinities theory to examine and critique polarised constructions of the 'fearless' male and 'fearful' female. An edited collection by Newburn and Stanko (1995) provides insight into gendered constructions of crime, victimisation and vulnerabilities; while Mirrlees-Black and Byron's (1999) Home Office-funded research on domestic violence introduces results that challenge stereotypes about victimisation. Finally, my own work on gender and 'fear of crime' (Goodey 1997) brings together ideas in relation to gendered displays of vulnerability and age, and explores these ideas in relation to masculinities theory.

Notes

1. Other surveys in other countries also use this question, or a very similar one, as a measure of 'fear' (Smith et al., 2001).
2. For example, the 1989 Home Office Standing Conference on Crime Prevention emphasised the 'reality' of criminal risk, which, it was hoped, would assist people to become less fearful of crime.

3. Possible emotive responses to victimisation included: none; angry; upset or tearful; fear or fearful; shocked; suffered insomnia; invaded; disappointed or fed up; other; don't know.
4. Crime type included: housebreaking; vehicle crime; assault; vandalism.
5. CASI allows respondents to read survey questions directly from a laptop, which has been passed to them by an interviewer. Respondents then input their responses into the laptop. It is thought that CASI affords respondents more confidentiality when answering sensitive questions. The method was first used in the 1994 BCS to examine illegal drug use and sexual victimisation.
6. All the results reported here are significant at the 99.9 per cent confidence level using a chi-square correlation.

Chapter 4

Academic victimology, victim advocacy and social policy

Introducing themes for discussion

The previous two chapters set out to describe and critique what we know and understand about the nature and extent of victimisation, fear of crime, and vulnerabilities. How we have come to this knowledge, and what drives political and activist-led interest in victim-centred issues, are the subject of this chapter.

Taking academic victimology and victim advocacy as the starting point for discussion, the chapter outlines why these two 'camps' have, in the main, failed to work together towards an informed and critical interpretation of victim-centred justice that can influence social policy. The under-development of a critical victimology, compared with the unstoppable development of victim-centred justice initiatives based on, among other things, political expediency, is critiqued here. In asking 'what is academic victimology?' and 'what is the so-called "victims'" movement?' the chapter draws on examples from victim advocacy to explain the development and current context of victim-centred initiatives. The point at which the academic and the activist can meet and inform social policy in the interest of victims is explored towards the end of the chapter with a discussion of the promotion of 'good practice' in victim-centred justice.

Labelling academic victimology and victim advocacy

Different streams of academic victimology and victim advocacy have been ascribed various labels over time. And, as Chapter 1 notes, competing criminal justice models are variously pitched against each other in an effort to assert the dominance of so-called victim-centred or offender-centred justice. Academic victimology and victim advocacy are often reduced to categories that reflect the competing interests of those promoting different models, frequently with political goals in mind.

In developing their theory of a 'critical victimology', Mawby and Walklate (1994) identify three broad categories in academic victimology:

1. *positivist*: defines victimisation according to the criminal law; wedded to ideas of victim precipitation/blaming; proposes victimology as 'science';
2. *radical*: includes victimisation beyond the confines of the criminal law; encompasses human rights; examines the role of the capitalist state in victimisation;
3. *critical*: combines aspects of positivism and radicalism to reconceptualise the victim; looks at experiences of individual victims and the influence of social-political powers on them; critiques the victim's construction as a 'consumer' of victim services.

Within and between each broad category, different sub-categories in victim-related research can also be identified. For example, as outlined later, feminist victimology can lie within a radical or critical victimology; and left realism adopts aspects of positivist, radical and critical criminology.

In turn, along with Karmen (1990), Mawby and Walklate identify three socio-political victim trends that variously cross-cut and reflect academic victimology:

1. *conservative*: focuses on victims of street crime; renders people account-able for their actions; focuses on retributive justice;
2. *liberal*: extends the conservative focus to include fraud/white-collar crime; encourages restitution and rehabilitation for victim and offender;
3. *radical-critical*: all forms of human suffering are considered as politically valid; the criminal justice system is critiqued as the cause of much 'secondary victimisation'; focuses on institutional wrong-doing and violation of human rights.

This three-pronged characterisation can incorporate other sub-categories. For example, administrative and managerialist criminology, in their respective efforts to 'count' crime and promote an efficient response to it, can both fit under the generic label of a conservative socio-political response to crime and victimisation. At the same time, managerialism can borrow ideas from the neo-liberal market economy to promote the man-agement of crime as private enterprise: for example, through the intro-duction of private security firms to police high crime neighbourhoods.

Alternatively, van Dijk (1999), outlining the history of victimology and victim advocacy, simplifies these divergent strands by distinguishing between two that can variously include conservative, liberal and radical responses to research and victim assistance:

1. *penal victimology*: confined to the criminal law and the dynamic rela-tionship between victim and offender; encompasses positivism;

2. *general victimology*: includes victimisation outside the criminal law; employs research methods other than positivism; incorporates victim assistance and medical/psychiatric intervention with victims.

But, broadly speaking, most commentators, when tracing the development of victimology and victim assistance, distinguish between two approaches: (1) academic 'scientific' victimology, and (2) activist-led 'humanistic' victim assistance (Cressey, 1988). However, while theoretically based academic research can be separated from atheoretical activist lobbying, this distinction is often difficult and unhelpful as 'scientific' and 'humanist' approaches also merge in practice in consideration of actual victim policy. In this regard, a third element needs to be brought in to understand the development of victim-centred research and victim assistance: that is (3) policy initiatives. Herein, all three strands – research, activism, and policy – should be considered alongside each other as informing and shaping the focus and direction of victim-centred research and criminal justice policy. In other words, research can inform activism and policy development, and, in turn, activism and policy shape research.

To this end, recent developments in the field of restorative justice have promoted connections between academic victimology, victim assistance and policy development – notably the European Science Foundation's COST Action A21 on restorative justice, and the European Forum on Victim–Offender Mediation and Restorative Justice (see Chapter 7). At present, restorative justice presents, arguably, the healthiest field – in terms of debate, growth and synergy – in victim-centred research, advocacy and policy. Other victim-centred issues do not enjoy the same level of exchange and multi-agency working partnerships that restorative justice does. However, this situation can change as the spotlight on restorative justice moves on to consider other areas of victim-centred research and policy (see Chapter 8). Just as the victim survey and fear of crime were in the ascendant in the 1980s – through a combination of academic interest, localised initiatives and the politics of the period – they can now be described as having 'had their day'. Circumstances join together to promote certain criminal justice issues in particular periods. With examples from the past and present of victim-centred research, policy and practice working in partnership, the possibilities for seeing victim-centred justice as something other than a debate between polarised camps, with different standpoints to protect, seems plausible.

Bringing academia and activism together to inform social policy

In outlining their vision of a critical victimology, Mawby and Walklate state (1994: 21–22):

The view of science suggested here places the academic and the activist
on the same critical plane. They are part of a social reality in which as
knowledgeable actors both have the capacity to influence the processes
of social change. They have much to learn from each other.

What Mawby and Walklate suggest is a combined critical reading of
academic victimology and victim advocacy. Herein, research-based and
activist responses to victims are interpreted in the context of a 'social
reality' that reflects social and political developments in relation to appropriate responses with respect to, for example, gender and ethnicity. In
positing the academic and the activist together, Mawby and Walklate erode
some of the divisions that are commonly placed between the two.

The academic victimologist and the victim activist can both describe
themselves as working towards the promotion of victims' interests. However, on the basis of long-held stereotypes, these two camps are seen as
approaching victim-centred justice from opposing standpoints. Where
academic victimology has been labelled 'scientific' and 'rational' in its
efforts to understand the origins and experiences of victimisation, victim
advocacy has been labelled 'emotive' and 'anti-offender' in its quest to
promote victims' interests at, seemingly, all costs.

Academic research should play a greater role than it currently does in
reviewing policy developments, and in particular activist-led developments,
that are purportedly 'for' victims. However, academic victimology suffers
from something of a tainted image as the wayward sub-discipline of
criminology because of its association with right-wing retributive justice
and victim advocacy. As a consequence, victimology's potential as a tool
both to advocate and to critically assess victim-centred criminal justice
policy has been underplayed. At present, victim-centred criminal justice
policy is commonly adopted without an insight into what victims really
need and want.

Some recent research, funded by the Home Office and British research
charities, presents developments towards 'rounded' research where the
satisfaction of victims is considered alongside that of professionals and
offenders when weighing-up the 'success' of criminal justice policy initiatives. Chapter 6 explores in detail the impact of two recent criminal
justice initiatives on victims – victim statements and probation-based
victim contact work. These were piloted in England and Wales in response
to the Victim's Charter requirement that the 'success' of Charter initiatives should be tested (Crawford and Enterkin, 1999; Hoyle et al., 1998).
The reports from these pilot studies examine the impact of initiatives
from the standpoint of practitioners *and* victims.

In general, the UK, through generous government funding, has
enjoyed a prolonged period of extensive research on victim-centred justice.
The same can be said for the Netherlands and the USA, which also have
a tradition of government-funded research on victims and victim-centred
criminal justice developments, although in all three jurisdictions research

has not always taken sufficient account of the victim's satisfaction with services. However, most notably in the USA, the association between right-wing retributive justice and victim-centred research has served to mar victimology's progress as an academic discipline. And, while crime surveys in developed and developing countries have done much to inform us about the impact of crime on victims and the general public, it remains the case that research on crime remains focused on 'the criminal' rather than 'the victim'. Arguably, the flipside of criminality, in the shape of 'the victim', does not benefit from the same level of research enthusiasm as it did in the 1980s and early 1990s when interest in the crime survey peaked. More recently, what we do have in England and Wales, as in many other common law jurisdictions, is a growing interest in alternative dispute resolution (restorative justice interventions) for offenders and victims. But these initiatives, from mediation through to family group conferencing, have been critiqued for their use of non-traditional dispute resolution as a means of diverting offenders from traditional justice at the expense of victims; in other words, whether restorative justice can be said to be 'victim-centred' or 'offender-centred' is still under debate (see Chapter 7).

While both academic victimology and victim advocacy share an interest in victim-centred justice, the two camps, and individuals and organisations within them, often appear to be acting in opposition. Given that victims' issues are increasingly politicised, and often used for politicians' own ends, there is an obvious need to bring academics and activists together in an effort to identify and respond to the needs of crime victims, and to critically assess interventions that are supposedly 'for' victims. To this end, the different and sometimes convergent paths that academic victimology and activist-led victim-centred initiatives have taken need tracing before we can suggest means of bringing them together in the interests of victim-centred policy.

Victimology: two dominant influences

Victimisation proneness: resurrection of an old idea

Academic victimology came into its own in the second half of the twentieth century, but it has not always had an auspicious history. Early proponents of the discipline, notably von Hentig (1948) and Mendelsohn (1956), set the tone for victimology's subsequent development by focusing on characteristics of victim proneness. Problematically, victim proneness came to be associated with victim culpability, with Mendelsohn devising a scale from the 'completely innocent' through to the 'most guilty' victim. According to this scale, those who threw the first punch in a fight, and subsequently found themselves with a broken jaw, could be assigned the label of 'guilty victim'. In comparison, an elderly person who is mugged could be described as an 'innocent victim'.

As a defence lawyer, Mendelsohn was keen to develop a scale of victim proneness that could point to mitigating factors in support of the defendant. His work, like other early victimological attempts to explain victimisation, reflected established wisdom about the nature of the ideal and innocent victim: the very young, the very old, the sexually vulnerable, and the socially respectable could be considered as 'innocent' parties in their own victimisation. In comparison, those who were regarded by the establishment as living or acting outside the parameters of acceptable social behaviour, such as the unemployed and the homeless, were to be regarded with suspicion when assessing their degree of culpability in their own victimisation. These stereotypes tended to work on the basis of dichotomies that served to distinguish the victim (us) from the offender (them). From this tradition, ideas about the part played by victims in their own victimisation have come to be associated, most damagingly, with 'victim blaming'.

The leap that is made from victimisation proneness to victim blaming has cast a negative shadow on victimology as the discipline that is supposed to be on the 'side' of the victim. In contrast, the criminal law has long used provocation on the part of the victim (sexual availability, nagging) as a contributory factor to help explain and excuse the actions of the defendant – often a man who has murdered, raped or sexually assaulted a female victim (Ashworth, 1975; Morris and Blom-Cooper, 1964). To an extent, provocation might be considered acceptable in some cases relating to negligence: for example, the person whose car is stolen after they forget to lock the door. However, to consider provocation as a mitigating factor in support of the defendant in crimes of violence and sexual violence, where the offender is often stronger than the victim, is to excuse the actions of the stronger party. Understandably, victim advocates, particularly feminists, are unhappy with suggestions of victim culpability that can be inferred from work such as Amir's account of rape and victim provocation (Amir, 1971), and the common usage of this defence under the criminal law (Lees, 1996, 1997; Radford and Russell, 1992). But, at the same time, provocation on the part of the victim has been successfully applied in recent years to lessen or remove charges of manslaughter from women who have killed their partners after years of abuse (Kennedy, 1992).

While research on victimisation proneness is controversial – particularly in relation to rape and sexual assault cases – it has served to raise some important issues with respect to victim and offender populations, and the nature of relationships between victims and offenders. As noted in Chapters 2 and 3, victims and offenders are often from the same background; and offenders are often themselves victims, and vice versa. What this tells us is that distinctions between offender and victim populations are not always helpful; one thinks here of the high incidence of offending and victimisation among young males in marginalised socio-economic positions. However, this information is rarely used by victim advocates because it undermines their need to distinguish offenders (them) from victims (us).

More recently, work on repeat victimisation, as detailed in Chapter 2, has revisited victimology's search for a typology of victimisation proneness by examining who is likely to be re-victimised and where. What this research has unearthed is a high incidence of repeat victimisation, of both personal and property crime, for certain individuals and social groups, and in particular neighbourhoods. This research has been employed by policy makers for target hardening and urban planning initiatives to tackle crime. Feminist victimologists and other researchers, for example those examining racist abuse (Sampson and Phillips, 1992), have also made inroads into social policy by using evidence of repeat victimisation that reflects aspects of social power and powerlessness within and between social units and communities, such as the family and deprived multi-ethnic neighbourhoods.

Looking at the impact of targeted and repeat victimisation, a certain theme emerges: patterns of criminal victimisation, and for that matter financial victimisation, impact most on the physically, socially, economically and politically vulnerable. Victimisation proneness, if looked at through the lens of victim vulnerability (as a code-word for absence of 'power'), is a useful measure for identifying likely targets. However, then to blame the victim for their own victimisation, because of negligence or provocation, is to enter the controversial waters of victim blaming. Ideally, as promoted by conservative/administrative criminology in the 1980s and 1990s, people should lock their doors and stay away from 'no go' neighbourhoods. However, particularly when we look at victimisation of the least powerful in society, we have to reconsider the extent to which blame can be assigned.

The criminal law likes to employ the image of the 'rational actor' when describing what might, in an ideal situation, be expected to happen in the run up to, during, and after a criminal event. But this image serves to distance crime, and those intimately involved in it, from social realities and, in particular, the repeat nature of many criminal acts against and between individuals over time. Finding patterns in victim proneness can alert us to both similarities and differences between victim and offender populations, and, importantly, highlight the role of social-structural inequalities in shaping victimisation. To this end, academic victimology, in searching for patterns in criminal victimisation, should explore causal factors related to inequalities – inequalities that are also highlighted by some victim advocate groups in their quest to combat secondary victimisation of victims (such as women and children) by the criminal justice system. Whether these inequalities, in relation to victim proneness, are considered as useful anti-crime fodder by policy makers is, however, largely dependent on the political climate of the day.

Positivism: promise and challenges

Arguably, academic victimology has prospered most under positivism. By employing quantitative research methods and tools of analysis, such as the research survey and statistics, positivism allowed victimology to claim its position as a 'science'. Because of this legitimating label, the crime/ victim survey has been enthusiastically adopted by conservative and administrative criminology/victimology as a means of 'counting' crime/ victimisation patterns.

Early victimological research that sought to identify victimisation proneness through identification of victim typologies was ideally suited to the adoption of quantitative research methods. Positivist methods could produce a taxonomy of victimisation proneness based on the identification, counting, and statistical analysis of different variables. However, according to Marxist and critical criminologists, positivism established itself under a narrow framework that negated wider considerations about crime and victimisation that touched on social realities such as poverty and social marginalisation. Positivism offered explanations of victimisation proneness that succeeded in individualising the problem of crime and victimisation on the basis of variables related to the instance of crime in question, and the circumstances and characteristics of the individual victim and offender.

With the emergence of crime surveys as an alternative to police recorded crime figures, the 1970s and 1980s were the high point for positivist research methods in victimology. Through the wholesale adoption of quantitative methods to map the extent and nature of crime, crime surveys were able to unmask the 'dark figure' of crime. Early crime surveys limited their analysis of crime to the criminal law and, in the main, street crime that induced 'fear' among the public. In this regard, crime surveys became a tool of conservative victimology that, in highlighting the extent of the crime problem, called for a tough response to increasing crime rates. By focusing on street crimes, however, these early surveys did not uncover victimisation in the workplace or the private domain: that is, the home and institutional settings.

In contrast, feminist researchers (Hanmer and Saunders, 1984) took the evidence of early crime surveys, on women's experiences of petty incivilities and sexual/physical abuse, and explained these findings in relation to patriarchal social structures. Arguably, in the 1980s, feminists were the most important group within criminology/victimology to link academic research with activist-led calls for social change. In so doing, feminism offered a new application for positivist victimology that challenged the establishment's use of crime survey figures in conservative law and order campaigns. And, while the UN-sponsored International Crime Victims Survey that emerged at the height of the positivist revolution included reference to abuse of power, the majority of crime surveys continued to focus narrowly on 'street crimes' that reflected the establishment's concerns to combat the 'crimes of the streets' rather than the 'crimes of the suites' (fraud, corruption).

In Britain, crime surveys were a document to the political and public mood of the time that saw crime as the biggest problem facing society. The British Crime Survey, overseen by the Home Office, emerged at the instigation of the Conservative government. Its findings supported a tough response to crime, and more funding for criminal justice authorities such as the police. In turn, local surveys were commissioned by local government authorities, and academic criminologists obtained contracts to carry out the research.

The Islington Crime Survey, referred to in Chapter 2, exemplifies a particularly British marriage between local government and positivist research methods in academic victimology. Alongside feminist inroads into victimology, this particular survey also reflects the development of left-wing academic responses to crime as it impacts on people's lives at the local level. In its effort to take crime 'seriously', by looking at the impact of criminal victimisation on different socio-demographic groups in one area, the Islington Survey identified the influence of unequal social-structural factors on people's experiences of victimisation. The survey saw the birth of 'left realism' in British criminology: 'left' because it focused on social inequalities as an explanation for crime and victimisation, and 'real' because it looked at people's lived realities.

Left realism offered new insights into how research and political agendas could be used to identify and respond to people's experiences of victimisation. However, left realism has also been critiqued on three counts: (1) feminists berated its over-emphasis on class and its lack of understanding of gender as a contributory factor towards victimisation; (2) in unveiling some uncomfortable truths about the victimisation of the poor by the poor, the survey succeeded in undermining the radical left's claim that responsibility for crime should largely be attributed to the rich (Box, 1983); and (3) in employing quantitative surveys, the left realists had adopted the tools of 'pure science', and in the process were accused of co-opting the same research methods as the conservatives, which served to restrain respondents' answers and neglected qualitative research.

These critiques have been partially responded to by advocates of left realism (Young, 1997). In turn, a number of quantitative surveys have incorporated a feminist agenda (Goodey, 1994; Morris, 1999), or one which does not set 'class' as the variable by which to judge different experiences of crime – for example, explorations of age, vulnerability and victimisation (Pain, 1995). In the main, the important ramifications of local crime survey research, besides challenging official police statistics on the 'true' extent of crime, can be said to rest with their analysis of results based on social inequalities. To this end, feminist and left realist research on crime victimisation has: (1) challenged conservative ideologies about crime that usually employ crime surveys to highlight the need for tough criminal justice intervention; and (2) brought into focus the differential impact of crime as it affects different social groups.

But, in general, positivism, in its application of variables and statistics to social problems, has lost favour in recent years to postmodern and critical analyses of crime and victimisation that challenge universal claims to knowledge based on selected interpretations of 'the truth'. Whereas positivism has traditionally made claims to objective value-free research, postmodern and critical research, typically employing qualitative methods (interviews, participant observation), has revealed research to be a value-laden process that is dependent on the standpoint of the researcher, the practitioner, and the policy maker. However, positivist research methods such as the crime survey remain popular among policy makers because they provide an easy means for documenting social problems related to crime and victimisation. The validity of the research survey and quantitative analysis is, in itself, the subject of critical enquiry through publications such as the *Journal of Quantitative Criminology*. And in North America, quantitative research methods remain the basis of research on crime and victimisation for many graduate students, while in parts of the developing world the victim survey offers fresh insights into the extent and nature of victimisation where research on crime and victimisation is either absent or patchy.

Victim advocacy: towards a 'victims' movement'?

The study of victims and victim assistance can be understood only when contextualised alongside wider political and policy issues. For example, common threads can be drawn between a conservative victimology and a conservative victim advocacy: namely, using established scientific methods (such as the victim survey), conservative victimology sets out to count conventional crime, and in so doing conservative advocates use evidence of crime rates, as they impact on the 'man in the street', to support calls for increased investment in law and order and a tough response to criminals.

However, crime surveys, as the tools of a positivist conservative victimology, have been employed in turn by the conservative right, left realists, and feminists in support of their own stance on victimisation and appropriate responses to it. In this regard, it can prove difficult to separate and categorise the uses and ends to which victimological ideas and research methods are put. While a radical victimology that focuses on theoretical arguments about human rights abuses (Schwendinger and

Schwendinger, 1970) can appear far removed from the current focus of criminal justice practice, in time, mainstream discussion and criminal justice practice can turn to ideas that once appeared radical. For example, radical victimology's identification of the criminal justice system as a main cause of victims' secondary victimisation is now widely accepted, and is incorporated in law as safeguards to protect victims from unnecessary, prolonged and aggressive questioning by criminal justice personnel.

While there is an obvious overlap between some branches of victimology and victim advocacy, the ascription of *a* 'victims' movement', to denote a common political movement for victims, is both confusing and inaccurate. As Williams comments (1999: 129): 'A social movement emerges when members of excluded groups mobilise (or threaten to do so) to seek recognition and influence.' Previously disparate camps might appear to merge their methods for describing victimisation and promoting victim-centred interests, but this belies deep-seated differences. Although feminists and right-wing lobbyists both ask for increased recognition of victims' rights in the criminal justice process, they approach the subject from different angles and with different aims in mind. For example, feminists might call for safeguards against aggressive cross-examination of rape victims in court, and right-wing lobbyists might call for use of victim impact statements prior to sentencing – but this does not make them *a* social 'movement'. Williams goes so far as to argue that only when criminal victimisation and its social causes are explicitly linked to its higher incidence among members of oppressed groups does it become a social and political movement. But, with the example of the United States, we can also see how the 'victims' movement' label can emerge to describe a collection of predominantly, though not exclusively, right-of-centre victim advocate groups with little interest in the socially oppressed but a commitment to give victims 'a voice' as the politically marginalised.

From the popularisation of the term since the 1970s, the description of a 'victims' movement', on both sides of the Atlantic, reflected a combination of factors that served to put victims' interests, or at least what victim advocates claimed was in the interests of victims, centre-stage in social and criminal justice reform. At their core, these factors included the following:

- a rising crime rate and, at the same time, a rejection of the rehabilitative criminal justice model as a response to offending;
- the emergence of the centre-right in British and North American politics, and, with it, a tough approach to law and order;
- growth in the feminist movement, and, with this, an emphasis on women and children as victims of interpersonal patriarchal violence.

This list can be added to, but what it illustrates is the range of factors that together encouraged the emergence of a diverse academic and policy response to victims of crime in North America and Britain that should more accurately be described as a series of disparate victim interests that coalesced at the same time.

Elias (1993), like Williams commenting later on the UK experience (1999), suggests that the term 'victims' movement' should refer to a social or political phenomenon seeking fundamental social change. Given this, he concludes that the victim lobby groups that fell under the term in the USA, many of which were largely conservative and in support of the government's right-wing law and order response to crime, should not have been considered as part of a 'movement'. As Elias states (1993: 48): 'If it [the so-called 'victims' movement'] was a movement, it ceased to be so when it became partners with government.'

At the same time, similar influences were working in some parts of Europe and Scandinavia, and, most notably, in other common law jurisdictions such as Australia and New Zealand, to promote interest in victim-centred justice. The first symposium of the World Society of Victimology, which took place in Jerusalem in 1973, marked the birth of international recognition for victim-centred justice and academic victimology. In turn, while early victimology meetings tended to be dominated by research and practitioner initiatives from developed countries, this pattern has changed in recent years. The 'rest of the world' can now advertise the fact that there is a wealth of victim-centred research, activism and policy initiatives in developing countries. With the emergence of post-communist and post-conflict societies in eastern and central Europe, new trends in victimology and victim advocacy can be identified that present different challenges to research and activism. The example of victims in post-conflict societies will be returned to in the last chapter of the book; suffice it to say here that the label of a 'victims' movement', let alone a 'movement', is at best an inadequate description for what is a diverse international array of academic, activist and politically-based developments, and at worse an inaccurate label for what hides a conservative law and order agenda.

Victim advocacy and political influence

If we apply the description of a 'victims' movement' to the USA of the 1980s/1990s, and the height of the conservative Reagan/Bush administrations, then this label reflects the right-wing response to crime and victim advocacy that reached its zenith during this period in this particular country. However, the reach of right-wing victim advocacy, encompassing calls for harsher sentences and victim allocution in consideration of sentencing, has spread beyond the borders of the USA. Adopting a hard-line response to law and order, in the name of victims and citizens as potential victims, has proved to be a vote winner in Britain too. But the more extreme manifestation of a right-wing victims' movement has not evolved in the UK for a number of reasons that reflect social and political differences between the two countries, and the particular history of victim support in each (Walklate, 2000).

If we take 'victim support' to mean organisations that work to practically assist and emotionally support victims, by providing services from something as simple as an information pack through to counselling, we can characterise the USA and UK as having two distinct approaches. In general, the development of victim support in the USA can be characterised as having an abundance of politically vested interests, and in the UK victim support can be characterised by its tempered political activism. While there are obvious exceptions to these generalisations, these two 'models' have dominated victim support in both countries since the 1970s. Explanations for these differences have tended to rest with the importance assigned to victims' rights in the USA, in comparison with the welfarist model of responding to victims' needs in the UK. Where, on the one hand, demands for victims' rights can challenge the political status quo, reliance on provision of services to victims means that, on the other hand, changes are brought in through the 'service backdoor'.

The following paragraphs focus on the development of Victim Support and on single-issue victims' groups in the UK, and examine their evolution with respect to underlying principles of how best to promote victims' interests.

Victim Support

In the UK, support for victims of crime is dominated by one organisation – Victim Support (VS). The first local scheme was launched in Bristol in the early 1970s. It emerged from a victim–offender initiative, and, after a faltering start, was relaunched with more funding and administrative support from NACRO (the National Association for the Care and Resettlement of Offenders). With a steady increase in the number of local schemes offering support to victims, the National Association of Victim Support Schemes (NAVSS) was established in 1979 (Williams, 1983). Three decades later, the renamed Victim Support is a national organisation with over 17,000 volunteers and a London head office with a core of around fifty paid staff. On average, VS offers assistance to around 1.5 million victims each year.

Over the years VS has acted as a source of support to millions of crime victims. Victims can directly approach the organisation for support, and the police refer a large proportion of victims to the organisation, who are then first approached by means of a letter and subsequently, in certain cases, by direct contact. In effect VS provides the sticking plaster for many victims in the aftermath of crime. What it does not do is pick up the pieces for victims at a deeper and more long-term level; that is, it is not a counselling service. Rather, what VS offers victims is a 'listening ear' and practical advice on what victims can expect from the criminal justice system and, where appropriate, State compensation.

In terms of its year-on-year growth and the number of victims it supports, Victim Support is an unparalleled success story when compared alongside other national organisations (INAVEM (Institut National d'Aide aux Victimes et de Médiation) in France; Weisser Ring (White Ring) in Germany; NOVA (National Organisation for Victim Assistance) in the USA). But, when one looks at its quasi-official status, the organisation represents something of a contradiction.

VS receives somewhere in the range of £30 million in funding each year from the Home Office, and sits on most government panels that touch on victims' issues as the definitive 'voice' of victim support (Rock, 1998a). At the same time, VS is a registered charity that likes to maintain its image as an independent apolitical organisation. With the bulk of the organisation's funding coming from central government it is understandable that VS steers clear of offending its paymasters. Yet, despite presenting itself as apolitical, VS is anything but a neutral organisation. In other words, VS has been able to survive successive changes of government, and has increased its funding from government over the years, because it has presented a 'conservative' response to victim-centred justice. As the victim organisation to which government defers, VS's influence in shaping government policy has been significant.

With its stated apolitical agenda, and its army of volunteers, mostly women with time to do charity work, VS has epitomised the 'safe' victims' movement in the UK – 'safe' because the organisation has tended to steer clear of difficult questions about the underlying causes of crime and victimisation, and their disproportionate impact on certain groups in society. As Williams comments (1999: 88): 'The feminist-inspired organisations have been marginalised at the expense of the more conciliatory Victim Support precisely because they do remain committed to a political conception of victimisation.' In maintaining an apolitical stance, VS has not asked 'why' women suffer from domestic violence and sexual assault, or 'why' minority ethnic people suffer from racist attacks. In comparison, Britain's Rape Crisis, with its overtly feminist agenda, asks the establishment uncomfortable questions about the causes of women's victimisation at the hands of men, and frames arguments in the context of patriarchal social structures. Where Rape Crisis marches to protest its agenda, VS regularly sits with government representatives to work for change for victims from within the system. As a reflection of these two different approaches, VS has enjoyed extensive government funding over the years, while Rape Crisis has struggled financially to survive. However, this characterisation of VS as a 'safe' apolitical organisation has more recently been changing, and, when looked at against VS's track record of work since the beginning of the 1990s, is increasingly tenuous.

From its origins working predominantly with victims of burglary, VS has increased its area of competence to include assistance to a range of vulnerable victims including rape victims, families of murder victims, and victims of racial harassment. For example: in 1990 VS convened a national, inter-agency working party on domestic violence; in 1994 VS convened a working party to look at support for families of road death victims; in 1996 VS published guidelines on *Supporting Victims of Racial Harassment*, as well as *Women, Rape and the Criminal Justice System* and *Children in Court*. These working parties and publications reveal a number of changes that have taken place in VS over the last decade or so as the organisation has increasingly come to work with vulnerable victims, such as victims of rape and domestic violence. Recognising the particular challenges these victims faced in the criminal justice system, VS saw its duty to respond to their needs. In particular, the 1996 VS publication on rape victims pointed to inadequacies in the way in which these victims were treated by the criminal justice system.

In its expansion of services to rape victims and families of murder victims, Victim Support has entered the traditional territory of other organisations such as Rape Crisis, Women's Aid, and SAMM (Support After Murder and Manslaughter). Understandably, there are elements within these smaller organisations that are resentful of the way in which VS has encroached on their areas of expertise (Williams, 1999). But, while VS, as the most financially and politically powerful victim support organisation in the UK, can offer victims an introductory service about what to expect from the criminal justice system, and a 'listening ear', it cannot offer the degree of long-term specialist assistance that certain victims need. Selected VS workers receive training to work with rape victims and other vulnerable victims, but the usefulness of the service they provide is questionable given that victims are usually referred on to the smaller specialist organisations. In this regard, the smaller victim support organisations that have built up their expertise over the years, and have struggled to fund their work, are cautious about what VS can offer. Recognising this, VS has made efforts to work alongside members of women's aid agencies in an effort to promote each other's work and provide support where it is needed.

VS's development as a politicised organisation continued throughout the 1990s. Most significantly, in 1995 VS published *The Rights of Victims of Crime*, and in so doing established itself as anything but an apolitical organisation. This report followed in the footsteps of the 1990 UK Victim's Charter, and earlier ground-breaking instruments like the 1985 UN Declaration for Victims of Crime and Abuse of Power. The 1995 report outlined five major responsibilities of the State to victims: (1) compensation; (2) protection; (3) services; (4) information; and (5) responsibility. With respect to 'responsibility', VS made it clear that victims should be free of what the organisation referred to as the burden of decisions relating to the offender. In other words, VS stated that victims should have no role to play in deciding the kind of sentence an offender should receive, or whether they should receive bail and parole. These decisions, according to VS, are the remit of the State. In doing this, VS positioned itself as far as possible from the demands of right-wing victim advocates, largely emanating from the USA, for inclusion of 'victim impact statements', as a statement of victim opinion on the impact of crime, prior to sentencing. In making a policy statement about victims' rights, both their extent and limitations, VS implicitly delivered a political statement about the 'place' of victims in criminal justice.

More recently, VS published the report *Criminal Neglect* on its website.[1] Using research findings from the 2000 British Crime Survey – which indicate that only half of all crime is reported to the police, and less than 5 per cent of all crime is processed through the criminal justice system – *Criminal Neglect* suggests that victim-centred criminal justice developments do very little to support the majority of victims: 'these provisions do nothing to help 96 per cent of victims. These are the people whose offenders are not detected and whose cases are not processed through the criminal justice system.' *Criminal Neglect* argues that all public services – schools, public employers, and hospitals – should recognise their shared responsibility to help people cope with the damaging experiences of crime (Shepherd and Lisles, 1998). Echoing the content of the JUSTICE report (1998), *Criminal Neglect* presses for 'joined-up' services between agencies in an effort to support all victims. The report both praises and challenges the achievements that have been made for victims of crime in the last 25 years. However, in recognising the number of neglected victims, and their need for assistance outside the narrow framework of the criminal justice system, the report steps into the realm of what was once considered radical victimology.

With the publication of *Criminal Neglect*, VS questions the lack of assistance received by victims who fall outside the remit of the criminal law. At the same time, the organisation reaffirms the government's stance on victims' rights with the publication of *The Rights of Victims of Crime*. As an established organisation that is valued and respected by the criminal justice establishment, VS is in an enviable position to challenge the status of victims without at the same time appearing to rock the boat. In deliberately avoiding an overt political standpoint, VS has been able gently to push through victim reforms, and has received millions of pounds in government funding that has been to the benefit of millions of victims.

Single-issue groups

Single-issue victim groups exist to support and promote the cause of certain victims. In the UK these groups tend to be formed and run by volunteers who have either directly experienced victimisation, such as rape or domestic violence, or whose loved ones have been the victims of crime, such as murder. These self-help organisations usually operate on shoestring budgets to assist victims and survivors of particular crimes, and often lobby government and criminal justice agencies in an effort to improve services for victims. Single-issue groups epitomise the realisation of the slogan 'the personal is political'.

Rock (1998a, 1998b) provides a detailed account of the emergence, division, and splintering of different UK groups that set out to support families of murder victims.[2] The first of these groups, The Compassionate Friends (TCF), was founded in 1969 to support parents and relatives bereaved by the death of a child, including victims of manslaughter/ murder. The emphasis of the group was on bereaved parents helping each other. Two members of The Compassionate Friends, recognising a special need, broke off from the organisation to form Parents of Murdered Children (POMC). In 1984, POMC constituted itself as a separate entity to The Compassionate Friends.

From herein POMC and TCF took a different course. POMC emerged as the more activist-based of the two organisations. By 1990 POMC had cemented its own identity when it was awarded charitable status independently of TCF. For a period in the mid-1980s POMC and VS worked together to offer mutual support and expertise. But in time the more radical members of POMC broke away to form the Victims of Crime Pressure Group and, later, Justice for Victims. As the names of these groups suggest, their central remit was to be politically active, public and bold in offering a concerted challenge to the insensitivity of the criminal justice system to the suffering and needs of bereaved relatives. Justice for Victims has organised marches on Parliament to petition for, among other things, a Bill of Rights for Victims (based on the US model), and victim impact statements.

In turn, POMC, reflecting its shift away from a narrow focus on parents, evolved into Support After Murder and Manslaughter (SAMM), formally launching itself in 1994. SAMM has enjoyed close support from Victim Support, and its office is located in the same building as VS's National Office. According to Rock (1998a), some members of POMC viewed the allegiance between VS and SAMM with suspicion, and, under- standably, some degree of envy.

The development of these single-issue groups for relatives of murder victims was aided and abetted by a number of factors in the 1990s. Generally there was an increased government focus on the language of victims' rights if not actual substantive rights, in the form of the 1990 and 1996 Victim's Charters (see Chapter 6). Then there was the media's focus on one single case that came to epitomise the decay of civil society in Britain – the James Bulger case, in 1993, in which a toddler was brutally murdered by two children. Rock has said of this period and the part played by the nation's media in fanning the flames of bloodlust and calls for vengeance (1998a: 229): 'the new [victim] groups, and Justice for Victims amongst them, were to rise up as part of just such a media-engendered cycle in the mid 1990s. Most were new and brash.'

The James Bulger case, and years later the release of his two young murderers, has seen repeated calls for retribution from members of the murdered boy's family and certain victim lobby groups. With this, the more modest victim lobby groups, such as SAMM, have been keen to distance themselves from the taint of vigilantism that marks some of their more retributive cousins. The human interest stories portrayed by groups such as Justice for Victims readily play to the media. However, the wider picture of what justice is, and the potential part for victims to play beyond retribution, is often left out by the populist tabloid media in what is for them a story and a means of selling papers. While Justice for Victims appeared to have a sympathetic ear under the Conservatives, and particularly Home Secretary Michael Howard, their single-issue message did not carry the weight and the support of the more universal and neutral stance of Victim Support. Single-interest victim lobby groups can have their time in the limelight, but, in England and Wales, one could argue that an overt political stance, coupled with aggressive lobbying, does not serve an organisation's cause in the long term. In comparison, single-issue lobby groups in the USA, such as Mothers Against Drink Driving, have fared well.

In the USA's more conservative and retributive political climate, where the death penalty exists alongside chain gangs, victim lobby groups can more readily bend the ear of politicians, who cannot afford to ignore calls for 'justice' that are sometimes based on a desire for retribution. In the 1980s, because of this, the USA began two decades of intense victim lobbying where the voice of single-interest victim groups could always be heard: 1980 saw the first Victim Bill of Rights passed; 1981 saw the declaration of National Victim Rights Week; in 1982 the President's Task Force on Victims of Crime was commissioned, and in the same year Congress passed the Federal Victims and Witnesses' Protection Act; and in 1984 Congress passed the Victims of Crime Act.

But as crime rates rose unabated throughout the 1980s and 1990s in the USA, it has to be asked whether these initiatives actually assisted victims, and to what extent they were primarily enacted as a vote-winner for politicians who needed to be seen to be doing something about crime. According to Elias, writing at the height of the 'war on crime' in 1993, the victim 'torch' passed from one single-issue victim group to the next during this period, so serving to create new victim 'celebrities' but doing little to address the underlying causes of social inequalities that lead to much victimisation.

The end of academic victimology?

Alongside the rapid rise of victim advocacy groups since the 1970s, academic victimology has also moved on as a discipline. But, marred by its association with right-wing victim advocacy, academic victimology remains under-developed and under-utilised as a serious area of academic study with huge potential for policy input.

Friday, acting as rapporteur at the end of the 1988 symposium of the World Society of Victimology, writes a clarion call for the 'science of victimology' to be resurrected (1992: 8):

> It is very clear that the predominant themes addressed during the Symposium were clinically oriented. But when did treatment become part of victimology? Where have all the academics gone who were prominent during the last Symposia? Isn't OLOGY used to described a science? What has happened to the field; what's happened to the scientific discipline, the primary basis of developing scope?

Looking at the contents of subsequent victimology symposia (Adelaide in 1994; Amsterdam in 1997; Montreal in 2000), it would appear that Friday's fears remain valid as the 'science' of victimology is overtaken by applied and largely uncritical victim advocacy. Keynote speakers, such as Fattah and Elias, have addressed symposia delegates about the absence of a scientific and critical victimology. But their opinions appear as a sideshow, as, in the main, victimology symposia tend to be dominated by presentations from victim advocates who relay the positive outcomes of their work with victims with little room for critical interpretation. What tends to be left out is an independent evaluation of victim programmes themselves. In turn, more fundamental questions such as 'what do victims need?' and 'what do victims think of the service they receive from agencies?' are often conspicuous by their absence. But as most agencies that work with victims of crime operate on small budgets, it is understandable that they are keen to promote the positive outcome of their service, and are less keen to highlight instances of victim dissatisfaction. As mentioned earlier, initiatives such as the European Science Foundation's COST Action A21, on restorative justice, provide some indication that critical assessments of criminal justice practice for victims are being developed through some funding channels.

The UK is fortunate to have a number of bodies that regularly fund independent research on the impact of crime and victimisation on individuals and communities, and the effect of criminal justice interventions: namely, the Home Office's research and statistics directorate; the government-funded Economic and Social Research Council; and a number of charities such as the Nuffield Foundation and the Leverhulme Trust.

Although the lion's share of research is government-funded, it is largely undertaken by academics with a remit to conduct independent and objective assessments of government and non-government policy into pressing social issues. For example, the regular British Crime Survey, as a government-funded initiative, cannot disguise 'bad' results that present government policy in a poor light.

However, this is not to be smug about the state of British victimology as 'science'. While British victimology/criminology is relatively well funded when compared to research undertaken in countries with similar levels of criminal justice development, the bulk of research relates to government policy in an effort to reduce *crime* rates. What research is not about is victims defining the field of services they should be in receipt of, and evaluating the services they receive. Rather, evaluations are of the services themselves based on criteria set by government, researchers, or employees. This charge is not exceptional to victimology, and applies to most of criminology. But to resurrect some aspects of a radical and critical victimology – one that challenges what victimisation is and can be, and how we might most effectively respond to it – research needs to step outside the accepted frame of reference to victims that has been dominated, since the 1980s, by 'administrative' or 'managerialist' concerns to manage crime.

Administrative criminology's 'counting' of victims, epitomised by the crime survey, and managerialist criminology's 'measurement' of criminal justice responses to these victims, by looking at efficiency, effectiveness and economy, do little to question 'what' we are studying. As Friday asks (1992: 8): 'Is Victimology a science or a service? Is Victimology a discipline or a movement? Is Victimology a phenomenon or a *cause célèbre?*'

Rather than position victimology as either one thing or another, we can attempt to move towards an accommodation of both science and service through the interplay of academic victimology, victim advocacy and victim policy. However, a wall has been built up between critical victimology and victim advocate groups, which has no equal in criminology meetings. The 'style' of both groups is often in direct opposition to each other. Where one uses theory and critical analysis, the other employs deeply personal and traumatic accounts of victimisation to position itself as the platform for victim-centred justice (Bowers-Andrews, 1992; Madigan and Gamble, 1991).

As an illustration, compare here two extracts from papers taken from the 1997 ninth international symposium on victimology: the first from Marlene Young (1999: 180–1), director of the National Organisation for Victim Assistance in the USA, and the second from Ezzat Fattah (1999: 193 and 196), professor of criminology at Simon Fraser University in Vancouver:

> Despite reductions in numbers, there are continuing patterns of rape, robbery and murder that are devastating to victims in any context, but that reflect even more social horror when perpetuated by increasingly younger offenders who seemingly have no social conscience and no regard for life . . . The sheer cumulative effect of observing from a distant or not-so-distant view the horror of our times takes its toll . . . I know personally the effects of that toll. I wake up nights after dreams in which I smell or taste the mixture of smoke, metal and blood after a fiery airplane crash . . . I hear in my mind the terror in a little girl's voice in Union, South Carolina . . . I feel palpable anger and frustration at the plight of the Oklahoma City bombing victims and survivors . . . I sense the shame of a young Japanese victim who was stalked, sexually assaulted, doused with

kerosene and burned, and who now faces the world through a scarred and mutilated face and wounded soul.

In our society, there is a tendency to stress – even overblow – the negative effects of victimisation. Even physical injuries resulting from victimisation do not carry the same weight everywhere . . . It is undeniable that psychological wounds heal faster and better in some cultures than in others . . . I wondered then [in the mid-1980s], as I do now [1999], whether the outpouring of sympathy for crime victims was doing more harm than good.

Even the title of these papers clearly marks their opposed standpoint; where Young's is titled 'Justice for All – Even the Victim', Fattah's is titled 'From a Handful of Dollars to Tea and Sympathy: The Sad History of Victim Assistance'. However, while Young's paper recounts harrowing tales of victimisation, she also calls for victim assistance providers to care for a range of victims outside the remit of the 'ordinary' – including victims of aeroplane crashes, natural disasters, and technological or biochemical accidents. She goes on to highlight the point that trauma victims are more at risk of other traumas (repeat victimisation), and are themselves at high risk of becoming offenders. With this last point, tucked in the midst of a paper that relates horror stories of victimisation before outlining a detailed list for a professional victim 'code of care', Young briefly refers to the links between victim and offender populations. However, this point is not pursued in the paper.

In contrast, Fattah, who is also a proponent of research on links between victim and offender populations, acknowledges that practical support for victims, such as repair to property, is welcome, but unregulated counselling, therapy and treatment can, he contends, do victims more harm than good. Fattah draws on the now widely discredited example of 'repressed memory syndrome'. This was popular for a period in the 1990s among therapists, in both the USA and UK, as a means of getting patients to recall suppressed childhood abuse. Reflecting the criticism of the 'culture of complaint' that is levelled at what some critics see as a 'victim industry' (Hughes, 1994), Fattah debates the usefulness to victims of the 'victim' label and associated therapies.

Given these examples, there is much reparation work that needs to be done if the present gulf between some proponents of critical victimology and victim advocacy can be mended so that they can work together to advance both the theory and practice of victim-centred justice. This division is not aided by the fact that victimology, as 'science', is in the doldrums. In recent years restorative justice has risen to fill the gap in the discipline's impetus to push towards 'new' victim-centred developments in social and criminal justice. But, as Chapter 7 comments, restorative justice proponents often sidestep negative criticisms of their 'movement', including its offender-centred rather than victim-centred merits.

It would seem, on reading the contents of victimology symposia, that victimology, as 'science', has lost direction. To this day, old ideas centred on victim blaming resurface in academic victimology. In the published selected proceedings from the sixth international symposium on victimology, two lengthy papers by Knudten were included that contained ideas about victim precipitation, victim responsibility and victim blaming. In his effort to outline a comprehensive victimology, Knudten uncritically describes a range of theories and, in doing so, betrays old ideas about the 'innocent' and 'deserving' victim (1992: 61): 'All victims are not fully innocent, just as all alleged offenders are not totally guilty.' Knudten proceeds to outline a victim–offender contributory continuum, on a nine-point scale, ranging from 'offender – full initiation' through to 'victim – full initiation', and later looks at victim responsibility for his/her vicimisation in relation to a six-point scale. As Friday rightly says of Knudten's work (1992: 11): 'The problem with this model is that it is perhaps more of a comprehensive definition of victimology than a theory of it for it incorporates nearly every contingency. It explains all and it explains nothing.'

Friday's critique reflects the wider state of victimology – that is, a discipline that now covers almost every aspect of 'victimhood', from burglary through to human rights abuses, but pays disproportionately little attention to objective empirical research on how we come to be victimised, the effects of victimisation, what victims need, and the impact of victim assistance. Instead, victimology has become, according to some critics like Friday and Elias, a mouthpiece for victim advocacy and social policy that is not based on solid empiricism. In turn, the influence of victimological research on social policy is debatable.

Moving forward: marrying academia, advocacy and policy

Victim-centred social policy is the result of competing interests, or ideologies, between different political and victim advocate groups. And as evidenced by Rock's research (1998a and 1998b) on single-interest victim groups, victim policy is also the product of dominant personalities within these groups. The politics of the day and the personalities of the day change over time, and therefore so does social policy. Social policy also reflects changes in crime rates and patterns of victimisation.

Compared with political ideologies and the part played by victim advocate groups, the influence of academic victimology on social policy is, arguably, marginal. As Sebba comments (2001: 34): 'research is not generally the main guiding factor behind the formulation of policy but, in the best case, competes with other sources of influence'. According to Weiss (1987) (as reported by Sebba, 2001), most policy makers in the USA are not informed about relevant research and only consult research in certain situations. This would suggest that victim-centred justice in the USA is ideology-driven rather than research-driven. Whether the same can be said of the UK is debatable; suffice it to say that the UK has a tradition of government-funded research that is not influenced by radical victim advocate groups and calls for retributive justice. On the other hand, Victim Support, as the safe 'voice' of victim policy in Britain, is now becoming a significant research funder in its own right, and no doubt will set its own criteria to determine 'who' and 'what' is funded. Given that VS has thrived over the last decades largely as a result of adopting a steady, cautious and (some would say) 'conservative' approach to law and order, it is debatable whether groups that significantly challenge government-driven victim policy will benefit from Victim Support's funding.

Victim policy becomes problematic when it fails to consider evidence from a range of empirical research studies. The credentials of victim policies that are driven by victim advocates, and media calls for a tough response to crime and criminals, have to be set against sound victimological research that identifies what is in the interests of victims. For example, populist legislation allowing local communities to identify paedophiles who, having served their sentence, are placed on a list of sex offenders – such as Megan's Law in the USA and similar provisions in the UK (see Chapter 1) – may do potential victims more harm than good as paedophiles go undercover to escape community vigilantism.

Working from the standpoint that good victim-centred social policy has to be informed by empirical research, the next paragraphs suggest ways to develop victimological practice based on 'good practice' ideals. This calls for two things:

- a definition and interpretation of what 'good practice' in victimology should be;
- a marriage between academic victimology, victim advocacy and policy reponses.

In outlining the potential for 'good practice' development in victimology, emphasis is placed on transferable practice between different settings. In other words, 'good practice' should be transferable at both an institutional level and a geographical or jurisdictional level – that is, between similarly placed institutions, such as victim support initiatives, and, at another level, between different places.

Building 'good practice' in victimology

'Good practice', or 'best practice' as it is often referred to, is a much used and abused term. Descriptions of victim assistance projects are relayed on websites as examples of 'good practice'[3], sometimes with little thought as to what this term means. Evidence-based research from academic victimology should be at the forefront of comparative assessments exploring how different projects, from the same and different jurisdictions, might learn from and adapt each other's 'good practice' for victims. Before this stage, though, there are a number of questions that need positing with regard to what 'works' and doesn't work for some victims in some locations, and how 'good practice' might be transferred from one place to the next. Knowledge of the promise and problems of offering and transferring 'good practice' can only be built up over time using skilled researchers. Although in-house assessments of a project's work are a quick and cheap shortcut to results, they lack objectivity, often because of the need to secure further funding, and therefore can prove to be unreliable sources for other interested parties.

Generic 'lists' of what 'good practice' should be, be this a reference to the UN Declaration for Victims of Crime and Abuse of Power or a list of service standards from a victim agency, alongside descriptive 'success stories' of 'good practice', do not as a general rule provide information about what is meant by 'good practice' and how to transfer 'good practice' from one project to another. In an effort to build 'good practice' guidelines by offering examples from evidence-based research on legislation and practice in the same and different jurisdictions, the following three points need addressing (Goodey, 2004a):

1. *What is 'good practice'?*
   Good practice needs definition with respect to project goals, 'success' stories, and possibilities for replication in other settings. Who defines and interprets practice as 'good' is an important consideration; and, where possible, victims' voices should be heard alongside practitioners, policy makers, and academics.
2. *Comparative and cross-national*
   Comparative and cross-national examples of victim-centred 'good practice' need to be sensitive to the different social-cultural practices that are particular to each institution/community/country. Questions need to be considered about the different ascription of 'victim', and the limitations imposed on the transfer of some 'good practice' ideas between different legal cultures.
3. *The place of the victim*
   Different organisations and different criminal justice systems afford variable levels of significance to victims and victim-centred justice, and, in turn, assign particular significance to certain types of victims (children for example). The victim's 'place' in different contexts needs to be understood as this impacts on the successful transfer of project ideas.

Taking the first point, 'good practice' is a difficult concept to define. While 'practice' can refer to the plans and activities of criminal justice agencies and victim advocate groups, it is very hard to define and agree on what is meant by 'good'. Practitioners and policy makers assign the label of 'good' to practice they deem to be successful; yet the measure of 'success' is often left undefined. Subjectivity tends to dominate 'good practice' assessments without a clear map of how judgements are made.

Bearing in mind the above three-point criteria for undertaking 'good practice' research, the following represents a useful extended 'checklist', adapted from the author's work on victims of sex trafficking (Goodey, 2004a), of what needs to be considered when working 'with' and 'for' crime victims, in light of empirical evidence:

- *Positive results*: Identify projects, through results, with a positive tangible impact on victims. Results should define and distinguish between 'successful' and 'unsuccessful' practice according to users (victims), practitioners, policy makers, and researchers.
- *Innovative*: Identify projects that employ new and/or innovative responses to victims that have been deemed 'successful'. Identify and reject established practices that cannot prove they serve the interests of victims.
- *Sustainable*: Look for projects with a long-term and durable shelf-life that can, where appropriate, offer assistance to victims over a prolonged period.
- *Replication/transferability*: Seek practical solutions that can be transferred to other settings, be this locally, nationally or internationally. Encourage information exchange between projects about success stories and failures in an effort to replicate success.
- *Cooperation*: Cooperation needs to be encouraged between different agencies working with victims. This avoids competition for resources between agencies, and unnecessary replication of project ideas. Cooperation should be sought between, where appropriate, criminal justice agencies, victim advocacy agencies, academia, and policy makers.
- *Ethical*: Projects should employ ethical values towards victims. To this end, due consideration should be given to the experiences and opinions of victims.

This list is not prescriptive. In other words it does not specify what is meant by 'successful' and 'unsuccessful' practice as determinants of 'good practice'. Rather, the first point asks that projects identify what is meant by these terms before they embark on work with victims. However, the following two criteria can be added to the above list as practical evidence of 'good' work with victims:

- More victims are assisted as a result of the project.
- A majority of victims indicate their satisfaction with the project.

Absent victim voices

With respect to victim satisfaction, and the first point made earlier on the question of 'what is good practice?', too often victims' views are not sought either when developing so-called victim-centred criminal justice interventions or when assessments of practice initiatives are undertaken. In other words, victim-centred justice programmes often evolve without or with very little direct critical input from victims[4]. For example, Ready et al.'s research on the role of crime victims in American policing employed a national (US) telephone survey of police departments and victim organisations (VSOs) that set out to (2002: 181) 'establish a baseline of policies and practices regarding the involvement of victims and VSOs in community policing' – but at no point did the research engage directly with victims. The survey asked police and VSO respondents to indicate whether they thought victims of crime are better placed than citizens who have not been victims to contribute to policing efforts to detect and prevent crime. The general response was that there are benefits to be had from victim involvement in policing efforts, but that any special knowledge that victims possess in relation to crime was unlikely to be of more use than assistance provided by non-victims. One statement from the director of a Californian VSO is particularly telling (Ready et al., 2002: 186):

> Utilizing victims as resources in domestic violence I don't think could
> happen, either in prevention, solving the crime or preventing
> revictimization. They would have to be a survivor because of what their
> mindset is. They still think like a victim and 90% of victims are not
> thinking logically. They're not even thinking about their own safety
> because they've been victimised so long.

What this statement indicates is the extent to which victim services can 'speak' on behalf of victims in what they perceive to be their best interests. In their efforts to protect victims, some victim services and the police deny victims input into services that directly affect them. Patronising assumptions abound that victim services or the police 'know best' when it comes to the state of mind and role that crime victims can play in criminal justice; in this regard, Ready et al.'s research found that only 27 per cent of police agencies that reported some kind of training to officers on assistance and working with crime victims included the participation of actual victims in their training.

Similarly, research by Blomberg et al. (2002) on the Jacksonville Victim Services Center in Florida, a 'one-stop' location for comprehensive victim services, was able to report that (2002: 168):

> According to various staff from the Center and in other collaborating
> agencies, its unique program implementation success reflects several
> different factors . . . a Center supervisor explained that its major strength
> lies in its capacity to provide comprehensive services that are achieved
> because of its quality of staff who have the skills, training and necessary
> professionalism to effectively assist crime victims.

This may be the case, but overall conclusions about the Center's success as a 'one-stop' victim service were reached by interviewing staff members at the Center, law enforcement agencies, and other agencies; in other words, victims' assessments of the Center's work were absent from this $100,000 evaluative study (Blomberg et al., 2002: 150).

Restorative justice has most recently taken on board the need to incorporate victims' assessments of programme initiatives that include the objective to be responsive to victims' needs (Braithwaite, 2002). The critique that has been levelled at restorative justice is that it uses victims in an effort to divert, primarily, young offenders from traditional justice by channelling them into mediation and conferencing programmes (see Chapter 7 for full explanation and critique). In response to this, restorative justice advocates are keen to advertise the victim-centred nature of their programmes. Bradshaw and Umbreit, recognising that (2003: 71) 'Victim satisfaction is one of the essential components of program evaluation', document the development and application of a standardised tool for assessing victim satisfaction with mediation programmes. Their unwieldy named 'Victim Satisfaction with Offender Dialogue Scale' (VSODS) sets out to advance a standardised tool for measuring victim satisfaction, across a range of questions, using an incremental scale to measure satisfaction. The authors propose that their standardised tool, much like the International Crime Victims Survey, can be applied to different restorative schemes in an effort to compare 'success' rates.

Transferability

Other authors, most notably in the crime prevention field, have critiqued crime reduction initiatives according to a variety of measures that also resonate with victims and potential victims (Crawford and Newburn, 2003; Ekblom and Pease, 1995; Pawson and Tilley, 1994). Evaluations have tended to focus on the temporal durability of projects (that is, how long their impact lasts), and the displacement effects of projects (that is, whether they increase the crime rate in the surrounding neighbourhoods outside the crime reduction scheme). More broadly, some crime prevention evaluations have explored and critiqued the possibilities of transferring 'good practice' crime prevention initiatives from one place to the next. However, for these 'good practice' benchmarks to work, both in victim assistance and in crime prevention, one factor is essential: knowledge about successful and unsuccessful project work with victims should be shared between practitioners and policy makers. In this regard, academic victimology has a key role to play in the monitoring, assessment, publication and transfer of 'good practice' examples and guidelines between different user groups. The willingness of agencies to share knowledge of successful and unsuccessful practice is key to this process.

Victimology can take advantage of organisations such as the World Society of Victimology and international victimology symposia to relay and critically assess interventions for victims that might be applicable in other settings. Besides the above list of 'good practice' descriptors, consideration needs to be given to further criteria when attempting to transfer 'good practice' between countries. As far as possible jurisdictions should be 'matched'; that is, they should have:

- similar legal and criminal justice structures: for example, adversarial or inquisitorial justice;
- similar levels of development with regard to victim-centred justice: for example, comparable levels of victim assistance or State compensation;
- comparable levels and types of crime: for example, comparing victim interventions in post-conflict Yugoslavia with contemporary Japan is unlikely to yield useful results.

While comparative research can be undertaken between countries with very different experiences of crime and criminal justice, the transfer of 'good practice' ideas is more likely to succeed where countries share similar mechanisms for responding to crime and victimisation. All countries suffer from crime, but their responses are diverse and often reflect the limitations and possibilities they have on offer in the context of their own political, social and economic settings. To take practice out of context is to run the risk of losing the best of what it can offer (Nelken, 1997).

When looking at practice for victims in comparable settings, both at home and abroad, researchers should offer practitioners and policy makers some useful assessments of common assumptions about what victims 'need' in terms of good practice, and what services should be provided. Looking at practice between different but similarly matched agencies, researchers should point to assumptions about existing practices that are and are not on offer to various victim categories. For example, by asking why a service is provided in court X to children, but in court Y the same service is provided to children and mentally disabled adults, agencies can compare and assess practice initiatives.

Careful investigation of what 'good practice' is and should be, by independent researchers trained in the methods of comparative assessment, can assist practitioners and policy makers to transfer ideas and experiences of 'good practice'. The implications of this can mean the transfer of knowledge and practice at the local, national and international level. Assessment of 'good practice' should not be left to practitioners and policy makers as their results can be labelled as partisan. There is an obvious role for academic victimology to play here.

Concluding comments

This chapter set out to look at the contradictions between academic victimology and victim advocacy, and their influence on social policy. In the process, dangerous and promising developments in both the 'science' of victimology and the manifestation of the 'victims' movement' have been highlighted. The interplay between academic victimology, victim advocacy and victim policy has also been explored in the chapter with the aim of promoting 'good practice' intervention for victims. Without providing a prescriptive account of what 'good practice' with victims should be, the chapter has mapped a route for a critical and constructive response to victim practice in different settings.

Informed social policy for victims can offer a better response to victims' needs that is measured by 'good practice' criteria. To this end, victim advocacy and political interests cannot be allowed to lead victim-centred justice initiatives. Rather, academic research needs to critically inform victim advocacy and policy initiatives that, in due course, can feed back into new research avenues.

Suggested reading

Mawby and Walklate (1994) present a good introduction to the various strands in academic victimology and their overlap with victim advocacy. Williams (1999) provides a solid overview of the politics of victim advocacy and policy as they impact on practice with victims in a British context. In comparison, Elias's (1993) seminal work is a rallying call to critique the politicisation of victim-centred developments in the USA that resonates with British experiences. Two papers by Fattah (1979 and 1999) span twenty years of developments in academic victimology, victim advocacy and social policy, which he, alongside Elias, roundly critiques as having 'sold out' to the so-called 'victims' movement'. For suggestions of how academic victimology and victim advocacy might enlighten victim policy through transfer of 'good practice', see Goodey (2004a); and for a critique of victimology's failure to sufficiently inform victim-centred criminal justice practice see Sebba (2001).

Notes

1. www.victimsupport.org.uk/about/publication/neglect.
2. Kenney (2002) presents an interesting piece of research on the impact on the 'self' when a loved one is murdered, taking gender as a key factor influencing an individual's responses to murder. His qualitative research is based on interviews with 32 individuals who experienced the murder of a loved one; a mail survey with 22 respondents; and information obtained from 108 homicide files. He also presents a thorough overview of the literature on victimisation, self and bereavement.
3. See www.victimology.nl; www.cabinet-office.gov.uk/servicefirst/2000/guidance.
4. In February 2003, the UK government website, CJS online, reported on a proposed panel of ten crime victims to advise the government on criminal justice reform.

Chapter 5

Looking at victims' needs and rights

Introducing themes for discussion

Chapter 4 mapped out how academic victimology, victim advocacy, and victim-centred social policy might be married through application of 'good practice' principles to victim-centred initiatives. A key element in this is that due consideration should be given to the experiences and opinions of users of these services – namely victims – when determining whether they can be considered a 'success' or not. Herein, the careful identification of victims' needs and the establishment of victims' rights are central to the success, or otherwise, of interventions 'with' and 'for' victims.

This chapter introduces important provisions for victims in the context of established debates concerning victims' needs and victims' rights, or service standards and legal provisions. In looking at the interconnections between needs and rights the chapter poses questions around the idea of rights and responsibilities and citizenship and consumerism. Towards the end, the chapter focuses on the example of State compensation, referring to examples from Britain and around the world as illustrative of some of the dilemmas and practical realities facing the needs/rights debate.

Determining needs

In the aftermath of crime different victims have very different needs. Victims' needs can be practical and material, emotional and social, and can encompass any or all of the following:

- reassurance and counselling;
- medical assistance;
- financial and practical assistance to secure property;

- information about case progress;
- guidance about what to expect in court;
- the chance to express how the crime has affected them;
- assistance with filling out a form for State compensation;
- information about the release date of their offender.

Needs can be both immediate and long term, and can range from practical assistance such as repair of doors and windows after a burglary, through to counselling over a period of months. Once victims decide to report a crime and actively become engaged with the criminal justice system, they are confronted with a series of requests that place further demands on them. If a case goes to trial victims have to face the prospect of being in the presence of their offender in court, and of undergoing potentially harsh questioning at the hands of a defence lawyer. They may also face intimidation at the hands of the defendant's family and friends. Victims' feelings and concerns develop as they pass through the pre-trial, trial, and post-trial stages of their case. As a reflection of this, what victims say they want, and what they actually need, changes as their situation develops.

Victims' needs reflect the nature of their victimisation and are shaped by their personal characteristics and circumstances. While we can assume that victims of sexual assault are more affected by their victimisation than victims of car theft, there can be great variation in how victims are affected by similar crimes. For example, Ruback and Thompson (2001: 106) refer to different research studies that indicate different levels of distress suffered by women as a result of sexual assault by a stranger or known assailant, with no clear agreement between researchers that stranger rape results in more distress than acquaintance rape. Factors such as the degree of violence involved, the presence of third parties, and the nature of care and support offered after the crime, all impact on the victim's physical, mental and social recovery. The nature and degree of post-traumatic stress disorder (PTSD) experienced by victims in the aftermath of crime hinge on a range of variables that reflect the crime itself and a host of other factors.[1]

Personality, coupled with previous experience of victimisation, and the circumstances surrounding a criminal incident, work together to influence the impact of crime. Whether someone can be considered a nervous or resilient character, whether a crime was particularly brutal in nature, and other events surrounding a crime, such as recent bereavement or loss of employment, are some of the factors influencing the impact of crime. In combination, these factors influence the impact of both personal and property crime on victims (Maguire, 1980). While there is no neat matrix by which we can determine the impact that different crimes will have on individuals according to their gender, age, ethnicity, disability, sexuality and income – to name but a few variables – there are general principles that can guide our understanding of victim vulnerability and resultant needs.

The degree of physical and social power individuals possess is key to understanding their experience of crime, and how they (and others) perceive their own vulnerability as potential victims (see Chapter 3).

Physical power affects the impact of crime on victims, and the extent to which they can be expected to make a full and speedy recovery after an assault. In this regard, when comparing different groups of people, some are obviously more physically vulnerable than others: women compared with men; the disabled and infirm compared with the able-bodied; children compared with adults; and the elderly compared with younger able-bodied adults. But within each group there is great variation in physical strength that correspondingly impacts on an individual's ability to recover from crime. In turn, the same degree of violence can have very different consequences for different victims; a baby can die from a hard punch, while a young fit man may suffer only bruising.

Social power impacts on how individuals experience victimisation, and how they come to terms with victimisation, as both physical and non-physical harm. Intra-familial and institutionalised abuse preys on the social powerlessness of certain groups who do not have the means to confront abusers in positions of power over them. For example, while the elderly are less likely than young men to be victims of violent crime in public places, they are more vulnerable to violent and/or sexual victimisation in private places such as the home and institutionalised care because of their combined lack of physical and social power.

These broad categorisations can be variously added to as they are cross-cut by other influential factors. For example, mental ability or state-of-mind, reflecting a particular mental history and circumstances, can help to determine how people cope in the short and long term post victimisation. Obviously, those suffering from depression and mental disability might not be expected to cope as well as others. But the ability of the mentally disabled, among other vulnerable victims, to cope in the aftermath of crime is cross-cut by those factors already mentioned – such as social power/powerlessness, as provided by work, and by family and support networks. While general categorisation of victims according to physical and social attributes can help determine need, it can also result in stereotypes that neglect the needs of victims who are considered as being able to cope.

While the very young, the very old, and female victims of sexual assault and domestic violence need special recognition as vulnerable victims and witnesses, mainstream victimological research has also begun to recognise the vulnerability and experiences of particular categories of male victims. As Chapter 3 points out, just as all women cannot be constructed as 'victims', so all men cannot be constructed as aggressors, offenders, and as indifferent to their own vulnerability and victimisation. As a reflection of the shifting emphasis on 'who' can be constructed as vulnerable, male rape is now acknowledged as a crime which, like male on female rape, reflects abuse of power and has consequences for determining need amongst a hitherto neglected group of victims (Allen, 2003).

The 'deserving' victim

Ideas about vulnerable victims are restricted by social constructions of appropriate victimhood rather than the actual needs of victims. In other words, 'who' can be a victim is formulated around the idea of the 'innocent' and 'deserving' victim. Victims whose character, past conduct, or actions can be considered as undesirable, or as somehow contributing to their victimisation, are unlikely to be responded to sympathetically by the criminal justice system as deserving victims with particular needs to be met. In this atmosphere, girls and women who step outside the boundaries of respectable female behaviour, such as prostitutes or heavy drinkers (Cain, 1989; Smart and Smart, 1978), and men with criminal convictions (O'Donnell and Edgar, 1996, 1998; Sim, 1994) or associations with 'lawless' communities (such as communities living in the midst of paramilitary groups in Northern Ireland: Hamill, 2002; Knox, 2001), are not generally considered as deserving and innocent victims. The social vulnerability of these particular groups, often exposed to dangerous situations where violence is normalised, has not, until relatively recently, featured in the criminal justice system's appraisal of vulnerability. Although much has changed in recent years, and attacks on a witness's character in court are now being curbed by new guidelines and legislation, the idea of the deserving and innocent victim arguably still holds sway through much of the criminal justice system. As a reflection of this, the needs of other victims – 'men' as a generic group, and in particular 'blameworthy' victims – have been and continue to be sidestepped as the focus remains with accepted notions of vulnerability and need constructed around ideas of the deserving and innocent victim.

My own research into criminal justice responses to vulnerable and at risk victims of crime in eight European Union (EU) member states[2] shows that experts in the field of victims and criminal justice generally agree that certain victim categories are prioritised as 'vulnerable' by the police and other criminal justice agencies (Goodey, 2003). Top among the list of vulnerable victim categories are child victims, and in particular child victims of sexual and physical abuse. In comparison, other personal characteristics and other crimes do not warrant the same degree of attention from criminal justice agencies: typically, victims of homophobic crimes, victims of repeat victimisation, illegal immigrants and former criminals. What the research revealed, among other things, is that while vulnerable and at risk children are deservedly recognised as being in need of special attention and services by criminal justice agencies, other deserving victim categories are not prioritised to the same degree. Here, the idea of innocence, and non-complicity in one's own victimisation, as

Chapter 3 pointed out, is central to understanding how certain people and certain experiences of criminal victimisation are typically excluded from consideration as victims. As a result, the very real needs of certain 'undesirable' victim categories are neglected in a number of criminal justice jurisdictions in Europe.

At the time of writing, the government's July 2003 paper *A New Deal for Victims and Witnesses* states that 'The Criminal Justice Bill currently before Parliament proposes that any witness – not just the vulnerable and intimidated – should be able to give evidence by live TV link where the court considers this appropriate.'[3] While this statement appears to promote concessions towards victims who have traditionally been neglected, it is unclear how this will work in practice given that the court determines who should have access to live television links. And, while recognising the needs that 'any witness' might have, the same government paper adds in a later paragraph: 'In developing the overall approach to making it easier to give evidence, close attention will be paid to the needs of particular victims and witnesses. These include children, victims of sexual crimes, domestic violence, victims of hate crime, people subject to repeat victimisation, people living in high crime areas, and people who are members of ethnic minority communities.'[4] The need to address the needs of some of the most obviously vulnerable victims while broadening the scope of victim-centred justice is a difficult challenge for the government to live up to.

The question that arises here is whether some victims' needs are greater than other victims' needs, and whether all victims should receive similar levels of service provision irrespective of need. Recognising that there is a range of needs that different victims may have under different circumstances, it is not the case that every victim wish should be considered as a legitimate victim need. To do so is to run the risk of over-stretching and misappropriating precious resources that governments and non-governmental organisations set aside for victims. Instead, basic standards of service provision need recognition and enforcement to ensure an adequate and sensitive response to victims of crime. And, within a broad-based set of standards for all victims, there should also be recognition of particularly vulnerable and at-risk victims, such as children, victims of homophobic and racist crimes, and the elderly.

While some victims can readily articulate their needs, others are not in a position to do so or may be unaware that services are available to them as victims of crime, such as State compensation for victims of violent crime. In turn, as the previous chapter has illustrated, some victim advocate groups are in a better position than others to demand services for certain victim groups. In focusing on the needs of particular victim groups, the question of access to and equality of justice for all victims emerges. Herein lies the question of if and when victims' needs should become victims' rights, and whether these rights should be universal or targeted at particular victim groups and victims identified as vulnerable and intimidated.

While victim legislation is usually drawn up to protect and enhance the interests of the most vulnerable victims, providing universal rights to all victims of crime will mean that the needs of 'deserving' and 'undeserving' victims are met. But to attempt to distinguish the 'deserving' from the 'undeserving' victim, as has been the case in the past, is to miss the ready connections that are often there in the lives of victims and offenders in particularly high crime communities. As Chapter 3 has pointed out, the biographies and circumstances of victims and offenders are often one and the same.

Recognising rights

There is an ongoing discussion in criminal justice about the 'place' of victim-centred justice with respect to victims' needs and rights. This discussion has surfaced after centuries of responding to crime as, first, an act that challenges the authority of Sovereign and State, and, second, as an act against the individual as a victim of crime. As Nils Christie (1977) pointed out, in his seminal paper on the marginalisation of the victim in 'western' criminal justice, the victim's role has been relegated to that of witness once a criminal act comes to the attention of the authorities and is drawn into the criminal justice process. As the 'ownership' of crime has moved away from victims to the State, any 'rights' victims have to 'own' their own experience of victimisation and its aftermath have been eroded over time.

However, since the latter half of the twentieth century, victims' needs have increasingly been pushed to the fore by governments and non-governmental organisations. This process has evolved in an effort to redress the imbalance between State and victim in the 'ownership' of crime. It also evolved in response to rising crime rates that brought with them fear of a non-cooperative public who, as the police's main reporting source, would be less than willing to assist the authorities if their needs as victims were inadequately met. The early work of feminist and other grass-roots organisations, encouraged by the civil rights movement in the USA and accompanying challenges to authority such as protests against the Vietnam War, saw increasing calls for recognition of and adequate responses to large swathes of vulnerable victims, such as battered children and women, and victims of sexual assault and rape (Brownmiller, 1975).

However, these early victim-centred criminal justice developments should not be characterised as the sole work of radical organisations. In Britain, government and mainstream organisations had an equal role in the development of victim-centred initiatives. Chief among these, and pre-dating women's refuges by a decade, was the foundation of the State compensation scheme for victims of violent crime in England, Wales and

Scotland in 1964 – that is, the Criminal Injuries Compensation Scheme that is now administered by the Criminal Injuries Compensation Authority. In the same vein, the probation service was pivotal to the development of the first victim support initiative in England and Wales in the early 1970s, with the first scheme established in Bristol in 1974, and the national association established in 1979. Both State compensation and the national association that is now Victim Support benefit from significant funding from central government.[5]

These developments, together with changes to legislation and criminal justice practice, have variously been working towards parity of justice between victim, offender and the State. As victims' access to justice has increased in the last few decades in response to their real and perceived needs, so the question of victims' rights has emerged. When and if victims' needs should be redefined as victims' rights is a debate that touches on underlying principles of justice. To put the victim at the heart of the criminal justice system is to reinterpret centuries of practice where the role between State and offender has been central to the resolution of crime and the administration of justice in common law systems, and the victim has been relegated to the role of witness.

At the beginning of the twenty-first century, victim-centred justice now forms one of the three central pillars of criminal justice reform in England and Wales. The July 2002 government White Paper *Justice for All* sets out its goals as: (1) tough action on anti-social behaviour, hard drugs and violent crime; (2) rebalancing the criminal justice system in favour of the victim; and (3) giving the police and prosecution the tools to bring more criminals to justice. *Justice for All*, written under a Labour administration, is pre-dated by the Conservative government's publication of the first Victim's Charter in 1990. The Victim's Charter was written at a time when there was a 'Charter' for any number of services, including the 'Rail Charter' for the railways, and formed part of a broader 'Citizen's Charter'. While the 1990 Charter was written with the aim of improving services for victims of crime, and was principally targeted at service providers, it was justly accused of falsely raising victims' hopes by dressing service standards in the language of 'rights' (Fenwick, 1995).

Six years later, the second Victim's Charter set out service provision standards that the victim of crime could expect to receive from criminal justice agencies, and covered the following areas: help from the police; victim support; compensation; what happens if someone is caught; being a prosecution witness; witness service; help at court; special help for certain witnesses; what happens in court; after the court case; victim helpline; and information about the offender's release. It also covered what to do in case of complaints about: the police; the Crown Prosecution Service; the crown courts and magistrates' courts; judges and magistrates; the probation service; Victim Support and the witness service; and the Criminal Injuries Compensation Authority. This extensive list, taken from the 1996 Charter, is worth relating here in detail because it outlines key elements of what have variously been constructed as victims' rights. However, the Victim's Charter is not a statement of victims' rights. In this regard the second charter was written with the purpose of clarifying the meaning of a 'charter', and to this end clearly stated that it was a document that set out to inform victims about what they 'can expect' in the way of help and service from criminal justice agencies.

Rights in context

The 1996 Victim's Charter is a product of its time and place. It reflects the position that victims of crime have held for a long time in England and Wales; that is, victims are a group to which the criminal justice system, from the police through to probation, owes some services. However, these services are not a right that victims can demand. Instead, victims might receive an apology or compensation if they complain of inadequate service provision. What the Victim's Charter does is indicate standards of service provision that victims can expect to receive. This position reflects the history of victim-centred criminal justice developments in England and Wales, a history that has been characterised as needs-based, and as stemming from a welfare tradition marked by volunteerism (Mawby and Gill, 1987; Mawby and Walklate, 1994). This 'needs-based' approach to victim services is highly discretionary as it distinguishes between those victims who are eligible for special service provision and those who are not, both overtly and covertly basing need on the idea of the deserving victim.

Victim Support, with thousands of volunteers, making up 92 per cent of its staff, exemplifies this tradition of charitable work for deserving victims. The opening statement on Victim Support's national website reads: 'Victim Support is the independent charity which helps people cope with the effects of crime.'[6] However, Victim Support and other charity-based victim groups in England and Wales, such as Support After Murder and Manslaughter (SAMM), have more recently turned their attention towards a rights-based approach to victims' needs, with the opening statement on Victim Support's national website going on to read: 'Victim Support also works to promote and advance the rights of victims and witnesses.' With this statement, Victim Support is acknowledging a number of points. First, a needs-based approach to victims is vulnerable to changing political priorities that easily shift focus away from victims to other causes. Second, a needs-based approach can enhance discretionary allocation of services. In comparison, a rights-based approach can do two things. First, it can emphasise rights in law which are less vulnerable to changing political priorities. Second, a rights-based approach can, at least in theory, provide a service to all victims and witnesses.

In comparison with Britain, the history of victim-centred criminal justice developments in the United States has been characterised as rights-based and therefore as grounded in law. For example, while the

UK introduced a set of service standards laid out in the Victim's Charter, with no legal redress for victims, the USA saw the introduction of Victims' Rights Acts across different states as statutory legal instruments affording rights to a range of victims. In turn, continental or inquisitorial European justice systems have been characterised as offering victims more substantive rights than the adversarial common law systems of England and Wales and North America. Comparing compliance in twenty-two European jurisdictions with the 1985 Council of Europe Recommendation on the Standing of Victims in Criminal Law and Procedure (Recommendation (85)11), Brienen and Hoegen (2000) divide their overview into three core themes that summarise the main points of the Recommendation: the victim and information; the victim and compensation; and treatment and protection of the victim. What they find at the end of their comprehensive overview challenges accepted wisdom about the role and place of victims in adversarial and continental justice systems: while victims might have more rights on paper on the continent, their experience of criminal justice practice is often less than satisfactory when compared with victims in England and Wales.

Brienen and Hoegen's research supports the age-old assertion that there is the law in theory, the 'law in the books', and then there is the law in practice. It also serves to highlight the importance of following up national and international promotion of victims' rights, through adoption of legislation, with rigorous implementation programmes that also monitor standards of service provision for victims. Brienen and Hoegen's remit to look at the implementation of the 1985 Council of Europe Recommendation was in response to calls from the Council to monitor take-up of the Recommendation. Over a decade after the Recommendation, Brienen and Hoegen found that very few states were meeting the criteria it laid out. Much like the gap between the 1970 Equal Pay Act in England and Wales, which set out to provide equal pay for equal work undertaken by men and women, and the reality of women's unequal pay over three decades later, there is much that needs to be done to monitor the implementation of victims' rights, in law, with the reality of how victims' needs are responded to in practice. Rather than characterise victims' rights as unattainable 'gold standards', there needs to be greater monitoring of what happens in the aftermath of legislation.

Progress towards victim-centred justice in England and Wales reflects broader developments at an international level concerning the need for enforceable victims' rights and standards of service provision. Chief among these is the 1985 United Nations Declaration of Basic Principles of Justice for Victims of Crime and Abuse of Power, and more recently the 2001 Council of the European Union Framework Decision on the Standing of Victims in Criminal Proceedings. The 1985 UN Declaration is wide-ranging in its definition of victimhood, and goes beyond national legislation to include internationally recognised norms relating to human rights. The Declaration also refers to victimisation with respect to environmental harm and corruption by public officials. In this regard the UN Declaration is more challenging than the later 2001 Framework Decision by the Council of the European Union. However, unlike the Framework Decision, the UN Declaration can be described as 'soft law' because it is not legally binding on UN member states. In comparison, the Framework Decision presents binding legislation and is therefore more cautiously framed.

Looking at any number of legally binding and non-legally binding international instruments that purport to be 'victim-centred', a common 'checklist' of core 'rights' runs through each:

- compassion and respect;
- information on proceedings and rights;
- presentation of victims' views;
- legal aid;
- swift case processing;
- protection of privacy and identity;
- protection from retaliation and intimidation;
- compensation from the offender and the State;
- recognition of victims with special needs.

There are numerous binding and non-binding international instruments, alongside those already mentioned, that focus on victims' rights, from the UN's 1948 Universal Declaration of Human Rights through to the more recent 2000 UN Protocol Against Trafficking in Human Beings (which forms part of the UN Convention Against Transnational Organised Crime). Looking at the range of instruments available to victims is encouraging as it illustrates the political will to be doing something for victims of crime, but at the same time one gets a sense of the wheel being reinvented. There is a great deal of 'progress' on paper, but, at least in many parts of the world, very little to show in practice. While there are obvious exceptions to this generalisation – such as the South African government's Movement for Truth and Reconciliation in the aftermath of human rights abuses under apartheid – it is also the case, as Brienen and Hoegen's research illustrates, that many developed countries, let alone developing countries or countries in transition, such as South Africa, are doing poorly when it comes to the *practice* of victim-centred justice. With this critique in mind one begins to question the focus on victims' rights without accompanying enforcement.

The 1999 UN *Handbook on Justice for Victims* (UNODCCP, 1999a) and the 1999 UN *Guide for Policymakers* (UNODCCP, 1999b), published some years after the 1985 Victims Declaration to which both documents refer, set out to provide victims and policy makers with a list of appropriate standards of service provision. To this end both documents go some way towards addressing the gap between evocation of rights and implementation of victim-centred justice in practice using 'best practice' guidelines.

The UN *Handbook* and *Guide for Policymakers* promote victims' rights along-side victims' needs as practical and achievable goals, whereas too often victims' rights can be interpreted as the 'gold standard' to which, once enshrined in law, we simply refer. Some middle ground should be found to promote one at the same time as the other: to see rights reflect needs, and to see needs become rights. This process needs constant revision so that legislation and guidelines reflect the changing position and needs of victims in society and in the criminal justice process.

Towards victim-centred and service-centred justice: merging needs and rights

How victims' needs are identified, and who determines what these needs are, and whether these needs are in turn constructed as rights, are important considerations when interpreting whether criminal justice developments that are supposedly victim-centred are victim-driven or service-driven: in other words, whether a 'victim-centred' development is really for the benefit of victims, to assist their recovery in the aftermath of crime and help them through the criminal justice process, or whether it is envisaged primarily as an aid to obtaining useful witness information and testimonies.

In England and Wales, since the 1980s/1990s, victims have been constructed as 'consumers' of services, be these public services such as the police, or non-governmental services such as Victim Support. The victim's construction as 'consumer' is a new development in the history of state law and order (Zauberman, 2000), and reflects three things: first, by focusing on 'customer satisfaction' with victim services the question of rising crime rates is sidelined; second, the State recognises that it relies on victims to report crimes and therefore must keep its customers 'happy'; and third, the State's legitimacy to govern effectively is questioned if it fails to meet victims' needs. As Wemmers comments (1996: 215):

> Besides enhancing victims' suffering, negative experiences with legal authorities are associated with diminished victim co-operation with authorities, decreased support for authorities and reduced respect for the law. This realisation has triggered governments to introduce policy changes in order to improve the treatment of victims of crime.

However, as a reading of the 1996 Victim's Charter indicates, victims are consumers of services with very little recourse to justice should these services fail to match what they indicate victims can expect to receive. In this regard, the Victim's Charter not only fails to establish the victim as a consumer with encumbent consumer rights, but it also fails to establish the victim as a citizen with substantive rights, as one might expect of a Charter, and therefore it is misleading in terms of what it can deliver.

The 1998 Home Office report *Speaking Up for Justice* put forward a comprehensive list of 78 recommendations to build on the Victim's Charter by encouraging and supporting vulnerable and intimidated witnesses through the criminal justice process, and in particular the adversarial trial. *Speaking Up for Justice* presents a significant development for the acknowledgement and promotion of vulnerable and intimidated victims' needs, as they pass through the criminal justice system. However, the force of these recommendations can only be measured in relation to their practical implementation. *Action for Justice* is the implementation plan to take forward the recommendations outlined in *Speaking Up for Justice*; and Part II of the Youth Justice and Criminal Evidence Act 1999 provides legislative change for those recommendations in *Speaking Up for Justice* that set out to assist young, disabled, vulnerable or intimidated witnesses to, in the words of the Home Office, 'give their best evidence in criminal proceedings'.[7] In other words, the recommendations outlined in *Speaking Up for Justice* can be interpreted as being in the interests of vulnerable and intimidated victims, to ease their path through the adversarial trial process, *and* in the interests of a criminal justice system that wants to obtain useful witness evidence and testimonies. To this end, the special measures outlined in the Youth Justice and Criminal Evidence Act 1999 include provision for, amongst other things, screens (to ensure that the witness cannot see the accused in court), and allow the possibility for a witness's evidence-in-chief to be given as a video-recorded interview.

In theory, the Youth Justice and Criminal Evidence Act 1999 provides ample measures to assist certain vulnerable and intimidated victims *and* the criminal justice system, by offering safeguards for the delivery of best evidence in the course of a criminal trial. However, there are a number of factors that militate against the Youth Justice and Criminal Evidence Act being put to its best use:

- there is the significance given over to the discretionary powers of the judiciary, to decide whether a victim should be considered as a vulnerable or intimidated witness and afforded certain safeguards;
- there is a lack of consistent service provision between and within agencies that should consistently recognise and respond to the needs of vulnerable or intimidated witnesses;
- the deep-rooted traditions of the adversarial trial in England and Wales continue to work against alternative means for presenting evidence such as pre-recorded evidence and use of live television links.

Herein lies the conundrum between the law in theory and how it is practised. Human discretion, misinformation and error play a large part in determining which victims are offered innovative services that are designed to ease their path through the criminal justice process. To rely on a culture of responding to need is to offer victims, at best, a discretionary service, and at worst, a service that is discriminatory. Arguably, with the establishment of victims' rights in law, victim-centred criminal justice practice stands a better chance of reaching as wide a range of victims as possible – provided, that is, that the fair and equal application of legal provisions is monitored. As Jackson (2003: 326) comments in his critique of the 2002 government White Paper *Justice For All*, in which 'rebalancing the criminal justice system in favour of the victim' is identified as one of three central priorities: 'A true 'justice for all' policy, arguably, needs to take a more explicit rights-centred approach than the government is willing to take.'

The government's July 2003 paper *A New Deal for Victims and Witnesses* outlines the administration's attempts to rectify this imbalance between talk of rights and actual statutory provision for them, and is supported in this effort by the 2002 government White Paper *Justice For All. A New Deal for Victims and Witnesses* refers to the proposed introduction of a Victims and Witnesses Bill that will establish a statutory Victims' Code of Practice covering protection, support and advice, and information about case progress. The intention is that the new Code sets out a series of specific responsibilities in relation to the service that each criminal justice agency and Victim Support service should deliver to victims. Most importantly, victims who are dissatisfied with the service they receive, as specified under the terms of the new Code as a service responsibility, will be able to refer their complaint to the Parliamentary Ombudsman for investigation. In this respect, if the proposed Victims and Witnesses Bill comes to fruition it will effectively put the Victim's Charter on a statutory footing where victims actually have recourse to rights.

However, the 2003 government paper *A New Deal for Victims and Witnesses*, in which reference to the proposed Victims and Witnesses Bill is briefly made, is written in the language of victims' needs rather than victims' rights. The paper provides some useful pointers in its use of language with respect to the dominant thrust of the government's focus on victims. For example, in paragraph 4.1, the paper states that victim-centred justice should be 'based on an understanding of their [the victims'] needs, not determined by the agencies' systems and priorities'. With this statement, and in the paper's chapter headings that refer to victims' needs rather than victims' rights, it is clear that government policy on victims can be constructed as:

- victim-centred rather than criminal justice-centred; that is, justice based on victims' needs rather than the needs of the criminal justice system;
- prioritising victims' needs and not victims' rights as the focus of victim-centred criminal justice developments in England and Wales.

Although victim-centred criminal justice in England and Wales can be characterised in the tradition of a needs-based rather than a rights-based approach, the proposed Victims and Witnesses Bill hints at more substantive rights. Along with the Criminal Justice Act 2003 and the Courts

Act 2003, the Victims and Witnesses Bill will offer a number of improvements to meet the needs of victims in the criminal justice system on a statutory basis. In this regard, the Criminal Justice Act allows *any witness* to refer to their original statement when giving evidence. It also allows for evidence to be given by live television link when there is good reason, and disallows gratuitous attacks on a witness's character in court. In turn, the Courts Act sets out to combat threats and intimidation of witnesses by improving security in court.

With the Criminal Justice Act 2003 recognising that *any witness* can refer to their original statement when giving evidence, there is a real indication that victims' rights are turning towards the rights of *all* victims, and not just those who have traditionally been considered as vulnerable or intimidated. But, the government's focus remains with easing the victim's path through the adversarial trial process, and in this respect, provision for *all* victims is limited to those few who actually reach the trial stage.

It can be argued that victim-centred recommendations and guidelines have, to date, served victims, or more correctly vulnerable victims, reasonably well in England and Wales without the need for legislation referring to substantive rights. However, legislation can go hand in hand with 'soft law' options, such as recommendations for standards of service provision. In turn, service standards should not be seen as the lesser cousin of substantive rights, particularly as 'soft law', by its very nature, can be more challenging in what it offers victims as it does not have to answer to statutory rules that need to balance the needs of victim, offender, State and regulatory authorities. In turn, by giving victims rights, there is also the implication that they have responsibilties to the State. The language of 'rights and responsibilities' is now commonplace, and imposes duties on victims as citizens. In this regard, to move wholesale towards victims' rights, without considering the implications this might have to the benefit and detriment of victims, is foolhardy.

Rights and responsibilities

While *Speaking Up for Justice*, as the forerunner of recent victim-centred criminal justice developments, emerged from a criminal justice culture that recognises and responds to 'needs' before 'rights', the paper does introduce the language of citizenship and responsibilities at one point. Paragraph 3.3 under the heading 'Role of a Witness' states: 'A witness to a crime is expected, as a civic duty, to report the crime to the police and eventually they may be asked to give evidence in court.' Although this statement is innocuous in itself, it uses language that is inappropriate given the absence of actual rights, rather than standards of service provision, that are afforded victims of crime in England and Wales. By saying that witnesses have a civic duty to the State to report crime and give evidence, the idea of responsibility is evoked. However, to talk about civic duty and responsibility without reference to victims' rights, as citizens, is to negate one half of a balanced approach to justice that recognises rights and responsibilities. Given that the main focus of *Speaking Up for Justice* is meeting victims' needs, this brief reference to civic duty appears out of place. What it throws up, however, is the unspoken reference to duty and responsibility that runs through much of the government's current emphasis on meeting victims' needs.

The emphasis on rights and responsibilities is exemplified in the approach that is currently adopted with respect to the probation service's statutory duty to consult with and notify victims of serious crime about release arrangements for offenders. This statutory duty to victims is a rare obligation for any criminal justice agency in England and Wales, and was introduced with a great deal of debate and reservation, given the probation service's long-standing duty to offenders rather than victims, under the terms of the Criminal and Court Services Act 2000. Under the terms of the Act, the probation service has a duty to inform victims of serious violent and sexual offences, where the offender received a minimum twelve-month sentence, of the expected release date of their offender *should* the victim indicate their wish to be informed. In this regard, the victim has the opportunity to opt in to a service. But, in referring to the probation service's statutory duty as an example of successful victim-centred innovation, the 2003 government paper *A New Deal for Victims and Witnesses* adds (paragraph 1.4): 'Victims can now make a contribution to risk management of offenders in the community, including Multi-Agency Protection Panels, through this process.' In other words, not only does the probation service have a duty to victims of serious sexual and violent offences, but these victims also have a duty to contribute to community safety. The unstated implication of this is that if victims decide not to be kept informed of their offender's release arrangements, they are not contributing to 'risk management of offenders in the community'.

In turn, the current thrust of government victim-centred policy, which focuses on providing a comfortable and non-threatening environment for victims in the court room and other criminal justice settings, comes with the implication that victims should cooperate with the criminal justice authorities to see that justice is done. As *A New Deal for Victims and Witnesses* states with respect to tackling witness intimidation (paragraph 5.15): 'strategies need to be developed to normalise reporting crime and playing an active part in the criminal justice system as part of one's role in the community. Clearly this is part of the wider rights and responsibilities agenda which links in with public confidence in the criminal justice system . . .' The same paper then refers to the need to encourage 'active citizenship', particularly in high crime and socially deprived areas. In other words, the State will assist victims of crime in the most crime-ridden and socially marginalised areas, but this assistance comes with a duty to assist the State through cooperation with the criminal justice authorities. Herein lies the pay-off between the provision of services to victims, and the implication that victims have duties to the criminal justice authorities who provide them with these services. As the government increasingly refers to citizenship in the context of civil society, so the idea is introduced that rights come with responsibilities. However, there are problems with constructing victims' and witnesses' rights around the idea of citizenship.

Citizenship, consumerism and the market economy

Increasingly, since the 1980s, aspects of public life that have traditionally been under the control of the State have shifted to the private sector. As a consequence, citizens' rights can be eroded when public life becomes the domain of private enterprise. For example, shopping malls have taken the place of street shopping in many towns and cities; and because the mall, unlike the street, is privately owned, private security firms can police these areas and eject those they regard as less than desirable. The private security sector has put security guards on housing estates and in businesses, and has covered large parts of Britain with closed circuit television (CCTV) cameras that monitor our every move (Painter and Tilley, 1999). Even prisons and correctional institutions are not immune from this process of profit through privatisation, with Britain having embarked on the privatisation of prisons since the 1990s (Bottomley et al., 1997). In sum, large parts of formerly State monopolised criminal justice, principally policing, have moved into the hands of private enterprise. As a reflection of a general trend towards non-State governance of public life, the 'least desirable' members of society, namely the very poor, are increasingly unable to participate in certain activities because they are either excluded from doing so or because they cannot afford to do so – money being a great excluder. The point here, in relation to victims and citizenship, is that while citizenship might appear to afford all victims equal and fair rights in principle, the reality is different and complicated for the following reasons:

- aspects of public life are increasingly being removed from State control, and as a result citizenship offers little recourse to rights in these settings;
- the individual's place in society is increasingly governed by consumer 'choice' that is largely determined by relative income rather than citizenship;
- citizenship brings with it exclusion of non-citizens as large swathes of society currently live in states where they have no rights of citizenship (i.e. asylum seekers and illegal immigrants).

Herein, victims' needs and victims' rights need interpreting with respect to both citizenship and the liberalisation of the market economy.

The market economy, encompassing shops through to correctional facilities, ideally wants to attract those 'customers', or 'clients', who cost the least in the quest for profit. In other words, the difficult customer or the undesirable client is best avoided. Under this scenario, the victim who consumes a great deal of an agency's resources, be this manpower or time, is a drain on any agency that has a finite number of resources that need to be shared between a large pool of victims. Where funding is available from State sources it might be the case that subsidies are provided to meet the number of clients, or victims, assisted in the previous year. However, this money tends to be based on an average per person; as a result, difficult cases place a strain on an agency's resources. In this regard, victim cases that warrant a great deal of counselling, information and general assistance are best avoided.

As an illustration of this, Victim Support, as the national point of reference for victims of crime in England and Wales, traditionally concentrated its efforts on victims of burglary and to a lesser degree on victims of interpersonal violence. While Victim Support would admit that its volunteers did not have the expertise to handle cases of interpersonal violence in the early years of the organisation, one can add that cases of sexual and interpersonal violence also presented the organisation with more difficult cases to process than the average burglary. Because of Victim Support's focus on less serious cases of victimisation, the organisation was able to show a year-on-year increase in the number of cases it had assisted. However, this profile hides the fact that more difficult cases were left to the underfunded and marginalised work of Rape Crisis and women's shelters.

More recently, Victim Support has turned its attention to victims of interpersonal violence including rape, sexual assault and domestic violence, partly as a reflection of the organisation's growing confidence and professionalism, aided by significant government support and funding, and partly in response to the organisation's failure to assist significant numbers of vulnerable victims. In turn, *A New Deal for Victims and Witnesses* (paragraph 4.8) has indicated the government's willingness to put more funding into what have traditionally been conceived as radical victim organisations such as Refuge and Women's Aid, although the bulk of government funding for victims continues to be allocated to the 'safe' apolitical organisation that is Victim Support. However, with Victim Support turning its attention to victims of interpersonal violence, it appears that recognition of and response to some of the most vulnerable victims in society, such as rape victims, is finally being mainstreamed by an agency that has hitherto neglected their needs.

While all victims of crime in England and Wales can benefit from the 'free' services offered them by Victim Support and the National Health Service, and can also freely apply for State compensation in the aftermath of violent crime, victims on higher incomes have an extra safety net that incorporates private home and health insurance, and access to additional funds and resources. It is also clear that the least marginalised victims have more resources at their disposal to enquire about and challenge the services they are offered as victims of crime. In this regard, the least marginalised victims tend to have knowledge about their 'rights' and entitlements as victims of crime as they are active consumers of both public and private services. In contrast, the most marginalised and, arguably, the most vulnerable victims have no access to private services they can ill afford, and are often unaware of public services to which they may be entitled. Therefore, it would appear that three central factors are key to understanding the place, role and importance of 'care' in response to victims' needs and rights:

- purchasing power;
- knowledge;
- citizenship.

Purchasing power

The individual's power to purchase certain services, either to prevent victimisation or effectively deal with its aftermath, erodes the impact of universal services to victims of crime as a matter of right. The individual-isation of aspects of social life and criminal justice means that the top income earners can:

- choose to buy homes in safer neighbourhoods;
- send their children to safer schools;
- insure their home, property and health;
- easily replace stolen consumer goods regardless of insurance cover;
- employ private security;
- avoid encounters with undesirable 'others' in crime-ridden neighbour-hoods through use of private transportation;
- employ lawyers to ensure that justice is done on their behalf.

While the government might like to construct crime victims in the language of consumers of services, it is more accurately the case that victims are comprehensive consumers when they have access to individual purchasing power. In turn, individualisation of the victim through purchasing power succeeds in turning attention away from collective responses to victimhood that are based on social marginalisation and vulnerabilty. In this regard, the radical voices of 1970s' and 1980s' feminist groups that highlighted the plight of victims of rape and sexual assault have no place in a market where purchasing power, based on the individual's ability to pay for services, buys improved access to care.

Knowledge

Access to knowledge about service entitlement ensures that inadequate service provision, from the police through to the probation service, can be readily challenged. Here, information is key to understanding how justice and aspects of care provision are accessed by different victims. In this regard, consumer purchasing power is less important than a sound knowledge-base about one's rights and service entitlements as a victim of crime, and how to make use of them effectively. Government, primarily, is responsible for making people aware of their rights and entitlements as victims of crime. Individual agencies, from the police through to Victim Support, are in turn responsible for advertising and making accessible their victim services. Accessibility is a central factor that determines 'who' gets to know about victim-centred services. Whereas the educated and those on high incomes are able to access and question the services made available to them, typically because they occupy positions of authority themselves, the under-educated and socially marginalised do not enjoy a similar status where they are able to challenge the system because they themselves are on the peripheries of that system. In this regard, it is the duty of victim-centred criminal justice and non-criminal justice agencies to make their services accessible by providing appropriate access to information that can instil a knowledge-base that is necessary to gain access to care and justice.

In turn, the individual's purchasing power as a victim of crime or a potential victim, together with access to knowledge about services and justice, is affected by another factor in the debate about the victim as 'citizen' and 'consumer' with encumbent rights and responsibilities: namely, the construction of the 'citizen victim'.

Citizenship

The idea of the 'citizen victim' conveniently ignores the fact that many of the most vulnerable and marginalised victims in society are not citizens. Illegal immigrants, from those working in illegal sweatshops through to women working as prostitutes, present some of the most vulnerable and victimised people. However, their status as 'illegal aliens' or 'undesirable other' has, until very recently, robbed them of access to justice. If illegal immigrants are physically or sexually assaulted, or if their property is stolen, they cannot go to the police for fear of being deported. And those charities that might be able to assist them, from Victim Support through to housing associations, are not geared to their particular needs. At the same time, these victims are unlikely to approach these services for a number of reasons: namely, fear of repeat victimisation and intimidation from their abusers; lack of information about agencies' existence and how to access them; problems with language; and mistrust of agencies given the cultural background of many illegal immigrants that reinforces their suspicion of all agencies as corrupt.

However, given the above critique, *A New Deal for Victims and Witnesses* has, for the first time in a general paper about victims and witnesses, recognised the particular plight of victims of trafficking. This move reflects the government's obligation to respond to trafficking victims as it is a signatory to the 2000 United Nations Convention Against Transnational Organised Crime and its accompanying Protocol Against Trafficking in Persons. What is interesting here is that the government will have to respond to the needs of trafficking victims, who are typically not citizens of European Union member states, while at the same time promoting the idea of victims' rights and responsibilities as citizens (see Chapter 8).

Herein lies a problem with governments continuing to focus on the idea of citizenship – encompassing civil, political and social rights (Marshall, 1950) – as a means of framing victims' rights and corresponding responsibilities. Ideas of citizenship based on the nation-state are becoming increasingly outmoded in a world where both legal and illegal migration are normalised. Hammar has forwarded the term 'denizens' to denote alien residents or non-nationals who enjoy social and civil rights but not full political inclusion (Hammar, 1990). In other words, these are legally resident foreigners who enjoy some degree of rights in their host society, but not full political representation. Here one thinks of a US citizen legally residing in a member state of the European Union. In comparison, the cumbersome term 'citizenless alien' can be used to describe the status of illegal immigrants who enjoy no or very few rights in the States they reside in. These 'citizenless aliens' represent the most vulnerable victims in society, to whom governments are only gradually turning their attention.

Finally, in the language of rights and responsibilities, citizenship and community – all keywords of government policy in the first decade of the twenty-first century – restorative justice, or communitarian justice as it is sometimes referred to, exemplifies the integrated and active part that victims, as citizens, are being asked to play in the resolution of conflicts and in the management of public order. In asking victims to engage with offenders in an informal setting, it can be argued that the State is placing more duties on victims than would be the case in the formal setting of traditional adversarial trials. Arguably, where lawyers and the whole machinery of criminal justice have, until now, stepped in to 'do justice' on behalf of victims, restorative justice has seen a refocus on victims with the idea being that they should come to some kind of arrangement with offenders towards the resolution of conflict and its subsequent management. As with the probation service's statutory duty to keep victims informed about the release date of offenders, and victims' corresponding duties to take this offer up in order to 'make a contribution to risk management of offenders in the community', victims are also given the duty to work with offenders in the resolution of crime through restorative justice. Arguably, the State has its duties lightened in the process, but with increased attention given over to 'rights and responsibilities' this is only to be expected.

The example of State compensation: who benefits?

In the final part of this chapter, the example of State compensation to victims of violent crime is offered as illustrating some of the dilemmas and practical realities facing the needs and/or rights debate.

State compensation schemes tend to focus on victims of violent crime, and are financed either through taxpayers' money (Britain's Criminal Injuries Compensation Scheme) or through a combination of taxpayers' money and payments, or fines, collected from offenders (as is the case with compensation schemes in the United States). Given that the State and/or offenders need the financial resources to support State compensation schemes, it is hardly surprising that their existence is limited to wealthier countries in the developed world, and even then tends to be narrowly framed around the physical needs of victims of violent crime.

State compensation responds to the needs of victims of violent crime who are injured as a result of their victimisation, and who may sustain temporary or permanent disability requiring additional support and services beyond what the State usually offers in terms of social benefits. Compensation can cover lost income, specialist medical care, counselling, and adjustments to the home as a result of disability resulting from victimisation. On the other hand, while many victims of violent crime do not suffer from prolonged physical incapacity, many do suffer from psychological damage over a long period. However, State compensation schemes tend to recognise physical injury before they recognise psychological harm as 'pain and suffering'. In this regard it needs to be asked 'who' State compensation really serves? In other words, is it little more than a political gesture for some governments, and a pragmatic response to high crime rates, or does State compensation respond to a real victim need?

The rationale behind State compensation

The introduction of State compensation to victims of violent crime can be interpreted with respect to four key rationales that States may adopt individually or in combination:

1. the 'legal duty' of the State to compensate crime victims for its failure to prevent crime;
2. the 'moral duty' of the State to assist victims on humanitarian and welfare grounds;
3. a form of 'loss distribution' along the lines of social insurance from taxpayers' money;
4. as a 'benefit to the State' because it affords political credibility to those who introduce and administer State compensation schemes.

The first rationale responds to the State's failure to prevent crime or guarantee monetary restitution from offenders to victims by evoking the

State's legal duty to provide compensation. This rationale makes State compensation a right, and therefore presents an unworkable ideal given the extent of violent crime and the amount of money that the State would have to distribute to victims. In comparison, the second rationale presents State compensation as an expectation, rather than a right, based on discretionary application of funds to 'deserving' and 'innocent' victims. As a result, the 'moral duty' rationale is preferred by governments that pay for State compensation, using tax-generated income, as a less expensive option. The third rationale interprets crime as unfortunate but unavoidable, and as something that society should share the cost of by collectively insuring against harm, particularly as those in vulnerable and marginalised social positions are most likely to be victims of crime but are least likely to be able to insure themselves. Finally, the fourth rationale presents an astute political response to the problem of crime by focusing attention on the State's efforts to deal with its aftermath, victimisation, without actually tackling the more difficult problem of crime itself.

Most governments would, of course, not admit to employing this last rationale. However, looking at the actual worth of many State compensation schemes across the developed world it is clear that the existence of a State compensation scheme on paper is no guarantee of its successful application to victims in practice. Miers argues in his book *Responses to Victimisation* (1978: 51), comparing the introduction of State compensation schemes in Britain and Canada, that 'political factors were the single most important determinant behind the introduction of victim compensation schemes'. Burns (1980) goes so far as to suggest that the number of persons applying for State compensation and the final number receiving it is irrelevant, when measuring a scheme's success, if the scheme's political goal is to placate public criticism of the criminal justice system while at the same time encouraging victims to assist the authorities with their investigations. In this regard, according to Burns, it is enough for the State to be seen to be doing something for victims of crime. However, while it may be the case that political considerations to be seen to be doing something for victims were important in the early days of State compensation schemes, it is less likely given time that States can sustain a veneer of victim-centred justice if legislation is not followed through with actual compensation to victims.

Maguire and Shapland (1990) argue that State compensation in Europe is founded on ideals of humanitarianism and welfarism, and, as a reflection of this, State compensation as a mere symbolic act is less applicable in Europe than in other parts of the world. They state (1990: 214): 'where European countries have set up schemes, they have attracted applications and made awards'. But, according to evidence comparing State compensation schemes in the EU (Greer, 1996; Mikaelsson and Wergens, 2001), the reality is that some European schemes are less than generous. And, although the preamble to the Council of Europe's 1983 European Convention on Compensation of Victims of Violent Crime vaguely indicates that State compensation is justified on the grounds of 'social solidarity and equity', and would seem to support Shapland and Maguire's claims about European compensation schemes, the same document also makes it clear that compensation from offenders should be prioritised in preference to State compensation. In this regard, as in later European documents that refer either directly or indirectly to compensating crime victims,[8] it is made abundantly clear that State compensation is not to be considered as a victim right in Europe but rather as a goodwill gesture loosely based on ideas of 'moral duty'.

Britain's Criminal Injuries Compensation Authority (CICA) has, since its origins in the early 1960s, framed its awards of compensation as an expression of public sympathy to innocent victims of violent crime. As Victim Support comments on its website: 'scrutiny of the character of the victim has remained a feature of the CICS [Criminal Injuries Compensation Scheme] ever since [its inception]'.[9] In this regard, State compensation for victims of violent crime is not a right in the eyes of the State under the terms of the CICS's remit.

Britain's State compensation scheme for victims of violent crime emerged in 1964, a few months after New Zealand became the first country in the world to legislate for State compensation.[10] The British scheme was established in response to the following:

- the ineffectiveness of court-awarded offender compensation to victims of violent crime;
- the need for State intervention to ensure that victims of violent crime receive some level of monetary compensation when no offender is found;
- the need for the State to intervene to assist victims of violent crime as a reflection of the State's duty to assist innocent victims who have been wronged;
- the campaigning efforts of penal reformers such as Margery Fry who called for State compensation in response to the above (Fry, 1959).

The British scheme was founded on the back of welfare state developments in the second half of the twentieth century. As the country extended social provision to various groups in society, so innocent crime victims were included as a special category in need of recognition. State compensation in Britain emerged without a clear philosophical underpinning, but more as a pragmatic response to need loosely based on ideas of 'moral duty'. In other words, it can be said that State compensation was promoted in Britain on humanitarian and welfare grounds, and also as a form of loss distribution along the lines of social insurance. Britain's State compensation scheme also expanded in line with the overall growth in victim-centred justice in Britain from the 1970s (Shapland, 1984). In this regard, the scheme can also be viewed as an astute response to rising crime and increases in interpersonal violence that warranted action by a State that – once again – needed to be seen to be doing something for victims. However, this somewhat cynical interpretation of Britain's State compensation scheme, as a 'sticking plaster' response that fails to address the underlying causes of increased crime and victimisation, should not overlook the significant impact that awards of State compensation have had on many people's lives (Victim Support, 1993).

When comparing State compensation schemes in different European Union member states with similar or larger populations and roughly equivalent levels of criminal victimisation, the British scheme far surpasses other countries with regard to both the number of applications received and total compensation awarded (Goodey, 2002a). A survey of State compensation in the EU, based on data from either 1999 or 2000 (Mikaelsson and Wergens, 2001: 262), estimated that Britain received 78,165 applications for compensation in one year and distributed a total of €340,926,000 in compensation, while France received 13,353 applications and awarded €147,550,000 in compensation, and Germany, with a larger population than either Britain or France, received 9,787 applications and distributed €106,694,000 in compensation. In contrast, two of the fifteen EU member states, Greece and Italy,[11] had no general State compensation scheme for victims of violent crime at the time of the survey. And in the same period as the European survey was conducted, the USA – with a population of 290 million, and each state having a crime victim compensation programme – distributed US$265 million in compensation nationwide (roughly the equivalent in euros) to or on behalf of more than 115,000 victims.[12]

State compensation versus offender-based compensation

The striking difference in the figures for State compensation between EU member states can be explained by two key points.

First, the presence or absence of State compensation, and the generosity of its awards, reflects the overall significance given over in each jurisdiction to victim-centred justice. In other words, if there have been few victim-centred criminal justice developments this tends to be reflected in the absence of or low priority given to State compensation.

Second, and of equal importance to the first point, is the reliance given over in each criminal justice jurisdiction to legal provision for compensation from the offender to the victim *before* compensation from the State to the victim, or before the payment of a fine from the offender to the State.

Many EU member states have legal provision for the victim to act as '*partie civile*' in the course of a criminal trial. This right allows victims to bring a civil claim for compensation from the offender during a criminal trial. It is generally assumed that the victim's right in continental Europe to act as '*partie civile*' is illustrative of the more significant role played by victims in non-adversarial systems. By adopting the role of '*partie civile*' under the 'adhesion principle', the continental victim has the right to play a more active role in criminal proceedings than is the case in adversarial justice systems. However, there is the theory of law, and then there is criminal justice practice. As Brienen and Hoegen (2000) point out, while a victim's right to play an active role in criminal justice proceedings exists in law in most continental justice systems, this right is rarely evoked in practice, and when it is victims experience no or very little assistance from the State to reclaim any compensation from their offender that has successfully been awarded in the course of a trial. In comparison, while victims have no equivalent right of '*partie civile*' in England and Wales, victims enjoy the most generous State compensation scheme in Europe, although the scheme is not offered as a right and is run as a discretionary award scheme.

When State compensation is financed in the main from State funds, most jurisdictions prioritise offender-based compensation before State compensation for obvious financial reasons. Offender-based compensation is legislated for in most jurisdictions, either by recognising a crime of violence as a tort for which the offender is liable in a civil court (Schuck, 2003), or by the victim evoking the role of '*partie civile*' in the course of a criminal trial. But these alternatives to State compensation offer the majority of victims little recourse to justice for the same reasons that were given for the introduction of a State compensation scheme in Britain: (1) most offenders are not caught and brought to trial; (2) of those that are, many are unable or unwilling to pay significant amounts of compensation to victims; and (3) many judges and lawyers are unwilling to mix compensation claims, which are traditionally seen as the remit of civil law, with the process of criminal law, and as a result victims are often ill-informed of their rights to bring a civil claim for offender-based compensation.

In England and Wales, in an effort to rectify this last point, the compensation order from offender to victim, which was first introduced in England and Wales under the 1972 Criminal Justice Act, was prioritised before the payment of a fine to the State under the terms of the 1982 Criminal Justice Act. To bolster the effectiveness of the 1982 Act, the 1988 Criminal Justice Act stipulated that courts had to give reasons for not awarding a compensation order from offender to victim in cases where there was an identifiable victim who was eligible for compensation. At the same time, Home Office Circular 20/1988 gave the police the duty to ensure that all relevant information about injuries and losses suffered by a victim were passed to the Crown Prosecution Service as part of the case file which would assist the court in the award of any compensation from the offender. However, given these developments, awards of offender compensation have not always been consistent. Research has also found that although victims tend to welcome compensation from offenders as a form of direct restitution, dissatisfaction sets in when awards are considered too small, when the courts fail to inform victims of the amount due to them and the means being taken to enforce payment, and finally when victims are not informed of reasons for non-payment (Maguire and

Shapland, 1990). In this regard, State compensation offers the only real viable means for receiving compensation for harm and injury suffered for the majority of victims of violent crime.

Eligibility for State compensation

Britain's Criminal Injuries Compensation Authority was only put on a statutory footing under the terms of the 1995 Criminal Injuries Compensation Act, which came into force in 1996 – two decades after the State compensation scheme was established. The Act states that it sets out to compensate victims of violent crime for: (1) personal pain and suffering; (2) loss of earnings; and (3) costs of care. Awards are made in addition to the free healthcare that victims automatically receive from the National Health Service in Britain. In comparison, medical care represents one of the chief costs incurred by compensation schemes in the USA, and as a general rule US schemes do not compensate victims for non-economic loss such as pain and suffering.

'Who' is eligible for State compensation, under the rationale of 'moral duty', is limited in practical terms in Britain to the deserving and innocent victim. Membership of an organisation engaged in criminal activity, having a significant criminal record or unspent convictions,[13] and engaging in actions that are seen as contributing to victimisation, are all factors that weigh heavily against particular victims being awarded State compensation. The Criminal Injuries Compensation Authority (CICA) has a scale of penalty points, based on the above criteria, that can reduce the amount of award received or the actual allocation of an award. Roughly one-third of all applications to the CICA are turned down on the grounds of the applicant's current or prior association with criminal activity. This may be a sensible way of ensuring that one of the most generous State compensation schemes in the world does not stretch funds any further by giving awards to the 'wrong' people. But what this scheme appears to disallow, in its strict application of penalty points, is the idea that serious offenders can be rehabilitated and that they should not be re-punished by the State for past criminal acts. What also needs consideration is the impact that non-payment of an award can have on the families of former criminals who are innocent parties to their relative's past criminal acts, but who may suffer as a result of non-payment of an award. In comparison, in Finland, the Netherlands and Sweden, a victim's relationship to organised crime does not automatically bar them from State compensation.

Additional factors influencing eligibility for State compensation awards are 'where' crime occurs, and the citizenship status of the victim. According to a survey conducted by the US Federal Office for Victims of Crime (US Department of Justice, 1999), 28 countries have crime victim compensation programmes throughout the world, and there is great variation between programmes with respect to 'who' is eligible to receive compensation. While some State schemes will award compensation to anyone victimised on their territory, other schemes are restricted to citizens of that State and those who are legally resident in the country, or whose country of origin is otherwise connected with the country in which the crime occured – such as joint membership of the EU. In this regard, illegal immigrants are usually excluded from receipt of State compensation, yet they represent groups who are often victimised by citizens of their host countries or by organised criminal gangs that clandestinely employ them and transport them across borders.

Other important factors for denying State compensation in EU jurisdictions include reference to the applicant's financial circumstances. In this regard, State compensation is not generally offered as a right regardless of income, but often comes with a cap on the upper limit of awards. These caps make it clear that State compensation schemes are not to be considered in the same vein as awards under tort law which can, at least in theory, reach into the millions. Caps also make sure that State funds are not overdrawn and focused on a few expensive cases.

Controversially the 1995 Criminal Injuries Compensation Act introduced a tariff-based system of awards for criminal injury ranging from a minimum of £1,000, at level 1, for an injury such as blurred or double vision lasting six weeks, through to a maximum award of £250,000, at level 25, for paralysis of all four limbs.[14] While this tariff system is a means to stem the tide of petty claims, and can speed up the processing of claims that were formerly assessed on a discretionary basis, the tariff denies the positive impact that an award of less than £1,000 can have on victims on low incomes. In addition, the CICA stipulates that victims in receipt of social security payments from the State, or any insurance and pension payments, that cover the period claimed for State compensation, can have their benefits reduced in line with any compensation they are awarded. Again, this rule hits hardest at those on low incomes who are most likely to benefit from any award of compensation. In turn, relatively small awards of money, in cases involving less serious injury, are also important to victims as they symbolise State recognition of harm suffered under the scheme's remit to address 'pain and suffering' in the aftermath of violent victimisation.

Under the terms of the British Criminal Injuries Compensation Scheme, the absolute maximum that can be awarded for criminal injury coupled with 'lost earnings' and 'special expenses' is £500,000. This means that victims who suffer horrific injuries and are unable to work again, and have to make alterations to their homes to accommodate their new disabilities, will receive no more than £500,000. In comparison, successful claims for compensation under tort law can far exceed this sum; however, as the role of the '*partie civile*' in continental European justice systems shows, successful awards of compensation from offenders to victims are difficult to obtain through civil claims in both continental and common law jurisdictions.

Case study: compensating victims of 9/11 – generous awards with limited rights

Finally, as an interesting illustration of eligibility for State compensation and discriminatory payment of awards, we can turn to the example of the US administration's Victim Compensation Fund (VCF) that was established in the first days after the terrorist attacks of 11 September 2001 on the United States.

The VCF can be described as a 'one-off' fund that was introduced, in the first instance, to save US airlines from financial collapse through threat of tort actions against them in the aftermath of the attacks. The Fund was introduced as part of the Air Transportation Safety and System Stabilization Act, and set out to significantly limit the tort options of those seriously injured, or the families of those killed, by capping the liability of the airlines in line with their existing insurance coverage. As a result, victims and their dependants were pushed to use the newly established Victim Compensation Fund, and in doing so had to waive their rights to file a civil action against the airlines. This action may have saved US airlines from financial collapse but it has also been on the receiving end of negative critique with respect to the victim-centred nature of the VCF (Dixon and Stern, 2003).

In opting to apply for compensation under the VCF, victims receive a flat payment of US$250,000 for non-economic loss, and an additional US$100,000 per spouse and dependant child. These may seem like generous payments when read alongside other State compensation schemes. However, two of the rules governing payments from the Fund have proved highly controversial. First, payment for economic loss is based on a calculation of lifetime earnings and is limited to incomes up to the 98th percentile of all wage earners in the USA: that is, US$231,000 per year. Second, life insurance payments can be deducted from the awards given out by the Fund. In this regard, as many victims of the attacks on the World Trade Center were high income earners (above the 98th percentile) their remaining dependants feel they have been unfairly punished for their relative's ability to earn significant sums of money and insure for the future economic security of dependants. While most victims of violent crime would be more than pleased to receive awards of compensation covered by this special fund, it remains the case that victims and their families are less than happy about what they see as discriminatory payments against the very rich who have worked hard to achieve their incomes and guarantee their families economic security through life insurance payments.

While the Victim Compensation Fund is an unprecedented example of State compensation, it does highlight some of the questions and dilemmas that are thrown up in consideration of State compensation schemes alongside civil claims for compensation. When comparing the different capping systems employed by the VCF and Britain's Criminal Injuries Compensation Scheme we can see how both the wealthy and the poor can feel left out of schemes that base awards on upper and lower limits and which quite clearly have ulterior motives to their establishment other than a simple 'moral duty' to victims. However, when we compare the generosity of these two schemes with the absence of any State funds for victims of violent crime in most countries of the world, including developed countries, it becomes harder to critique them.

Concluding comments

Having presented an overview of victims' needs and victims' rights, and what these can mean with respect to the specific example of State compensation, the reader should be reminded of central questions and points for discussion in consideration of the needs/rights debate and associated issues of citizenship and consumerism.

First, much discussion of needs and rights currently takes place almost without due consideration being given to what victims actually need, and what they say they need. Much of the debate on victims' rights occurs without recourse to what needs might be and how they might have changed over time. International and national instruments tend to reiterate the same points with respect to an established 'list' of victims' assumed needs. In the process of highlighting victims' needs and discussing how these needs might become rights, the victim's voice has been lost. Instead the victim has been constructed by governments as a 'consumer' of services. However, as in the marketplace, victims' access to certain services may be limited by income, access to knowledge and citizenship status. In this regard some victims, as 'consumers', have ample access to services they need, while other victims have access to basic services which in the main are not offered as a right.

Whether victims' needs are usefully served by becoming rights is dependent on the successful application of these rights in practice. Herein, the desirability of merging needs and rights becomes clear when the language of 'citizenship' and 'consumerism' is applied to victims without having established a bedrock of rights. Victims will only enjoy access to the kind of justice they need, as people with distinct experiences of victimisation, when rights are not limited by relative income and access to knowledge/information. Criminal justice services, together with victim-focused non-governmental organisations, have a duty to ensure that rights practically respond to need, whilst reflecting upon changing political preferences that at present focus on the victim as citizen and consumer.

Suggested reading

The Home Office website details the government's approach to and services for victims and witnesses, including the 1996 Victim's Charter; see also, for example, *Justice for All* (July 2002) and *A New Deal for Victims and Witnesses* (July 2003) – www.homeoffice.gov.uk. Jackson's 2003 article provides a nice critique of current government policy as victim-centred. In contrast, Mawby and Gill's 1987 book examines victims' services and the role of the voluntary sector at a time (the mid-1980s) when the needs/ rights debate was gathering steam. The example of State compensation, and its development over the years, illustrates some of the dilemmas and practical realities facing the needs/rights debate. Fry's ground-breaking 1959 article succinctly presents the arguments for State compensation, and the 1978 book by Miers sets the political scene for the development of State compensation schemes in Britain and North America (see also Burns, 1980). Comparative European responses to State compensation versus civil claims can most readily be found in Brienen and Hoegen's comprehensive book (2000). For the current response to State compensation in England and Wales see the website of the Criminal Injuries Compensation Authority: www.cica.gov.uk.

Notes

1. PTSD has been extensively researched by psychologists and medics and, as a particular area of expertise, is beyond the scope of this book; however, in relation to its manifestation in the aftermath of crime the following present some useful findings for those who are interested: Falsetti and Resnick (1995); Norris and Kaniasty (1994); and Resick and Nishith (1997) for a general introduction about the psychological impact of sexual assault; and Wortman et al. (1997) for a general introduction to parents' and spouses' responses after the death/murder of a family member.
2. Austria; Belgium; England and Wales; Finland; France; Germany; Italy; The Netherlands.
3. www.homeoffice.gov.uk/docs2/vicwitstrat.pdf – paragraph 5.7.
4. Ibid., paragraph 5.8.
5. The National Association of Victim Support Schemes, the umbrella organisation for Victim Support, receives funding from the Home Office and makes grants to local Victim Support groups to pay for staff, offices and other costs. Victim Support is a registered charity whose expenditure for the year ending 31 March 2002 was £25.3 million, £20.5 million of which went to local groups. See www.victimsupport.org.uk.

6. www.victimsupport.org.uk.
7. http://www.homeoffice.gov.uk/docs/crimevint.html: Youth Justice and Criminal Evidence Act.
8. European Parliament Resolution on Victims of Violence, OJ C 256, 9.10.1989, p. 32; and European Parliament Resolution on Crime Victims in the EU, OJ C 67, 1.3.2001, p. 308. Also the 2001 Council of the European Union Framework Decision on the Standing of Victims in Criminal Proceedings, and the 2001 European Commission Green Paper on 'Compensation to Crime Victims', COM (2001) 536 final.
9. www.victimsupport.org.uk.
10. The New Zealand Criminal Injuries Compensation Act (No. 134).
11. While Italy has no general State compensation scheme for victims of violent crime it has a special scheme in place for victims of terrorist violence and organised crime. Law No. 302, from 1990, can award State compensation to victims injured as a result of an act of terrorism or organised crime, and extends awards to dependants of persons who die as a result of violent acts of terrorism or organised crime; but according to research published in 1996, maximum awards payable for total disability or death are set at 150 million lire or £61,000 (see Piva, 1996: 382).
12. National Association of Crime Victim Compensation Boards (2000) *Crime Victim Compensation: Program Directory*, p. 1.
13. 'Spent' convictions are past convictions with prison sentences of less than 30 months which applicants no longer have to declare. Prison sentences of 30 months or more can never be considered as 'spent' convictions under the terms of the CICA's scheme.
14. See Criminal Injuries Compensation Authority website: www.cica.gov.uk.

Chapter 6

Balancing victims' and offenders' rights

Introducing themes for discussion

The previous chapter explored what is meant by 'victims' needs' and recognition of 'victims' rights'. The example of State compensation was used to illustrate some of the political reasons for and practical realities of adopting so-called victim-centred initiatives. This chapter concentrates on recent criminal justice developments in England and Wales to ease the path of victims of crime in the run up to, during, and after a criminal trial. Particular attention is paid to developments that set out to give victims a 'voice'. Specific examples referred to at the end of the chapter include 'victim statements' and probation-based victim contact work.

The chapter critiques so-called victim-centred initiatives for their impact on the rights of both victims and defendants. The adversarial nature of criminal justice in England and Wales provides the backdrop to debates forwarded here with respect to the need to balance victims' and defendants' rights. Evidence is also drawn from the European Court of Human Rights as its influence encroaches on the practice of justice in England and Wales, with implications for both defendants and victims. Victim-centred developments are outlined with an eye to the balance of interests that now faces criminal justice agencies, such as the probation service, as its remit is extended to include consideration of the needs and rights of both offenders and victims. Whether developments that are supposedly 'for' victims can correctly be said to be in their interests, or in the interests of defendants/offenders, is considered in the course of the chapter.

Justice for victims and offenders

As Chapter 4 illustrated, to be 'for' victims is often positioned as being 'against' offenders. However, rather than portray victim-centred justice in opposition to defendants' rights, we need to examine how victims can be successfully included in a criminal justice system that is traditionally constructed on the basis of conflict between offender and State, with victims excluded from this process. Initiatives to assist victims to give their best evidence at trial, such as use of live television links between the court room and an adjoining witness room, need to be interpreted for what they bring to the trial process and, in particular, the presentation of evidence. It is not useful to view such initiatives as primarily a threat to defendants' rights and the traditions of the court room.

Alternatively, a working partnership needs to be achieved between due process in law (the essence of which is to protect the rights of defendants and offenders) and victim-centred justice/crime control (the essence of which is to promote the rights of existing and potential victims). In recognising victims' freedom to participate at some level in the criminal justice process, but not in decision-making concerning offenders, the rights of suspects/defendants need not be eroded. For example, providing victims with information, such as the release date of their offender, does not affect offenders' rights, but it does inform victims and satisfy society that victims' interests are being taken into account. In comparison, asking victims to comment on whether an offender should receive bail, in the form of a victim statement, has potentially negative consequences for some offenders, and arguably does little to help victims beyond satisfying the needs of some individuals for retributive justice.

In this regard, Sanders and Young (2001) advance a justice model whereby inclusion of victims does not impinge on defendants' rights or freedoms. They call this the 'freedom model'. The model can accommodate the rights of both victims and offenders, providing, that is, that application of victims' rights does not impinge on the freedom of offenders beyond what has been ordained in a court of law. The subjective opinions of victims, for example with respect to sentence severity, are not valid in this model because they have different consequences for different offenders according to the retributive nature of the individual victim. Sanders and Young, in outlining their 'freedom model', are searching for a justice model that is both participative and inclusionary for victims *and* offenders. Drawing on Sebba's work (2000), they note that the old rehabilitative model of justice, based on reform of the offender, existed without active participation of offenders on whose behalf decisions were made. And, in the same way, traditional justice models exist with victims as outsiders with no participatory rights. In contrast, giving due weight to both offenders and victims in the criminal justice process, without impinging on either party's freedoms, can help us move towards a participative and inclusive justice model.

Sanders and Young develop their idea of a participative and inclusive 'freedom model' within the framework of current criminal justice practice. The 'freedom model' is different from but closely aligned to restorative justice, as restorative justice challenges established ways of doing justice in an effort to actively include victim, offender, and community in a restorative justice process. Chapter 7 focuses on this latest 'challenge' to established criminal justice practice; suffice it to say here that criminal justice in England and Wales is currently a long way from embracing restorative justice as an alternative to current practice.[1] At present, any effort at inclusive justice for victims and offenders has to work within the existing framework of established criminal justice practice. New ways of doing justice, which can include the participatory rights of victims and offenders without infringing either parties' freedoms, are faced with a number of challenges, principal among which is the nature of adversarial justice in common law jurisdictions such as England and Wales.

The adversarial nature of justice in England and Wales

The common law of England and Wales is an adversarial system of justice that emphasises the principle of *orality*. What this means in practice is that when cases are brought to the attention of the criminal justice system and go to trial, all evidence must be produced in court, and it must be orally introduced. In other words, evidence has to be presented in person by witnesses in court, and has to be spoken rather than written down. The witness must be physically available in court to be cross-examined face to face either by a defence lawyer, on behalf of the defendant, or by the defendant if he or she has opted for self-representation. In comparison, inquisitorial or continental justice systems, as in mainland Europe, place their faith in written documents contained in a case file that is compiled prior to trial by an examining magistrate. Here, the principle of 'truth' finding allows a diverse range of evidence to be collected by different means that would be regarded as 'hearsay' in common law systems, and therefore as uncorroborated and unreliable evidence that cannot be tested in open court. Witnesses can be called before a court and questioned on their evidence in inquisitorial systems, but this is not regarded as an essential element of a 'fair trial' as emphasis is placed on the contents of the case file.

By its very name, adversarial justice is constructed as a contest between State and defendant in the guise of lawyers for the defence and prosecution. Traditionally, witnesses have simply been tools through which lawyers do battle to win 'their' case. Difficult and often aggressive cross-examination is considered the norm in a system that emphasises the ability of defence lawyers to undermine the credibility of prosecution witnesses. While trial judges have a common law duty to restrain unnecessary, improper or oppressive questioning of witnesses, and the Bar's Code of Conduct for lawyers also includes similar provisions,[2] it remains the case that aggressive cross-examination takes place. As the somewhat understated comment in the comprehensive government report *Speaking*

Up for Justice sums up the problem: 'There are concerns that witnesses feel intimidated by cross-examination by defence counsel, particularly when the manner of questioning is perceived to be aggressive.'[3]

Plotnikoff and Woolfson's (1998) research on witness care in magistrates' courts and youth courts in five sites in England and Wales provides some insights that are relevant to witnesses' experiences at crown court. Their research is interesting because it explores the experiences of both defence and prosecution witnesses. While the focus of this book lies with victims of crime, it is useful to be aware, as this chapter highlights, of how the criminal justice process impacts on other players – be these defendants or witnesses for the defence. Plotnikoff and Woolfson interviewed 275 witnesses and others attending court, and found that witnesses for the prosecution and defence were respectively worried about 'Being asked questions I could not answer' (46 per cent / 35 per cent) and 'Not understanding what was happening in court' (41 per cent / 42 per cent). Since Plotnikoff and Woolfson's research there have been a number of improvements in all courts to assist witnesses through the criminal justice process; for example, there is now a witness support service, run by Victim Support, in every crown court and magistrates' court in England and Wales. However, these improvements do not alter the fact that witnesses still have to undergo cross-examination, and are only permitted to speak when asked questions.

Stages in a criminal trial

A criminal trial in an English crown court follows a series of steps that appear normal to criminal justice personnel, but which place victims and first-time defendants in a situation that is both alien and intimidating. Witnesses and defendants are only allowed to speak about events at certain points in the trial, and their responses are framed by questions that are put to them by lawyers. In brief, the pattern of events in a criminal court is as follows (Gibson and Cavadino, 1995; Rock, 1993).

The prosecution lawyer opens a case. Witnesses for the prosecution, including the victim or victims, are called in turn by the prosecution and questioned on the evidential statement they made to the police, some time ago, about the crime – the examination-in-chief. Witnesses are not asked to give an account of events as they remember them, nor are they asked their opinion as to what actually happened. Instead, the prosecution guides witnesses through a series of questions that set out to provide answers in support of original statements made to the police. Prosecution witnesses are then turned over

(Box continued)

to be questioned by the defence counsel – the cross-examination. While witnesses for the prosecution naturally undergo a mild form of questioning at the hands of the prosecution, with leading questions disallowed, defence lawyers present a different challenge. As the chief purpose of the defence lawyer is to extract information and impressions that are favourable to the defendant, witnesses for the prosecution are undermined by questions that seek to discredit them. A broader set of questions is allowed by defence lawyers than is permitted from prosecution lawyers, and tactics are employed under cross-examination that centre on a witness's way of life, social standing, past convictions, and any possible motives they may have to harm the defendant's reputation. Having been cross-examined, witnesses can then be re-examined by the prosecution in an effort to repair any harm done by the defence to the evidence and character of the witness. Defence counsel can then call its own witnesses for questioning, if it chooses to, who, in turn, can be cross-examined by the prosecution.

Rock (1993) describes this process as a deliberate simplification of events that obscures certain issues and limits the 'facts' presented. In other words, alongside the common law's reliance on oral evidence at trial to substantiate statements made to the police, another central feature of a 'fair trial' is its investigation of circumstances and evidence surrounding a *single event*. The context and history of a case, including the complex social and emotional relations that are often involved between defendant and witness, are stripped away. Non-revelation of previous charges and convictions may be in the interests of the defendant, but it is not in the interests of the victim. The history and circumstances surrounding instances of repeat victimisation against individual complainants, by the same offender or offenders, is lost in the process of reducing evidence to the single event.

Although efforts have been made to curb the worst excesses of unnecessary and aggressive questioning of child witnesses and complainants in cases involving sexual assault and rape, moves are still afoot to change the method and style of cross-examination for all witnesses. The heart of the problem lies with the culture of the criminal court as a setting for combative justice. Whereas inquisitorial systems can, somewhat ideally, be characterised as platforms for finding the 'truth' through the careful collection and sifting of evidence contained in the case file, the adversarial system can be characterised as a 'contest' to find the most convincing line of argument between lawyers. Lawyers are raised in an adversarial system that rewards those who 'win' the most trials. The criminal trial represents the stage where lawyers clash, and where aggressive cross-examination is too often permitted. Judges are drawn from a population of top barristers, and, as a result, a culture of aggressive justice becomes normalised and self-perpetuating. Witnesses and victims exist at the periphery of this culture, and are often simply viewed as accessories to the main event which rests in the hands of lawyers, judges, court ushers, court clerks, and the police.

In evidence presented to the Working Group behind the 1998 government paper *Speaking Up for Justice*, Rape Crisis quoted a statement from Northumberland police that the threat of aggressive, humiliating and irrelevant questioning in court was the single biggest factor making women withdraw from pressing charges in rape cases.[4] Aggressive and embarrassing cross-examination has effectively served to put complainants on trial themselves in sexual assault and rape cases, so much so that many feel they have suffered *'secondary victimisation'* at the hands of the criminal justice system. Secondary victimisation is not isolated to sexual assault and rape cases, but it is particularly problematic in these cases given the nature of the crimes and their impact on victims. Lees (1996), a critical feminist criminologist, and Kennedy (1992), a prominent barrister and advocate of women's rights in the criminal justice system, are two voices that paint a vivid picture of some of the worst excesses of cross-examination and treatment encountered by women complainants in sexual assault and rape cases. Since the latter half of the twentieth century these voices of dissent, coupled with collective criticism from Rape Crisis and Victim Support, have pushed for changes in the way that vulnerable and intimidated victims are treated at trial.[5]

Cross-examination by defendants

In response to the above, a number of legal and procedural safeguards have been established in England and Wales that set out to ease the victim's path through the criminal justice process and alleviate some of the most gruelling aspects of the criminal trial. The forerunner of more recent developments was the introduction of Section II of the 1976 Sexual Offences (Amendment) Act, which set out to limit questioning about a complainant's previous sexual history, except, at the judge's discretion, when directly relevant to the case – that is, when a woman has a history of making false allegations of rape. The 1976 Act was a landmark move against secondary victimisation of complainants; however, to this day, it continues to be undermined by judges who allow questions about witness credibility and reliability to enter into cross-examination. And it was only in the 1990s that legislative reform removed the right from an unrepresented defendant to personally cross-examine a complainant in certain cases.

The 1991 Criminal Justice Act removed the defendant's right to cross-examine a child in person in cases involving sexual or violent offences.

This provision was extended by the 1999 Youth Justice and Criminal Evidence Act, which removed the right of an unrepresented defendant to cross-examine an adult rape complainant at trial. The 1996 Ralston Edwards case, in which the victim was cross-examined over several days by her rapist, was a catalyst for reform as it alerted the public to the imbalance between protecting a defendant's right to represent himself at trial and the witness's absence of rights in circumstances where a judge failed to limit cross-examination. Measures are now in place to prevent a defendant from representing himself in rape cases, but provision must be made for his legal representation in such cases to ensure the principle of a 'fair trial'.

Questioning by police and lawyers

A similar event in the early 1980s, when a BBC television 'fly on the wall' documentary showed the aggressive police interrogation undergone by a complainant in the early stages of a rape investigation, led to public outrage and subsequent calls for the police to change their treatment of complainants in sexual assault cases (Dunhill, 1989). Arguably, while the police have made significant inroads towards improved treatment of victims and witnesses in preliminary investigations, and there has been a cultural shift in practice policy towards 'service provision' for victims and the public, other criminal justice personnel, and in particular trial judges and defence lawyers, have been slow to change. Institutional racism, as highlighted in the MacPherson Report on the investigation into the racist murder of Stephen Lawrence, remains the most significant problem that the police have yet to tackle; but their treatment of victims is far in advance of the judiciary. Given that the aggressive culture of police questioning of victims has changed, it has to be asked, in light of a plethora of recent victim-centred developments at trial, whether the same cultural change will be seen among the judiciary who have to implement these changes.

The Crown Prosecution Service (CPS) – which oversees the work of prosecution lawyers – has made inroads into improving the Service's treatment of victims, at least on paper. The Service's 'Code for Crown Prosecutors' (2000) includes the following paragraphs which are relevant to victims: paragraph 6.7 addresses the Service's need to take into account 'the consequences for the victim of the decision whether or not to prosecute, and any views expressed by the victim or the victim's family'; and paragraph 6.8 states that 'it is important that a victim is told about a decision which makes a significant difference to the case in which he or she is involved'. The CPS website includes a 'Statement on the Treatment of Victims and Witnesses' which it relates to the Victim's Charter and the Citizen's Charter.[6] But a central theme that runs through both the 'Code' and the 'Statement' is that the CPS is bound to act in the 'public interest' rather than that of an individual victim; as the Statement says (paragraph 2.1): 'The CPS does not act directly on behalf of individual victims or represent them in court in criminal proceedings because it has to take decisions reflecting the overall public interest rather than the particular interests of any one person.' In this regard, while 'victim-centred' service might be expected of a Service which relies on witness cooperation to prosecute guilty defendants successfully, the extent of the CPS's victim-centred approach is constrained by the Service's principle of answering first to the 'public' rather than the 'private' interests of individual victims.

The police have responded more comprehensively than the CPS to the need to change their culture, especially with regard to witness interrogation. Not only did it make for bad public relations when the police were seen to bully rape complainants aggressively, but the danger was that the public would withdraw from reporting serious crime to the police for fear of the kind of treatment they would meet. Collectively, a combination of stark realities and political will pushed the police towards their new role as service providers:

- recognition that the police are reliant on the public to report crime, as very little crime is detected by the police first-hand;
- rising crime rates in the 1980s, and the political will of government to be seen to be doing something about crime by focusing on victims.

While crime rates have begun to fall since the late 1990s, the political focus on crime and victims of crime has not gone away, and if anything has grown stronger. This helps to explain the continued growth of victim-centred justice developments in England and Wales over the last two decades.

Victim Support now provides a government-funded witness support service in all crown courts and magistrates' courts in England and Wales. The service informs witnesses about what to expect at trial, and thereby ameliorates some of the more intimidating aspects of the court appearance for first-time witnesses. However, victims still face a culture where aggressive face-to-face cross-examination in court remains a real possibility. It can be said that defence lawyers are the last bastion of 'victim unfriendly' justice. Given that an essential remit of defence lawyers is to undermine witness credibility, it is hardly surprising that the culture of the court room is, perhaps, the last aspect of criminal justice to move towards victim-centred justice. While developments are being put in place to lighten the witness's progress through the criminal trial, it remains to be seen whether the culture of the judiciary is up to the challenge of changing its age-old way of conducting business at trial as a face-to-face adversarial contest.

Enhancing victims' rights: recent victim-centred developments

Since the mid-1990s there has been a wealth of so-called victim-centred criminal justice developments that, besides those already referred to in the previous paragraphs, have set out to rectify some of the worst excesses of the criminal justice process, and in particular the criminal trial, for victims and witnesses. As outlined in the previous chapter, key developments in the 1990s for victims include:

• The second Victim's Charter (1996);
• *Speaking Up for Justice* (1998), the government report on vulnerable and intimidated witnesses, and its follow-up implementation plan *Action for Justice*;
• The Youth Justice and Criminal Evidence Act, Part II (1999), which took up recommendations set out in *Speaking Up for Justice*.

There are, of course, other victim-centred criminal justice initiatives from the mid-1990s onwards: for example, Home Office Circular 41/1996, directed at chief constables, on 'Witness Care in the Criminal Justice System', and, more recently, the Criminal Justice and Police Act 2001, which sets out to challenge intimidation or harm of witnesses. Also, more recently, two criminal justice Acts are now in place that will further add to victim-centred criminal justice developments: the Criminal Justice Act 2003, emerging after the government's White Paper *Justice For All*, which sets out to enhance a number of provisions for alternative witness testimonies other than in open court; and the December 2003 Domestic Violence, Crime and Victims Bill, which has been described as 'The biggest overhaul of domestic violence law in 30 years, heralding tough powers for the police and the courts to protect victims and prosecute offenders.'[7]

However, put together, the 1996 Victim's Charter, along with *Speaking Up for Justice* and the 1999 Youth Justice and Criminal Evidence Act, represent arguably the most ground-breaking generic set of victim-centred developments in England and Wales since the mid-1990s. Notably, Part II of the 1999 Youth Justice and Criminal Evidence Act put in place a wide-ranging set of 'special measures' to assist vulnerable and intimidated witnesses to give their best evidence in court:

• screens – to ensure that the witness does not see the defendant in court;
• video-recorded evidence-in-chief – allowing an interview with the witness, which has been video-recorded before the trial, to be shown as the witness's evidence-in-chief;
• live television link – allowing a witness to give evidence from outside the court room in a neighbouring room;

- clearing the public gallery of the court – so that evidence can be given in private;
- removal of wigs and gowns in court – to provide a more informal atmosphere;
- video-recorded pre-trial cross-examination – allowing a witness to be cross-examined before the trial about their evidence, and a video recording of that cross-examination to be shown at trial instead of the witness being cross-examined live at trial;
- intermediaries – allowing an approved intermediary to help a witness communicate with legal representatives and the court;
- allowing a witness to use communication aids.[8]

This list of initiatives is to be welcomed; however, it can be faulted for two central reasons:

1. The use of special measures is limited, at the judge's discretion, to children under 17, and those suffering from mental or physical disability or impairments, or those whose evidence is likely to be affected by fear or distress.
2. The onus remains with giving live oral testimony at trial, either in the court room or somewhere else by means of a live link.

According to Ellison (2001: 160), in her critique of *Speaking Up for Justice* and its implementation through the Youth Justice and Criminal Evidence Act 1999 (YJCE Act):

> So unreserved is the commitment to cross-examination that no serious consideration has so far been given to the possibility of alternative methods of evidence testing. Until such a re-examination takes place there can be no meaningful integration of a witness perspective within the criminal justice process.

In other words, the various developments set out in the YJCE Act fail to challenge the underlying principles of adversarial cross-examination at trial.

The more recent Criminal Justice Act 2003, sets out its key provisions offering 'a better deal for victims and witnesses' at trial as: (1) allowing witnesses to give evidence using television links from remote locations if this would be more efficient or effective; (2) witnesses' previous statements would become more widely admissible at trial including allowing witnesses to refer to their statement while giving evidence in court; and (3) greater use of video-recorded statements for crucial evidence in serious cases. While *Justice For All* dressed up these developments as being for 'all victims', it remains to be seen whether they will be implemented beyond a few high-profile cases as new initiatives always remain at the mercy of a judge's discretion and are up against a legal culture committed to live cross-examination.

Enhancing victims' rights: a problem for the defence?

An underlying principle that is working against the wider adoption of new developments in law to allow witnesses to give best evidence is the idea that victim-centred justice impinges on defendants' rights. According to a report published by the Queensland Law Reform Commission in Australia, judges are reluctant to exercise their discretion in favour of live television links between the court room and a witness room, allowing the witness to be cross-examined away from the defendant and the public, because they believe that the defendant's right to a fair trial is compromised in the process.[9] In England and Wales the same argument was forwarded with respect to early developments that set out to assist child witnesses to give best evidence in court (Spencer and Flin, 1993).

Oral evidence versus other means

The 1988 Criminal Justice Act was an early victim-centred and child-centred initiative that made it possible for child witnesses to give evidence by live television link from a room adjacent to the court. This initiative was supported by the report of Lord Justice Pigot in 1989 on use of video evidence for child witnesses. He also recommended that, in certain cases, the entire evidence of children be routinely taken in advance of trial and recorded on video tape, and that the admissibility of these video interviews be decided at a preliminary hearing attended by the accused and counsel for both defence and prosecution. The 1991 Criminal Justice Act went on to allow the possibility of video-taped investigative interviews to replace a child's examination-in-chief in open court. However, these innovative and welcome developments to assist children to give best evidence were grudgingly adopted against the backdrop of a culture that was reluctant to let go of age-old traditions of live face-to-face cross-examination.

Defence lawyers argued that child witnesses who were cross-examined using live television links could more readily lie under these circumstances than if they were challenged through direct cross-examination in court, though there is no concrete evidence that this occurs (Ellison, 2001). However, in the early application of video-recorded evidence there was a problem with interviewers using leading questions. The 1992 'Memorandum of Good Practice on Video Recorded Interviews with Child Witnesses for Criminal Proceedings', directed at police officers and social workers conducting interviews, set out clear guidelines on how to avoid leading questions and other failings in interview style that could make a recording inadmissible in court. Also, if more than one video session were recorded, defence lawyers were keen to point out that interviewees could be influenced on what to say and how to act between sessions. In response, the single recorded session is now promoted to counter accusations of witness prompting. One session also serves to alleviate the stress caused to interviewees by multiple sessions asking about the same harrowing events.

At the same time, in the interests of managerialist goals of efficiency, one recorded video session is cheaper than two or three. In this vein, the preamble to the 2003 Criminal Justice Act, in outlining its key provisions for victims and witnesses, indicated that use of live television evidence from remote locations would be desirable if proved to be 'efficient and effective': that is, if it assists evidence-giving and produces evidence that can be used in court (effective), and, equally, if it costs less in terms of money, personnel, time and management (efficient). So, alongside concerns that victims should be able to give best evidence, without impinging on defendants' rights, is the managerialist concern to be doing justice efficiently.

Witness demeanour and lying

Besides the emphasis placed on oral evidence in open court, both defence and prosecution lawyers place great importance on a witness's demeanour in court: for example, how they stand, and where they look and how. Juries are similarly affected by the demeanour of a witness. A strong argument against live television links and pre-recorded video evidence is that the meaning behind non-verbal gestures is lost when questioning takes place outside the setting of the court room. Defence lawyers maintain that witnesses might be in a better position to lie when alternative methods of testifying are available, as witnesses are saved from closer scrutiny of how they present what they say. In contrast, prosecutors often see it as being to their advantage when witnesses testify in open court. The prosecution witness who breaks down in tears, or who is otherwise visibly disturbed when having to recount events, presents the prosecution with the emotional weight they need to convince a jury that a witness is telling the truth. The stress caused witnesses by having to appear in open court may not be in their own immediate interests, although it can have the desired effect of securing a conviction, but it is undoubtedly in the interests of prosecution lawyers if their witness appears emotionally vulnerable in court.

However, the assertion that juries miss subtle non-verbal gestures when evidence is presented other than through direct cross-examination in court, either as a video recording or via a live television link, assumes two things: first, that non-verbal gestures are somehow lost using alternative methods of evidence giving; and second, that juries are in a position to interpret non-verbal gestures correctly. As Spencer and Flin comment (1993: 280): 'In tests designed to discover how good people are at telling whether another person is lying, subjects rarely manage a success rate that is much above chance level, or what they would achieve by shutting their eyes and ears and making a guess.' There is no blueprint about how we should respond when recounting events in the unusual setting of a police interview room, witness room, or court room. And the usual signs we might interpret as indiciators of lying – sweating, not looking people directly in the eye, fidgeting – are also signs of stress that can be brought on during cross-examination. Given that every witness is different and experiences crime differently, it is doubtful whether verbal information and non-verbal gestures can always be accurately read. To an extent we can assume that jury members, like criminal justice personnel, often judge witnesses on the basis of stereotypes. As juries are not trained to interpret witnesses' verbal evidence and non-verbal gestures, people rely on their own personal experiences and prejudices when it comes to 'truth' seeking. Equally, consideration needs to be given to how juries respond to evidence presented in the form of a video recording, or cross-examination using a live television link. The very fact that a witness gives evidence or is cross-examined away from the court room can imply their need for protection and, correspondingly, in the eyes of the jury, can imply the defendant's guilt.

Accepting change

Many of the early teething problems with recorded video evidence, such as leading questions that direct a witness to respond in a certain way, have been alleviated to a great extent. However, while lawyers and judges now concede that there is a place for children to testify using live television links or to give evidence in pre-recorded video interviews, these measures are less welcome in cases involving other categories of vulnerable and intimidated witnesses. Although the 1999 Youth Justice and Criminal Evidence Act includes provision for live television links and pre-recorded evidence-in-chief for vulnerable and intimidated witnesses other than children, it remains the case that these provisions are narrowly applied to adults at the discretion of trial judges.

Ashworth, a key commentator in the debate about advances in victims' rights and their impact on defendants' rights, asks: 'Is it true that the only way to ensure that a defendant has a fair trial, with full and fearless representation, is to attempt to discredit prosecution witnesses in a degrading way?' (Ashworth, 2000: 187–8). In answer, Ashworth asks what is a fair trial? And do witnesses have rights at trial? He contextualises these questions with respect to the judicial-legal culture in England and Wales that continues to work with stereotypes about victims and witnesses. Prejudices about who makes a credible or good witness, and acceptable ways of behaving in the run up to and after victimisation, permeate how and why the legal profession responds to members of the public, as victims and witnesses, in certain ways.

But established ways of conducting criminal justice business are increasingly coming under scrutiny as Victim Support and other organisations call for improvements to be made in how victims and witnesses are treated by the criminal justice system. Given that, from 2003–4, the government now provides funding that enables Victim Support to have a witness service in every court in England and Wales, the evidence on the ground is that the once impermeable fortress of the court house and the court room, as the province of the legal profession, is gradually being encroached on by witnesses and victims who were once outsiders in the criminal justice process.

Focus: victim statements and victim contact work

Having outlined some general considerations with respect to improvements in treatment of victims in the criminal justice system, and resultant implications for defendants, the next section focuses on two examples of so-called victim-centred justice in England and Wales that appear to impinge on defendants'/offenders' rights.

The 1996 Victim's Charter announced that 'victim statement' projects would be piloted in England to allow victims to make written statements about the impact crime had had on them. At the same time, the Charter committed the police to the provision of information to victims on the progress of their case, in the form of the One-Stop-Shop, and reaffirmed the probation service's committment, since the 1990 Victim's Charter, to securing information from victims in serious cases prior to any consideration about offenders' release (victim contact work). This section focuses on some of the questions that are raised in relation to: (1) the 'victim statement', or 'victim impact statement' as it is commonly referred to; and (2) the work of the probation service with respect to victim contact work.

Victim statements

Background

According to its advocates the 'victim statement' developed in common law jurisdictions to give victims a greater 'voice' in the criminal justice process by allowing them to give a statement about the impact of crime on them. Its proponents suggest that the 'victim statement' (VS) permits victims to give an account of how their victimisation has affected them psychologically, physically, socially and financially. However, opponents of the VS suggest otherwise.

Proponents of the VS suggest:	**Opponents of the VS suggest:**
• it legitimates the victim as a party to criminal proceedings;	• it allows victims' subjective accounts to influence criminal justice decision-making, which is particularly worrying in the case of sentencing;
• it allows the victim to give an account of harm suffered;	
• information contained in the VS helps criminal justice agencies to understand the impact of crime, and, correspondingly, influences their decision-making;	• as a result, defendants' rights are eroded;
• it encourages victims to cooperate with the criminal justice authorities who appear to be taking their victimisation seriously.	• in giving a VS, without making its purpose clear, victims' expectations can be unrealistically raised if their VS has no discernible impact on case outcome.

More than any other recent criminal justice initiative, the VS confronts established ways of doing justice by offering the prospect of a personalised account of how crime has impacted on the individual victim. Most controversially of all, the use to which the VS can be put has implications for sentencing severity depending on individual victims and their response to victimisation. In allowing victims to describe the wider impact of crime on them, including feelings of anxiety, the VS differs from a victim's evidential statement to the police as it can include uncorroborated 'hearsay' comments. Because of this, the VS, as it exists in England and Wales, can only be referred to in the criminal justice process if a guilty plea has been entered, or once a guilty verdict has been returned at trial. These limitations are there to respect the offender's right to due process in law, as retributive victims are not given the opportunity to influence verdicts and sentencing through the VS.

In comparison, in some US states 'victim opinion statements' are permitted that allow the victim's opinion in relation to sentencing (Morgan and Sanders, 1999). Sometimes these statements can be given orally to the court – something that carries great emotional weight for both victim and listener, including the judge and members of the jury. However, in England and Wales the VS is limited to a written statement about the impact of crime on the victim, and its content is narrowly framed. The opinions of the victim and those of his or her family are not seen as relevant, and are excluded from the VS. To this end, the Home Office-funded researchers who conducted the first pilot study on VSs in England (Hoyle et al., 1998) purposely referred to 'victim statements' rather than 'victim impact statements' to distinguish the English-based initiative from its more controversial US counterparts. But, as Hoyle et al. (1998) note, the 1996 Victim's Charter, in framing the VS, hints at it having procedural rights:

> You can expect the chance to explain how the crime has affected you, and your interest to be taken into account. The police will ask you about your fears about further victimisation and details of your loss, damage or injury. The police, Crown Prosecutor and judges will take this information into account when making their decisions.

This wording implies that a VS will be taken into account when judges decide on sentencing. At the same time, the Director of Public Prosecutions, in a publication on the Victim's Charter pilot projects,[10] seemed to envisage that the VS would have a role to play in sentencing. In contrast, Victim Support, as *the* victim support organisation influencing UK government policy, is keen to remove the burden of decision-making from victims, and therefore is cautious in its interpretation of the uses to which VSs should be put. As a result of these conflicting standpoints, the VS has been used in a discretionary way by individual criminal justice personnel, who, without clear guidance, have been forced to interpret the remit of the VS as they see fit.

Pilot studies

The VS was piloted in five areas in England in the mid-1990s. Under the terms of the VS pilots, victims of the following crimes were admitted to participate: domestic burglary, domestic violence, assault occasioning grevious bodily harm, sexual assault, robbery, criminal damage over £5,000, racially motivated offences, and attempting or conspiring to commit any of these offences. Victims could choose to write a VS. Having done so, they either completed a VS form themselves, or received assistance and guidance from the police in filling out a form.

A team of researchers from Bristol University examined the impact of the first VS pilots (alongside the outcome of the One-Stop-Shop police initiative to keep victims informed of developments in their case[11]). They contacted 564 victims across the five pilot areas and interviewed 289 using, predominantly, telephone-based interviews. Of these 289 interviewees, 148 had made a VS. The researchers found that 30 per cent of eligible victims from all five pilot areas made a VS.

According to Hoyle et al.'s survey results, and allowing for the fact that respondents to the survey could give more than one answer, 60 per cent of victims who made a VS did so for expressive reasons: that is, to get the incident 'off their chest', or to tell the offender or his/her family how they had been affected by the offence. Significantly, given this chapter's focus on the impact of victims' rights on defendants' rights, 55 per cent offered an instrumental reason for writing a VS: that is, to influence the court. According to the research, victims expressed a particular desire to 'persuade sentencers to give tougher sentences'.[12] In turn, a substantial minority of victims hoped their VS would influence the verdict in their case or their claim for victim compensation, and 8 per cent hoped the VS would influence any decisions regarding bail/remand. Finally, 43 per cent of victims made a VS for procedural reasons: that is, in support of their evidential statement to the police.

Interviewing victims some weeks after they had made a VS, the research found that over three-quarters felt they had made the right decision in doing so. However, there were a number of factors that did not assist the VS as an informative and cathartic process. For example, in relation to the timing of the VS in the aftermath of crime and the intervention of the criminal justice authorities with the victim, the research found that VSs were able to capture the medium-term effects rather than the immediate or long-term effects. In addition, the VS pro forma was formulated in such a way as to restrict and shape victims' responses in a manner that did not fully reflect the impact of the crime on them. Also, the attitude of the police and information supplied by them, as the key personnel responsible for VS implementation, often failed to assist victims in how best to complete a VS form, what could be contained in it, and how it would be used.

The research found that approximately 90 per cent of victims did not know at the end of their case what had happened to their VS; they did not know who saw it, what use was made of it, and what impact it had had on their case and its outcome. In sum, the research concluded that the VS 'raised more hopes, for many victims, than it was able to satisfy'.[13] This was largely due to victims' raised expectations, particularly regarding the opportunity to influence sentencing, that were not kept in check by clear explanations of the limited uses to which a VS could be put. Additionally, criminal justice personnel were often woefully ignorant of the uses to which a VS should be put. In this regard, while victims might expect the VS to have an impact on sentencing and other decisions related to the defendant's or offender's release, the reality is that the VS is primarily a tool for criminal justice personnel to use or ignore at their discretion.

Eroding defendants' rights?

According to Erez, a prominent US exponent of victim impact statements (2000: 173):

> Providing victims with a voice in the form of victim impact statements has not affected fundamental principles underlying the adversarial legal system. The research suggests that the VIS has not transformed victims into parties to proceedings, nor has it compromised defendants' rights.

This comment suggests that VSs are not the revolutionary development for victim-centred criminal justice intervention that we might have expected, nor have they served to erode defendants' rights. Hoyle et al. (1998) compared the VSs of twenty victims with their evidential statements to the police to see if the VSs added anything new or vengeful. They found that (1998: 28): 'Rather than, as is sometimes feared . . . VSs encouraging exaggeration, inflammatory statements and vindictiveness, the opposite appears to apply: they tend to understate, rather than over-state, the impact of offences.'

Looking at similar research undertaken by Erez in South Australia (1994), which showed that VSs tended to underplay the impact of crime on victims, Hoyle et al. (1998) found support for their findings: that is, VSs do not provide a place for vengeful victims to air their views on sentencing. But these findings could simply reflect the conditions under which VSs were applied in these particular studies: that is, the content of VSs was closely monitored and controlled by criminal justice personnel to limit information about the victim's opinion regarding sentencing, and victims were unclear about the purpose of VSs and what they could contain.

In conclusion, VSs can offer an opportunity for victims to tell some-thing about the impact of crime on them, which can, where appropriate, be used to inform decisions made by criminal justice personnel. The purpose and limitations of VSs should be clearly articulated to victims by informed personnel. Victims need to be clear that any decisions on sentencing and release are the remit of the judiciary. In this way, victims will not be misled into thinking they can influence sentencing and release dates for offenders. However, the VS provides an opportunity for victims to inform the court of any loss and damage they have suffered, to person or property, which can influence decisions regarding compensa-tion. Close monitoring of the content and uses to which VSs are put can ensure that defendants' rights are safeguarded.

This safe and watered-down version of the VS, far removed from the content and purpose of the victim opinion statement or its weaker cousin the victim impact statement, does not rock the boat for criminal justice. Much as Erez suggests (2000), the VS does very little in practical terms to change either the position of victims in criminal justice or the rights of defendants. While the VS, in its current form, does not make victims active parties in criminal proceedings, it has the potential, if properly used, to inform criminal justice personnel about the impact of crime on victims.

Victim contact work

Background

The 1990 Victim's Charter created an obligation for the probation service to contact victims of life sentence prisoners, or their families, to enquire whether they had any anxieties about their offender's release from custody. If victims expressed anxieties, this information would be used to place restrictions on offenders' movements after release. However, the probation service was given this obligation without any clear guidance about how they should go about implementing it. At the same time, no new funds were allocated to assist the service with its increased workload (Williams, 1996).

In 1991, the Home Office issued a circular to chief probation officers, and later the Association of Chief Officers of Probation (ACOP) issued its own advice (1993, 1994) concerning probation's new obligations to victims. However, the clearest statement about probation's victim-centred obligations came in 1995 in the form of Home Office Probation Circular 61. This set out probation's remit as: 'To provide information to the victim about the custodial process, and to obtain information from the victim about any concerns he or she may wish to be taken into account when the conditions (but not the date) of release are being considered.'[14]

Further, probation's 1995 Code of Practice, the 'National Standards for the Supervision of Offenders in the Community', included reference to probation's new obligations to victims, and extended these obligations to victims of serious violent or sexual offences where previously only victims of life sentence prisoners had been considered. In turn, the 1996 Victim's Charter reiterated probation's obligations to victims by stating that victims could expect that:

> Within two months of the sentence a probation officer will get in touch with you to find out whether you want to be told when the prisoner may be released from prison. They will ask you if you have any worries about them being released. Your worries can be taken into account when considering whether conditions need to be attached to the offender's release.

Also in 1996, Victim Support issued a Joint Statement with the ACOP to outline and distinguish each organisation's victim-centred work. The ACOP reiterated the contents of the 1995 Probation Circular, to give and receive information from victims, and Victim Support stressed its emotionally and practically supportive role to victims alongside its remit to assist probation with its victim contact work. Crawford and Enterkin (1999) critique this Joint Statement for its failure to outline clearly the practical arrangements for probation and Victim Support to work in harmony, beyond an obligation for both parties to refer to each other's work. In particular, they criticise the Joint Statement's absence of detail regarding Victim Support's work in the area of 'emotional support'.

This lack of clarity is symptomatic of the general lack of foresight with which victim contact work was introduced into the remit of the probation service. For a service that has traditionally been offender-centred, the requirement to consider victims' worries with regard to offender release dates has thrown up a conflict of interests for probation in consideration of the needs and rights of offenders and victims (Nettleton et al., 1997).

Pilot studies

Johnstone (1995, 1996) undertook an early piece of research on victim contact work by West Yorkshire Probation Service. He outlined some of the problems involved with probation contacting victims a long time after an offence had taken place, and the corresponding need for sensitive intervention practices with victims to ameliorate secondary victimisation. He also specified the need to avoid a conflict of interests for probation officers, for example to make sure that an officer does not contact the victim/s of the offender for which he/she is responsible. Johnstone noted that early work with victims is essential if worries about offender release are to be taken into account. And, importantly, he identified the problems of under-resourcing and an absence of clarity with respect to working partnerships between agencies with a responsibility towards victims.

Johnstone's study informed later research by Crawford and Enterkin (1999) on victim contact work undertaken by West Yorkshire Probation Service in comparison with the work of Northumbria Probation Service. Crawford and Enterkin conducted face-to-face interviews with victims, probation officers and other criminal justice personnel to determine the impact and effectiveness of probation's victim contact work in light of requirements set out in the Victim's Charter. In total, they interviewed 80 victims, 40 from each area. The victim sample included the relatives of victims in 13 murder or manslaughter cases, 37 victims of serious sexual offences, and 30 victims of other violent offences. In 15 victim cases offenders were serving a mandatory or discretionary life sentence. Information gathered from victims or their families by victim contact workers was placed in a 'victim report'.

Of the seventeen probation officers interviewed for the research, all agreed with the principle of incorporating victims' needs and concerns into criminal justice. However, probation officers interpreted their victim-centred work as having a narrow agenda, and were generally of the opinion that victim reports should only be used to establish conditions in consideration of an offender's release. Even then, this was qualified by concerns that excessive restrictions imposed on an offender's release or denial of parole, informed by the content of a victim report, could engender feelings of resentment among criminals. In turn, this could jeopardise offenders' reintegration into the community as it might increase their risk of reoffending.

Crawford and Enterkin's research pointed to various problems arising from victim contact work; these largely centred on mis-administration and lack of professional coherency. Depending on the probation service area, victim contact workers could include probation officers or mediators and/or Victim Support workers affiliated to probation. Victims who were interviewed revealed a lack of coherency between different victim contact workers with regard to what they were told about the uses to which a victim report could be put. Herein, Crawford and Enterkin's research indicates that victim contact workers, be they from probation or Victim Support, need to give victims identical and clear advice about the purpose of collecting information from victims prior to their offender's release.

A central message to emerge from Crawford and Enterkin's report is that different criminal justice agencies, from the police through to probation and prison staff, need to consider victims as part of a criminal justice 'whole', and not in terms of the narrow responsibilities of a particular agency. Echoing the 1998 report of the JUSTICE committee on *Victims in Criminal Justice* (JUSTICE, 1998; Shapland, 2000), Crawford and Enterkin's report emphasises the need for agencies to adopt cross-cutting horizontal accountability towards victims to challenge the current focus on each agency's own branch of criminal justice and a set of limited responsibilities. In this regard, the probation service should look beyond the Victim's Charter when framing its response to victims.

With a more coherent working relationship developed between probation and the various agencies responsible for victims' needs, probation's response to victims can be framed as part of a 'victim responsible' system.

Eroding defendants' rights?

Contrary to popular belief concerning probation's pro-offender bias, and as many probation officers stated to Crawford and Enterkin in the course of their research, the probation service has long taken victims' needs into account. To frame probation's victim contact work as posing a new threat to defendants' rights, and as presenting a conflict of interests to probation's work that has traditionally rested with offenders, is to forget the service's earlier inroads in the area of victim support initiatives and mediation. The Bristol Victims–Offenders Group was established in 1970, and, with administrative support from the National Association for the Care and Resettlement of Offenders, was able to relaunch itself to renewed success in 1975 as the forerunner of Victim Support. And in the 1980s the probation service engaged in mediation and reparation work that both directly and indirectly involved work with victims.

Mediation and reparation units were established under the wing of the probation service, with probation professionals or volunteers, supervised by the probation service, acting as mediators. Mediation tended to adopt one of two forms: (1) indirect mediation, often in letter form, with a mediator acting as a go-between between offender and victim; or (2) direct face-to-face mediation between offender and victim with a mediator present.

Arguably, victim–offender mediation schemes were established in England and Wales with the principal aim of diverting adult and young offenders away from the courts and prison by offering them the alternative of mediation. However, at the same time, mediation was able to offer victims information and answers to questions about the offence and their offender that they otherwise could not receive from the traditional criminal justice process. While both parties, offender and victim, had to take part in mediation voluntarily, the possibility of offenders being coerced into mediation was raised. In an effort to divert themselves from the traditional justice system or, where mediation was applied post-sentencing, in an effort to secure their early release from prison, offenders might be tempted to volunteer for mediation. But, as a number of studies have shown, contrary to the forebodings of some just deserts' proponents, mediation schemes (or reparation orders as they have more recently been defined under the terms of the 1998 Crime and Disorder Act) have proved to be anything but a soft option for offenders (Dignan, 2002).

With regard to offenders' rights in relation to probation's latest commitments under the terms of the Victim's Charter, Crawford and Enterkin's research found that some probation officers raised concerns that victims might lie or exaggerate to increase the likelihood of restrictions being placed on offenders post-release. Allowing for the uncorroborated testimonies of victims to inform decisions about parole and release raises the spectre of vengeful victims acting against offenders. Similar concerns have been raised regarding information presented in victim statements. However, the uses to which victim reports are put raises additional concerns in consideration of offenders' rights: namely, should offenders who have been sentenced and punished be subjected to further restrictions on their liberty post-release? Having 'served their time', offenders whose victims express particular concerns about their offender's release face the double jeopardy of being 'punished' once again. Contrastingly, other offenders with similar criminal records, and victims who express no such concern, may not be faced with restrictions on their movements post-release.

Other common law jurisdictions inform victims about their offender's release and any conditions imposed. For example, New Zealand allows victims to request notification concerning the release or escape of prisoners, and to request dates of parole hearings at which the Parole Board is required to have any submissions made by victims. In New South Wales, Australia, victims have the right to make submissions to the Parole Board for consideration. And in Canada, victims may apply to be an observer at their offender's parole hearing. But, as Préfontaine (2000) notes in relation to Canada, conflicts arise between a victim's need for information and the offender's right to privacy. Conversely, a victim's need for confidentiality to protect his or her safety, when raising concerns about an offender' release, are compromised by the fact that offenders usually know their victims and can assume their influence on any restrictive parole and release practices.

In England and Wales, under the terms of the European Convention on Human Rights (as incorporated into the 1998 Human Rights Act), offenders are allowed to see the content of the probation officer's report, which may contain information supplied by the victim. In contrast, victims can receive only limited information about their offenders. A victim's 'right' to have their concerns detailed in a victim report, which is then incorporated into a probation officer's report, is therefore a double-edged privilege; it may allow victims' legitimate concerns to be taken into account, but it also raises the prospect of offenders, having seen the report, becoming more vengeful towards victims who have requested restrictions. As Crawford and Enterkin state (1999: 88): 'The findings from this research suggest the urgent need to clarify issues regarding the lack of confidentiality of the information provided by Victim Reports.' Victims need to be aware of the potential dangers posed by airing their concerns about an offender's release in a victim report. Some of these implicit dangers should be alleviated by a filtering process that moderates victims' concerns through probation officers' reports. However, offenders are always free to interpret the cause of any restrictions placed on their release as they see fit.

External influences: the European Convention on Human Rights and other instruments

Finally, any discussion of victims' and offenders' rights, as they exist in England and Wales at the beginning of the twenty-first century, cannot take place without consideration of external European influences on domestic law.

The criminal justice system in England and Wales is now open to scrutiny by European legal instruments and institutions. When looking to question underlying principles of justice, with respect to what is a 'fair trial' and victims' rights, we can turn to the example of the European Convention on Human Rights, and its platform for action, the European Court of Human Rights, as providing the benchmark against which to question established principles of justice.

In addition to the European Convention on Human Rights and the European Court of Human Rights, a range of international instruments exist that reflect and enhance changes in criminal justice cultures towards recognition and implementation of victim-centred justice. These include the Council of Europe's Recommendation (85)11 on the Position of the Victim in the Framework of Criminal Law and Procedure, and the more recent 2001 Framework Decision by the Council of the European Union on the Standing of Victims in Criminal Proceedings. While the Framework Decision, unlike Council of Europe Recommendations, is binding on all member states of the European Union, the decisions of the European Court of Human Rights, in line with the Convention, have the greatest impact on how justice is done in England and Wales. Since the Human Rights Act 1998, all courts in England and Wales are now required to apply the European Convention on Human Rights to national law.

Although witnesses have, in reality, very few substantive rights in England and Wales, their rights are inadvertently established through careful application of international law on admissibility of evidence and the defendant's right to a fair trial. Specifically, Article 6 of the European

Convention on Human Rights focuses on the rights of the defence to a fair and public trial. Other articles in the Convention deal with life, liberty and security of the person, and therefore have implications for both defendants and witnesses (victims) as they progress through the criminal justice process.

The European Convention on Human Rights: Article 6

In setting out defendants' rights in Article 6, the Convention indirectly indicates what can and cannot be done with respect to witnesses. For example, Article 6 refers to the need to protect the private life of the *parties* involved, and gives weight to special circumstances where publicity would prejudice the *interests of justice*, therein referring not only to defendants' rights but also to those of witnesses.

Defence, cross-examination and legal representation

Importantly, given the new provisions in England and Wales that prevent defendants from personally cross-examining witnesses in rape cases, Article 6 refers to the defendant's right to (paragraph 3.c) 'defend himself in person or through legal assistance of his own choosing or, if he has not sufficient means to pay for legal assistance, to be given it free when the interests of justice so require [sic]'. And paragraph 3.d is relevant as it entitles the defendant to 'examine or have examined witnesses against him and to obtain the attendance and examination of witnesses on his behalf under the same conditions as witnesses against him [sic]'. In other words, according to paragraphs 3.c and 3.d, the defendant does not have the absolute right to defend himself or herself and directly cross-examine witnesses in every case, but his or her rights are guaranteed through legal representation; herein, the victim can, in special circumstances, be saved from cross-examination by the defendant.

Public trials and admissibility of evidence

Ideally, in instances of actual or potential witness intimidation, such as those related to organised crime, exceptions should be made to permit witnesses to testify using alternative means other than having to appear in open court. As a general rule, according to judgments made by the European Court of Human Rights, special measures for witnesses should be used sparingly and in exceptional circumstances. The Convention guarantees that trials are undertaken in the public domain as a safeguard against the private administration of justice, and Article 6 secures everyone's right to have a charge against him or her brought before a court of law. However, as a result of judgments by the Court,[15] these rights are not absolute, and therefore are subject to certain limitations depending on the case in question. So, for example, the media and the public can be excluded from all or part of a trial when this is seen as being in the interests of justice. Where these provisions prove insufficient, in cases involving witness intimidation, other measures can be adopted.

Specifically, in cases where the defendant has threatened the complainant or a witness, the European Court of Human Rights has interpreted the Convention as providing for the exclusion of the defendant from court providing that his or her defence lawyer is present and can put questions to the complainant or witness. In the same vein, statements made to the police or judicial authorities prior to the trial can be used as evidence providing that the defence has the opportunity to challenge the credibility or reliability of the witness and his or her evidence. And, in exceptional circumstances, a statement made by an anonymous witness can be used at trial providing there is corroborative evidence to support it.

The anonymous witness

The idea of the anonymous witness presents perhaps the greatest challenge to the idea of a fair trial under Article 6. The Council of Europe, in its explanatory memorandum to Recommendation (1997) 13 on 'Intimidation of Witnesses and the Rights of the Defence', outlines the risks involved in allowing anonymous witnesses:[16]

1. the anonymous witness could be unreliable for subjective reasons associated with his or her personal history – which could not be brought to light without the defence knowing his or her identity and verifying his or her personal history;
2. the anonymous witness might have had in the past some undisclosed relationship or contact or indirect connection with the defendant – which might be the source of a prejudiced attitude towards the defendant;
3. the anonymous witness could be plotting against the defendant.

However, given these reservations and others concerning alternatives for witness testimony and cross-examination, such as video-recorded evidence-in-chief, the Council of Europe suggests, in relation to Recommendation (1997) 13, that:

> under certain circumstances, where criminal proceedings deal with very serious allegations in the field of organised crime and the life and freedom of the witness is in danger, the rights of the defence must be weighed against the rights of the witness and the duty of the state to do justice. The recommendation emphasises, in accordance with the rulings of the European Court of Human Rights, the need for striking a balance between the interests of society and the rights of the defence.[17]

As an illustration, the case of *Doorson* v. *The Netherlands* was challenged in the European Court of Human Rights because witnesses who knew the accused, an alleged drug dealer, were allowed to testify anonymously.[18] However, in its ruling the Court accepted this procedure, particularly as the original court's conviction was not solely based on the evidence of anonymous witnesses, and defence counsel was able to cross-examine witnesses at an earlier pre-trial hearing. The Court ruled that the defendant's interests were outweighed by considerations for the safety of witnesses.

Doak (2000: 388), commenting on the European Court of Human Right's ruling in the case of *Doorson* v. *The Netherlands*, states:

> For too long the state versus offender duality has meant that reform of the treatment of witnesses in court has been slow moving . . . The European Court of Human Rights has effectively embarked upon an interest-balancing approach through the extension of the 'right to a fair trial' in Doorson to victims as well as witnesses.

But in contrast to Doak's reading of *Doorson* v. *The Netherlands*, Spencer and Spencer (2001: 9) argue that this particular case is exceptional, and they therefore call for preservation of the status quo with respect to the current place of the witness in a criminal trial:

> The witness, including the victim-witness has no substantive claim
> against the state in the court arena because her life or liberty are not at
> stake . . . Gratuitous intimidatory cross-examination should of course be
> banned if it is obscuring truth-finding or is irrelevant but the consideration
> of the discomfort of adult witnesses should not permit inroads into the
> rights of the defandant . . . The victim does not have the right to a fair trial,
> only to courtesy and protection that does not impinge on the fairness of
> proceedings.

Generally speaking, in the interests of a fair trial, special provisions, such as witness anonymity, are only admissible in exceptional circumstances and providing defence counsel has the right to put questions to witnesses. In the 1990s, Germany and Austria amended their Codes of Criminal Procedure to allow for witnesses' personal details to be kept secret from the case file that forms the bulk of evidence presented at trial.[19] In this way, in an effort to secure their safety, a vulnerable or intimidated witness's personal data does not become public knowledge but, at the same time, defence counsel has the right to question witnesses. However, as Spencer and Spencer (2001: 10) argue: 'In the increasing emphasis on the admittedly seductive concept of finding a balance between competing rights there is some risk of eroding defendants' rights by stealth, by the cumulative imposition of restrictive provisions.'

Changing European responses to victims

Commentators such as Spencer and Spencer depict the enhancement of victims' rights as being in direct opposition to defendants' rights. In so doing they fail to grasp that the adversarial trial process, as it currently exists, is perhaps not the best advert for a 'fair trial', and is not always in the best interests of either offenders or victims.

A guilty plea in common law stops the trial process in its tracks, and proceedings move on to sentencing. In comparison, inquisitorial systems continue the trial process and examine the contents of the case file to ascertain what actually happened. In this regard, principles of what constitutes 'truth finding' and a 'fair trial' differ greatly between common law and inquisitorial systems of justice. In turn, how evidence is collected and what evidence is admissible in court is judged differently between common law and inquisitorial systems, with far more scope for hearsay evidence in continental justice systems. Providing that defence counsel has the opportunity to question evidence and the reliability of the witness, it is generally concluded that the principle of a fair trial is upheld in inquisitorial systems without the need for direct face-to-face cross-examination of witnesses.

Finally, while international legal instruments have tended to focus their attention on protection of witnesses in high-profile cases involving organised crime and terrorism, there is great scope for extending these measures to a range of cases where witness security is needed. The Council of Europe's explanatory memorandum for Recommendation (1997) 13, on witness protection and the rights of the defence, specifically refers to the need for enhanced witness protection in cases involving organised crime *and* intra-familial violence as these cases are particularly difficult to prosecute because of witness intimidation. The explanatory memorandum identifies primary responsibility for witness protection as lying with the police and/or other specialist agencies that take care of witnesses. The memorandum lists a range of initiatives ranging from the relatively simple, such as non-disclosure of a witness's address, through to the time-consuming and costly, such as change of identity and relocation, which can be put in place to protect witnesses in both low-profile and high-profile cases.[20]

As most jurisdictions place the average witness under a legal obligation to testify in court once summoned to do so, with notable exceptions under 'professional privilege', such as priests and medical doctors, a witness's refusal to do so is generally punishable under law. In England and Wales, the wilful non-attendance of a witness summoned to court constitutes a contempt of court. However, in recognition of the problems of intimidation that 'ordinary' witnesses can face, and not just witnesses in organised crime cases, jurisdictions are gradually responding by providing witnesses with protective measures before, during and after a criminal trial (Fyfe and McKay, 2000; Fyfe, 2001). These protective measures serve to alleviate the worst aspects of threatening behaviour towards witnesses from the defence and his/her family, friends and associates, but at the same time they challenge the principle of a 'fair trial' that is wedded to the rights of the defence.

For too long, many jurisdictions failed to match the civil duty of witnesses to appear before a court of law and testify with adequate insurances that they would be safe to do so. The responsibility to testify was not matched with the right to security. Jurisdictions are now gradually responding to the general neglect of intimidated witnesses in the criminal justice process, and much of this is due to the influence of the European Convention on Human Rights and the case law of the European Court of Human Rights. At the same time as the needs and rights of intimidated witnesses are being addressed, the treatment of vulnerable witnesses, such as children, is now a central feature of early twenty-first-century justice in many European jurisdictions, such as England and Wales, the Netherlands, and Scandinavian countries. Significant changes are afoot in criminal justice systems that have for too long expected witnesses to appear in court without adequate provision for their well-being and safety.

Concluding comments

Victim statements and victim reports that are carefully moderated through the appropriate criminal justice channels can serve to provide information about victims that can usefully inform sentencing and release decisions for offenders. In the case of victim statements, threats to defendants'/offenders' rights are only possible when this information is used prior to sentencing in a manner that allows for the discretionary impact of crime to take precedence and inform sentencing decisions. Sentencing policy that is based on the impact of crime according to the individual victim can only lead to justice inequality and the erosion of defendants' due process in law. In this regard, victim statements and victim reports need to be carefully monitored by criminal justice agencies and discarded when found to incorporate inaccurate or exaggerated information about the impact of crime on victims.

Whether victim statements and victim reports can be said to enhance victims' rights is debatable. Undoubtedly they give victims a 'voice' in common law systems where previously they were silenced. But at the same time they tend to raise victims' expectations about their impact on sentencing and release decisions, expectations that cannot be met because of due regard for defendants'/offenders' rights. At present, any criminal justice developments in England and Wales that serve to take account of victims in the run up to, during, and after a criminal trial only scratch the surface of a system that is based on protecting the rights of the defence/offender against the might of the State in its role as prosecutor. Defence lawyers cling to the terminology of 'complainant' to ensure that the status of 'victim' is not evoked in a case until the defendant is proved guilty. However, in the same vein, reference to the 'defendant' assumes innocence when guilt might be the case. But, as defence lawyers would be all too keen to point out, the defendant has much more to lose if found guilty as, in serious cases, their freedom can be removed by the State. In comparison, while the State does not threaten to revoke a victim's freedom, the victim's freedom to go about their business in the aftermath of crime is often severely restricted because of fear, intimidation and post-traumatic stress.

To position defendants' rights in opposition to victims' rights is to misrepresent new avenues for criminal justice development. The biggest challenge for victim-centred criminal justice initiatives is to convince the criminal justice establishment that they do not erode defendants' rights. The culture of adversarial justice in England and Wales, and other common law jurisdictions, is not well-placed to incorporate victim-centred developments that challenge established ways of doing justice. Arguably, victim-centred initiatives, as set out in the 1999 Youth Justice and Criminal Evidence Act, and subsequent developments on it, only chip away at the edges of a system devoted to confrontational cross-examination in open court. Under the present common law of England and Wales, there is little evidence to support the contention that defendants' rights are being undermined by a more victim-friendly justice system. The European Court of Human Rights along with new restorative justice developments (outlined in the next chapter) are challenging the current system, from outside, to balance the needs and rights of both victims and offenders.

With this in mind, the next chapter introduces some of the debates surrounding the current promotion of 'restorative justice' as an alternative to traditional forms of adversarial conflict resolution.

Suggested reading

Rock's detailed critical account of the workings of an English crown court, though over a decade old (1993), still provides a good introduction to the processes that underpin the adversarial trial. From here, the Home Office's comprehensive paper *Speaking Up for Justice*, together with Ellison's (2001) monograph on vulnerable witnesses and Fyfe's (2001) on intimidated witnesses, present a rounded introduction and thorough critique of the shortcomings of adversarial justice with respect to vulnerable, intimidated and at-risk victims/witnesses. Arguably, publications by Ashworth (1993, 2000) offer the best read – that is, the most succinct and rounded – in consideration of developments in the area of victims' rights and their impact on defendants' rights and criminal procedure, with respect both to England and Wales and to the recent influence of European legal instruments. Some of the most developed arguments on balancing offender and victim rights have evolved in response to the introduction of victim (impact) statements in North America and, more recently, England and Wales; see Erez (1994, 2000); Hoyle et al. (1998); Morgan and Sanders (1999).

Notes

1. Examples do exist of other common law jurisdictions where restorative justice principles and practice function as alternatives to traditional retributive justice: notably, New Zealand's juvenile justice system, and, closer to home, Northern Ireland, which is in the process of reviewing its criminal justice practice and making considerable inroads towards inclusion of restorative justice principles (Dignan, 2000; O'Mahoney et al., 2002).
2. See www.barcouncil.org.uk – Conduct in Court, paragraph 708.
3. Home Office (1998) *Speaking Up For Justice*, London: Home Office, paragraph 8.50.
4. Home Office (1998) *Speaking Up For Justice*, London: Home Office, paragraph 9.58.
5. Using evidence from an Australian case study of Aboriginal and non-Aboriginal women, Cossins (2003) offers a recent feminist interpretation of how women complainants experience rape trials according to their race/indigenous status; she concludes that sexual assault law reforms, in their construction of a generic 'woman', fail to challenge deeply held and harmful stereotypes about the sexual behaviour of Aboriginal and black complainants.
6. www.cps.gov.uk.
7. www.cjsonline.org/news/2003/november/domestic.html.
8. www.homeoffice.gov.uk/docs/faqwitnesses.pdf.
9. Reported in Ellison (2001: 62, fn 158).
10. Home Office's Victim's Charter Pilot Project Information Pack, 1996, as referred to in Hoyle et al. (1998: 6).
11. The 'One-Stop-Shop' pilots (see Hoyle et al., 1998) consisted of the following. Of the 289 victims interviewed as part of the research, 46 per cent opted to receive information via the OSS pilot. Victims were supplied with information, via the police, about the progress of their case through the criminal justice process; for example: charge laid against the defendant; date of first hearing. Most victims who opted in wanted to know everything about the progress of their case, but the OSS was limited with regard to what it could reveal. The research indicated that the OSS helped most victims opting in to know more about the criminal justice system, and to be slightly more satisfied with it. But one-fifth of victims who opted in felt they did not get the information they wanted; a third thought information came too late; and almost half would have liked to get information in a different manner. These victims' expectations of the criminal justice system, and the information they would receive about their case, seemed to be raised unrealistically as a result of opting in to the OSS pilots.
12. Hoyle et al. (1998: 26).
13. Hoyle et al. (1998: 32).
14. Home Office Probation Circular 61/1995, 1, paragraph 4.

15. Golder (judgment of 21 February 1975, Series A, No. 18); Deweer (judgment of 27 February 1980, Series A, No. 35); see Council of Europe, Committee of Ministers, Explanatory Memorandum on Recommendation (1997) 13 on 'Intimidation of Witnesses and the Rights of the Defence', paragraph 33.
16. Council of Europe, Committee of Ministers, Explanatory Memorandum on Recommendation (1997) 13 on Intimidation of Witnesses and the Rights of the Defence; see: http://cm.coe.int/ta/rec/1997/97r13.html, paragraph 37.
17. Ibid., paragraph 64.
18. *Doorson* v. *The Netherlands* (1996) 22 EHRR 330.
19. Council of Europe, Committee of Ministers, Explanatory Memorandum on Recommendation (1997) 13 on Intimidation of Witnesses and the Rights of the Defence; see: http://cm.coe.int/ta/rec/1997/97r13.html, paragraph 59.
20. Ibid., paragraph 50.

Chapter 7

Restorative justice: victim-centred paradigm shift?

Introducing themes for discussion

The previous chapter addressed the problematic demands of attempting to balance the needs and rights of victims and offenders in the setting of an adversarial justice system that has, until recently, disproportionately focused on upholding defendants' rights. As traditional criminal justice comes to terms with the need to integrate a victim perspective, so a 'new' challenge to its established focus on the offender has emerged in the guise of 'restorative justice'. This chapter asks whether restorative justice can, as some proponents argue, offer a victim-centred paradigm shift away from the limitations of traditional justice. At the same time, the chapter discusses the limitations of restorative justice as 'victim-centred' in its practical application, its deference to offenders, and its appeals to abstract ideas concerning 'community'.

The chapter begins by asking what is 'restorative justice'. The origins and application of restorative justice are introduced with respect to its development across different continents in various forms from mediation through to family group conferencing. With examples of restorative justice from around the world, the chapter turns to legislative and practical applications of restorative justice in Britain in terms of restorative elements in the 1998 Crime and Disorder Act, the 1999 Youth Justice and Criminal Evidence Act, and recent initiatives by Thames Valley Police. Having presented a range of examples of restorative justice, the scope and potential of restorative justice are critically reviewed in light of its claims to be variously victim-, offender- and community-centred.

The chapter sets out to question 'who' restorative justice benefits. Ultimately, it asks whether restorative justice presents a challenge to traditional criminal justice practice or whether it should be more accurately viewed as an additional resource for case disposal.

What is restorative justice?

Defining restorative justice

The definition of restorative justice is anything but clear-cut. There is a great deal of disagreement between restorative justice advocates, and to the non-specialist observer this can serve to confuse restorative justice with other initiatives that do not stem from restorative principles. Because of this, as Dignan notes (2000), the conflation of restorative justice with other criminal and non-criminal justice based reform initiatives, which emerge from different philosophical and policy agendas (particularly retributive justice), is not helpful when attempting to interpret and evaluate restorative justice as a distinctive justice ideology.

Tony Marshall, as one 'voice' in the restorative justice field, defines 'restorative justice' as (1997: 15) 'a process whereby all the parties with a stake in a specific offence come together to resolve collectively how to deal with the aftermath of the offence and its implications for the future'. Marshall proceeds to break down the individual components of this definition to clarify how restorative justice is different from established forms of criminal justice.

Referring to the 'parties with a stake in an offence', Marshall includes victim and offender, together with the possibility of incorporating the families of each, and members of their wider communities who are affected by and can contribute to the resolution of the offence or conflict. He adds that the 'parties' concerned may also include representatives from criminal justice and social agencies. It is with this tentative inclusion of criminal justice representatives that restorative justice emerges as essentially different from established forms of criminal justice. In other words, lay people, who are directly affected by an offence or an interpersonal conflict, are central to the restorative justice process. Professionals are not at the centre of the restorative justice process. In turn, the parties involved 'come together' in an informal setting, away from the restrictions of the court room, to resolve the circumstances and aftermath of the event in question. This 'coming together' can take a variety of forms from a one-off meeting between victim and offender that is supervised by a professional or volunteer mediator (mediation), through to an extensive meeting, or a series of meetings, involving all those with a stake in the offence (restorative conference).

There are variations on a theme with respect to the above. For example, Bazemore and Walgrave (1999) critique Marshall's definition as 'too narrow' and, significantly, note its failure to refer to 'restoration'. Instead Bazemore and Walgrave offer a wider definition of restorative justice which recognises that some sanctions can be restorative without being part of a restorative process, and, likewise, restoration can occur without the presence of all parties involved. Their interpretation of restorative justice refers to it as (1999: 48) 'every action that is primarily oriented towards doing justice by restoring the harm that has been caused by a crime'. Following the lead of Bazemore and Walgrave, the central remit of any meeting which calls itself 'restorative' should be the desire to 'repair the damage done' to, and between, victim and offender, and, potentially, other key parties involved in an offence.

In turn, other descriptions of restorative justice stress different elements: for example, *reconciliation* between victim and offender, often with the inclusion of a sincere apology from offender to victim; *restitution* from the offender to the victim, often in the form of monetary compensation or the performance of a specific task; *rehabilitation* of the offender is also seen as a desirable outcome of restorative justice practice in an effort to reduce recidivism and therefore prevent further victimisation.

Dignan (2000) offers a more generic description of key attributes underpinning restorative initiatives. These are (2000: 1): (1) the principle of inclusivity; (2) an attempt to balance the different sets of interests that are acknowledged to be affected when a criminal offence is committed; (3) a form of practice that is based on the principle of non-coercion; and (4) a problem-solving orientation. Dignan returns restorative justice to its underlying principles in an effort to distinguish it from non-restorative practices that are often 'dressed up' as restorative, such as mediation involving elements of non-restorative offender 'shaming'.

In centrally considering the needs of victim and offender in the resolution of conflicts and the reconciliation of events, the focus of restorative justice is far removed from a traditional criminal justice concern of retribution against the offender. Here, Marshall's reference to the 'aftermath' of the offence and its 'implications for the future' denotes that the well-being of victim and offender, in light of the wider involvement of family and 'community', is central to the restorative process at the time of the restorative meeting and afterwards.

Marshall (1997: 15) sets out what he refers to as 'the features of restorative justice that virtually every proponent would advance':

1. prevention of reoffending;
2. helping victims more;
3. preventing the escalation of formal justice (and resources);
4. the re-creation of community.

In turn, these objectives are to be achieved through:

1. making room for personal involvement;
2. seeing the problem in its social context;
3. looking to the future (problem-solving).

The Home Office, in its recent claims to adopt restorative justice principles through the 1998 Crime and Disorder Act and the 1999 Youth Justice and Criminal Evidence Act, provides a definition of restorative justice that encompasses 'restoration, reintegration and responsibility'. This trium-virate of restorative principles can be variously victim-centred and/or offender-centred depending on the particular approach of different (so-called) restorative initiatives. For example, 'responsibility' can imply the offender's responsibility to make amends to his/her victim(s) and the wider community, but it can also relate to the victim's responsibility to follow through any reparation agreement with an offender, and, in turn, the community's responsibility to see that justice is done to offender and victim. Later sections in the chapter elaborate on the theme of 'who' so-called restorative practices serve; suffice it to say here that inter-pretation and application of the 'Three Rs' is not as clear-cut as some restorative justice proponents suggest.

In sum, restorative justice is a wide-ranging philosophy and a diverse range of practices that can be variously labelled and defined according to the interests of 'who' is defining it. For example, Sebba (1996), in his discussion of mediation and other forms of alternative dispute resolution, employs the term 'informal justice' rather than 'restorative justice'. Other terms include 'relational justice', 'reparative justice', 'communitarian justice' and 'peace making' (to name but a few). Victims and offenders may place a different emphasis on what it means in comparison with the definitions offered by the organisations running diverse forms of justice intervention that can be labelled 'restorative'. In turn, no two victims or offenders can be expected to agree on its definition as befits their own circumstances. What this apparent 'confusion' illustrates is, at best, a healthy diversity of interpretation and practical application of diverse restorative justice ideals. In light of the intense debates by academics and practitioners that currently surround restorative justice (Hirsch et al., 2003; McEvoy and Newburn, 2003; McLaughlin et al., 2003), it would appear to be anything but a foregone solution to some of the problems of tradi-tional justice.

Ancient ideas resurrected

Restorative justice might appear as a new development to challenge established criminal justice practice. However, as Christie points out in his seminal article on 'conflicts as property' (1977), restorative justice is anything but a 'new' idea. Rather, restorative justice is an old idea resurrected in new guises that reflect particular cultural origins and practi-tioner/community settings.

Christie argues that the modern criminal trial has effectively 'stolen' conflicts, or crimes and disputes, from the people and the communities directly affected. As he states (1977: 4): 'Lawyers are particularly good at stealing conflicts. They are trained for it.' In comparing the ancient practice of justice in rural Tanzania with the setting of the criminal trial in Scandinavian countries, Christie makes a number of points in his effort to highlight the neglect of the victim by modern criminal justice. He argues that in the modern criminal trial two important things have happened to marginalise the parties most affected by crime. First, the professionalisation of justice has resulted in the interests of both defendants and victims, as the central parties involved, being represented by lawyers and the State. Second, he asserts that victims are so over-represented by the State that they are pushed to the very margins of criminal proceedings. In other words, victims are over-represented by others to the extent that their experience of victimisation pales alongside the interests of the State to see that justice is accomplished, primarily on behalf of the State.

What Christie is centrally berating in his article is the evolution of 'western' criminal justice that has repositioned crime from a harm committed against the individual, and the community, to a harm committed against the State. With the example of rural Africa, alongside historical references from 'western' culture (Davis, 1992; Mawby and Walklate, 1994), Christie proffers other times and places where victims play, or played, a more central role in the solution of their own conflicts. In these settings, the victim's 'voice', rather than the lawyer's 'voice', is central to the initiation and practice of justice in the resolution of conflicts. Having noted western society's shift in the ownership of conflicts and 'victimhood', Christie acknowledges how the law has come to reflect the segmentation of society in developed industrial nations and the re-establishment of what he refers to as a 'caste society'. In other words, as personal life becomes more complex, as society moves from an agrarian state to an industrialised state, so our personal points of reference, in identifiable local communities, become diluted and fragmented with respect to the demands of work, relationships, leisure and travel. In light of this, the professionalisation of criminal justice has become a necessary cornerstone of the modern state. Christie goes on to suggest that late modernity represents the depersonalisation of social life to the extent that crime against people's 'honour' is absent and, as a consequence of this, the State has come to 'own' people's experiences of crime, conflict and injustice. While Christie notes that certain interpersonal conflicts, such as domestic violence, have been made visible in this new social order, he suggests that they are without solution in the context of the modern trial setting.

Having outlined the State's progressive 'theft' of people's conflicts, through the professionalisation of criminal justice, Christie suggests possibilities for victim-centred justice by focusing his attentions on the criminal trial and the establishment of a three-stage trial process. In his simple three-stage setting, the first stage, as with current practice, establishes whether the law has been broken and, if so, by whom. From here, the trial evolves into the second stage, the 'victim stage', whereupon every detail relevant to the victim is aired at the trial. Having established the defendant's guilt, the victim stage proceeds to consider what can be done for the victim by, in turn, offender, local neighbourhood, and

State. Finally, the third stage of the trial process focuses on the offender's punishment and the circumstances of the offender. With this three-stage trial process Christie is not offering a thoroughly considered alternative to the established practice of the criminal trial. Rather, he is attempting to invert the criminal trial's skewed focus on the defendant's needs and rights, and those of the State, by placing consideration of the victim as a central focus in the trial process. But whether Christie's ideas can be described as 'restorative', in light of the above definitions, is debatable.

What Christie offers is an idealistic but nonetheless thought-provoking critique of the modern criminal trial in the tradition of what Sebba (1996) refers to as the 'radical romantics' (see also Danzig, 1973). With his example of community justice in Africa he is guilty, along with others (Nadar and Todd, 1978), of a certain romanticism in the worst traditions of anthropological investigation. More recent advocates of restorative justice have come to critique the idealisation of aboriginal justice as neglectful of the power imbalances in any society which, as in the modern trial setting, are difficult to avoid (Daly, 2000, 2002). However, idealisation of variously labelled 'aboriginal' or 'native' practices, containing elements of restorative justice, is still found in calls for recognition of restorative justice (Winfree, 2000). Idealisation tends to stem from a limited interpretation of restorative justice as something in opposition to established criminal justice, which is conceived as essentially 'bad'. However, in their efforts to advance a challenge to the established norms and practices of criminal justice, early advocates of restorative justice can be excused for their depiction, somewhat uncritically, of an idealistic alternative (Zehr, 1990). While it is easy to negatively critique aspects of Christie's article, his ideas reflect a groundswell of developments from the 1970s, both practical and academic, which advanced the cause of restorative justice.

Mediation as restorative justice?

In the 1970s, Christie was not a lone voice in his expressed desire for an alternative model of justice that would centrally involve people in the resolution of their own conflicts (Barnett, 1977; Danzig, 1973). Developments were taking place in North America and Europe that would set in motion mediation practices between victims and offenders.

Having provided a brief explanation of what restorative justice should, ideally, aim to encompass, this chapter goes on to describe and critique these early initiatives, which were alleged to be reconciliatory for victims and offenders, as they developed in North America and Britain. These various initiatives were based on mediation between victim and offender, either directly (face to face) in the presence of a trained mediator, or indirectly through a go-between in the form of a mediator. In some cases, mediation has involved meetings between small groups of victims and offenders who are not directly linked by the same crime, although they will be indirectly linked by the same type of offence (Dignan, 1992). However, mediation generally refers to cases where mediators work with victims and offenders whose experience of crime is directly linked. The point at which mediation enters the criminal justice system, or remains outside it, is as varied as the initiatives themselves. Mediation can take place as an alternative to prosecution, prior to sentencing, or after sentencing. And, in briefly characterising mediation, it has to be noted that, to a large extent, it focuses on young offenders more than adult offenders, and therefore tends to be utilised in less serious cases of offending.[1]

Whether the initiatives described below can be viewed as 'restorative', in light of later theoretical and practical developments in restorative justice, is questionable. Similarly, whether they are more accurately described as offender-centred, rather than victim-centred, is open to debate.

Early mediation developments in North America

Martin Wright (1991) charts the progress of various mediation initiatives, from the 1970s onwards, that emerged in North America. What is striking about his account of developments in North America is the important part played by religious organisations, or individuals' religious affiliations, in the promotion of mediation. For example, a Mennonite Protestant probation officer, Mark Yantzi, was instrumental in involving Ontario's Mennonite Central Committee in the development of an initiative that brought together offenders and victims for the purpose of conflict resolution and monetary reparation. This personal initiative fed directly into the development, in 1975, of Ontario's Victim/Offender Reconciliation Project (later programme) (VORP) under the direction of the Ontario Ministry of Corrections and the Area Probation Officer. In turn, VORP's ideas were adopted by the Mennonite community in Indiana, from where probation, in collaboration with the local community, developed mediation initiatives. Howard Zehr, the director of a Mennonite organisation for ex-offenders in Indiana, became involved in Indiana's community-based VORP scheme and subsequently, having written about VORP (Zehr, 1990), has become a significant North American figure in the promotion of, and discourse concerning, victim–offender reconciliation.

Wright's (1991) documentation of VORP's emergence is interesting for its portrayal of how religion played a role in the development of mediation practices in North America. While 'Christian' values of forgiveness and reconciliation are found in liberal western cultures, 'Christian' values are also replete with conservative references to retributive justice. However, rather than focus on VORP's religious origins, it is more useful to examine criminal justice's neglect of certain ideals such as forgiveness and reconciliation. The dominant retributive tone of criminal justice, set against the apparent failure of rehabilitation initiatives for offenders during the 1970s (or the 'treatment' model), is partially responsible for the development of alternative practices, for offenders and victims, that originate both from within and without criminal justice. On top of this, alternatives to punishment, including those which appear to emphasise victim–offender reconciliation, are also promoted for the practical purpose of diverting offenders from imprisonment and as a response to the fiscal problems of balancing the criminal justice purse. However, there is no guarantee that restorative initiatives, if carried out with due care and thought for the causes and aftermath of crime, are a cheap alternative to imprisonment.

What is important in consideration of 'how' and 'why' victim–offender mediation emerged, more so than the religious affiliation of individuals who personally promote ideals of reconciliation, is the institutional origins of different mediation initiatives. While the Mennonite community, alongside the Quakers, was instrumental in the North American promotion of VORP, its key players were also directly working with the criminal justice system. In this respect, 'where' restorative justice emerges, be this with a local community initiative, a school programme, the probation service, or local judges, is important with respect to the emphasis that a particular initiative adopts as being part of or external to the established system of criminal justice. In this respect, we can trace how the idea of restorative justice as a wholesale challenge to established criminal justice is, to some extent, dependent on 'where' significant programmes originated: that is, which organisations or institutions were primarily responsible for promoting reconciliation programmes. In turn, the offender-centred or victim-centred emphasis of reconciliation initiatives reflects the particular remit of different criminal justice institutions. So, for example, juvenile justice focuses its application of potentially reconciliatory or restorative programmes on young offenders. Herein, the victim-centred focus of reconciliation initiatives, or the actual reconciliatory nature of so-called 'reconciliation' or 'restorative' programmes, cannot be assumed.

In practice, it appears that the early Canadian VORP initiatives emphasised restitution from the offender to the victim, in the form of monetary compensation, while playing down the potential for reconciliation, which it was felt could dissuade victims from taking part in the process (Dittenhofer and Ericson, 1983). Likewise, monetary compensation featured significantly in the US VORP initiatives (Coates and Gehm, 1989). While monetary compensation may be a strong incentive for victims to take part in programmes, the reconciliatory or offender-centred agenda of various schemes must not be hidden from them. To this end, victims cannot be misled about the motives of particular initiatives and their expected outcomes. Similarly, in emphasising monetary restitution, programmes are in danger of misinforming victims with regard to the amount and the actual payment of compensation they are likely to receive.

Early mediation developments in Britain

In Britain, the probation service and parts of the criminal justice system concerned with young offenders have played a significant role in promoting initiatives that have, to a greater or lesser degree, advanced ideals which can be described as 'restorative'. Mirroring the evolution of restorative events in the United States, 1979 saw the foundation of a reparation scheme for juvenile offenders by the Exeter Joint Services Youth Support Team (Harding, 1986; Wright, 1991). As in the United States, individual probation officers in one part of the country, the south-west, were particularly important in developing victim–offender reparation schemes. In the same period, and in the same area of the country, probation officers were also involved in a ground-breaking initiative to develop a scheme specifically supporting victims of crime – NAVSS (the National Association of Victim Support Services, the forerunner of Britain's Victim Support; see Chapter 4).

One could argue that the early arrival of alternatives to custody in England and Wales, in the form of the 1973 community service order, served to encourage ideas about offender reparation to victims. However, criminal justice attempts, throughout the 1970s and 1980s, to divert young offenders from prosecution and internment at Her Majesty's pleasure, through, most significantly, application of the police caution, did not result in reconciliation and reparation for the victims concerned (Cavadino and Dignan, 1996). Arguably, at the height of its efforts to divert young offenders from prosecution, British criminal justice succeeded in sidelining the concerns of victims who were directly affected by the actions of young offenders. For example, as Wright (1991) notes, the Northamptonshire restoration scheme, as an example of one of the earliest British victim–offender reparation schemes, established in 1981, was primarily set up to increase the use of police cautions for young offenders in an effort to divert them from prosecution. In other words, and confirming the critiques of Ashworth (2000), victims, in the name of reparation, can be used in the service of offenders and criminal justice. In this respect, these schemes cannot strictly be referred to as 'restorative'. However, if reparation schemes which are primarily set up to divert young offenders from prosecution inadvertently assist victims, either through indirect or direct mediation, then this is not in itself a bad outcome.

Besides these individual efforts to promote victim–offender reparation, the real breakthrough in British experimentation with restorative justice came with Home Office funding of four pilot mediation projects in Cumbria, Coventry, Wolverhampton and Leeds (Marshall and Merry, 1990). The projects worked with either police or court-based referrals, and the focus was on young offenders. Theft and criminal damage featured prominently in police-based projects, which predominantly worked with younger offenders with lesser criminal records than their counterparts in court-based projects, who were older and who tended to be charged with more serious offences such as burglary and violence. Mediation, between victim and offender, was offered in two-thirds of police-based schemes and in the majority of court-based schemes. Having been offered mediation, the majority of offenders in both types of scheme, over 90 per cent, were keen to take part, while 79 per cent of victims in police-based schemes, and only 51 per cent of victims in court-based schemes, agreed to mediation (Marshall and Merry, 1990).

The 'success' of the various mediation projects, from the victims' point of view, is partially measured by the fact that over 80 per cent of victims who agreed to mediation felt that meeting their offender had been a valuable experience. Similarly, nearly all offenders who took part in mediation indicated they were glad to have met their victims. In the case of offenders, this willingness to take part, and the satisfaction they received in having done so, may appear as an obvious reaction to circumstances. Given their apprehension and their appearance in a police- or court-based scheme, offenders are likely to view mediation as a means of displaying their willingness to 'make amends' for the harm they inflicted. Cynically, or somewhat naturally, offenders can use mediation in their favour, particularly if mediation is offered prior to sentencing. As Wright (1991) notes with respect to one of the Home Office schemes – while 57 per cent of offenders initially gave mitigation of sentence as a reason for taking part in mediation, this figure dropped to 17 per cent post-mediation, indicating, perhaps, that offenders came to view mediation as more than a means of reducing their sentence. Likewise, we cannot assume that victims' cooperation with mediation is always undertaken for altruistic purposes. Some victims agree to take part in mediation for the sake of retribution, while others may be encouraged by the thought of receiving compensation or some other form of restitution from their offender.

In the case of the Home Office pilots, agreement was reached regarding a mediation settlement in the majority of police- and court-based schemes. However, as 49 per cent of victims in court-based schemes did not take part in mediation, the 'success' of this scheme was already in question. The nature of projects, with respect to the crime and the criminal in question and, importantly, 'who' was victimised, was of crucial importance to the 'success', or otherwise, of each mediation and the initial willingness of victims to take part. With respect to victim profiles and victim–offender relationships, there are a couple of interesting points worth noting from the Home Office pilots. First, two-thirds of victims in police-based schemes and one-third of victims in court-based schemes were businesses and local authority agencies. Second, one-quarter of victims in police-based schemes and one-half of victims in court-based schemes had some previous relationship or acquaintance with the offender; in cases of violence, these figures rose to 76 per cent and 64 per cent respectively (Marshall and Merry, 1990; Wright, 1991). Together, these two factors serve to challenge how we tend to stereotype victimisation as the experience of an individual victim against an offender, and of a victim with no previous relationship to the offender.

As Tudor (2000) points out, in her discussion of the use of mediation in cases of violent crime, a great deal of interpersonal violence, if not 'domestic', involves young men who are acquainted with one another. In these cases mediation has, perhaps, an interventionist role to offer before the escalation of violence between the parties involved. Similarly, as the above highlights, a great deal of crime – such as theft and vandalism, and sometimes violence committed in the course of these crimes – is against businesses and other institutions. There is evidence that these experiences of victimisation, as R. Young points out (2002), can also benefit from restorative justice intervention, though it appears that most restorative justice promoters are less keen to engage with 'corporate crime' as victimisation because businesses do not fit the mould of the 'ideal' and 'deserving' victim.

Ultimately, in the case of England and Wales, victim–offender mediation has not received the support and recognition it deserves. More recently, mediation has re-emerged as one course of action under 'reparation orders' (which were introduced as part of sweeping youth justice reforms under the 1998 Crime and Disorder Act). The 'reparation order' and the more recent 'referral order', which was introduced as part of the 1999 Youth Justice and Criminal Evidence Act, are critiqued later in the chapter as offender-centred initiatives; suffice it to say here that both reparation and referral orders have been dressed up in the language, if not the actual practice, of restorative justice.

Given the traditional remit of probation and youth justice services to work with offenders, new calls to work with victims, through mediation, and latterly reparation and referral orders, have presented something of a conflict of interests. Throughout the late 1980s and 1990s, certain probation services, such as Leeds and Bradford, continued to push mediation in appropriate cases; however, there was no discernible knock-on effect to other regions. A reluctance to work with victims can also be readily understood when due consideration is given to the underfunding of mediation initiatives.

Without the political will and funding supporting mediation initiatives, it is hardly surprising that mediation did not become widespread in the 1980s and early 1990s in England and Wales. Successive governments failed to promote mediation, and it was only in the late 1990s, with the Crime and Disorder Act, that mediation was given a new lease of life through the reparation order.

Towards a holistic restorative justice

It is doubtful whether mediation can, in its past and present incarnations, be accurately described as 'restorative justice'. As Walgrave asserts, in his 'maximalist' interpretation of restorative justice (2000: 263): 'it is not correct to consider mediation (in whatever form) as a synonym for restorative justice'. Much of this wary appraisal of mediation as 'restorative' rests with its principal incarnation as a form of diversion for offenders from prosecution/imprisonment.

Recent developments in restorative justice, such as family group conferencing, appear to advance a more holistic interpretation of what 'restorative' means in practice. An essential difference between mediation and forms of conferencing which have recently taken up the challenge to be restorative, in the face of traditional justice, is the inclusion of a wider 'community' and multiple victimhood in the resolution of conflicts. While mediation is usually limited to an offender, a victim, and a mediator, either in direct or indirect mediation, family group conferencing or community conferencing involves more people in the restorative process – though whether family group conferencing can be described as 'victim-centred' is, in turn, questionable (see later critique of restorative justice as 'paradigm shift').

In searching for 'victim-centred' justice we can display a limited conceptualisation of 'victimhood' which reflects a legal tradition that focuses on the lone victim and the lone offender, with the State as go-between, in the resolution of criminal conflicts. In light of conferencing's attempt to recognise and include multiple 'victimhoods', from the immediate victim through to the wider 'community' and even the offender, we can readdress our hitherto narrow critique of justice as offender *or* victim-centred.

Trail-blazing from New Zealand and Australia

The most significant practical development in recent years towards a holistic form of restorative justice has taken the form of 'family group conferencing'. New Zealand has led the way in family group conferencing, which latterly has been adopted and adapted in England and Wales.[2] At the same time as family group conferencing emerged, Australian criminologist John Braithwaite introduced his ideas on 'reintegrative shaming' as a theoretical and practical response to complement conferencing initiatives.

Maori lessons: the family group conference

Restorative justice, through the application of the family group conference, was able to gain a strong foothold in New Zealand as a result of the 1989

Children, Young Persons and their Families Act. The Act encouraged diversion of young people away from traditional youth justice and, importantly, the courts, through the introduction of an alternative form of dispute resolution in the form of the 'family group conference'. The Act encouraged family group conferencing in cases of minor and serious juvenile offending, both prior and subsequent to arrest. In sum, the Act tried to secure family group conferencing as a prerequisite when dealing with young people and crime.

The Act focused on the idea of rights and responsibilities as a fundamental part of juvenile justice. At the same time it was heavily influenced by traditional Maori concepts of conflict resolution. To this end, the Act set out to get young offenders, their families and their communities to take responsibility for offending. In doing so, the Act asserted that victims' rights, as citizens, should be taken more seriously in a restorative process including offenders, families, communities and victims. However, having encouraged a broad set of people to take on their responsibilities, as citizens, against crime and reoffending, the Act also expected victims, as responsible citizens, to shoulder their responsibilities in the restorative process. In this respect, one might critique the Act for placing too much emphasis on the victim's role in the restorative process, which in traditional criminal justice is normally left to the State (see Chapter 5).

The Act's practical outcome is the 'family group conference'. This (normally) includes the following participants:

- the offender;
- the offender's family (which can extend beyond the immediate family);
- other people invited by the offender's family;
- the victim;
- the victim's support people (these can be family members);
- a representative from the police;
- the conference facilitator in the form of a youth justice coordinator.

Social workers can also attend conferences in cases where a young offender is already under their supervision. Similarly, if the conference takes place subsequent to arrest, once the young person has been involved with the formal justice system, then a lawyer or youth justice advocate can also attend. However, as indicated in research by Morris et al. (1997), only half the youth justice advocates they surveyed indicated that they regularly attended conferences on behalf of their clients. More interestingly, and given Christie's resounding criticisms, other professionals tended to regard the presence of a youth justice advocate as unessential and in some cases as a hindrance to events.

Away from the formal justice system, the nature of family group conferencing is ordered informality. The stages of the conferencing process, at least in the early years of its incarnation, have been characterised as follows.

A 'typical' conference

In a room with chairs arranged in a circle, the conference facilitator introduces everyone present and proceeds to outline the purpose of the conference. From here, the usual order of events is that the police representative reads out a summary of the offence, which the young person is asked to corroborate. Variations in the young person's interpretation of events are noted, but should the young person deny their guilt with respect to the offence, then the conference is stopped for the case to be deferred, usually, to the Youth Court. Having agreed to their culpability in the offence, the young person then listens to the victim, or a representative for the victim, relate the event and its impact on them. There then follows a general discussion, involving the various conference participants, regarding the offence and, importantly, its underlying causes. Offender accountability and possibilities for 'making amends' are aired during the discussion. At some point the discussion is broken off and the young offender and his or her representatives are left alone to discuss options for 'making amends' as part of the long-term restorative process for all those involved with the offence. The victim and other conference participants then return to the room to hear the proposals for making amends. After discussing the proposals and, hopefully, agreeing to them, there is often an apology from the young person to the victim. The conference facilitator then formally records the agreement, in order to follow it through at a later point. The agreement is most often in the form of an apology and some kind of community work, with few agreements, given the limited means of most young offenders, involving financial restitution. If adopted by everyone present, the agreement then becomes formally binding.

Only half of the New Zealand family group conferences monitored by Morris and Maxwell in the period 1990–91 succeeded in getting victims to attend (Maxwell and Morris, 1993). Their research indicated that, of those victims who did attend a conference, only 48 per cent were 'satisfied' with the process, in comparison with 84 per cent of young offenders and 86 per cent of youth justice coordinators. An important reason why victims did not enter into conferencing when offered, and their dissatisfaction with the process itself, can be attributed to poor practice in the management of the conferencing process. Lack of information, and disinformation regarding what to expect, was rife. Professionals also neglected their duties to monitor subsequent events or to inform victims when agreements were successfully completed. It would appear, on the basis of this evidence, that family group conferencing, at least in its early days, suffered all the pitfalls of traditional justice when it came to recognising victims' needs for information about 'their' case (Shapland et al., 1985).

On the evidence of these early research findings, it would seem that family group conferencing has to be cautiously interpreted as a 'victim-centred' initiative. For example, it was only in 1994, five years after the 1989 Act introducing conferencing, that the victim was given due regard when the site of the conference was suggested by the offender and his/her family – perhaps, tellingly, one of the reasons why victims were less than 'satisfied' with conferencing in comparison with other participants. Also, as New Zealand's adaptation of conferencing drew from Maori traditions, and was frequently utilised for Maori juvenile offenders, it has to be asked whether conferencing was an idealistic attempt to resurrect 'community' in the image of traditional Maori culture. As Maxwell and Morris (2000) inform us, conferencing can also take place in Maori meeting houses – *marae*. While *marae* may, for offences involving young people with Maori origins, be regarded as suitable sites for the resolution of conflicts involving the Maori 'community', one has to ask whether victims of non-Maori origin, with Maori offenders, feel the same about the appropriate location for conferences. Importantly, one has to question the extent to which, in striving for 'community' involvement in conflict resolution, a 'different', or perhaps secondary, form of justice is being applied to young offenders, their victims and, in turn, indigenous people such as the Maori.

These criticisms are not unique to New Zealand and are taken up towards the end of the chapter. The absence of victim satisfaction with family group conferencing may reflect more than misinformation or lack of information regarding the conferencing process, and may, at another level, reveal deeper misgivings regarding the kind of 'justice' that is being meted out.

Reintegrative shaming: restorative justice?

In his book *Crime, Shame and Reintegration,* John Braithwaite (1989), an Australian academic, develops his ideas on 'reintegrative shaming' as a cornerstone of applied restorative justice. Reintegrative shaming has been adapted by various 'conferencing' initiatives, but to a number of practitioners and academics working in the restorative field his ideas remain controversial. However, what Braithwaite does achieve in the field of restorative justice, which can be variously accused of lacking a clear theoretical focus, is a theory which can be applied and tested in practice.

Reintegrative shaming stems from the ideals of civic republicanism. A key concept in the civic republican tradition, as grounded in the French Revolution's ideals of liberty, equality and fraternity, is citizenship (Braithwaite and Pettit, 1990). In particular, the 'fraternity' part of citizenship appeals to a sense of community and belonging. In this sense, civic republicanism looks to the citizen's response to crime, victimisation and fear of crime through the lens of 'community'. Herein, Etzioni's (1995) ideas on 'communitarianism' are evoked in a community-based restorative process.

What is meant by 'shaming'?

A basic remit of reintegrative shaming is to avoid long-term stigmatisation of an offender in order to reintegrate him or her back into society. Reintegrative shaming seeks an alternative to the negative labelling of offenders that generally occurs with the intervention of traditional criminal justice. This is achieved by means of a restorative process involving shame followed by reintegration of an offender into the 'community'. Shame is utilised in the restorative justice process in order to instil remorse in the offender for the harm caused to victim, family, friends and 'community'. A central tenet of this process is that shame is emphasised in reference to the offence in question, rather than the offender him or herself. In other words, the emphasis is on the 'act', the offence, as warranting shame and disapproval, within a context of general social approval for the 'actor' in the form of the offender.

Braithwaite's ideas echo Christie's earlier call for recognition of the State's 'theft' of conflicts which deny the role of people and community in the resolution of their own conflicts. However, reintegrative shaming, in its reference to and application of 'shame', can be readily critiqued for its evocation of retribution in the restorative process. Here, as Braithwaite would argue, a clear distinction needs to be made between shaming without subsequent restoration, as is the case with traditional criminal justice, and shaming as utilised prior to reintegration of the offender back into the community. As any attendance at a court of law illustrates, at the point where the judge passes sentence, traditional criminal justice tries to inject feelings of shame and remorse in the offender. However, given that there is little scope in the traditional trial setting for the victim and the wider community to impart how the crime has affected them, it is hardly surprising that most offenders will feel distanced from a judge's appeals to shame. In itself, shame, with regard to breaking the law, is not useful unless it results in the reformation of the offender's character. There is no evidence to date that shame in the traditional trial setting results in reduced recidivism rates. Nor is there consistent evidence that 'reintegrative shaming', through conferencing, results in reduced recidivism rates. As Levrant et al. (1999: 9) argue: 'Although programs with a restorative orientation may occasionally reduce recidivism . . . the current knowledge base on offender change would suggest that restorative interventions are likely to have effects on recidivism that are modest, if not inconsequential.' But one could argue that shame, if expressed to a victim, is a much-needed display of remorse that certain victims need to hear. However, feelings of shame, unless developed, are not long-term solutions to either problem of offending or victimisation.

Morris and Maxwell (2000), in light of their own experiences with restorative justice in New Zealand, critique the use of shaming in the process of family group conferencing. They suggest that 'reintegrative shaming' is 'a concept difficult to operationalize and arguably at odds with restorative ideals' (Morris and Maxwell, 2000: 208). Their main objection, in reference to findings from reintegrative shaming practices in Australia (Sherman and Strang, 1997; Strang and Sherman, 1997), is that a ready connection tends to be made, by advocates of reintegrative shaming, between offenders' feelings of 'shame' and their sense of having 'made amends' to society. Morris and Maxwell argue that the two concepts are not necessarily linked in the eyes of an offender. Likewise, they challenge researchers' suggestions that reintegrative shaming produces the 'right kind of shame', when compared with traditional criminal justice, given the fact that police officers are often present at reintegrative shaming ceremonies and serve to reinforce a certain authority with their presence.

Practical initiatives have been developed in Australia which variously set out to employ Braithwaite's ideas on reintegrative shaming. Notable among these are the police-run family group conferencing models in Wagga Wagga (O'Connell, 1995), now defunct, and RISE (the Reintegrative Sharing Experiment) in Canberra (Sherman and Strang, 1997). Past and present practitioners of these and similar initiatives would argue that a central aim of reintegrative shaming, as with other interpretations of restorative justice, is to reintegrate the offender back into the 'community'. However, whether 'shaming' needs to be employed as a central element of restorative praxis is debatable. Ultimately, one has to question the extent to which shaming is 'useful' for the offender *and* the victim. Herein, appeals to certain damaged and disgruntled victims' need for retribution can be aroused by conferencing models that include an element of 'shaming'. Whether victims are willing or prepared to progress from shaming to reintegration is a point needing careful consideration in the selection of both offenders and victims, and their wider families and 'communities', for conferencing.

The resurrection of restorative initiatives in Britain

Compared with our European neighbours, notably Austria and Germany where mediation schemes thrive with the support of legislation and financial backing (Dünkel, 1996; Dünkel and Rössner, 1989; Kilchling and Löschnig-Gspandl, 2000), England and Wales have never taken to mediation as a serious alternative to traditional justice. However, interest in restorative ideals was rekindled in England and Wales as responsive practitioners, including those from existing and defunct mediation schemes, took notice of developments in other countries.

Thames Valley Police

Thames Valley Police have taken the initiative in this area and have drawn on practical examples of police-led conferencing in Australia, together with early British examples of restorative initiatives such as the Milton Keynes 'Retail Theft Initiative' (where young offenders came together with victimised shop owners; *Police Magazine*, 2003). Aspects of Braithwaite's reintegrative shaming theory have also been adapted by Thames Valley Police for practical application in the restorative process.

The Aylesbury 'restorative cautioning' initiative, carried out in the Thames Valley Police area, was the forerunner of further restorative developments by Thames Valley Police. Young and Goold (1999) undertook a small-scale study of this initiative in the summer of 1997. They reported that reintegrative shaming principles were incorporated in the cautioning process – this invited people affected by an offence, including those suffering from any second order and indirect harm, to a meeting which sought to see how the interests and the relationships of the parties damaged by the offence might be restored by the offender. The Aylesbury initiative applied the principles of reintegrative shaming by making offenders ashamed of their behaviour in a way that sought to promote their reintegration back into the 'community'. Appeals to 'shame' were seen as most effective when exposing offenders to disapproval of their actions by those they cared about the most, and by making offenders aware of the consequences of their actions by hearing from victims. Young and Goold argue that reintegration occurred when stigmatisation of offenders was avoided in a context of caring. By 'making amends' for their behaviour, to their victim and significant others who 'care' for them, offenders were allowed to gain self-esteem.

Young (2000) argues that the Aylesbury initiative was effective because it recognised the need to work with a broader sense of 'victimhood'. In other words, if the Aylesbury experiment had relied on the individual victim, its restorative ideals would not have come to fruition. Recognition of indirect victims allowed restorative principles to be applied to those not directly implicated in the offence, which in turn was utilised for more effective reintegration of the offender back into the community by evoking the harm done by crime on a wider social canvass.

Since the Aylesbury initiative, Thames Valley Police have adopted a number of restorative responses to crime that can be applied to both juvenile and adult offenders. On their promotional website, Thames Valley Police state: 'Restorative policing is part of a cultural shift within the entire Criminal Justice System, within which conventional criminal justice and restorative justice techniques will work in tandem.' From the late 1990s, with restorative principles firmly set in their remit, Thames Valley Police have sought to deliver restorative justice at a number of levels from the 'restorative caution' through to the 'restorative conference' and the 'community conference'. In deciding on the nature of restorative intervention, the police, in cooperation with multi-agency youth justice panels in the case of young offenders (now Youth Offending Teams (YOTs) since the 1998 Crime and Disorder Act), give due regard to the seriousness of the offence and the individual circumstances of the case. At the most comprehensive level of restorative intervention the 'community conference' is applied to cases where there has been a significant impact on the victim, the community or the offender. All parties involved must indicate their willingness to participate in a face-to-face conference with the aim of a positive, rather than a purely retributive, outcome. In this respect, the police stress the voluntary nature of restorative justice interventions for all those involved.

In their promotional literature, Thames Valley Police offer a number of goals with respect to restorative justice intervention. Among these is the aim to divert young offenders from the traditional court setting, and to give victims the opportunity to relate the impact that crime has had on their lives. At the end of a restorative conference, the police set out to elicit a reparation agreement from the offender to the victim in the form, initially, of a verbal apology, followed by a written apology and financial compensation, or some other form of restitution. The police also stress that restorative conferencing, while giving victims a 'voice', should placate their worst fears concerning the offender as an unseen 'ogre', and at the same time reassure victims that their victimisation is 'normal'.

The Thames Valley restorative initiatives evolved at the same time as major legislative changes in England and Wales at the end of the 1990s towards the development of restorative justice practices, particularly in the case of juvenile offenders. Most important among these, and reflecting discourse and developments concerning the shape of youth justice (Audit Commission, 1996 report *Misspent Youth*), were the 1998 Crime and Disorder Act and the 1999 Youth Justice and Criminal Evidence Act.

Reparation orders: restorative practice?

The 1998 Crime and Disorder Act, which was implemented in England and Wales on 1 June 2000, includes specific legislative measures towards 'reparation orders' for children aged 10 to 17 convicted of any offence other than one for which a sentence is fixed by law. According to Dignan (2002: 68), the reparation order was envisaged with two aims: first, to help prevent further offending by making young offenders aware of the consequences of their actions; and second, to require young offenders to make amends for their offending behaviour either to their victim or to the wider community.

Reparation orders are a means for young offenders to undertake some practical reparative activity on behalf of the victim, if the victim so wishes. At the same time, the orders afford the opportunity for victims to have some insight into 'why' an offence occurred, and can give offenders an insight into the distress and inconvenience their actions have caused. In the language of restorative justice, the Act attempts to instil responsibility in offenders for their actions while giving them the opportunity to 'make amends' to the victim and/or the wider community (particularly in cases where the victim wants nothing to do with the offender or where there is no identifiable victim).

Reparation orders can include any of the following, either alone or in combination: a letter of apology; a meeting or restorative conference between the parties involved; several hours a week of practical activity intended to benefit the victim or the wider community. Reparation orders should not consist solely of financial restitution from the offender to the victim. However, they can be combined with a compensation order and other sanctions such as a custodial sentence or a community service order. A breach of a reparation order can result in an offender incurring a fine or another sanction such as an attendance centre order or a curfew order.

According to researchers responsible for appraising the introduction of reparation orders in four pilot areas, their take-up and 'success' largely reflected the particular criminal justice culture in the area where they were piloted, and the willingness of criminal justice workers to adopt and promote reparation (Dignan, 2000, 2002). In the four pilot areas, Youth Offending Teams (YOTs), which were established under the 1998 Act with a responsibility for contacting and informing victims about reparation, differed considerably in the mode of victim consultation policies they adopted. Some YOTs, contrary to many victims' desire to be kept informed about their case, adopted a policy of non-consultation with victims when direct reparation between victim and offender was unfeasible. Other YOTs made no attempt to contact victims about reparation when offenders appeared hostile to the idea, for fear of causing secondary victimisation. Overall, the piloted YOTs indicated that victims were consulted about reparation orders in two-thirds of cases where there was an identifiable victim. However, different practices by different YOTs meant that the percentage of contacted victims who agreed to some form of reparation ranged from 20 per cent in one pilot area through to 75 per cent in another, while the proportion of victims who were willing to receive direct reparation ranged from just over 50 per cent to over 90 per cent (Dignan, 2002: 78).

Reparation orders are just one of many new criminal justice initiatives for responding to youth offending in England and Wales, among which is the replacement of multiple police cautions by the 'final warning', and provision for supervision orders. Principally, what these legislative and practical reactions to youth offending have in common, along with the reparation order, is a desire to divert young offenders away from the criminal justice system in the attempt to stop reoffending and ultimately limit the costs of future arrests, trials and incarceration to the public purse.

The language of restorative justice might be invoked in the 1998 Crime and Disorder Act but the central focus of the Act is on offenders, rather than their victims and the wider community. In this respect, reparation orders are primarily employed for the benefit of young offenders and exist within the confines of the traditional justice system. As Dignan comments (2002: 81):

> while the reparation order has helped to establish some basic elements of a restorative justice approach as part of the mainstream response to youth offending behaviour for the first time, the context and manner in which it operates is still largely shaped by the traditional criminal justice process. The result has been the introduction of a hybrid form of justice that is neither purely restorative nor purely retributive, but incorporates elements of both approaches.

In comparison, the 1999 Youth Justice and Criminal Evidence Act, with respect to the criminal evidence part, gives extensive and much overdue attention to 'vulnerable' and 'at-risk' victims and witnesses to ease their path through the ordeal of the adversarial trial. To some extent, these elements of the 1999 Act are 'restorative' because they give victims greater recognition as valuable players in the criminal process (see Chapter 6). Whether the 'referral orders' contained in the 1999 Act can also be considered 'restorative' is the subject of the next paragraphs.

Referral orders – restorative practice?

The Youth Justice and Criminal Evidence Act 1999 introduced the referral order as a sentencing disposal for 10–17-year-olds pleading guilty and convicted for the *first time* in a court of law. Under the terms of the Act, a Youth Offender Panel (YOP), consisting of volunteer Community Panel members, is responsible for drawing up a 'contract' with the young person stipulating how they will make amends for their offence. YOPs are assisted in this by YOTs. A court can make a referral order for anything between three and twelve months, but it is up to the YOP to decide the terms of the referral order, with the advice of YOT staff, as agreed in the contract with the young person. YOPs can meet a number of times to monitor the young person's compliance and non-compliance with the contract, and, where appropriate, changes can be made to the contract.

Drawing on the principles of restorative justice, YOPs provide an informal setting where the offender, his or her family, and, where appropriate, the victim, meet to consider the circumstances of the offence in question and its impact on the victim. A parent or parents of a child under 16 are expected to attend all panel meetings. And, in an effort to replicate restorative justice practices from New Zealand and elsewhere, other people may be invited to attend panel meetings, such as a victim supporter and a supporter of the young offender.

According to a report by researchers who monitored the first YOPs in eleven areas in England and Wales (Newburn et al., 2001; see also Crawford and Newburn, 2003), YOPs and referral orders were received positively by offenders, Community Panel members who made up the YOPs, and YOTs who worked alongside the YOPs. However, these conclusions were reached largely in the absence of victims taking part in YOPs; for example, of 566 initial panels examined as part of the YOP pilots, a victim was present at only 36. As a reflection of this, 44 per cent of contracts involved some form of community reparation, 34 per cent involved a written apology, but only 4 per cent involved referrals to mediation or direct work for victims (Newburn et al., 2001: vii).

The pilot YOPs failed to attract sufficient numbers of victims to the panel meetings. This reflected difficulties experienced in identifying and contacting victims, and attracting them to take part in panels on a voluntary basis. The shortfall in victim attendance can also be attributed to confusion and non-performance of duties by YOT personnel, which in turn reflects lack of resources and time constraints on overstretched staff. Because of the absence of victims at YOP meetings, only three young offenders, of forty interviewed in the pilot study, had attended an initial panel meeting with a victim present (Newburn et al., 2001: viii). These three agreed that the victim's presence was right and had made them think differently about things. In comparison, very few offenders who had attended a panel meeting without a victim present indicated they would have liked a victim to be there. As a reflection of the general absence of victims attending YOPs, observational data from the pilots found that one-quarter of all panels made no mention of the victim's perspective. As the Home Office report on the pilots states (Newburn et al., 2001: viii): 'In the absence of significant victim attendance there are obvious concerns that victims' issues are insufficiently represented.'

Given the failure of the pilot referral orders to incorporate victims in the initial stages of YOPs, the 'success' of this new initiative, which purports to be 'restorative', is obviously limited. Most contracts focused on community level reparation in the absence of actual victims. While community reparation is part of restorative justice, the lack of direct victim reparation means that a 'holistic' restorative label cannot be assigned to referral orders. Perhaps the most positive outcome of the referral order and the establishment of volunteer YOPs was the way in which the YOPs' Community Panel Members (CPMs) and the professional YOT staff were able to work closely together. Professionals and volunteers gained mutual respect and understanding through their contact in the YOPs. This 'result' appears to promote restorative principles of community involvement in the resolution of conflicts. But, given that CPMs were largely ethnically white (91 per cent), female (69 per cent), over 40 (68 per cent), and employed in professional or managerial occupations (50 per cent), it is incorrect to suggest that these volunteer community members represent a broad cross-section of society (Newburn et al., 2001: ix). CPMs are much like magistrates in England and Wales, who, as a volunteer force, are largely drawn from members of the middle classes with time and resources to spare for voluntary work. Although the culture of voluntarism in England and Wales is laudable and can, in abstract terms, be evoked as a representation of community, the criminal justice system's reliance on volunteers can also be critiqued as a form of cheap, non-professional labour that is not in a position to appreciate the lifestyles and circumstances of the young offenders with whom they come into contact.

In conclusion, the reparation orders in the 1998 Crime and Disorder Act and the referral orders in the 1999 Youth Justice and Criminal Evidence Act are, given their limitations as essentially offender-centred tools, significant developments towards the implementation of restorative justice practices in England and Wales. However, as noted, restorative initiatives are in danger of being hidden under the array of responses currently available to tackle youth *offending*. Individual police force initiatives with restorative principles, such as those undertaken by Thames Valley Police, together with restorative developments in the 1998 and 1999 Acts, will undoubtedly promote restorative justice interventions in England and Wales with the benefit of legislative backing. Yet what is required, besides the willingness of individual chief constables and YOT staff to back legislative reform, is financial support for restorative programmes which need staff training, time and multi-agency cooperation. In this respect, it has to be seen whether criminal justice, if inclined, is able to adopt 'holistic' restorative justice reforms given the ever-present demands on personnel, time and money from different quarters both inside and outside the justice system.

Restorative justice – a victim-centred paradigm shift?

Having explored various incarnations of restorative justice from around the world, from mediation through to family group conferencing, I now return to a number of questions and critiques of restorative justice that have been referred to throughout this introductory overview. Central among these is the extent to which restorative justice can be considered as the 'victim-centred' paradigm shift in criminal justice that some of its more enthusiastic proponents would have us believe.

International developments

Proponents of restorative justice as 'paradigm shift' can point to developments at an international level that indicate the growing significance of restorative justice as both theory and practice. For example, at the level of the UN, a draft resolution on 'Basic principles on the use of restorative justice programmes in criminal matters' was recommended in 2002 by the UN's Commission on Crime Prevention and Criminal Justice for adoption by the UN's Economic and Social Council.[3] This draft resolution represents a step on the road towards international legal recognition and adoption of restorative justice principles as an adjunct to criminal law. Its emergence reflects intense lobbying by restorative justice practitioners at the Tenth UN Congress on the Prevention of Crime and Treatment of Offenders (held in Vienna, April 2000), which was followed by a meeting of experts, in Canada, to refine and promote the draft resolution in an effort to advance its adoption. As a reflection of the different legal and social cultures represented by the member states of the UN, the Economic and Social Council is still some way off adopting the draft resolution.

Some restorative justice commentators have noted the problems involved in trying to promote restorative ideals at the level of the UN as most member states – representing the countries of the world – are ill-informed and openly suspicious about restorative justice (Aertsen, 2002). However, at the European level, more progress has been made towards adoption of some restorative principles, partly, perhaps, as a reflection of shared European ideals and innovations in criminal justice reform. The European Union's Framework Decision on the Standing of Victims in Criminal Proceedings (2001) includes reference to mediation, while the Council of Europe's Recommendation (1999) 19 is specifically concerned with mediation in penal matters; however, while the former is legally binding on EU member states, the latter is not.

Interesting developments are also taking place in Europe with respect to the marriage of restorative justice theory and practice. In 2002 the European Science Foundation, under COST Action A21, financed a four-year networking programme for European researchers in the field of restorative justice. The network explores three core themes in restorative research: evaluation research on restorative justice practices; policy-oriented research on restorative justice developments; and theoretical research. Belgian academics, based at the University of Leuven, have been particularly active in promoting European links on restorative justice research and practice. Leuven University is the contact point for the European Forum for Victim–Offender Mediation and Restorative Justice, which has an online newsletter and hosts conferences every other year, the first of which was in 2000. The European Forum has drawn up a constitution governing its operation, which is accompanied by a memorandum describing restorative justice and its development.

These various developments, at the level of the UN and the EU, and with regard to the emergence of initiatives such as the European Forum, are encouraging developments in the field of restorative justice. However, we are still some way off before a 'paradigm shift' can be declared. The following paragraphs sketch some of the obstacles facing restorative justice's development in the face of traditional criminal justice practice.

A challenge to traditional criminal justice?

Howard Zehr, an early proponent of restorative justice, saw criminal justice's failure to solve the 'crime problem' and the resultant crisis of legitimation in criminal justice – prison overcrowding; public fear of crime – as the catalyst for a paradigm shift in criminal justice, led by reformers, towards restorative justice. As Sebba notes (1996: 275): 'many advocates of informal alternatives have not regarded these alternatives exclusively as second-best substitutes for the "real thing". The more radical or romantic advocates have viewed informal proceedings as a desirable end in themselves.'

Walgrave (2000), a founding member of the European Forum, distinguishes between two dominant responses to restorative justice. First, there are those, including Walgrave, who advocate restorative justice as an alternative to retributive and rehabilitative responses to crime. Although the main focus of this approach, to date, has been on young offenders, Walgrave refers to restorative justice as a 'maximalist' option with the potential to respond to a diverse range of offending and offenders, while at the same time giving due consideration to victims and the wider community. However, Walgrave, in line with the European Forum's memorandum on restorative justice, proceeds to note the role of the State in upholding the rights of those involved in restorative justice and, where necessary, its duties to step in where restorative justice is unworkable.

Much of Walgrave's enthusiasm for and criticism of restorative justice comes from his experience of legislative reform in his own country, Belgium. The 1994 Belgian law on 'Regulation of a Procedure for Mediation in Penal Matters' allows the public prosecutor to dismiss a case which could incur a maximum penalty of less than two years' imprisonment if the offender agrees to cooperate in reparation, treatment, training, community service, or a combination of these. A 'mediation magistrate' has been appointed in each of the 27 Belgian 'courts of first instance' to select, supervise and chair mediation sessions as part of the above law's drive towards non-custodial responses to minor offending by, principally, young offenders. To date, around half of cases which are eligible for mediation under the 1994 law have resulted in reparative orders. However, Walgrave critiques the implementation of the law for its marginalisation of victims to the sidelines in most mediation sessions, and for the punitive, rather than restorative, undertones of the final stages of mediation which are, according to Walgrave, evocative of a 'mini-trial'.

While Walgrave notes the 1994 law's possibilities for working with victims, he also remarks (2000: 256): 'it [the Belgian law] may be an exemplar of what a victim perspective risks if it agrees too easily to be integrated within criminal justice'. Similar criticisms have been levelled at the practice of mediation initiatives in France (Crawford, 2000), where, as in the case of Belgium, well-intentioned initiatives that could benefit offenders, victims and the wider community have been subsumed under a dominant criminal justice ideology.

The second dominant response to restorative justice, reflecting the majority of restorative justice developments in Belgium and other countries, includes those who see restorative justice principally as a form of diversion from established criminal justice. Marshall, who falls under this category of proponents, states (1997: 14):

> The truth is that restorative justice is not an alternative paradigm of justice capable of replacing current processes . . . Criminal justice represents the application of force by society in protection of its members . . . The role of restorative justice is to perform those tasks that the force-based system cannot fulfil. It is complementary to criminal justice, not antithetical to it.

At present, restorative justice initiatives cohabit the same universe as traditional criminal justice. There is a tendency for alternative dispute resolutions to be used in less serious cases and, more often than not, for the primary purpose of diverting young offenders from a punitive criminal justice system. When more serious cases come to the attention of the criminal justice system they are usually dealt with through the medium of established practices. Where restorative justice does exist, current criminal justice forms the dominant backdrop to alternative forms of dispute resolution. Ultimately, should a victim or an offender claim dissatisfaction or absence of due process and legal rights in the course of restorative justice intervention, then the law is there to reassert its dominion.

Arguably, the challenge of restorative justice lies not with its establishment as a wholesale paradigm shift in criminal justice, but rather as a practical response to some of the worst excesses and neglectful practices of established forms of justice. The usefulness of presenting a dichotomous model of restorative justice in opposition to traditional justice, or as everything that traditional justice is not, is a misleading attempt to create difference where, more often, agreement and practical solutions can be found between the two systems of justice (Hirsch et al., 2003). For example – as Marshall notes (1997: 13) in his adaptation of Zehr's polarised depiction of retributive 'versus' restorative justice – whereas retributive justice sees crime as a violation of the State and restorative justice sees crime as a violation of a person or persons, synthesis of the two sees crime as having repercussions for society and its individuals, of which the State and communities form a part. Dignan (2000) identifies four main implementational strategies for restorative justice which range on a continuum from limited attempts to incorporate restorative justice-style reforms within a traditionally retributive system, through to a fully integrated restorative justice approach to justice. Between these two extremes lie the other two approaches: namely, the compromise strategy of a 'partially integrated' restorative justice, and the separatist 'stand alone' approach in which restorative justice initiatives are developed outside the regular criminal justice system. In summarising his review of global experiments with restorative justice, Dignan concludes that a fully integrated restorative justice approach, where restorative principles lie at the heart of mainstream criminal justice, is the only way to avoid the various pitfalls that currently beset *ad hoc* implementation of restorative justice practice.

Finally, a basic but fundamental problem with restorative justice's claim to represent a serious challenge to traditional criminal justice's neglect of the victim is the fact that most crimes and, hence, experiences of victimisation do not involve the apprehension of a known offender. In other words, there is no offender with whom the majority of victims could undertake restorative justice practices should they wish to. With, in the case of England and Wales, the average proportion of cases 'cleared up' by the police hovering around 5.5 per cent, of which not all result in an offender being caught, claims that restorative justice represents a 'paradigm shift' seem woefully inadequate. While restorative practices are possible between offenders and victims who are not linked by the same criminal event but are linked by the same type of crime, as in the Milton Keynes 'Retail Theft Initiative', the impact of restorative justice appears greatest where victims meet 'their' offenders (Coates and Gehm, 1989).

In asking whether restorative justice offers a challenge to traditional criminal justice, practical considerations are equally valid in any ensuing discussion alongside more abstract considerations of what restorative justice is or should be in theory. Levrant et al. (1999) question whether restorative justice can be regarded as a 'substantive' or 'symbolic' challenge to established criminal justice, and pose three practical issues when determining this.

- First, they note the degree to which criminal justice staff, such as police and probation officers, are committed to a new philosophy of justice as an essential component in determining its success.
- Second, staff have to be willing to change their roles from 'service provider', traditionally to offenders, to that of 'community service facilitator'.
- Third, restorative justice programmes can only succeed where sufficient human and financial resources have been secured for this purpose.

At best, in light of current practical realities, restorative justice might more accurately be described as an adjunct to traditional forms of criminal justice in England and Wales. In this respect, restorative justice appears to pose a symbolic and piecemeal reform, rather than a substantive and wholesale reform, of criminal justice.

Evoking 'community'

As Crawford notes (1997), and in reference to Etzioni's (1995) promotion of 'community' ideals through 'communitarianism', there is a slippage between what 'community' is and what it ought to be. The idea of 'community' is more often than not thrown into restorative justice discourse without due regard for what 'community' means and is in reality. While restorative justice evokes 'community' as the place for the resolution of conflicts and 'making amends', it needs to be recognised that 'community' is also the place of crime and disorder. Restorative justice, in its most holistic form, can only work given the existence of 'community'; but, at the same time, restorative justice sets out to revive 'community' through the application of family or community conferencing. Just as restorative justice bemoans loss of 'community' in developed industrialised nations, 'community' is held up as the third pillar, after offenders and victims, underpinning successful restorative justice interventions. In this respect, one can readily accuse restorative justice advocates, through reference to 'community', of advancing a symbolic rather than a substantive and practical challenge to established criminal justice practice.

Community involvement in restorative justice works best where there already exists a sense of 'community', as is the case with New Zealand's indigenous Maori people who were instrumental in castigating their country's 'western-centric' criminal justice system. Conversely, conferencing initiatives might be expected to fail in high-crime inner-city neighbourhoods where a sense of 'community' never prevailed or, through time, has been gradually eroded. Much as Neighbourhood Watch schemes, in the tradition of crime prevention, tend to have a limited impact because they attempt to instil 'neighbourliness' where it does not exist, so absence of community cannot be rectified through a restorative justice programme. The problems of high-crime areas, which ironically are most in need of restorative initiatives, cannot be solved without a comprehensive response to the causes of crime and the absence of 'community'. While restorative measures to 'make amends' between offenders, victims and the wider 'community' provide more scope for potentially reconciliatory and rehabilitative responses to crime than existing retributive justice, there is inconclusive evidence that restorative justice has any meaningful impact on recidivism in the community (Levrant et al., 1999). Although reducing reoffending is not the only goal of restorative justice, one has to ask whether the 'community', as used and promoted by restorative justice, and in turn victims, would like to see reduced recidivism as a key remit of restorative justice. In appealing to 'community', restorative justice should also work 'for', and not simply 'with', the 'community' in an effort to achieve positive long-term results – reducing recidivism being one such long-term goal.

Restorative justice evokes an image of community that addresses some of the power differentials of established criminal justice, notably in the adversarial trial process. However, it would be naïve to assume that these power differentials are not transferable to restorative justice. Just as traditional criminal justice has been criticised for its unequal treatment of people, both offenders and victims, according to their class, gender and race (Carlen, 1985; Lees, 1997; Smith, 1997), so restorative justice can be critiqued for its failings in this area. Delgado (2000) presents a sharp critique of restorative justice, focusing on racial inequalities. Drawing from examples of mediation in the United States, Delgado asserts that victim–offender mediation (2000: 768):

> sets up a relatively coercive encounter in many cases between an
> inarticulate, uneducated, socially alienated youth with few social skills
> and a hurt, vengeful victim. This encounter is mediated by a middle-class,
> moralistic mediator who shares little background or sympathy with the
> offender, but has everything in common with the victim. To label this
> encounter a negotiation seems a misnomer, for it is replete with overt social
> coercion.

Delgado focuses on inequalities in mediation as they are primarily felt by the offender as a socially marginalised member of society: that is, typically, African-American or Latino, and from a deprived social background. However, while his picture of mediation may paint a grim reality of worst-case scenarios, he fails to acknowledge the extent to which victimisation, as property or personal crime, is experienced as an intra-class and intra-racial event. In other words, poor urban African-Americans tend to victimise poor urban African-Americans. Although, from a radical victimological perspective (Quinney, 1972), the State and 'big business' are primarily responsible for crimes of social inequality that have marginalised society's urban poor, the crimes that are brought to the attention of mediation are, typically, interpersonal crimes contained within racial and social groups. In this respect, mediation might appear as 'second-class' justice for marginalised social groups – offenders, victims and their 'communities'.

Delgado's critique of mediation is most useful for its elucidation of deeper social inequalities that are unlikely to be rectified by the process of mediation. Without adequate revitalisation of 'community', for those offenders (and, one should add, their victims) who come from the most deprived backgrounds, one has to ask 'what' kind of society are people, post-mediation, supposed to be restored to? In some senses the worst excesses of mediation that Delgado highlights might be rectified through more holistic restorative initiatives, particularly those in the framework of conferencing, which attempt to involve the wider 'community' in the resolution of conflicts. In these settings the role of mediator, in the form of a conferencing facilitator or a police representative, should be tempered to that of an umpire. However, social inequalities between offenders, victims and their supporters, if uneven to begin with, will tend to surface during these encounters if the conferencing facilitator does not quell their excesses. Likewise, dominant personalities can harm the goals of a mediation or conferencing session if facilitators fail to temper and address these dynamics. Here, the practical reality of the 'family' group conference, given the power inequalities present in many families and the diverse make-up of 'the' family in today's society, gives rise to more concerns regarding the management of the conferencing setting and the dominance of certain 'voices'. However, given the alternatives of the traditional justice system, where the power and the dominant 'voice' are invested in professionals, appeals to community and family involvement in restorative justice initiatives would, in theory, appear to offer a more balanced participatory process.

Who benefits?

Discussion of restorative justice tends often to caricature its practice as either offender- or victim-centred. But a narrowly focused victim-centred or offender-centred critique of restorative justice neglects to promote the advantages and disadvantages of restorative justice for both parties. While early mediation initiatives can be readily accused of an offender-centred remit, they endeavoured to respond to the punitive excesses of retributive criminal justice by evoking a more humanistic social justice with positive repercussions for both offenders and victims.

Victims, as critics such as Ashworth (2000) indicate, can be utilised as tools in the service of offenders and restorative justice practitioners. Taken further, this point suggests that victims' compliance with restorative initiatives allows offenders to escape a punitive justice system. However, having said this, restorative justice is not the 'easy option' for offenders that many critics of the process take it to be.

As noted earlier, current restorative justice practice does not tend to exist in isolation from established criminal justice. In this respect, an offender who fails to comply with a restorative justice agreement will, in most cases, face the full impact of the law. That is, having agreed to 'make amends' to victim and 'community', failure to do so can result in the offender appearing before a court to be admonished and punished for non-compliance. The degree to which non-adherence to restorative agreements is punishable depends on the law in the jurisdiction in question and the seriousness of the offence. In petty cases, such as a juvenile's first misdemeanour, where the criminal law would normally not intervene, non-compliance with restorative agreements should not involve the full force of the criminal justice system. But, given the application of restorative justice to minor misdemeanours involving young offenders, one can readily criticise restorative justice for 'net widening', as Dittenhoffer and Ericson (1983) pointed out in their early critique of Canadian victim–offender reconciliation work. In other words, restorative justice intervenes where traditional justice does not, and in so doing succeeds in widening the net of what might otherwise have been ignored as a minor wrong.

In turn, the sanctions imposed on offenders who take part in restorative initiatives need to be compared with the level of sanctions imposed on offenders who are processed through the criminal justice system. The principle of proportionality with respect to offence and sanction needs to be upheld by restorative justice practitioners. While the criminal law judges criminal intent, restorative justice looks at the harm done by offenders to victims and 'community'. As the damage inflicted on a victim can be greater than the intent, restorative justice should ensure that restorative agreements do not exceed the punishment an offender would receive under the existing criminal law. Once again, the restorative justice facilitator needs to make certain that the demands of retributive victims are not met through alternative dispute resolution. Retributive victims should be quickly eliminated from restorative programmes in order to avoid punitive encounters that usurp restorative principles.

While early mediation initiatives were predominantly offender-centred, often as a result of their instigation by probation services, conferencing initiatives have a stronger remit to consider the needs of victims, the family and 'community'. The 'multiple victim' perspective is increasingly recognised by restorative justice practitioners as a comprehensive response to crime. However, within this process, the immediate victim's voice should not be lost beneath the voices of family and community members. Who speaks 'for' the victim needs careful consideration if, as noted earlier, power differentials are to be avoided in a restorative setting. Facilitators need to ensure that victims are content with a restorative agreement as reached between offender, victim and representatives of both parties.

Restorative initiatives are only 'restorative' if they result in both victim and offender feeling that the harm inflicted by an event has been amended through restorative agreements and actions – be this an apology, monetary compensation, or an act of restitution. Although the wider concerns of family and other participants are important to the restorative process, the needs of victims and offenders should take precedence. Rather than pitch the needs of offenders against the needs of victims, restorative justice should respond to victims' anxieties and feelings of anger with respect to their experience of victimisation, while imparting to offenders their part in this and their means for 'making amends' to the victim and the wider community. Restorative agreements reached between victim, offender and community should be reasonable and not onerous. Likewise, in agreeing to an offender's apology, and any other restorative gestures, the victim is being asked to do far more than would be the case under the terms of traditional justice where the State speaks 'for' the victim. Having a participatory role should not be made an onerous task for victims.

Finally, the applicability of restorative justice to more serious cases of offending, and the implications of this for victims, needs consideration. There are no hard and fast rules that restorative justice should only be applied to minor offences and first-time young offenders. To date there has been a range of restorative initiatives that variously work with serious offences and adult offenders. One could argue that providing victims agree to a restorative initiative, having been briefed on the nature and implications of this, then justice should not deny victims this opportunity. However, serious doubts are generally raised about the applicability of restorative justice in cases of 'domestic' violence, sexual violence, and murder (Presser and Gaarder, 2000).

Given that women and children are the predominant groups victimised by 'domestic' and sexual violence, one can object to the inclusion of these crimes in restorative initiatives on a number of grounds:

- First, by taking these crimes out of the criminal justice system they are in danger of being demoted to a 'secondary' form of justice; in other words, the State, with the full force of traditional criminal justice, needs to be seen not to condone these crimes.
- Second, the power differentials that sustain violence against women and children are in danger of resurfacing in the setting of an informal restorative meeting, particularly where families or people in relationships are involved.
- Third, restorative justice should not play the part of a marriage counsellor; its duties are not to resurrect relationships.
- Fourth, restorative justice should not play the part of a therapist; in other words, particularly in the case of intimate relationships, the restorative facilitator cannot be expected to help resolve some of the deep-seated problems that result in sexual and physical abuse.
- Fifth, the repeat nature of these crimes, often covering serial abuse against the same person (or persons) over a number of years, demands that their severity be recognised as more than 'one-off' events, which restorative justice is not yet sufficiently equipped to handle.

This list is not exhaustive but should serve to illustrate some of the limitations of restorative justice as a wholesale response to crime in its widest context. In turn, one can consider the benefits and pitfalls of restorative justice intervention with respect to corporate crime (Braithwaite, 2000) and work-based conflicts. The potential for restorative justice to be utilised for a range of conflict interventions, beyond the limitations of the criminal law, is seemingly endless; for example, restorative justice is currently used for local housing disputes (Mulcahy, 2000) and school bullying projects. While the potential application of restorative initiatives is wide, one has to return to fundamental questions which ask 'who' benefits – victims, offenders, communities or the State?

Concluding comments

The application, across different continents, of alternative forms of dispute resolution, which might come under a loose definition of restorative justice, suggests two things: (1) restorative justice is presenting a new challenge to traditional forms of justice; and (2) there is a crisis of legitimation in traditional justice. While different criminal justice jurisdictions have, since the 1970s, variously experienced increasing levels of crime and escalating prison numbers, restorative justice can be read as only one response to these developments. Restorative justice needs to be contextualised with respect to other victim-centred initiatives since the 1970s. For example, Britain's Victim Support, which has always cautiously responded to mediation and restorative justice initiatives, also emerged in the 1970s. Victim Support developed as a response to the neglect of the victim by traditional criminal justice, rather than as a wholesale challenge to traditional justice. In turn, if we are to consider restorative justice as a 'challenge' to traditional criminal justice, one might add that Victim Support currently impacts on many more victims than restorative justice reaches. Arguably, the scope for restorative justice initiatives, within the realms of the criminal law, can be thrown wider to include more serious offences, more adult offenders, and hence more victims. However, this does not escape the fact that restorative justice, in its most holistic form, requires a known offender and a known victim. In reality, restorative justice can only respond to a limited number of offences and can only work with a limited number of victims.

With these considerations in mind, restorative justice might be more accurately interpreted as one of a number of victim-centred developments since the 1970s. This is reflected in the United Nations 1985 Declaration of Basic Principles of Justice for Victims of Crime and Abuse of Power, which refers to 'restorative' practices as one of many victim-centred standards. More recently, the UN's Congress on the Prevention of Crime and the Treatment of Offenders, in April 2000, included extensive reference to restorative justice, from panellists, member state delegations, and non-governmental organisations (NGOs), with respect to the agenda item 'Offenders and Victims: Accountability and Fairness in the Justice Process'. Following on from here, in 2002, the UN's Economic and Social Council considered a draft resolution towards the development of a Declaration of Basic Principles on the Use of Restorative Justice Programmes in Criminal Matters. And, in addition to developments at the level of the UN, the Declaration of Leuven (1997) (an international document by academics and practitioners), and legislative and practical initiatives at the national level, have variously contributed to the steady take-up of restorative initiatives. What these developments illustrate is a growing interest, acceptance and adoption of restorative justice at both the national and international level.

However, I would contend that restorative justice presents, at best, a fragmented 'movement' towards a more humanistic and inclusive form of justice for victims, offenders, and members of the wider 'community'. Restorative justice does not, as yet, represent a 'paradigm shift' in criminal justice, nor does it represent a wholly victim-centred development. Its proponents can point to a diversity of initiatives, from early mediation to the latest implementation of conferencing, which can, to a greater or lesser degree, be described as 'victim-centred'. However, rather than focus attention on particular parties, to the detriment of others, it is preferable that restorative initiatives attempt to balance the needs of victims, offenders and the wider community. But, in an effort to spread their remit wide, restorative initiatives must manage limited resources. The 'restorative' element of restorative justice can easily become diluted as it attempts to appeal to different parties.

At present, restorative justice, with respect to the criminal law, can best be described as 'bolted-on' justice: that is, as an alternative to retributive justice that can still invoke the full force of the law, and criminal justice practice, should this be necessary. Restorative justice is, perhaps, just one more variation of 'justice', such as 'rehabilitative justice' or 'welfare justice' (see Chapter 1), that has been advanced in an effort to challenge the worst excesses of retributive justice. Given its diversity and the debates surrounding it, it has to be seen whether restorative justice can present a forceful challenge to traditional justice, and, ultimately, whether in the future it will come to present a victim-centred paradigm shift in criminal justice.

Suggested reading

Restorative justice is an increasingly popular field for practitioners, policy makers and victimologists. While it has suffered from an absence of critical theory, recent initiatives such as the European Science Foundation's COST Action A21 and the European Forum for Victim–Offender Mediation and Restorative Justice reflect developments towards the marriage of theory, critical evaluation studies, and practical initiatives. This is reflected in the recent growth in publications that document and variously critique the implementation of restorative justice initiatives around the world, including edited collections (Hirsch et al., 2003; McLaughlin et al., 2003), and more focused assessments of initiatives as restorative endeavours (Crawford and Newburn, 2003). Key texts in the field include Christie's seminal piece from 1977, which set the scene for restorative justice critiques about the 'theft' of crime (conflicts) from the people by the State. Braithwaite's 1989 text *Crime, Shame and Reintegration* provides much-needed theory in a field that is often replete with practice but lacking critical theoretical insight. For a brief overview of some of the key features and developments in restorative justice, Tony Marshall's short article, from 1997, presents a good introduction. This can be read along with his 1984 Home Office paper to get some insight into the development of restorative initiatives in England and Wales from mediation on. More recent assessments of restorative justice practice in England and

Wales include Young and Goold (1999), Young (2000), and Dignan (2002) with respect to reparation orders. Bazemore and Walgrave's edited collection (1999) includes some good chapters, particularly their own, on the 'place' of restorative justice as a challenge to established criminal justice practice, and presents case studies from around the world. Examples of North American restorative justice initiatives can be found in Wright (1991) and Zehr (1990), and New Zealand examples can be found in Morris and Maxwell (2000).

Notes

1. Restorative justice interventions are typically concentrated on interventions with juvenile offenders. At the time of writing, the University of Sheffield, UK, was in the process of evaluating adult-based restorative justice initiatives for the Home Office.
2. Scotland and, in particular, Northern Ireland are also promoting restorative practices (Dignan, 2000; O'Mahoney et al., 2002).
3. E/CN.15/2002/L.2/Rev.1 – 'Basic principles on the use of restorative justice programmes in criminal matters' (18 April 2002).

Chapter 8

Neglected and emergent victim-centred research, policy and practice

Introducing themes for discussion

Certain experiences of victimisation are regularly featured in victimological research and policy initiatives. The focus tends to be on victims of property and personal crime that falls within the ambit of the criminal law. As Chapter 2 illustrates, victim surveys have traditionally steered clear of difficult-to-count crimes, or so-called 'victimless crimes', such as fraud and drug abuse. More recently some 'victimless crimes', such as drug abuse, have been considered by victim surveys that include young people within their sampling frame. However, a diverse body of victimisation experiences remains that is not explored by the bulk of researchers and policy makers. This variously includes both 'old' and 'new' experiences of victimisation, or rather, given that very little crime is really 'new', neglected and emergent experiences of victimisation.

Focusing on specific examples of neglected and emergent victim-centred research and policy, this chapter explores what is known about the extent and nature of victimisation under these crimes, reasons for their omission and recent (re)discovery, and current policy responses to them.

'Alternative' themes in victim-centred research and policy

Examples of neglected and emergent avenues in victim-centred research and policy include:

- *fraud*: against individuals and small businesses through to large financial institutions and multinational corporations, including government offices;
- *money laundering*: harming financial institutions and countries that are the source of 'capital flight';

- *internet/cyber crime*: incorporates fraud and money laundering, and exploitation of vulnerable groups, such as children, particularly through sex crimes;
- *environmental crime*: pollution by industry, power stations and farming enterprises that impacts on people's health, and which goes unregulated/unprosecuted;
- *conflict and post-conflict crime*: crime is heightened during war and civil unrest, and women and girls are particularly vulnerable to human rights abuses such as rape; genocide and terrorism are also features of crime in conflict and post-conflict societies;
- *sex trafficking*: victimisation of women and children who are coerced into situations of sexual exploitation, often involving physical and psychological violence, by (organised) criminal groups.

This list is not exhaustive: for example, it does not include victims of hazards related to health and safety at work; nor does it include victims of road traffic accidents; nor victims of dangerous goods and inadequate services. What is does provide is a 'taster' of what tends to be left out of mainstream victimology and victim-centred policy initiatives. Echoing Ruggiero's (1992) call for a realist criminology incorporating a broader sweep of 'invisible victims' than those typically included in victim surveys, the list points to the neglect of victimisation against 'ordinary people' by businesses, governments and international criminal networks (organised crime).

For the sake of convenience the categories above are listed separately. In reality, categories tend to overlap, and can be variously grouped together depending on the crime(s) in question. For example, with respect to fraud, money laundering and certain aspects of internet crime, there are obvious similarities as they can be collectively grouped under the general heading of 'white-collar crime'. Likewise, environmental crime can incorporate aspects of fraud and money laundering, but is manifested as physical harm against the environment and people. There is also a link between conflict/post-conflict crime and sex trafficking, as trafficked women tend to come from regions suffering from economic instability associated with political and civil unrest. Both conflict/post-conflict crime and sex trafficking could come under the general heading of 'human rights abuses', which can also include torture and genocide, and which are, again, supported by laundered money.

Many of the above crimes have been under-researched because they do not provide an easy means of identifying victims and counting victimisation. For example, environmental crime – with the exception of well-publicised large-scale disasters such as Bhopal (India) or Chernobyl (former USSR) – literally seeps into the environment and can go unchecked for years. While the criminal law has traditionally focused on crime as a one-off event in time and place, these 'alternative' experiences of victimisation present crime as a complex and often long-term enterprise.

In turn, many of the above crimes, or victimisations, share a global reach. They are not limited to the 'domestic' sphere of the locality or the nation-state. Crimes like large-scale fraud and sex trafficking take place in a global arena but manifest themselves as crime and victimisation at the local level.

In sum, these 'other' experiences of victimisation have been neglected for two main reasons:

1. they challenge assumptions about 'who' should be considered a victim, and what should be considered as victimisation;
2. they present a 'new' and difficult set of considerations about the place and time of victimisation that helps to contextualise current experiences of 'victimhood', and in so doing opens up areas for victim-centred research and policy intervention.

Challenges for mainstream victimology: 'who' and 'what' is a victim?

Returning to themes addressed in Chapters 2 and 3, with respect to questions about 'who' can be a victim, the above list of neglected and emergent avenues in victim-centred research presents yet another layer of 'hidden' victimisation. These examples serve to challenge our assumptions about 'who' and 'what' can be considered as areas for research and policy intervention by victimologists. This exploration, here, centred around a selected group of 'alternative' experiences of victimisation, is as much about the prejudices and history of victimology, and individual victimologists, as it is about the nature of funding that prioritises certain research areas over others. The political emphasis given to different victims in different periods is also influential in determining policy areas.

While radical and critical victimology bemoans the discipline's narrow focus on personal and property crimes related to the criminal law, conservative victimology is wary of the discipline's expansion to include 'all' areas of human suffering. The accusation that is thrown at a wide-ranging victimology is that it has fallen foul of victim lobbyists and the 'culture of complaint' where we can all be considered victims or potential victims (Hughes, 1994). An expansionist victimology also appears to erode the foundations of victimology as *the* discipline to focus on the flipside of crime and criminality as based on the criminal law. However, limiting victimology's remit precludes the discipline's need to respond to changing experiences of crime and victimisation as they develop on both a domestic and a global stage.

The following paragraphs briefly sketch the marginalisation of 'environmental crime' and 'conflict and post-conflict crime' by mainstream victimology, while in the next section a range of explanations is offered that helps to contextualise diverse experiences of victimisation at the end of the twentieth century/beginning of the twenty-first century. Later on, 'white-collar crime' and 'sex trafficking' are explored in detail as case studies.

Environmental crime

Academic victimology/criminology pays very little attention to the impact of environmental crime on individuals, society and the environment. In comparison, grass-roots environmental campaigns, much like single-issue victim groups, have received and continue to receive support from segments of the population, and draw our attention to both the environmental and personal impact of environmental disasters. But while criminology generates a significant literature on corporate and State activity that can be directly and indirectly associated with crime, the same interest is not paid to environmental crime as generated by the State and 'big business'. Although, as South (1998) notes, 'little' events of localised pollution accumulate to bring modest to devastating changes in people's lives, there is no corresponding body of research by victimologists on the impact of these environmental harms.

The *Oxford Handbook of Criminology* contains a chapter on 'Environmental Criminology' which would seem to offer hope to those looking for criminological research on crime against the natural environment and its impact on human beings. However, the chapter will disappoint because its study – as the chapter puts it – of 'crime, criminality and victimization as they relate, first, to particular places and, secondly, to the way that individuals and organizations shape their activities spatially' (Bottoms and Wiles, 2002: 620) is limited to the spatial patterning of crime and criminality in the urban environment. True to its traditions, environmental criminology is narrowly framed around the built environment and fails to consider the wider environment of space and place in relation to nature.

Explanations of why victimology has failed to take up the challenge of environmental crimes rest with the discipline's construction as a sub-discipline of criminology, and the limitations that both subjects impose on themselves with respect to what can constitute legitimate areas of study. Given that crimes against person and property, as defined by the criminal law, constitute most of criminology's and victimology's areas of interest, crime against the environment, which often falls under the control of regulatory bodies other than the police, does not appear at first glance to fall within the remit of either discipline. Instead, the Environment Agency or the Health and Safety Inspectorate are two government agencies with responsibility for regulating and reporting environmental abuse, and geographers and environmental scientists are two academic groups that engage with the subject of environmental damage. Yet, environmental pollution harms both people and property, and, if intentional, should be considered as part of everyday crime and victimisation.

The omission of environmental crime as an eligible field of study for victimology rests with the fact that environmental crime, like white-collar crime, evokes an abstract victim. While increasing competence is being given at national and international levels to the penalisation of environmental crime through the criminal law,[1] and real victims can be identified who have suffered physical harm, victimology fails, in the main, to take on board the damage wreaked by these crimes on the environment, people, businesses and farming. Part of the reason for this non-recognition lies with what Beck (1992: 25; quoted in South, 1998) calls 'loss of social thinking'. In other words, consideration of the natural environment challenges us to reconsider questions about civil (social) rights and responsibilities that rest with ideas located in the built environment of the city as a place of human interaction. South (1998) adds that research on crimes against the (natural) environment confronts ways in which western culture has traditionally understood and theorised about the place of 'man' in relation to nature. With the burgeoning of 'science', invention and engineering in the industrial powerhouse that was Britain from the eighteenth century on, the environment came to be seen as a place of exploitation in the search for minerals and fuels that could support the country's wealth. By looking at environmental pollution and means of policing and punishing it, we are called on to rethink our ideas about social responsibility to each other and to the environment in settings other than the city.

Conflict and post-conflict crime

In turn, there are crimes that present us with tangible victims but which have not, until recently, received sufficient attention from victimology/ criminology. For example, research on crimes in and around war zones and areas of civil unrest have largely been left to other disciplines such as political studies, peace studies, law, history and journalism. As Jamieson (1998: 480) comments: 'The disinclination of contemporary criminology to foreground war and armed conflict is all the more astonishing when one considers (a) that as an empirical area of study, war offers a dramatic example of massive violence and victimisation in extremis.' Where criminologists have engaged with this subject they have pointed to the fact that most crime is heightened in times of war and civil conflict for a number of reasons that include: loss of social conduct norms (anomie); breakdown of agencies of social control (the police, judiciary); economic collapse and a corresponding rise in theft and black market trading; availability of weapons; and an emphasis on exaggerated masculinity encouraging aggressive behaviour.

Ordinary civilians are dragged into war and civil conflict and, as a result, suffer heightened victimisation from conventional crime (theft, burglary, assault), as well as increased risk of human rights abuses including mass rape, mass killings/genocide, and torture. These acts of violence against civilians are often carried out by agents of the State, and in this regard pose a series of questions for victimologists who need to consider the role of the State in sanctioning crime against civilians. More recently, irregular fighting cells under the control of 'warlords' or 'terrorists', rather than regular armies with a clear line of command, have played an increasingly prominent role in armed conflicts around the world (Holsti, 1996); here one thinks of Afghanistan, the Democratic Republic of Congo, Liberia, Iraq, Somalia and the former Yugoslavia (to name but a few). With little or no central authority overseeing the actions of these rogue fighting units, and holding them accountable to codes of conduct in war such as the Geneva Convention, there is little to stop them committing crimes against civilians. At the same time, there is ample evidence, from twentieth-century wars through to more recent conflicts in Afghanistan and Iraq, that regular armed forces also engage in practices against the human rights of non-combative civilians and those deemed to be 'enemy aliens'.

A culture of lawlessness is promoted in times of war and civil unrest, which presents victimology with a new set of rules regarding the relationship between victim and victimiser. In times of peace, at least in democratic countries, the separation between criminal and victim is usually clear once a defendant has been found guilty in a court of law. While miscarriages of justice serve to challenge the State, it remains the case that offenders, and particularly those who have broken the criminal law, are constructed in the eyes of the public as the criminal 'other'. But during war and civil unrest this distinction between the criminal 'other' and the 'victim' is less clear. In this regard, while the western media tended to construct Serbs as the aggressor during the civil war in the former Yugoslavia, Serbs were also victims of crime at the hands of other nationalities and other Serbs, including Muslims (Nikolić-Ristanović, 2002). NATO bombing of the Federal Republic of Yugoslavia, over several weeks in 1999, also served to rally Serbs together as victims of an aggressive air campaign (Ignjatović, 2002). The same muddied distinctions between 'victim' and 'offender' groups can also be noted with respect to other conflict zones, such as Israel/Palestine and Northern Ireland. Depending on which 'side' you are on in an armed struggle, the labels of aggressor/non-aggressor, freedom fighter/terrorist, and victim/offender are subject to group identification. Nationality, ethnicity and religion serve to determine 'who' is constructed as a victim or offender in the eyes of those doing the labelling (Ewald, 2002).

In turn, the specifically gendered nature of certain crimes during war and civil unrest – namely mass organised rape and sexual abuse of women and girls – has been documented by feminists, human rights activists and historians for some time now (Brownmiller, 1975; Amnesty International and Human Rights Watch). Non-governmental organisations try to meet the medical, psychological and practical needs of victims of rape and abuse, but there is an obvious role for victimologists to play in understanding and responding to the particular problem of violence against women during war and civil unrest. While some victimologists from these conflict zones have alerted the 'west' to women's experiences of rape, sexual abuse and domestic violence during and after periods of war and civil unrest (Milivojević, 1999; Nikolić-Ristanović, 2000; Nikolić-Ristanović, 2002), and have sought to explain this phenomenon, their work remains on the margins of mainstream victimology. The crime of rape during war, with ample documented examples from the First World War through to more recent events in Africa (Zilli, 2002), raises uncomfortable questions for victimologists with respect to patriarchy, misogyny, racism and xenophobia.

The UN's International Criminal Tribunals for the Former Yugoslavia and Rwanda illustrate the extent to which war and post-conflict crimes, including the crime of rape, are now taken seriously at an international level. And, at a domestic level, South Africa's Truth and Reconciliation Commission has had some success in exposing and reconciling former offenders with victims. However, mainstream victimological research has generally failed to engage with these experiences of group victimisation *in extremis*, nor has it sufficiently explored the impact of international trials and tribunals on actual victims of human rights abuses (Garkawe, 2001). Instead, lawyers and human rights activists are left to address the issue of war crimes by former dictators, warlords, non-civilians and civilians who have been accused of either sanctioning or committing various atrocities. Conflict and post-conflict victimisation should be the domain of human rights lawyers, non-governmental organisations *and* victimologists.

The place and time of victimisation: from the global to the local

The above list of neglected and emergent areas for victim-centred research and policy demands one thing: that we explore crime and victimisation as events that can be interconnected in place and time at the local and global level. Crime, in late modernity, needs to be understood as part of globalisation (Castells, 1998; Giddens, 1991 – see Chapter 1).

White-collar crime, environmental crime, conflict and post-conflict crime, and sex trafficking, all impact on individual victims and communities in certain places at certain times. To this end they can be understood, in part, in much the same way as conventional crimes, such as burglary and domestic violence, which we tend to examine at the local level. But many aspects of these 'alternative' fields of victimological research and policy force us to consider crime and victimisation as events that manifest themselves at the local level, but which are best understood in a global context. Although it is not useful to interpret petty white-collar crime, such as theft of company stationery for personal use, as part of a global criminal network, large-scale fraud and money laundering have to be interpreted as crimes that take place in an international arena. Similarly, drug smuggling and trafficking in women for sexual exploitation are, by default, cross-border crimes. Yet in describing these criminal activities as 'global' we must be careful not to lose sight of their impact at the level of the individual and the local. That is, global crime has real victims at certain times and in certain places.

Victimologists often prefer to work 'at home' on subjects that are specific to their local or country-wide jurisdiction. Although the World Society of Victimology's international symposia attract delegates from around the world, the majority of researchers and practitioners report on their localised experiences of victimisation and responses to it. In this regard victimology is no different from many other disciplines, and it is understandable that researchers should concentrate on domestic experiences of victimisation and social policy to which they have ready access and knowledge. On the other hand, while every research initiative does not have to be cross-national and comparative in scope, there is increasing recognition, particularly in criminology, that crime needs to be explored as part of a global phenomenon that impacts on community experiences of crime and victimisation at the local level.

A number of factors at the end of the twentieth century and the beginning of the twenty-first century have contributed to criminology's recognition of crime as a global enterprise. These include:

- the collapse of communist regimes in the former eastern bloc;
- civil conflict and accompanying economic instability in many regions around the world;
- mass migration, both legal and illegal, as a result of war, civil conflict and economic instability;
- the increasing power of international drug cartels and associated aspects of organised crime;
- the growing significance of international terrorist organisations.

The above factors are closely related and are most usefully considered in tandem as having an impact on crime and victimisation. For example, war and civil unrest in the former Yugoslavia followed the collapse of the country's Communist regime, and saw mass migration within the region and into the European Union. As a reflection of these events the region continues to suffer from economic and social instability. Organised crime has taken advantage of this situation to smuggle drugs, weapons and people within and outside the region (Lewis, 1998). The unstable political, social and economic climate, coupled with a significant Muslim population and the availability of weapons, has also aided the recruitment and training of terrorists since the attacks on the United States in September 2001.

After 11 September 2001, when the twin towers of the World Trade Center in New York (as well as the Pentagon and other US government buildings) were targeted by Islamic fundamentalists, terrorism has been held up by the US government and its supporters as the biggest threat facing the civilised world. Yet the manifestation and impact of terrorism as a *global* phenomenon has to be carefully appraised with respect to 'who' its victims and perpetrators are, and 'where' it occurs in time and place (Grabbe, 2001).

Case study: the significance of 9/11

While the US administration under President George W. Bush has played out a global 'war on terror' after the events of 11 September 2001, aided by Britain as its strongest ally, terrorism does not present a 'new' threat to peace and stability in many parts of the world. Britain itself has a long history of terrorism related to civil unrest in Ireland, once a former colony, and, more recently in the twentieth century, a long and bloody struggle in Northern Ireland that has resulted in the deaths of more people than were killed in the attack on the World Trade Center. Other western European countries have also suffered from terrorism: France, Germany, Italy and Spain. Yet European governments, unlike the US administration, have tended not to construct their experiences of terrorism in a global context. Arguably this is because, in the main, European terrorism has been internally generated, whereas in comparison the 11 September attacks on the US were of external origin.

But this polarised description of internal (local) or external (global) manifestations of terrorism serves to simplify a reality that is more complex. Local terrorist action is often financially supported by diverse sources. For example, private US donations supported the IRA's (Irish Republican Army) campaigns in mainland Britain and Northern Ireland against British rule. Likewise, Islamic suicide pilots who were involved in the 11 September attacks were, in some cases, residing in the US on expired visas and/or were trained as pilots there. And, while focusing on the 11 September attacks, we must not overlook the 1995 Oklahoma city bombing, which was the worst terrorist attack on US soil prior to 11 September, and which was perpetrated by two ex-army US citizens (although the US authorities

(Box continued)

and media pundits were at first keen to point the finger of responsibility for the bombing at Islamic fundamentalists).

While some terrorist attacks are local in origin with respect to their perpetrators, victims, financing and resources, they may be backed by ideals that have their origins elsewhere and which are part of a loosely connected international 'movement'; here, at the time of writing, one thinks of Islamic fundamentalism. At the same time, the 'civilised west', particularly the US, has a history of supporting armed resistance against communist regimes based on its own anti-communist ideals (Woodiwiss, 2001). This 'armed resistance' can be recast, by those same regimes that the 'west' seeks to overthrow, as sponsored terrorism. When States do not like what opposition groups are doing, then so-called 'civilised' nations can engage in the terrorism they are so ready to condemn as the action of 'others'. As South states (1998: 447): 'States condemn "terrorism", but of course have always been perfectly capable of resorting to terrorist-type methods when in conflict with oppositional groups.' For example, in 1985 the French government backed the action of its secret agents in blowing up the flagship of the environmental organisation Greenpeace. This served as a warning against the organisation's coverage of France's nuclear test programme in the Pacific; one crew member was killed as a result of the bombing.

Terrorist attacks, as they occur in one time and place, need to be interpreted as *potentially* part of a diverse and complex support system involving legal and illegal international financial transactions, weapon smuggling, and connected cells of human activity from different regions. Just as contemporary organised crime is no longer limited to the jurisdiction of particular criminal families in certain city neighbourhoods – here one thinks of the Krays' notorious reign in London's East End of the 1960s – so terrorist action needs to be considered as part of a global phenomenon that manifests itself as localised experiences of victimisation.

Exaggerating the place of the global: scapegoating 'the other'?

In their exploration of the local realities of organised crime, Hobbs and Dunnigham (1998: 300) state: 'We experience crime as global only via the manufactured outpourings of media and control agencies.' In other words, people do not experience crime as a global phenomenon. Ordinary citizens usually experience crime as victimisation in, around, or on the way to places where they live and work. People are also victimised when on holiday or business trips, but these events are locally contextualised in certain times and places. Hobbs and Dunnigham argue that crime is constructed as a global threat by the media because it sells papers, and by control agencies, such as Interpol/Europol and MI5/MI6, because it serves to justify their work.

With the collapse of communist regimes, the 'west' had to create a 'new' enemy other than communism. The identification of new external threats, be this international terrorism led by Islamic fundamentalists or transnational (organised) crime, also directs the public's attention away from internal problems that are particular to each country. Rather than focus on social, economic and political problems at home, governments can focus on the threat posed to a country's internal security and external business interests by international criminal networks and terrorism. The announcement in February 2004 that the British Labour government is to launch a British FBI-style 'superforce' to tackle crimes related to drugs and money laundering at a national and international level – with the provisional title of the 'Serious Organised Crime Agency' – highlights the government's commitment to tackling crime as a *global* phenomenon.

By focusing on externally generated crime we can also blame 'outsiders', rather than ourselves, as the cause of our own country's crime problems. From the Chicago School of urban sociology onwards, the focus has been on crime committed by undesirable outsiders. More recently in the context of the European Union, this negative label of criminal 'Other' has rested with refugees, asylum seekers, and economic migrants from poor countries – in particular, neighbouring eastern European countries and the Balkans because they pose a more immediate threat in terms of location and their accession into the EU (Goodey, 2002b). Evidence tends to be overlooked that the most marginalised foreigners are usually criminalised by default (because of their illegal status in a country) or, if they do commit crime, they generally commit petty acts as a means of economic survival (Albrecht, 2002). Rather than scapegoat the 'Other' for our own society's ills (I.H. Marshall, 1997), countries could do more to identify and compare internally driven threats to their own stability that originate with their own citizens with externally driven threats that originate with 'outsiders'.

Undoubtedly, international criminal and terrorist networks do pose a significant problem to the internal security of each country as crime has become more internationalised in recent years. The globalisation of the market economy, combined with the rise in communications technology, and the ease with which people can travel, have, together with unstable political, economic and social climates, aided the growth of international crime and terrorism. But each era would appear to create new 'demons' or 'outsiders' that raise the spectre of threatening a country's particular social order. In assessing the danger posed by each new threat, we have to address a number of factors in relation to the demand and supply of criminal markets within and between countries. In other words, external criminal influences infiltrate home-grown internal criminal markets where there is demand for their services, be this illicit cheap labour or drugs. At the same time, in focusing on an external criminal threat we detract from internally driven crime trends that have a devastating impact on people's lives.

The majority of criminal victimisation, at least in Britain, remains:

- home grown (by and against citizens, as opposed to being by non-citizens);
- conventional (burglary and petty theft, as opposed to international drug smuggling);
- local (occurring locally rather than globally).

Case study: the example of drug markets

A large part of crime in Britain's most deprived communities is related to drugs and the need to buy and sell them – drug dealing, violent crime, burglary, car crime. There is an obvious connection between the local reality of crime in these communities and global criminal networks. In other words, drug trafficking and related crime and violent crime link 'at-risk' local communities with transnational criminal networks.

Drug addicts and those who are victimised in the crossfire of violent drug-related crime are at the end of a long international chain that begins with illicit crop production in countries such as Afghanistan or Brazil. While some illegal drugs are manufactured in laboratories closer to home, drug markets are largely transnational. The negative impact on communities of illicit drug markets, and the crime and violent crime associated with them, is immense. Above all, communities suffering from illicit drug markets see the flight of 'social capital': that is, the disappearance of social norms that exist in social relations, and through social institutions, which instil foundations of trust and obligation in society. Communities that lose social capital see changes such as loss of business and employment opportunities, and a decline in the local infrastructure (schools, housing). As a result, communities also experience heightened levels of fear of crime as people are afraid to use public spaces where drug dealing and associated crime occurs. The knock-on effect of crime and fear of crime related to drug markets also manifests itself in the domestic sphere as families, particularly those with children and teenagers, suffer the consequences of members' direct and indirect involvement in drug-related crime (McKeganey and Norrie, 2000;

(Box continued)

Salzinger et al., 2002). As an example, communities that have fallen foul of drug markets represent the local reality of transnational crime, a reality that governments are right to focus on as part of an international fight against organised crime and illicit drugs.

However, while much good work is undertaken to deter and reduce the influence of illegal drug markets on communities at the local level (UNODCCP, 2002), the bulk of international funding is focused on destruction and control of illicit crops at source, and law enforcement efforts against organised drug cartels (International Narcotics Control Board, 2004). There are a number of problems with this approach:

- supply reduction is prioritised at the expense of demand reduction;
- the 'fight' against organised criminals is prioritised at the expense of addict rehabilitation and assistance to local communities that suffer as a result of illicit drug markets;
- drug crime is approached as a 'global' phenomenon before it is approached as a local reality.

It would be in order for governments to focus on international drug cartels if they devoted as much time and funding to combat the victimisation and suffering caused by illicit drug markets at the level of communities. But 'fighting' crime and declaring a 'war on drugs', like the latest 'war on terror', are more attractive propositions to international policing and security agencies than efforts to rehabilitate and assist drug victims.

External threat: forgotten victims

By focusing on crime generated by 'outsiders' we focus on the threat 'they' pose to citizens of our own country. Although research has been carried out in a number of developed countries on racially motivated crime and violence against ethnic minorities, which can include non-citizens (Martens, 2001), and there is now a Vienna-based European Union Monitoring Centre on Racism and Xenophobia, the focus of popular attention rests with 'undesirable' immigrants as a social and criminal problem. The victimisation of non-citizens, and in particular those 'undesirable others' (in the form of refugees, asylum seekers and illegal economic migrants), is neglected in the simplified construction of these outsiders as having the potential to harm 'our' own citizens (Goodey, 2000b). But recent cases exposing the exploitation and death of marginalised non-citizens in the EU, at the hands of human traffickers and gang masters, have served to question the stereotype of the 'undesirable' immigrant as an 'economic scrounger' or 'criminal'.[2] Instead, the reporting of these cases has served to partially reconstruct some unwanted immigrants as victims. However, accountability for these people's victimisation tends to rest with other immigrants and foreigners in the migration chain, and stops short of blaming citizens of countries whose demands for immigrants' cheap services – be this cockle picking or prostitution – are a reason for their presence in 'our' country. The responsibility of governments, whose immigration control mechanisms fail to tackle the problem of illegal and exploitative immigration, is also marginalised by the public and a populist media that are keener to label 'outsiders' as 'undesirable others' and 'criminals' in a reactionary effort to stem the tide of unwanted immigration. Ironically, the physical and legal barriers that governments put in place to prevent unwanted immigration, be this in the European Union or on the border between the United States and Mexico, provide a ready market for human smugglers who provide a smuggling 'service' for a high fee (Morrison, 1998).

The human cost of enforced border controls and ever more desperate efforts to cross them illegally is high. Many people die in their attempt to enter wealthier countries: for example, by drowning en route to their destination in flimsy boats, or when their smugglers ditch their human cargo at the first sign of a police/immigration patrol. Those who do successfully arrive at their destination can be further exploited in sweatshops or on building sites where pay is low and where they have no access to unions, health and safety protection, and a range of other social benefits that citizens tend to enjoy in developed countries.

But, as some commentators note, particularly in the right-wing British tabloid press, illegal immigrants do not pay tax on any money they earn, and, in entering another country illegally, they must realise that certain risks exist in their passage from A to B. However, this argument fails to acknowledge a number of points:

- First, illegal immigrants are not all economic migrants; many are fleeing political instability – in other words they are legitimate refugees.
- Second, many refugees and illegal immigrants, particularly those trafficked for sexual and labour exploitation, would rather not leave their homelands if there was any possibility of social and economic stability.
- Third, in the process of being exploited in their host countries many illegal immigrants are victims of criminal acts, and therefore should be recognised as such.
- Fourth, a significant number of refugees and illegal immigrants are children for whom 'choice' does not apply, as they are moved from one country to another, and whose rights as children should be recognised.

Finally, and returning to the major themes addressed in this section – namely the relationship between the construction of global (organised) criminal/terrorist threats and local realities of crime, and the scapegoating of undesirable outsiders as the criminal 'Other' – the next section focuses on two cases studies in an effort to explore these themes further as they relate to victimisation: (1) sex trafficking and (2) white-collar crime.

Focus: victims of trafficking

What is trafficking in persons/sex trafficking?

As an example of 'who' or 'what' generally fall within the remit of victimology, 'sex trafficking' presents a particular case that has received a great deal of attention from the international community in recent years, but, in comparison, relatively little attention from victimologists considering its impact on human rights abuses.[3]

Sex trafficking is grounded in the long history of human slavery (Bales, 1999). Anti-slavery initiatives, from British reformer William Wilberforce through to the League of Nations (as the precursor to the United Nations), have variously sought to define and eradicate slavery. There are more than 300 treaties and agreements that incorporate prohibitions against slavery and trafficking in persons. Looking just at UN-based international instruments in the twentieth century, these notably include: the Universal Declaration of Human Rights (1948); the Slavery Convention and additional protocols (1926, 1953 and 1957); the Convention on the Elimination of All Forms of Discrimination Against Women and additional protocols (1979 and 1999); the Convention on the Rights of the Child and additional protocols (1989 and 2000); and the International Labour Organization Convention Concerning the Prohibition and Immediate Action for the Elimination of the Worst Forms of Child Labour (1999). This list is selective and does not include the most important international instrument for the generic category of 'victims', namely the 1985 UN Declaration of Basic Principles of Justice for Victims of Crime and Abuse of Power.

Most recently, in 2000, the UN Convention Against Transnational Organised Crime and its two supplementary protocols have, for the first time, provided internationally agreed definitions that distinguish the activities of human 'trafficking' and 'smuggling'.

Article 3(a) of the UN Trafficking Protocol states:

> 'Trafficking in persons' shall mean the recruitment, transportation, transfer, harbouring or receipt of persons, by means of the threat or use of force or other forms of coercion, of abduction, of fraud, of deception, of the abuse of power or of a position of vulnerability or of the giving or receiving of payments or benefits to achieve the consent of a person having control over another person, for the purpose of exploitation. Exploitation shall include, at a minimum, the exploitation of the prostitution of others or other forms of sexual exploitation, forced labour or services, slavery or practices similar to slavery, servitude or the removal of organs.[4]

In comparison, Article 3(a) of the UN Protocol against Smuggling states:

> 'Smuggling of migrants' shall mean the procurement, in order to obtain, directly or indirectly, a financial or other material benefit, of the illegal entry of a person into a State Party of which the person is not a national or a permanent resident.[5]

As reflected in the above definitions, both trafficking and smuggling entail the illegal movement of people for profit, either within or across national borders. The fundamental difference between the two activities is that smuggled people are free at the end of the smuggling process, whereas trafficking victims are held in slave-like conditions of bonded labour or sexual servitude. Human smuggling can become human trafficking when, having parted with money to be smuggled, people find themselves working in situations of bonded labour. Likewise, smuggled people are at the mercy of their smugglers until they arrive at their final destination. In this regard, smuggled people can suffer various levels of exploitation at the hands of smugglers in their journey from A to B, but on arrival at their destination they have some degree of autonomy. While, in the case of 'sex trafficking', for example, some women may knowingly be recruited to work in the sex industry, their experience becomes one of trafficking when they are exploited under slave-like conditions. As indicated by the UN Protocol, trafficking, by definition, incurs exploitation.

The activities of human trafficking and human smuggling are wide-ranging in their scope. Trafficking and smuggling can impact on adults and children, men and women. Both activities involve the exploitation of people, either within and between developing countries, or between developing countries and the developed 'west' as they are moved from, typically, poorer areas to more affluent ones. Given the broad scope and impact of trafficking and smuggling, this case study narrowly focuses on one aspect of 'human trafficking', as opposed to 'human smuggling': that is, trafficking in women[6] for the purposes of sexual exploitation, or 'sex trafficking', primarily as it is experienced in the EU.

While the UN's Protocol on Trafficking in Persons provides an internationally agreed common definition of the phenomenon, the scale of 'sex trafficking' is, like any activity associated with organised crime, difficult to quantify accurately. Problems of accuracy are not aided by the fact that, until recently, shared definitions of 'trafficking' did not exist. 'Human trafficking' and 'human smuggling' continue to be confused as activities, and agencies with a responsibility for recording trafficking do not always keep accurate records. Faced with these challenges, the UN has recently established a database on trafficking flows in an attempt to identify global trafficking trends, including the volume of trafficking, though it is debatable whether accurate figures can be arrived at.[7]

Intergovernmental and government agencies are no better placed than non-governmental organisations (NGOs) to provide accurate estimates of the extent of trafficking in women for the sex industry. In recent years, the International Organisation for Migration (IOM) has provided the most quoted attempt to quantify the extent of sex trafficking in the European Union – with the figure suggested for 1995 being 500,000 (IOM, 1995). Within the EU only a few police forces can produce figures on sex trafficking with any degree of accuracy. This largely reflects the extent to which sex trafficking, as opposed to the widespread problem of illegal alien smuggling, has traditionally not been considered worthy of police time and effort as a reflection of its political standing. In turn, figures on 'trafficking' must be cautiously read as they often represent combined figures on illegal alien smuggling and human trafficking.

The German Federal Police, the Bundeskriminalamt (BKA), provides perhaps the best example in the EU of official records on sex trafficking. The BKA's regular situation reports on the extent and nature of sex trafficking in Germany are based exclusively on official criminal justice statistics gathered by the police. In 1999, the BKA recorded 801 victims of sex trafficking, of which a mere two were male (BKA, 1999). Of these 801 victims, the majority were nationals of central and east European countries, while the highest percentage of suspects by nationality were German (38.9 per cent) and Turkish (15.3 per cent), with the remainder from central and east European countries. This pattern of victims and victimisers reflects, in the case of Germany, three factors: (1) the country's proximity to central and east European countries; (2) the economic, political and social circumstances that have exacerbated central and east European countries' slippage into crime and civil disorder since the collapse of communist regimes; and (3) discrimination in employment practices against women in central and east European countries (the 'feminisation of poverty') which traffickers exploit by offering women false promises of lucrative work abroad.

NGOs working with trafficked women in central and east European countries, such as La Strada and the IOM, have documented the circumstances under which women enter into trafficking and are exploited by traffickers and, in turn, brothel owners. According to NGO reports, women are typically recruited with offers of lucrative employment in bars and clubs, or as au pairs. It is not uncommon for women to be falsely recruited by men they know, sometimes even family members, who offer a sense of security. In the same vein, there is evidence to suggest that women who were themselves victims of trafficking are also used for the recruitment of other women. Admittedly, some women are aware that they are being recruited for prostitution; however, they are unaware of the nature of the abuse they will suffer as victims of forced prostitution. Without engaging in the extensive debates that variously rage around the legitimisation of prostitution, one has to recognise that sex trafficking, as forced prostitution, is a human rights abuse.

It is not uncommon for women to be raped by traffickers, brothel owners and 'clients'. Rape, or the threat of rape, together with other forms of violence, is used as a means of subjugating women into a submissive state to be abused by those who profit from their exploitation. Under 'slave-like' conditions of containment, women are not given free range to come and go as they please. Instead, passports and other means of identification are removed from them and they are held as virtual prisoners in brothels where they are expected to service up to twenty clients a day (Europol, 1996).

There are a number of reasons why trafficked women are unable to escape situations of sexual bondage, and, having done so, why they are reluctant to cooperate with the authorities in their attempts to prosecute traffickers and brothel owners. First, circumstances of virtual imprisonment leave women with few opportunities for escape to report their victimisation. Given the opportunity to report to the police, trafficked women are often unable or unwilling to do so for a number of reasons: at a basic level they may not possess the language skills to report their experience of victimisation; they often originate from cultures with limited confidence in, and respect for, policing, and so would not think to approach the police; and they may fear physical reprisal from their abusers if they report their abuse. Traffickers also pose the threat of exposing a woman's involvement in prostitution to her family back home who remain ignorant of her situation. Revelation of a woman's involvement in prostitution, even if forced, only serves to shame women and family honour in many developing countries where victims of sex trafficking are effectively blamed for their exploitation and abuse. Threat of exposure, or threat of violence against a woman's family, can often be enough to stop a woman's attempts at escape and reporting. Together, these factors combine to trap women in abusive circumstances of forced prostitution.

Finally, sex trafficking needs to be understood on two levels. First, it is a crime of violence, by men, against women. While evidence exists that some women play key parts in the recruitment of women for trafficking networks, trafficking remains, like most other (organised) criminal activities, male-led. In this respect, trafficking in women for sexual exploitation needs interpretation as a gendered phenomenon with respect to its perpetrators, victims and 'clients' (Goodey, 2004b). Second, sex trafficking needs to be responded to, primarily, as a human rights abuse rather than a national or EU-wide security problem related to illegal and unwanted immigration for economic gain. In this regard sex trafficking is distinguishable from human smuggling.

Policy responses to sex trafficking at the level of the EU

Writing in 2002, Levi critiques the inclusion of trafficking in women in the list of competencies of agencies charged with organised crime control. He states (Levi, 2002: 881, footnote 4):

Following feminist, human rights, and media campaigns, trafficking of women rose to a high priority in the US and the UN and, to a perhaps lesser extent, the EU. There are real concerns about whether some of this was just economic migration, despite low wage rates in host countries and the fact that many become sex workers and therefore part of the quasi-consensual crime market. Many may migrate voluntarily, but what proportion of them are then forced to work 'exploitatively' and by violence rather than from lack of job prospects for illegal immigrants is much disputed.

Levi's doubts about the validity of 'feminist, human rights, and media' claims about sex trafficking reflect a number of factors. First, accurate data on the extent of sex trafficking is difficult to come by; because of this, attention given to sex trafficking can be dismissed as overblown in proportion to the scale of the problem. Second, reference to 'sex trafficking' conjures up age-old images of a 'white slave trade' in women. These images satisfy media and public curiosity in the worst traditions of the gutter press, and only serve to dismiss the current focus on sex trafficking as media hype. Although images of a 'white slave trade' might ring true in the context of movements of women within Europe, sex trafficking is in the main characterised by movements of women (and girls) either within or between developing regions of the world. Third, the current focus on illegal economic migrants serves to confuse 'trafficking' with 'smuggling', so that suspicions are raised that trafficked women are really economic migrants sheltering under the banner of 'exploitation'. But, in response to the doubts raised by Levi and some other cautious critics (Beare, 1997), evidence by 'hardened' police officers on the nature and extent of sex trafficking,[8] rather than liberal and sympathetic feminists and human rights activists with a cause to promote, would appear to confirm rather than deny the fact that sex trafficking is a real problem, on a global scale, with large-scale human rights abuses.

The recognition given to sex trafficking by international organisations such as the UN, OSCE (Office for Security and Cooperation in Europe), and the Council of Europe cannot be dismissed simply as the end product of recent successful lobbying by interest groups seeking to promote recognition of sex trafficking. As noted earlier, the long history of UN treaties in response to slavery testifies that 'sex trafficking' is not a new phenomenon, but one which has been recognised to varying degrees over the years. And, contrary to Levi's claim that the EU puts less emphasis on sex trafficking than the UN or the US, European institutions have done much since the mid-1990s to develop a comprehensive response to sex trafficking that variously adopts a three-pronged approach to the problem based on the need for: (1) prevention; (2) prosecution; and (3) protection and assistance to victims (see Kartusch, 2001 and Pearson, 2002 for comprehensive overviews of all three approaches in Europe and globally).

Until recently, prosecution has been the central focus of European law enforcement agencies in their efforts against trafficking and organised criminal networks. The recent shift towards victim-witness protection and assistance in trafficking cases is, arguably, also part of the prosecution effort as these measures encourage witness testimonies against traffickers. At the same time, assistance can encompass housing and education/training initiatives for women, and, to this end, can be welcomed as victim-centred measures. While the central focus of policing and prosecution agencies rests with the need to prosecute those responsible for trafficking, other organisations are more focused on victim/witness protection and assistance, as well as prevention campaigns in women's countries of origin.

The Council of Europe, with its human rights agenda, has been particularly active in highlighting the plight of victims of crime and specifically victims of sex trafficking.[9] In this respect, the Council has done much to distinguish the plight of trafficking victims as *victims* of organised crime rather than accomplices. And, while the European Commission and the European Parliament continue to focus on the criminal activities of organised crime and illegal immigration, they have also turned their attention to victims of organised crime.[10] To this end, in 1997 the Council of the European Union adopted a comprehensive Joint Action Plan in its efforts to combat trafficking in women (and children) for sexual exploitation. Two important anti-trafficking programmes emerged from this. The STOP[11] programme funded research and initiatives that set out to combat the sexual exploitation of women and children, including trafficking, and was aimed at public officials and representatives of NGOs.[12] The STOP programme was complemented by the Daphne initiative, which supported NGOs working to combat violence against women, and included projects against trafficking. At the same time as the STOP programme was instigated, the remit of the European Drugs Unit (as the precursor to Europol) was extended to include the collection, analysis and exchange of information and intelligence on trafficking.[13]

While these various communications, recommendations and action plans provide the basis of a response to the problem of trafficking, and while trafficking is now a criminal offence in all EU member states, there is no guarantee of substantive action, and results, against trafficking in the EU. As Kelly and Regan note in their research on, and critique of, criminal justice responses to sex trafficking (2000: 12): 'it appears there has been much talk but limited action'. Kelly and Regan's critique contrasts with Turnbill's overview of EU cooperation in the area of justice and home affairs, in which she suggests that trafficking in women and children 'appears to be an area where there has been significant success' (Turnbill, 1997: 203). EU initiatives with practical implications against trafficking, such as STOP and Daphne, present some measure of 'success'. However, it is relatively 'easy' to support the efforts of selected NGOs and government agencies in their fight against traffickers. It is a great deal harder for EU member states to collaborate on effective substantive measures against traffickers and in support of victims.

Since the initiation of the 1997 Joint Action Plan by the Council of the EU, there have been a number of attempts by the European Commission, the European Parliament and the European Council to realise an effective response to the crime of trafficking and, hence, the plight of trafficked women. In the conclusions of the October 1999 Tampere European Council, on the realisation of an area of freedom, security and justice in the EU, points 23 and 48 requested concrete initiatives to combat traffickers. But proposals have been slow to be adopted due to the absence of common definitions and sanctions against traffickers in the various member states of the EU. In this respect, the UN protocol on trafficking, to which the EU is a signatory, has provided the impetus for the latest legislative reforms from the European Commission against human trafficking.

Drawing heavily on the UN trafficking protocol, the Commission proposed, in January 2001, a Council Framework Decision on combating trafficking in human beings that has subsequently been adopted by the Council of the European Union.[14] This Framework Decision replaces the 1997 Joint Action and sets out to rectify the ineffective implementation of Tampere's conclusions, and subsequent initiatives, with respect to the absence of a harmonised legislative response to trafficking in the EU. Article 2 of the Framework Decision specifically details 'offences concerning trafficking in human beings for the purpose of sexual exploitation'. In turn, Article 8 refers to 'victims' and, in this respect, upholds the status of trafficked people as primarily *victims* of crime. The Framework Decision also includes the imposition of a minimum jail sentence for traffickers.

The effectiveness of this latest Framework Decision can only be gauged with time. The application of a common minimum sentence against traffickers has closed a loophole that, to date, has allowed traffickers to operate with relative impunity in different member states. However, common sanctions against traffickers do not directly serve the interests of trafficking victims; rather, this responds to trafficking as primarily a crime against the State. In this respect, one has to critique EU responses *against* traffickers in light of responses *for* victims.

The most recent comprehensive Commission response to trafficking, at the time of writing, is a February 2002 proposal for a Council Directive on short-term residence permits for victims of trafficking who cooperate with the authorities in their attempt to prosecute traffickers.[15] Looking at this Directive in some detail, it is apparent that its main concerns lie with the successful prosecution of traffickers through accommodating, to a limited extent, the needs of trafficking victims who usually face deportation once discovered by the authorities. The Directive is based on the premise that if cooperation between the competent authorities in a trafficking case serves the interests of victims, by giving them a residence permit, then victims are more likely to be a useful source of information against traffickers for the authorities.

What the Directive sets out to do is provide a residence permit, for an initial period of six months, for those who cooperate with the authorities against traffickers. 'Cooperation' itself covers a range of responses – from providing information about trafficking networks, through to testifying against traffickers in court. The Directive is not a victim protection or witness protection measure. Other international instruments are in place, such as the Resolution of the Council of the European Union,[16] together with the national laws of individual member states, that specifically respond to victims' needs for witness protection.

Concerns have been raised that the prospect of obtaining a residence permit in the EU, however temporary, might encourage women to falsely claim exploitation at the hands of traffickers. The 'success' and legitimacy of residence permits has yet to be determined. The authorities might regard them as successful if, as a consequence of their implementation, more trafficking victims are willing to provide information and give evidence against their traffickers. However, as far as trafficking victims are concerned, their 'success' is limited to the length of time they are permitted to stay in their 'host' country, and the degree of access they are afforded to other services while resident, such as welfare and health.

It can be argued that responses to sex trafficking, such as the 2000 Council Framework Decision and the 2002 Council Directive, are generally centred on the implementation of effective measures *against* traffickers in order to secure prosecution. While Decisions and Directives contain proposals that positively impact on victims of trafficking, one can argue that these primarily function as necessary tools in the effort to secure convictions. In this regard, one has to question the motives behind legislative and practical reforms against trafficking with respect to their impact on traffickers and victims, and the advantages they accrue for criminal justice authorities wishing to pursue trafficking cases. Whether anti-trafficking initiatives are 'victim-centred' is debatable.

Contextualising responses to sex trafficking

A number of juxtapositions emerge when considering criminal justice responses to offending and victimisation in the context of EU-wide efforts to stem the harmful effects of illegal immigration. Arguably, the focus of political and criminal justice activities, with respect to problems associated with unwanted immigration and crime, remains with offenders: their identification and punishment. In this regard, victims of organised crime – sex trafficking victims – have traditionally received less attention as 'equal players' in a crime equation that includes offenders, victims and criminal justice authorities.

For some time criminal justice authorities have not distinguished between organised criminals and victims of organised crime. In the case of sex trafficking, women's status as illegal immigrants has led to their criminalisation by default. Until relatively recently, the police have tended to respond to trafficked women, first, as illegal immigrants who are associated with organised crime, and, second, as vulnerable victims of organised crime. In this respect, victims of organised crime are doubly marginalised as victims and as 'outsiders'. In turn, with respect to women who are trafficked for the sex industry, one can argue that they are triply marginalised as victims, as 'outsiders', and as women who, through their 'work' as prostitutes, do not conform to stereotypes of 'vulnerable' and 'innocent' victims. There are a number of factors that, together, negatively impact on the treatment of trafficked women by criminal justice authorities: that is, their access to fair treatment and justice at different stages of the criminal justice system.

To a great extent, the secondary attention afforded victims of organised crime, when compared with offenders, reflects the limitations of broader responses to 'victims' in general. As victims of crime have until recently received scant attention within the criminal justice systems of EU member states (Brienen and Hoegen, 2000), it is hardly surprising that victims of organised crime, as particularly marginalised victims, should receive even less attention. Given the increased international recognition afforded to (1) victims of crime and (2) organised crime, it has yet to be determined where *victims of organised crime* 'fit' in this regard. While the latest European Commission Directive 'for' victims of organised crime can be positively viewed as a step in the right direction towards harmonisation of responses to victims of sex trafficking, this has to be read alongside broader responses to victims of crime in general. Given that many EU member states cannot, as yet, meet the demands of the 1985 UN Declaration of Basic Principles of Justice for Victims of Crime and Abuse of Power, one has to critically question the feasibility of the latest EC Directives for the specific category of sex trafficking victims. But, given criminal justice authorities' keenness to prosecute offenders in trafficking cases, increased assistance to victims seems likely in an effort to secure convictions.

Focus: victims of white-collar crime

Constructing a 'victimless' crime

White-collar crime is an all-encompassing term that can refer to fraud, money laundering and internet/cyber crime. Evoking the traditional class divisions between those who wore white collars to work in offices, and those whose blue collars denoted their work on the factory floor, 'white-collar crime' is crime that can be committed with the click of a computer mouse in the environment of the office. Because of this, as Nelken comments (2002: 860), 'The behaviour which constitutes white-collar crime is often indistinguishable on its surface from normal legal behaviour.' The setting for white-collar crime is the normal world of business interactions.

White-collar crime can affect individuals and small businesses, through to multinational corporations and the City of London's financial institutions. It can be the work of an individual or a sophisticated scam involving several partners. The economic and social impact of white-collar crime is significant (Slapper and Tombs, 1999), yet it is often constructed as 'complainantless' or 'victimless'. In the same way, crime against businesses such as theft, burglary and vandalism, and violent crime committed in the course of these crimes, is relegated to second place after personal and property crime against the individual. As R. Young comments, in his review of the neglect of corporate victims by restorative justice (2002: 137–8): 'All of the most influential victim studies and surveys, including the British Crime Survey itself, have focused on individuals as victims and have simply ignored corporate victims.' Yet the economic, social and personal costs of white-collar crime are significant.

The reasons for the neglect of white-collar crime as a legitimate area for victimological study are myriad. First, individuals who are victims of white-collar crime tend not to report their victimisation for a number of reasons: they fail to realise they have been victimised; they do not recognise themselves as 'victims'; they consider the crime too petty to report; or they feel there is nothing that can be done to recover their lost assets and apprehend those responsible. However, in cases involving credit card fraud, victims tend to report these offences more often as they are either aware of their card's disappearance and/or they notice purchases on their credit card bill that cannot be accounted for. In comparison, when individuals obtain the services of a professional – such as an accountant – when they cannot perform certain tasks themselves, then they are at risk of fraud because of their lack of expertise in the professional's field. Wrongful accounting or overcharging for goods and services are common practices that target unsuspecting customers.

Certain customers are particularly vulnerable to fraud at the hands of unscrupulous professionals who take advantage of people's frailty (the very old, the sick, the disabled) or lack of knowledge concerning the service they have hired the professional to perform. Croall (1995) suggests that long-held assumptions about women's ignorance in financial affairs has meant that female investors are targeted by fraudulent financial services and fraudulent sales of goods they typically consume – though this is perhaps less so as women are increasingly financially independent from men.

Everyday occurrences of white-collar crime against businesses, from taking of envelopes to fiddling company-car petrol receipts, do not usually merit detailed attention by businesses because this would entail use of valuable company resources (personnel, money and time). Many businesses tend to respond to fraud as an internal matter for their own disposal because the culprits are often employees and the sums involved are small enough to be written off as losses (Levi and Sherwin, 2000). Although more companies, particularly in the United States, are implementing fraud awareness programmes in an effort to prevent fraud and encourage employees to report instances of fraud, it is debatable whether these initiatives are cutting down on petty offences as opposed to more serious ones. Also, reluctance to reveal that a business has been the victim of fraud, whether by employees or external agents, is a reason for businesses not to report smaller instances of fraud to the police or another regulatory agency. To admit that your company is not secure from fraud does not encourage customer trust and loyalty, and is unlikely to attract new customers. However, large-scale fraud does get reported, and is increasingly coming under scrutiny as banking regulations become ever tighter (Joyce, forthcoming).

White-collar crime is also misconstructed as 'victimless' because it is difficult for people to raise much sympathy for crimes committed against big business. While we can feel pity for individual victims of fraud who have lost their life savings, or the small shop whose accountant fiddles the books, most people are hard-pressed to feel sympathy for financial institutions. But the human, social, political and, not least, economic costs to society from both small-scale and large-scale fraud are huge. Yet victimological research has not paid the degree of attention to these crimes, and their social impact, that they undoubtedly deserve. Instead, research remains fixated with personal and property crime against the individual. Much like the tabloid press, victimology can be accused of focusing on headline-grabbing crimes that evoke more interest than financial crimes which conjure up images of staid accountants. More print pages are given over to financial and white-collar crime by financial journals such as *The Economist* than by academic journals exploring crime and victimisation.

Where criminology does turn to explorations of white-collar crime, the focus is on the manifestation of the phenomenon and means of preventing and regulating it. The same degree of attention is not paid to white-collar crime as an experience of victimisation. In this regard, the immediate and long-term needs of individual victims of white-collar crime, which reflect far more than financial loss, are not given the kind of attention they deserve by either criminology or victimology, and, for that matter, the State. Large-scale fraud against financial institutions does receive a great deal of attention from criminal justice agencies and regulatory bodies for the fact that it threatens economic stability. In other words, what is bad for business is bad for the country. In comparison, individual victims do not benefit from the same degree of attention. For example, while the Criminal Injuries Compensation Authority for England and Wales compensates victims of violent crime for physical injury and emotional suffering, the State does not recognise victims of property and financial crime as eligible for compensation. Given that the majority of recorded crime is non-violent, it is understandable that the State cannot reimburse all those who suffer loss of property and money. At the same time, individuals and businesses are expected to take out insurance to cover financial losses and damage to property. Here the onus is on self-help. While responsibility for managing loss might seem in order for big business, this approach hits hardest against individuals with little cash to spare for insurance purposes. In the language of 'rights and responsibilities', some victims lose out more than others.

The 2001 collapse of Enron is a 'model' example of the kind of damage that large-scale fraud and mismanagement of company funds can do not only to a company but to an entire economy, and, more importantly, innocent company pension-holders. Enron, which was once the largest energy trader in the United States, saw losses in the range of US$40 billion amid disclosures of illegal deals that inflated company profits and hid billions of dollars in debt. The accounting firm Arthur Andersen was implicated in the financial mismanagement of Enron's collapse, which, at the end of the day, hit hardest at the company's pension-holders, who lost everything, while company directors sold their shares in Enron, before its collapse, at great profit. Commenting on this case Levi notes (2002: 879, footnote 2): 'it is tempting to ask which organized crime groups are doing more harm than Enron did'.

Ill-gotten money

Available data on the extent and nature of fraud and money laundering focuses on their impact on businesses, both as culprits and victims. The impact of these crimes on individuals, as share-holders or pension-holders, is less well researched. As a reflection of this, the next pages are limited to information about businesses.

Fraud

In Britain, notable detailed surveys on crimes against businesses include those published by the British Retail Consortium in their annual 'Retail Crime Costs', the Home Office's 1994 Commercial Victimisation Survey (Mirrlees-Black and Ross, 1995), and the 1998 Scottish Business Crime Survey (Burrows et al., 1999). The British Retail Consortium survey is a large questionnaire survey on crime against retail outlets which focuses on responses from head offices. In contrast, the Home Office's 1994 Commercial Victimisation Survey looked at crime against both retail and manufacturing premises, and directly interviewed staff in the workplace. The 1998 Scottish Business Crime Survey looked at a wide range of businesses, and employed a mixed methodology of head office interviews, surveys on business premises, and focused interviews. While all three surveys provide a wealth of information on businesses as victims of crime, all three exclude the financial sector from their research. As a reflection of this, the surveys are most useful as generic indicators of 'crime', but are not so informative about the extent, nature and impact of white-collar crime – particularly as it affects its most obvious victim, the financial sector.

We have to turn to large international surveys by auditors to get a measure of the extent, nature and impact of fraud and other white-collar crime against businesses, including the financial sector. Since the mid-1980s, Ernst and Young has undertaken fraud victimisation surveys of its clients throughout the world. Ernst and Young's 2000 survey revealed that in the twelve months prior to the survey, 45 per cent of respondents were the victim of between 1 and 5 frauds, 15 per cent were the victim of between 6 and 50 frauds, and 8 per cent were the victim of more than 50 frauds (Levi and Sherwin, 2000). Of businesses having suffered more than 50 frauds, the banking and financial services sector was over-represented. The survey also revealed that in the twelve months covered by the survey the largest single fraud was US$28 million, and total losses from the single worst frauds suffered by each respondent amounted to US$172 million, of which 29 per cent was recovered. This last figure compares favourably with the US$628 million which was reported as the sum of single worst frauds suffered by each respondent in the twelve months prior to the October 1998 survey. The difference between these two surveys for combined single worst losses could reflect an actual reduction in the scale of fraud during the two years between the surveys, or, conversely, reduced detection of fraud by businesses. But perhaps what this variation in figures illustrates most clearly is the difficulty of attempting to count accurately the cost of financial crimes.

As most fraud is perpetrated by employees, many of the larger businesses surveyed by Ernst and Young undertake some form of staff fraud awareness training to encourage 'whistleblowing' against colleagues who commit fraud. The 2000 survey revealed that half of companies with a turnover above US$1 billion provide staff with fraud awareness training, with US businesses particularly active in this area. Ernst and Young's surveys also look at businesses' perceptions of risk of fraud. While most businesses are particularly concerned about the damage that could be caused by a one-off 'big hit', facts show that most fraud occurs over a long period of time. Executives' nervousness about the threat of a one-off hit would be better placed looking at internal mechanisms against low-level cumulative fraud over time.

Alongside Ernst and Young, KPMG (now called 'Bearing Point') is another big accounting firm that undertakes fraud surveys. Reporting on KPMG's survey of Australian experiences of business fraud, Smith (1999) found that of 367 businesses that replied to the survey (20 per cent of the original sample) 57 per cent had at least one incident of fraud in the two years preceding the survey. Sixty-nine per cent of those who had been victimised had suffered more than one incident (with the majority experiencing anything from two to ten incidents). The financial service industry, the insurance industry and government organisations reported the greatest losses. And, unsurprisingly, fraud tended to be committed by employees rather than outsiders.

The scope for employees to commit fraud using computer and communications technology is increasing. A 1998 survey by Australia's Victoria State Police and the firm Deloitte and Touche (as reported in Smith, 1999), revealed that 33 per cent of 350 large Australian businesses had experienced unauthorised use of their computers within the previous twelve months – with one-quarter of misuse motivated by financial gain. In response, businesses are trying to pre-empt opportunities for employees to commit crime using new technologies.

Finally, credit card internet fraud has the potential to do a lot of damage to online retailers, who are potentially the biggest victims in any online scam. This is because the bulk of the cost of fraudulent transactions has to be met by the *online* retailers themselves, and not by credit card companies (as is normal practice with *regular* retailers and members of the public when they are defrauded on their credit cards). As yet, the impact of online credit card fraud against businesses and individual consumers who conduct credit card transactions over the internet is a relatively uncharted area of research and financial investigation (Levi, 1998).

Money laundering

According to a 1998 UN report on 'financial havens, banking secrecy and money-laundering' (UNODCCP, 1998: 34): 'Often described as the white collar crime of the 1990s, money-laundering is in fact a crucial accompaniment to many forms of criminal activity ranging from drug trafficking and organized crime to financial fraud.' Money laundering, or the process of making 'dirty' money (obtained by criminal means) 'clean', is, like fraud, an old crime that manifests itself in new forms. The distinction between dirty and clean money is often unclear. Many areas of business in late modernity operate in the shadow or grey economy where differences between legitimate and illegitimate transactions are murky.

For example, tourist resorts in the Caribbean may be financed by money obtained from drug deals which is then laundered through off-shore banks (see box). As illicit drug crops are grown in parts of the Caribbean, and transported to their North American and European markets to be bought and consumed, so people from these same markets can return to the Caribbean, where illicit crops are grown, for a luxurious resort holiday. At the same time as we now travel easily for business and pleasure, globalisation means that we can also sit in an office in London and secure a financial transaction to an off-shore bank in the Caribbean.

Off-shore banking

Banks that operate 'off shore' are legally domiciled in one jurisdiction and conduct business only with non-residents. Their legitimate role is to reduce taxes and avoid other restrictive regulations on income growth for customers that are normally imposed by banks. But because off-shore banks are exempt from a wide range of regulations that are imposed on ordinary banks they are also a magnet for drug money and other illegally obtained funds.

Money laundering itself has been made easier by the existence and proliferation of off-shore banking. Within Europe alone, major financial havens for off-shore banking include: Cyprus; Gibraltar; the Channel Islands; the Isle of Man; Liechtenstein; Luxembourg; Malta; Monaco; and, most notably, Switzerland. However, bank secrecy in financial havens such as Switzerland has changed dramatically in recent years as countries respond to the pressure placed on them for greater transparency in their banking procedures.

While the importance of off-shore banks is in decline as governments around the world reduce taxes, liberalise financial regulations, and generally clean up their act, off-shore banks will still play a role for illegitimate business for some time to come.

In order to disguise money obtained by ill-gotten means, money laundering requires a three-stage response (UNODCCP, 1998):

1. The funds have to be moved quickly so they are not directly associated with the criminal act.
2. The trail needs to be disguised to avoid detection and pursuit.
3. Once disguised, the money needs to be made available to the criminal for use.

In response, the international financial system and international financial investigators set out to find, freeze and forfeit criminal assets and income through a variety of means. However, they are not aided in this process by a number of factors, including the general trend towards financial deregulation of markets and the proliferation of off-shore banking, both of which make the trail of illegal money increasingly harder to trace.

Money laundering is most often associated with illicit drug transactions involving organised crime. As a reflection of this, the UN Convention Against Illicit Traffic in Narcotic Drugs and Psychotropic Substances (1988) was the first international legal instrument to establish an offence of laundering the proceeds of drug trafficking. In the same year, 1988, the Basle Committee on Banking Regulations and Supervisory Practices issued a 'Statement on Prevention of Criminal Use of the Banking System for the Purpose of Money Laundering' – in effect a code of ethics for bankers. The European Commission's (EC) adoption of Council Directive 91/308/EEC, in 1991, aligned itself to the 1988 UN Convention, and gave EU member states additional powers to extend the Directive to other criminal activities involving money laundering other than drug trafficking. More recently, the EC's Council Framework Decision, June 2001, on 'money laundering, the identification, tracing, freezing, seizing and confiscation of instrumentalities and the proceeds of crime',[17] has set out to extend these powers.

The basis on which anti-money laundering initiatives have been developed for the international community is the 40 recommendations set out in 1990 by the Financial Action Task Force (FATF) (subsequently revised in 1996 and 2003). The FATF meets regularly to set international standards against all forms of money laundering. Its recommendations, together with those of the Basle Committee, have been backed by the UN through the 2000 UN Convention Against Transnational Organised Crime, which requires governments to put in place a range of anti-money laundering initiatives. More recently, in light of the 11 September attacks, further strength has been given to anti-money laundering initiatives by the UN in an effort to combat financing of terrorism. The key developments here are UN Security Council Resolution 1373, which addresses the financing of terrorism through money laundering and other illicit means, and the UN Convention for the Suppression of the Financing of Terrorism which entered into force in April 2002.

Since the 1988 UN Convention Against Illicit Traffic in Narcotic Drugs and Psychotropic Substances and the 11 September attacks, greater importance has been placed on seizure of illegal assets as they underpin organised criminal activity, including terrorism. In the eyes of law enforcement agencies, recovery of criminal assets is increasingly seen as a way of financing their activities, and secondly as a means of compensating victims for loss suffered (UNODCCP, 1998: 4).

While large businesses have the financial means at their disposal to pursue significant cases of money laundering, individual victims of money laundering have neither the financial means nor the expertise to undertake such a task. International policing and regulatory agencies, from Interpol to the FATF, need to consider how assets can be more readily recovered and repatriated to those victims of money laundering who are most in need. Admittedly, the trail of victims is hard to follow. But if laundered money can be traced through businesses and off-shore banks, then the same degree of attention could be paid to compensating victims in cases where governments and individuals, including heads of state, have laundered their country's assets for private gain.

Given that most restitution from offenders to victims is hard to secure in conventional criminal/civil law cases, it is debatable whether large sums of money can be recovered for victims in money laundering cases. With respect to illegal drug money, some researchers suggest that relatively little ends up being laundered through the banking system, except in the case of major international drug syndicates; this is because profits are spent immediately on hedonistic pursuits, or, as Levi points out from anecdotal interviews (2003: 223), the impact of new financial regulations means that more illegal money is being kept away from banks as cash. When illegal money does enter the banking system cases are highly complex and often take years to resolve. And, the 'success' rate in these cases is also low given the resources it takes to bring a case to court. As an expert from the UN's Global Programme Against Money Laundering puts it (Joyce, forthcoming): 'It is rare that more than a small proportion of the illegal funds is repatriated to the country from which it was stolen and the amount of success in repatriating some assets hardly seems commensurate with the years of work and the expense incurred.'

In response to these obstacles, a new Asset Recovery Agency was established in England and Wales in 2003, with a remit to recover £64 million from the proceeds of crime.[18] But the costs of asset recovery usually mean that the most financially impoverished countries, and their citizens, do not have the means available to pursue cases. Arguably, only when (rich) countries with off-shore financial centres experience crime related to drugs and fraud themselves – only when their own citizens become victims of crime on a significant scale – will they heed the call from organisations such as the FATF and the UN to reform their banking sector. However, perhaps the greatest scope for improving financial regulation of illegal assets comes with the enforcement of 'corporate criminal liability' and 'individual liability' for the acts of corporations. What this means is that if a company and its directors can be held directly responsible for illegal financial transactions, then they are more likely to self-regulate their company's deals to make sure they are legitimate. Fear of being held personally responsible and of going to prison is perhaps the best incentive that businesses can have to 'keep clean'. In the same vein, 'constructive trust liability' has developed in common law countries as a means of responding to fraud and corruption cases. This holds bankers, accountants and lawyers – who act as intermediaries in financial transactions – liable to owners of funds, even if they themselves did not benefit from these funds other than through professional fees for their services. The idea behind 'constructive trust liability', as with corporate and individual liability, is to make individuals within the financial sector more responsible in self-regulating the funds they handle. Secondly, constructive trust liability, targeted at the 'middle men' in financial dealings, is seen as a means of securing compensation for victims of fraud and money laundering where the principal offenders and their assets are not recovered – as was successfully applied in the Maxwell pension fraud case where intermediaries (bankers and account-ants) contributed almost all the money required to compensate victims (UNODCCP, 1998: 54).

Capital flight and corruption

Perhaps the clearest illustration of the social and economic damage caused by money laundering is the example of 'capital flight' – that is, when commercial and private funds are moved from one country to another. Capital flight is assisted by corrupt government, business and banking practices. The UN's International Crime Victims Surveys (see Chapter 2) explore people's experiences of corruption alongside their experiences of property and interpersonal crime. In developing countries and coun-tries in transition, corruption, from low-level bribes to public officials through to large-scale capital flight, emerges as a significant problem affecting people's daily lives. Although corruption is also a problem for developed countries – Italy being a classic example – they are economic-ally better placed to weather its worst aspects.

Capital flight can be both legal and illegal. The legal component consists of properly documented post-tax money being moved between countries, and is consistent with a free market economy. The illegal component is, by comparison, improperly documented, tax-free, and almost always untraceable – in other words, money laundering. While legal capital flight occurs in order to safeguard funds in situations of political and economic instability, with the intention that funds be reinvested in their country of origin once stability returns, illegal capital flight is about accumulating private funds that rarely return to their country of origin.

Although numbers are notoriously difficult to gauge with any degree of accuracy, it is estimated that US\$100 billion of illegal capital flight enter the United States and Europe every year; and the US Treasury Department further estimates that 99.9 per cent of criminal money that is deposited in US banks finds its way into secure accounts (Baker, 2000: 1055–6). This money provides a cover for further money laundering. As Baker comments (2000: 1055): 'Illegal capital flight and criminal money laundering are two rails on the same tracks through the international financial system.' Even if these figures are an over-estimation of the scale of the problem, at one-tenth of their real value they represent a serious problem for those countries experiencing illegal capital flight in times of crisis. The countries hardest hit by illegal capital flight are in the developing world, and the people who are most vulnerable as a result of the exodus of funds are the poor. In comparison, the developed west, through its banks' failure to target illegal capital flight, benefits from the money that is laundered through its accounts to be reinvested in the economies of North America and western Europe.

Case study: Nigeria

Nigeria provides ample examples of illegal capital flight, money laundering and resultant social harm. An oil rich country with the largest population in Africa (107 million), Nigeria has suffered under a series of disastrous dictatorships since its independence from Britain in 1960. The case of the Abacha family is just one example of illegal capital flight and money laundering, and the role played by western banks in this process.

General Sani Abacha was military leader of Nigeria from 1993 to 1998. His regime has been widely condemned as one of the most corrupt and brutal in Africa. According to a 1999 report on Abacha, he 'may have stolen over US$3.5 million over the course of his five years in power', which resulted in severe consequences for the bankrupted Nigerian treasury.[19] Other sources estimate that between US$5.5 billion (Joyce, forthcoming) and US$12 to 15 billion (Baker, 2000) was taken out of Nigeria during the time of the Abacha regime. After Abacha's sudden death in 1998, his sons and his wife were implicated in large-scale money laundering and illegal capital flight. According to press reports at the time of Abacha's death, his wife was stopped at a Nigerian airport with 38 suitcases full of foreign currency, and one of his sons was caught with about US$100 million in his possession.[20] Abacha held money in several western banks throughout the world. According to the Swiss Federal Banking Commission, Abacha's money passed from Swiss banks to 524 banks in Liechtenstein, Luxembourg, the US and the UK. After his death and investigations by the new Nigerian government into the missing millions, Abacha's former accounts were frozen and money began to return to Nigeria – money which had been leached from the State and, in particular, the country's oil reserves. While this case has a partial 'success' story to report, in most cases funds appropriated through illegal capital flight do not return.

Case study: Russia

Russia offers an ongoing example of illegal capital flight and money laundering since the collapse of its former Communist regime. According to Baker (2000: 1056), in the decade since the fall of Communism, between US$150 billion and US$500 billion has been lost from the country. Although investment by western businesses and governments is also taking place in Russia, the initial free-for-all

(Box continued)

in capital flight did much to damage the country's already ailing infrastructure. Russian politicians and businessmen, together with western banks, are responsible for a plethora of problems that have continued to besiege Russia since it opened its doors to the legal and illegal market economy – problems that include heightened inflation, reduced government revenues, and a widening poverty gap between rich and poor.

Corruption is the key facilitator for illegal capital flight. Money leaves a country via a range of corrupt practices including misappropriation and embezzlement of public resources, falsification of import and export costs, and 'wire fraud' involving internet transactions and off-shore banking. Corruption has to be present in both the source and receiving country for illegal transactions to succeed. Recognising that a combination of corruption and greed lie at the heart of criminal activities involving illegal money transfers, the United Nations has recently adopted a Convention Against Corruption (adopted by the General Assembly of the UN by Resolution 58/4 of 31 October 2003). The Corruption Convention establishes a comprehensive range of responses to corruption focusing on prevention, criminalisation, international cooperation and asset recovery. Money laundering and illegal capital flight are at the centre of many of the Convention's areas for international intervention and cooperation. For example, among a range of new commitments, signatories to the Convention are required to establish criminal offences against the concealment and laundering of the proceeds of corruption, and must also undertake measures to support the tracing, freezing, seizure and confiscation of the proceeds of corruption. The Convention's reference to asset recovery is particularly important for developing countries, such as Nigeria, where high-level corruption has stolen national wealth. By emphasising asset recovery the Convention sets out to recover money for reconstruction and rehabilitation of societies under new governments.

In his statement on the adoption by the UN General Assembly of the UN Convention Against Corruption, UN Secretary General Kofi Annan said: 'Corruption hurts the poor disproportionately – by diverting funds intended for development, undermining a government's ability to provide basic services, feeding inequality and injustice, and discouraging foreign investment and aid.' By setting out a wide range of responses to fight corruption, the UN Convention Against Corruption is ambitious in its goals. But only with the cooperation of the private banking sector, combined with its control mechanisms such as the FATF, can the Corruption Convention hope to be truly effective. As with its predecessor, the 1985 UN Declaration of Basic Principles of Justice for Victims of Crime and Abuse of Power, the Corruption Convention has a long way to go before the theory of 'good practice' becomes a reality.

Concluding comments

This chapter set out to provide a broad overview of some of the experiences of victimisation that are often ignored by mainstream victimology and victim-centred policy – that is, neglected and emergent areas. Each of the selected areas challenges victimology to reconsider 'who' or 'what' can be considered victims. In particular, the chapter asks victim-centred research and policy to look beyond a narrow focus on crime and victimisation as experienced at the level of the local, and to consider the implications of victimisation as part of a global criminal enterprise.

The experiences of victimisation introduced in the chapter are not readily quantifiable, and for that reason alone present a challenge to victimology, which so often likes to 'count' crime and victimisation. What the examples reveal is the complexities of victimisation that are not readily identifiable under the terms of national criminal law, which in many instances is only waking up to the fact that certain actions have tangible victims. Money laundering and environmental crime, to name just two examples, have been constructed as 'victimless' crimes when in reality they have a devastating impact on people's lives throughout the world.

Part of the chapter's remit has also been to challenge how we understand victimisation by making us think about the construction of the 'Other', or social outsiders, as criminals before we consider them as victims. Some of the most marginalised victims, such as women trafficked for the sex industry, have been constructed first as unwanted illegal immigrants, or economic 'scroungers', before their experiences of victimisation have been recognised. In our desire to protect our own interests, the circumstances of some of the most vulnerable victims in society are often ignored. Intergovernmental agencies such as the United Nations and the Council of Europe have done much to highlight the plight of the world's most vulnerable victims – from trafficked women and children, through to the poor whose national wealth is looted by corrupt individuals, governments and banks. The financial sector in the developed 'west' still has a long way to go in recognising its responsibilities to reform banking so that criminals cannot hide illegally obtained funds, and the world's poor do not suffer as a result.

Research on and responses to some of the *crimes* mentioned in this chapter are being led by practitioners and policy makers, and to a lesser extent academics. The flipside of these criminal activities – *victimisation* – has more recently received attention, but not, in the main, from victimologists; an edited collection by Davies et al. (1999) goes some way to addressing some of this shortfall from academia. Rather than defer research into these experiences of victimisation, and policy responses to it, to those working in the fields of human rights, law, and political studies, victimology should recognise that it has a significant role to play in understanding and responding to wide-scale abuses that constitute victimisation.

Suggested reading

There exists a wealth of literature on white-collar crime – fraud, money laundering, internet crime – as 'crime' rather than 'victimisation'. To this end, Nelken (2002) provides an excellent overview of white-collar crime that concentrates on its *criminality* rather than its impact as victimisation; while Levi and Sherwin (2000) touch on white-collar crime as a victimising experience in their exploration of the effect of fraud on business. Davies et al.'s (1999) edited collection is a rare exploration of hidden crimes and victimisation, focusing mostly on white-collar crime and crime in the workplace. In comparison, 'sex trafficking' has received a great deal of attention since the 1990s as a victimising experience, with a good deal of research, commentary and policy emerging from non-governmental and international organisations such as the International Organisation for Migration (www.iom.int) and the United Nations (www.unodc.org/unodc/en/trafficking_human_beings.html). Kelly and Regan's report for the Home Office (www.homeoffice.gov.uk/rds/prgpdfs/fprs125.pdf) provides an excellent empirical introduction to the problem of sex trafficking from a UK perspective. My own publications on sex trafficking (Goodey, 2004a and 2004b) and, more generally, the criminalisation of migrants and the neglect of their experiences as victims (2000b and 2002b), address various points raised in this chapter.

Notes

1. For example, Council of the European Union Framework Decision 2003/80/JHA of 27 January 2003 on the Protection of the Environment Through Criminal Law; see also IMPEL (European Network for the Implementation and Enforcement of Environmental Law), an informal network of regulators, with its secretariat (administration) based in Directorate-General 'Environment' at the European Commission (http://europa.eu.int/comm/environment/impel/criminal.htm).
2. Two cases involving Chinese immigrants are of particular note. One was the discovery in Dover of 58 dead Chinese people in the back of a container lorry; they had attempted to enter Britain illegally, but suffocated to death as the air vent into the container was closed during transit (June 2000). Another was the death of 18 Chinese cockle pickers in Morecambe Bay; they drowned as they were cut off by the tide, having been put at risk by their gang masters (February 2004).
3. There are exceptions – in 2004, a special issue of the *International Review of Victimology* (11(1)) was devoted to sex trafficking.
4. Accompanying Protocol against Trafficking in Persons, especially women and children.
5. Accompanying Protocol against the Smuggling of Migrants by Land, Sea and Air.

6. As stated, sex trafficking affects women and girls, but, given the paucity of information on trafficked girls, the focus here is on women. See Defence for Children, an international children's rights organisation that highlights the problem of children's sexual exploitation, including sex trafficking, www.defenceforchildren.nl.

7. See www.unov.org – Global Programme Against Trafficking in Human Beings.

8. Evidence presented by EU police officers at Europol expert group meeting on Trafficking in Human Beings for the Purpose of Sexual Exploitation, The Hague, March 2001; attended by the author. OSCE (Office for Security and Cooperation in Europe), Stability Pact for South-Eastern Europe, meeting on development of a training manual for judges dealing in trafficking cases, Sofia, March 2003; attended by the author as speaker.

9. Council of Europe (1994) Final Report of the Group of Specialists on Action Against Traffic in Women and Forced Prostitution as Violations of Human Rights and Human Dignity, CDEG: Strasbourg.

10. European Commission (1996) Communication from the Commission to the Council and the European Parliament on Trafficking in Women for the Purpose of Sexual Exploitation, COM (96) 567, Brussels (20.11.96); European Parliament (1996) Resolution on Trafficking in Human Beings, OJ C 32 (5.2.1996).

11. STOP programme: Joint Action 96/700/JHA; OJ L.322 (12.12.96).

12. The STOP programme was followed by the STOP II programme. This has now been replaced by the Agis programme (2002–07).

13. Europol Drugs Unit: Joint Action 96/748/JHA; OJ L.342 (31.12.96).

14. Communication from the Commission to the Council and the European Parliament on 'Combating trafficking in human beings', Brussels, 22.1.01, COM (2000) 854 final.

15. COM (2002) 71, final.

16. OJ C 327 (7.12.1995), p. 5.

17. 2001/500/JHA (26 June 2001); http://europa.eu.int/eur-lex/pri/en/oj/dat/2001.

18. See Home Office Circular 43/2003 'National Best Practice Guide to Confiscation Order Enforcement'; www.homeoffice.gov.uk/docs2/hoc4303.html.

19. Congressional Research Service (CRS) Issue Brief No. IB98046, 'Nigeria in Political Transition'; as quoted in the report of the Committee on Governmental Affairs, United States Senate, 106th Congress, First Session, 9–10 November 1999, p. 925.

20. *The Observer* (22/11/98) 'How the grand lootocracy beggared Nigeria's people'; as quoted in the report of the Committee on Governmental Affairs, United States Senate, 106th Congress, First Session, 9–10 November 1999, p. 925.

End comment: some salient points for consideration

The successful marriage of academic victimology, as non-partisan empirical research, with victim-centred policy and practice, as the politicians' and practitioners' fields of influence, is, as Chapter 4 noted, a tall order that demands a clear set of 'good practice' objectives, outputs and outcomes. Advocates of restorative justice would construct this marriage in the framework of 'inclusive' restorative principles, while restorative justice sceptics would look to improve the victim's experience of criminal justice through the traditional channels of police and courts.

Given that most victims do not engage with the criminal justice system for a variety of reasons, there is, at present, no justice model that can comprehensively meet the needs of the majority of victims. For example, many victims do not report crime either because they consider the offence too trivial, or they have no insurance cover that would demand a police report, or they are wary of the kind of reception they will receive from the criminal justice authorities. Traditional retributive justice is narrowly limited to those instances of victimisation where there is a known offender, and where victims are willing to report crime. Restorative justice similarly demands participation by victims and offenders. Although restorative justice initiatives exist that pair offenders with victims of similar crimes, if not the offender's actual victim, these 'restorative' practices are limited in their impact and the extent to which they can be identified as wholly 'restorative'. In turn, of those victims who decide to report their victimisation, many find that their cases are either dropped by the police and the Crown Prosecution Service because of lack of evidence, or, if pursued, no suspect is found, and, if found, charges are not brought. For those victims whose cases actually reach the courts, there is also, depending on the nature of the crime in question (rape being a prime example), the very real possibility that the defendant is found 'not guilty'.

Perhaps explorations of the victim's place *within* traditional criminal justice, or restorative justice as its main 'rival', should look to the victim's place *without* 'justice' models: that is, the experience and needs of the majority of victims who never engage fully, if at all, with any justice model. Such an approach to victims (of crime) – moving away from a close examination of the various innovations and failings of law and criminal justice practice for victims – would demand a new set of 'justice' criteria that even restorative justice, in its incarnation most removed from traditional criminal justice, is unable to meet.

Chapter 8 touched on some examples that serve to raise questions about those victims who fall *without* victimology and victim-centred policy and practice. There are obvious lessons to learn from other disciplines and other policy and practitioner fields that may yet allow the study of victims to flourish beyond current discussions that tend to remain with the criminal law and the criminal justice system. Hospitals, schools, housing schemes, factories, offices and public transport – to name just a few settings – are all the scene of 'harms' or 'crimes' that may or may not be processed through existing criminal justice channels or some means of civil or informal dispute resolution. To understand people's experience of 'harm' as 'victimisation', and what they understand it to mean, and what they might need as a result of it, requires that we (and I am mostly referring to academic victimologists here) also develop alternative 'justice' models that are able to capture the range of people's victimising experiences that exist *without* the confines of current traditional/restorative justice models. Herein there is another set of neglected themes that victim-centred research, policy and practice can address:

- experiences of victims who don't engage with any justice model;
- needs (service standards) of victims who don't engage with any justice model;
- rights (legal provisions) of victims who don't engage with any justice model.

But recognising that most victims do not engage with any justice model is not to deny the importance of existing models as the foundation on which the power of law is meted out, and through which the interests of the State and the public, more recently in the guise of 'community', can be met. As evidenced in Chapters 5 and 6, traditional criminal justice, as manifested in the operational cultures of different criminal justice agencies in various settings from the police station through to the court room, continues to undergo a series of radical changes that are focused on improved service provision for victims. The needs (and rights) of victims are increasingly centre-stage in an arena that was once the sole preserve of criminal justice professionals, and, to a lesser extent, defendants/offenders who are acknowledged through reference to their rights of 'due process' in law. Calls for restorative justice, as an alternative to traditional criminal justice, have arguably been able to surface because of the victim-centred developments that have taken place in traditional criminal justice. On the other hand, restorative justice can also be constructed as a radical departure from traditional criminal justice that owes little to developments in established practice.

Debates that position one justice model against another, or that fail to reach some kind of consensus with respect to a particular model (here one thinks of current debates by some proponents of restorative justice), are best understood as affirming struggles for 'power' between competing interests. Too often these competing interests neglect to consider the damage wreaked on victims in their tug-of-war. As Chapters 4 and 7 highlight, the current philosophy and practice of justice in England and Wales are based on a traditional retributive model that is in the process of adopting aspects of restorative justice. The wholesale storming of the battlements that is proposed by some restorative advocates appears to bear little resemblance to reality, at least in the near future, in a jurisdiction which is founded on the principle of adversarial justice, and which has the highest incarceration rate in western Europe. Undeniably, restorative justice is making significant inroads in the area of juvenile crime, with, latterly, experimentation with adult offenders. Yet, once again, we have to remind ourselves that the 'inclusive' restorative justice model is not an option for many cases of victimisation where no crime is reported, no offender is found, or the crime in question is too serious. In twenty years time another justice model might be waiting in line to step in where restorative justice 'failed' or, more optimistically, a hybrid justice model, incorporating aspects of restorative justice alongside traditional justice, might be in place.

Research on 'fear of crime' and 'vulnerability', as outlined in Chapter 3, touches on issues that permeate people's lives more often than actual experiences of crime as offending or victimisation (as outlined in Chapter 2). Hence, other avenues of victim-centred research, policy and practice are just as important to follow as those that debate the benefits and costs of adopting different criminal justice models that manage the aftermath of crime which has come to the notice of 'the authorities'. As Chapter 1 reported, the manifestation of risk and insecurity in people's lives shapes how we experience the everyday of which crime/victimisation is one aspect. 'Risk management' is also the driving force behind insurance against crime and harm, as it impacts on individuals through to big business. As Chapter 5 outlines, with respect to compensation, risk management is largely the preserve of those with money. And, as Chapter 8 illustrates, while 'big business' can aim to protect itself against the financial outfall from white-collar crime, the most marginalised members of society – typically the poor – are not in a position to protect themselves through access to insurance as a form of harm (crime) prevention. As the example of sex trafficking shows, some women are coerced into taking up seemingly lucrative offers of jobs abroad in an effort to insure their own and their families' economic future against financial hardship and instability 'at home'. Yet this risky 'insurance policy' – putting oneself in the hands of traffickers – does not pay off for women who find themselves exploited and abused in situations of sexual slavery.

Echoing the refrain of human rights advocates, marginalised victims (such as trafficked women and poor victims of white-collar scams) need justice, and the criminal law and traditional forms of justice should be there to see that justice is done. While some restorative justice advocates argue for its application in 'serious cases', it seems strikingly obvious that the power imbalances in such cases, coupled with the threat of further victimisation to oneself or one's family, do not render restorative ideals and practice feasible.

On the one hand there exists a range of petty and not so petty offences that either do not come to the attention of the criminal justice authorities or are not registered and processed by them. On the other hand there are a range of serious offences – such as sex trafficking and environmental crime – that either continue to be neglected by victimology or have only recently received the attention they deserve. Much of this neglect can be attributed to the narrow focus of criminal law on personal and property crime against the individual, and on crime as a single event. Other underlying reasons for this neglect include the narrow focus of victimology on crime and victimisation as it occurs at the level of 'the local'. While victimologists and practitioners do refer to practice examples in other places and other jurisdictions, too often these examples are offered as 'good practice' with little interpretation given over to how practice might be successfully transferred from one setting to another. In turn, 'good practice' remains an under-defined and much misused term that is thrown around with little exploration of the real use to which comparative practical examples can be put.

Chapters 1 and 8 have attempted to engage the reader with the idea of victimisation as part of a bigger picture other than the one-off event, against a lone victim by an unknown offender, in time and place. Victimisation, like crime, demands contextualisation. Localised events are often part of broader considerations that reflect crime with respect to risk, insecurity and globalisation. Academic victimology, victim advocacy and social policy need to work in tandem towards a more enlightened reading and policy response to victimisation that reflects developments at the local and global level. To interpret victimisation, and criminal and social justice responses to it, in the narrow framework of domestic criminal law and criminal justice practice is to neglect international crime trends, and international instruments and bodies (such as the UN and the European Parliament), that shape domestic crime, law and practice intervention.

Academic victimology needs to be at the forefront of debates and empirically based research that can inform victim-centred policy and practice. Rather than let politics and penal populism determine victim-centred policy, informed research, undertaken with practical victim-centred initiatives, can lead the way. The politics of the moment shape how victims, as part of a 'crime package' encompassing offenders, are responded to as actors in the criminal justice process. At the present time it would appear that there is no going back to the 'bad old days' before victims were afforded due recognition in the criminal justice process. Victims, so we are told, are now centre-stage in criminal justice reform. But much of this development is taking place without enough regard for how victims themselves measure the desirability or 'success' of interventions that are supposedly 'for' them.

In England and Wales there is much that we can recommend with respect to innovative victim-centred developments – State compensation, Victim Support – but there should be no room for complacency. In thinking that victim-centred criminal justice reforms are now in place through provision of new legislation, we must not neglect to employ empirical research that can monitor the application of victim-centred initiatives to victims over time. Legislation is just one step on the road to victim-centred reform of criminal justice, and demands regular follow-ups to see whether and how it is being put into practice, and whether reforms are benefiting victims and at the same time impacting on other criminal justice actors (defendants/offenders, criminal justice personnel).

As the focus of academic interest is currently turned on restorative justice, we must ensure that traditional criminal justice practice, encompassing the police through to the courts, is not neglected as a setting for victim-centred reform as we search for alternative models of victim-centred justice. The traditional criminal justice system remains the central point of reference for most victims who engage with justice. For those victims who remain *without* justice intervention – be this traditional or restorative – other avenues of research, policy and practice intervention have yet to be explored by victimology as it currently manifests itself. Whether victimology, whose strength as a subject lies in its focus on victims of *crime*, should engage with experiences of victimisation that go beyond the boundaries of criminal law is questionable. Rather, victimological research, partnered with informed policy and practice, can continue to draw on its existing strengths – as the 'science' of victimisation – to enhance work with victims in the framework of existing and alternative justice models.

References

Adler, I. (1975) *Sisters in Crime*, New York: McGraw-Hill.

Aertsen, I. (2002) 'Editorial', *Newsletter of the European Forum for Victim–Offender Mediation and Restorative Justice*, 3(2).

Albrecht, H.J. (2002) 'Immigration, Crime and Unsafety' in A. Crawford (ed.) *Crime, Insecurity and Safety in the New Governance*, Cullompton: Willan Publishing, pp. 159–185.

Allat, P. (1984) Fear of Crime: The Effect of Improved Residential Security on a Difficult to Let Estate, *Howard Journal of Criminal Justice*, 23: 170–182.

Allen, S. (2003) 'Male Victims of Rape: Responses to a Perceived Threat to Masculinity' in C. Hoyle and R. Young (eds) *New Visions of Crime Victims*, Oxford: Hart, pp. 23–48.

Amir, M. (1971) *Patterns of Forcible Rape*, Chicago: University of Chicago Press.

Anderson, S., Kinsey, R., Loader, I. and Smith, C. (1994) *Cautionary Tales*, Aldershot: Avebury.

Ash, M. (1972) On Witnesses: A Radical Critique of Criminal Court Procedures, *Notre Dame Lawyer*, 48: 386–425.

Ashton, J., Brown, I., Senior, B. and Pease, K. (1998) Repeat Victimisation: Offender Accounts, *International Journal of Risk, Security and Crime Prevention*, 3(4): 269–279.

Ashworth, A. (1975) Sentencing in Provocation Cases, *Criminal Law Review*, 1: 3–46.

Ashworth, A. (1993) Victim Impact Statements and Sentencing, *Criminal Law Review*, 498–509.

Ashworth, A. (2000) 'Victims' Rights, Defendants' Rights and Criminal Procedure' in A. Crawford and J. Goodey (eds) *Integrating a Victim Perspective within Criminal Justice*, Aldershot: Ashgate, pp. 185–204.

Ashworth, A. (2002) 'Sentencing' in M. Maguire, R. Morgan and R. Reiner (eds) *The Oxford Handbook of Criminology* (third edition), Oxford: Oxford University Press, pp. 1076–1112.

Association of Chief Officers of Probation (ACOP) (1993) *Victim's Charter: Probation Service Responsibility for Ensuring Victims' Interests are Considered when Formulating Release Plans for Life Sentence Prisoners*, Wakefield: ACOP.

Association of Chief Officers of Probation (ACOP) (1994) *Victim's Charter*, Wakefield: ACOP.

Aye Maung, N. (1995a) 'Survey Design and Interpretation of the British Crime Survey' in M. Walker (ed.) *Interpreting Crime Statistics*, Oxford: Clarendon Press, pp. 207–227.

Aye Maung, N. (1995b) *Young People, Victimisation and the Police: British Crime Survey Findings on Experiences and Attitudes of 12 to 15 Year Olds*, Home Office Research Study 140, London: HMSO.

Baker, M.H., Nienstedt, B.C., Everett, R.S. and McClery, R. (1983) The Impact of a Crime Wave: Perceptions, Fear and Confidence in the Police, *Law and Society Review*, 17: 319–335.

Baker, R.W. (2000) 'Money Laundering and Flight Capital: The Impact of Private Banking' in *Hearings Before the Permanent Subcommittee on Investigations of the Committee on Governmental Affairs, United States Senate*, 106 Congress, first session, November 1999, Washington: US Government Printing Office, pp. 1053–1060.

Bales, K. (1999) *Disposable People: New Slavery in the Global Economy*, Berkeley, Calif.: University of California Press.

Barclay, G. and Tavares, C. (2000) *International Comparisons of Criminal Justice Statistics, 1998*, Statistical Bulletin 04/00, London: HMSO.

Barnett, R. (1977) 'Restitution: A New Paradigm of Criminal Justice' in R. Barnett and J. Hagel (eds) *Assessing the Criminal: Restitution, Retribution and the Legal Process*, Cambridge, Mass.: Ballinger, pp. 349–383.

Barry, A., Osborne, T. and Rose, N. (eds) (1996) *Foucault and Political Reason: Liberalism, Neo-Liberalism and the Rationalities of Government*, London: UCL Press.

Bauman, Z. (1998) *Globalization: The Human Consequences*, Cambridge: Polity Press.

Bazemore, G. and Walgrave, L. (1999) 'In Search of Fundamentals and an Outline for Systematic Reform' in G. Bazemore and L. Walgrave (eds) *Restorative Juvenile Justice: Repairing the Harm of Youth Crime*, Monsey, NY: Criminal Justice Press, pp. 45–74.

Beare, M. (1997) Illegal Migration: Personal Tragedies, Social Problems, or National Security Threats?, *Transnational Organized Crime*, 3(4): 11–41.

Beck, A. and Robertson, A. (2003) Crime in Russia: Exploring the Link between Victimisation and Concern about Crime, *Crime Prevention and Community Safety: An International Journal*, 5(1): 27–46.

Beck, U. (1992) *Risk Society: Towards a New Modernity*, London: Sage.

Beck, U. (2000) *What is Globalization?*, Cambridge: Polity Press.

Becker, C. (1981) 'Criminal Theories of Causation and Victims', unpublished Ph.D. thesis, University of Cambridge.

Becker, H. (1963) *Outsiders*, New York: Free Press.

Bennett, T. (1988) An Assessment of the Design, Implementation and Effectiveness of Neighbourhood Watch in London, *Howard Journal of Criminal Justice*, 27: 241–255.

BKA (1999) *Trafficking in Human Beings: Situation Report*, Wiesbaden: Bundeskriminalamt.

Block, R. (1993) A Cross-National Comparison of Victims of Crime: Victim Surveys of Twelve Countries, *International Review of Victimology*, 2: 183–207.

Blomberg, T.G., Gordon, P.W. and Chester, D. (2002) Assessment of the Program Implementation of Comprehensive Victim Services in a One-Stop Location, *International Review of Victimology*, 9: 149–174.

Bottomley, K., James, A., Clare, E. and Liebling, A. (1997) *Monitoring and Evaluation of Wolds Remand Prison*, London: Home Office.

Bottoms, A.E., Mawby, R.I. and Walker, M.A. (1987) A Localised Crime Survey in Contrasting Areas of a City, *British Journal of Criminology*, 27: 125–154.

Bottoms, A.E. and Wiles, P. (2002) 'Environmental Criminology' in M. Maguire, R. Morgan and R. Reiner (eds) *The Oxford Handbook of Criminology*, Oxford: Oxford University Press, pp. 620–656.

Bowers-Andrews, A. (1992) *Victimization and Survivor Services: A Guide to Victim Assistance*, New York: Springer.

Bowling, B. (1993) Racial Harassment and the Process of Victimisation: Conceptual and Methodological Implications for the Local Crime Survey, *British Journal of Criminology*, 33(2): 231–249.

Bowling, B. and Phillips, C. (2002) *Racism, Crime and Justice*, London: Longman.

Box, S. (1983) *Power, Crime and Mystification*, London: Tavistock.

Bradshaw, W. and Umbreit, M. (2003) Assessing Satisfaction with Victim Services: The Development and Use of the Victim Satisfaction with Offender Dialogue Scale (VSODS), *International Review of Victimology*, 10: 71–83.

Braithwaite, J. (1989) *Crime, Shame and Reintegration*, Cambridge: Cambridge University Press.

Braithwaite, J. (2000) 'Restorative Justice and Corporate Crime', paper presented at Fourth International Conference on Restorative Justice for Juveniles, Tübingen, Germany, 1–4 October.

Braithwaite, J. (2002) *Restorative Justice and Responsive Regulation*, Oxford: Oxford University Press.

Braithwaite, J. and Pettit, P. (1990) *Not Just Deserts*, Oxford: Clarendon Press.

Brienen, M.E.I. and Hoegen, E.H. (2000) *Victims of Crime in 22 European Criminal Justice Systems*, Nijmegen: Wolf Legal Productions.

Brown, S. (1998) *Understanding Youth and Crime*, Milton Keynes: Open University Press.

Brownmiller, S. (1975) *Against Our Will: Men, Women and Rape*, London: Secker and Warburg.

Burchell, G., Gordon, C. and Miller, P. (eds) (1991) *The Foucault Effect: Studies in Governmentality*, Chicago: University of Chicago Press.

Burns, P. (1980) *Criminal Injuries Compensation*, Toronto: Butterworths.

Burrows, J., Hopkins, I., Bamfield, J., Hopkins, M. and Ingram, D. (1999) *Crime Against Business in Scotland*, Edinburgh: The Scottish Executive Central Research Unit.

Cain, M. (ed.) (1989) *Growing Up Good: Policing the Behaviour of Girls in Europe*, London: Sage.

Carlen, P. (1985) *Criminal Women*, Cambridge: Polity.

Castells, M. (1998) *The Information Age: Economy, Society and Culture, Vol. III: End of Millennium*, Oxford: Basil Blackwell.

Cavadino, M. and Dignan, J. (1996) *The Penal System*, London: Sage.

Chadee, D. and Ditton, J. (2003) Are Older People Most Afraid of Crime?, *British Journal of Criminology*, 43: 417–433.

Chesney-Lind, M. (1997) *The Female Offender: Girls, Women and Crime*, Thousand Oaks, Calif.: Sage.

Christie, N. (1977) Conflicts as Property, *British Journal of Criminology*, 17(1): 1–15.

Clarke, R. (1980) Situational Crime Prevention: Theory and Practice, *British Journal of Criminology*, 20: 136–147.

Clarke, R. and Newman, J. (1997) *The Managerial State*, London: Sage.

Clarkson, C. and Morgan, R. (eds) (1995) *The Politics of Sentencing Reform*, Oxford: Clarendon Press.

Coates, R. and Gehm, J. (1989) 'An Empirical Assessment' in W. Wright and B. Galaway (eds) *Mediation and Criminal Justice*, London: Sage, pp. 251–263.

Cohen, L. and Felson, M. (1979) Social Change and Crime Rate Trends: A Routine Activity Approach, *American Sociological Review*, 44: 588–608.

Connell, R. (1987) *Gender and Power*, London: Polity Press.

Connell, R. (1995) *Masculinities*, London: Polity Press.

Cornish, D.B. and Clarke, R.V. (1987) Understanding Crime Displacement: An Application of Rational Choice Theory, *Criminology*, 25(4): 933–947.

Cossins, A. (2003) Saints, Sluts and Sexual Assault: Rethinking the Relationship Between Sex, Race and Gender, *Social and Legal Studies: An International Journal*, 12(1): 77–103.

Crawford, A. (1997) *The Local Governance of Crime: Appeals to Partnerships and Community*, Oxford: Clarendon Press.

Crawford, A. (1998) *Crime Prevention and Community Safety*, Harlow: Addison Wesley Longman.

Crawford, A. (2000) Justice de Proximité – The Growth of 'Houses of Justice' and Victim/Offender Mediation in France: A Very UnFrench Legal Response?, *Social and Legal Studies*, 9(1): 29–53.

Crawford, A. and Enterkin, J. (1999) *Victim Contact Work and the Probation Service: A Study of Service Delivery and Impact*, Leeds: Centre for Criminal Justice Studies, University of Leeds.

Crawford, A., Jones, T., Woodhouse, T. and Young, J. (1990) *Second Islington Crime Survey*, Centre for Criminology, Middlesex Polytechnic.

Crawford, A. and Newburn, T. (2003) *Youth Offending and Restorative Justice*, Cullompton: Willan Publishing.

Cressey, D.R. (1988) 'Research Implications of Conflicting Conceptions of Victimology' in P.Z. Separpvic (ed.) *Victimology: International Action and Study of Victims, Vol. I: Theoretical Issues*, papers given at the fifth international symposium on victimology, 1985, Zagreb.

Cretney, A. and Davis, G. (1997) Prosecuting Domestic Assault: Victims Failing Courts, or Courts Failing Victims?, *Howard Journal* 36(2): 146–157.

Croall, H. (1995) 'Target Women: Women's Victimization and White-Collar Crime' in R.E. Dobash, R.P. Dobash and L. Noaks (eds) *Gender and Crime*, Cardiff: University of Wales Press, pp. 227–245.

Cunneen, C. (1990) 'Zero Tolerance Policing and the Experience of New York City', *Current Issues in Criminal Justice* 10(3), pp. 299–313.

Daly, K. (2000) 'Ideals Meet Reality: Research Results on Youth Justice Conferences in South Australia', paper presented at Fourth International Conference on Restorative Justice for Juveniles, Tübingen, Germany, 1–4 October.

Daly, K. (2002) Restorative Justice: The Real Story, *Punishment and Society*, 4(1): 55–79.

Danzig, R. (1973) Towards the Creation of a Complementary Decentralized System of Criminal Justice, *Stanford Law Review*, 26: 1–54.

Davidson, N. and Goodey, J. (1991) *Street Lighting and Crime: The Hull Project*, Hull: University of Hull.

Davies, M., Croall, H. and Tyrer, J. (1995) *Criminal Justice: An Introduction to the Criminal Justice System in England and Wales*, London: Longman.

Davies, P., Francis, P. and Jupp, V. (eds) (1999) *Invisible Crimes*, London: Palgrave Macmillan.

Davis, G. (1992) *Making Amends: Mediation and Reparation in Criminal Justice*, London: Routledge.

Declaration of Leuven (1997) On the Advisability of Promoting the Restorative Approach to Juvenile Crime, *European Journal of Criminal Policy and Research*, 5(4): 118–122; *European Journal of Crime, Criminal Law and Criminal Justice*, 6(1): 421–425.

DeKeserdy, W. (1996) 'The Realist Perspective on Race, Class and Gender' in M.D. Schwarz and D. Milovanovic (eds) *Race, Gender and Class in Criminology*, New York: Garland, pp. 49–69.

Delgado, R. (2000) Goodbye to Hammurabi: Analyzing the Atavistic Appeal of Restorative Justice, *Stanford Law Review*, 52: 751–775.

Dignan, J. (1992) Repairing the Damage, *British Journal of Criminology*, 32(4): 453–472.

Dignan, J. (2000) *Restorative Justice Options for Northern Ireland: A Comparative Review*, Belfast: Northern Ireland Office.

Dignan, J. (2002) 'Reparation Orders' in B. Williams (ed.) *Reparation and Victim-Focused Social Work*, London: Jessica Kingsley, pp. 66–83.

Dignan, J. and Cavadino, M. (1996) Towards a Framework for Conceptualising and Evaluating Models of Criminal Justice from a Victim's Perspective, *International Review of Victimology*, 4: 153–182.

Dittenhoffer, T. and Ericson, R. (1983) The Victim/Offender Reconciliation Programme: A Message to Correctional Reformers, *University of Toronto Law Journal*, 33: 315–347.

Ditton, J., Bannister, J., Gilchrist, E. and Farrall, S. (1999a) Afraid or Angry? Recalibrating the 'Fear' of Crime, *International Review of Victimology*, 6: 83–99.

Ditton, J. and Farrall, S. (2000) *The Fear of Crime*, The International Library of Criminology, Criminal Justice and Penology, Aldershot: Ashgate.

Ditton, J., Farrall, S., Bannister, J., Gilchrist, E. and Pease, K. (1999b) Reactions to Victimisation: Why Has Anger Been Ignored?, *Crime Prevention and Community Safety: An International Journal*, 1(3): 37–54.

Ditton, J., Nair, G., Hunter, G. and Phillips, S. (1991) *Street Lighting and Crime: The Strathclyde Simultaneous Twin Study Site*, Glasgow: Glasgow University.

Dixon, D. (1998) Broken Windows, Zero Tolerance, and the New York Police Miracle, *Current Issues in Criminal Justice*, 10(1): 96–106.

Dixon, L. and Stern, R.K. (2003) 'Approaches for Compensating Victims of Crime: Lessons from the September 11th Attacks', paper presented at the National Roundtable on Victim Compensation, 10 June 2003, Washington DC: National Center for Victims of Crime; see www.ncvc.org.

Doak, J. (2000) Confrontation in the Courtroom: Shielding Vulnerable Witnesses from the Adversarial Showdown, *Journal of Civil Liberties*, 5(3).

Dobash, R.E. and Dobash, R. (1979) *Violence Against Wives: A Case Against the Patriarchy*, Shepton Mallet: Open Books.

Dobash, R.E. and Dobash, R.P. (eds) (1998) *Rethinking Violence Against Women*, London: Sage.

Downes, D. and Morgan, R. (2002) 'The Skeletons in the Cupboard: The Politics of Law and Order at the Turn of the Millenium' in M. Maguire, R. Morgan and R. Reiner (eds) *The Oxford Handbook of Criminology* (third edition), Oxford: Oxford University Press, pp. 286–321.

Drapkin, I. and Viano, E. (eds) (1974) *Victimology: A New Focus*, Toronto and Lexington, Mass.: Lexington Books.

Dunhill, C. (1989) *The Boys in Blue*, London: Virago.

Dünkel, F. (1996) Täter-Opfer Ausgleich: German Experiences with Mediation in a European Perspective, *European Journal on Criminal Policy and Research*, 4(4): 44–66.

Dünkel, F. and Rössner, D. (1989) 'Law and Practice of Victim/Offender Agreements' in M. Wright and B. Galaway (eds) *Mediation and Criminal Justice*, London: Sage, pp. 152–177.

Edwards, S. (1981) *Female Sexuality and the Law*, Oxford: Martin Robertson.

Ekblom, P., Law, H. and Sutton, M. (1996) *Safer Cities and Domestic Burglary*, Research Study 164, London: Home Office.

Ekblom, P. and Pease, K. (1995) 'Evaluating Crime Prevention' in M. Tonry and D.P. Farrington (eds) *Building a Safer Society: Crime and Justice: A Review of the Research*, vol. 19, Chicago: University of Chicago Press, pp. 585–662.

Elias, R. (1993) *Victims Still: The Political Manipulation of Crime Victims*, London: Sage.

Ellingworth, D., Hope, T., Osborn, D.R., Trickett, A. and Pease, K. (1997) Prior Victimisation and Crime Risk, *International Journal of Risk, Security and Crime Prevention*, 2(3): 201–214.

Ellison, L. (2001) *The Adversarial Process and the Vulnerable Witness*, Oxford: Oxford University Press.

Erez, E. (1994) Victim Participation in Sentencing: And the Debate Goes On, *International Review of Victimology*, 3(1–2): 17–32.

Erez, E. (2000) 'Integrating a Victim Perspective in Criminal Justice Through Victim Impact Statements' in A. Crawford and J. Goodey (eds) *Integrating a Victim Perspective within Criminal Justice*, Aldershot: Ashgate, pp. 165–184.

Etzioni, A. (1995) *New Communitarian Thinking*, Charlottesville: University of Virginia Press.

Europol (1996) *Situation Report on Organised Crime in the European Union*, The Hague: Europol.

Evans, D. and Shaw, D. (eds) (1989) *The Geography of Crime*, London: Routledge.

Ewald, U. (2002) Victimization in the Context of War – Some Aspects of a Macro-Victimological Research Project, *European Journal of Crime, Criminal Law and Criminal Justice*, 10(2–3): 90–97.

Falsetti, S. and Resnick, H. (1995) 'Helping the Victims of Violent Crime' in J. Freedy and S. Hobfoll (eds) *Traumatic Stress: From Theory to Practice*, New York: Plenum, pp. 263–285.

Farrell, G. (1992) Multiple Victimisation: Its Extent and Significance, *International Review of Victimology*, 2: 85–102.

Farrell, G. and Buckley, A. (1999) Evaluation of a UK Police Domestic Violence Unit using Repeat Victimisation as a Performance Indicator, *Howard Journal*, 38(1): 42–53.

Farrell, G. and Pease, K. (1997) Repeat Victim Support, *British Journal of Social Work*, 27: 101–113.

Farrington, D. and Dowds, E. (1984) Why Does Crime Decrease?, *Justice of the Peace*, 148: 506–509.

Fattah, E. (1979) Some Recent Theoretical Trends in Victimology, *Victimology: An International Journal*, 4: 198–213.

Fattah, E. (1999) 'From a Handful of Dollars to Tea and Sympathy: The Sad History of Victim Assistance' in J.J.M. van Dijk, R.G.H. van Kaam and J. Wemmers (eds) *Caring for Crime Victims*, New York: Criminal Justice Press, pp. 187–206.

Fattah, E.A. and Sacco, V.F. (1989) *Crime and Victimization of the Elderly*, New York: Springer Verlag.

Feeley, M. and Simon, J. (1992) The New Penology: Notes on the Emerging Strategy of Corrections and its Implications, *Criminology*, 30(4): 449–474.

Feeley, M. and Simon, J. (1994) 'Actuarial Justice: The Emerging New Criminal Law' in D. Nelken (ed.) *The Futures of Criminology*, London: Sage, pp. 173–201.

Felson, M. (1994) *Crime and Everyday Life: Insights and Implications for Society*, Thousand Oaks, Calif.: Pine Forge Press.

Felson, M. and Cohen, L. (1981) Modelling Crime Rates: A Criminal Opportunity Perspective, *Research in Crime and Delinquency*, 18: 138–164.

Fenwick, H. (1995) Rights of Victims in the Criminal Justice System: Rhetoric or Reality?, *Criminal Law Review*, 843–853.

Ferraro, K.F. and LaGrange, R.L. (1987) The Measurement of Fear of Crime, *Sociological Inquiry*, 57: 70–101.

Ferraro, K.F. and LaGrange, R.L. (1992) Are Older People Most Afraid of Crime? Reconsidering Differences in Fear of Victimization, *Journal of Gerontology*, 47: 233–244.

Finkelhor, D. (1997) 'The Victimization of Children and Youth' in R.C. Davis, A.J. Lurigio and W.G. Skogan (eds) *Victims of Crime*, Thousand Oaks, Calif.: Sage, pp. 86–107.

Fitzgerald, M. and Hale, C. (1996) *Ethnic Minorities, Victimisation and Racial Harassment*, Research Findings No. 39, London: Home Office.

Forrester, D., Chatterton, M. and Pease, K., with the assistance of Brown, R. (1988) *The Kirkholt Burglary Prevention Project, Rochdale*, Home Office Crime Prevention Unit, Paper No. 13, London: HMSO.

Forrester, D., Frenz, S., O'Connell, M. and Pease, K. (1990) *The Kirkholt Burglary Prevention Project: Phase II*, Home Office Crime Prevention Unit, Paper No. 23, London: HMSO.

Friday, P. (1992) 'The Faces of Victimology: Report of the General Rapporteurs, Part I' in S.B. David and G.F. Kirchhoff (eds) *International Faces of Victimology*, Mönchengladbach: WSV Publishing, pp. 1–15.

Fry, M. (1959) Justice for Victims, *Journal of Public Law*, 8: 191–194.

Fyfe, N.R. (2001) *Protecting Intimidated Witnesses*, Aldershot: Ashgate.

Fyfe, N. and McKay, H. (2000) Desparately Seeking Safety: Witnesses' Experiences of Intimidation, Protection and Relocation, *British Journal of Criminology*, 40: 675–691.

Gabriel, U. and Greve, W. (2003) The Psychology of Fear of Crime, *British Journal of Criminology*, 43: 600–614.

Garkawe, S. (2001) The Victim-Related Provisions of the Statute of the International Criminal Court: A Victimological Analysis, *International Review of Victimology*, 8: 269–289.

Garland, D. (2001) *The Culture of Control: Crime and Social Order in Contemporary Society*, Oxford: Clarendon Press.

Genn, H. (1988) 'Multiple Victimisation' in M. Maguire and J. Pointing (eds) *Victims of Crime: A New Deal?*, Buckingham: Open University Press, pp. 90–100.

Gibson, B. and Cavadino, P. (1995) *Introduction to the Criminal Justice Process*, Winchester: Waterside Press.

Giddens, A. (1991) *Modernity and Self-Identity: Self and Society in the Late Modern Age*, Cambridge: Polity.

Gilchrist, E., Bannister, J., Ditton, J. and Farrall, S. (1998) Women and the 'Fear of Crime', *British Journal of Criminology*, 38(2): 283–298.

Girling, E., Loader, I. and Sparks, R. (2000) *Crime and Social Change in Middle England: Questions of Order in an English Town*, London: Routledge.

Goldsmith, V., McGuire, P.G., Mollenkopf, J.B. and Ross, T.A. (eds) (2000) *Analyzing Crime Patterns*, New York: Sage.

Goodey, J. (1994) Fear of Crime: What Can Children Tell Us?, *International Review of Victimology*, 3: 195–210.

Goodey, J. (1996) 'Adolescence and the Socialisation of Gendered Fear' in D. Milovanovic and M. Schwarz (eds) *Race, Gender and Class in Criminology*, New York: Garland, pp. 267–291.

Goodey, J. (1997) Boys Don't Cry: Masculinities, Fear of Crime and Fearlessness, *British Journal of Criminology*, 37(3): 401–418.

Goodey, J. (1998) Examining the 'White Racist/Black Victim' Stereotype, *International Review of Victimology*, 5: 235–256.

Goodey, J. (2000a) Biographical Lessons for Criminology, *Theoretical Criminology*, 4(4): 473–498.

Goodey, J. (2000b) Non-EU Citizens' Experiences of Offending and Victimisation: The Case for Comparative European Research, *European Journal of Crime, Criminal Law and Criminal Justice*, 8(1): 13–34.

Goodey, J. (2002a) 'Compensating Victims of Violent Crime in the European Union: The Case for State Restitution' in B. Williams (ed.) *Reparation and Victim-Focused Social Work*, London: Jessica Kinglsey, pp. 16–33.

Goodey, J. (2002b) 'Whose Insecurity? Organised Crime, Its Victims and the EU' in A. Crawford (ed.) *Crime, Insecurity and Safety in the New Governance*, Cullompton: Willan Publishing, pp. 135–158.

Goodey, J. (2003) *Sex Trafficking in the European Union: Towards 'Good Practice' for Victims*, report of European Commission funded Marie Curie Research Fellowship, HPMF-CT-1999-00383.

Goodey, J. (2004a) 'Promoting Good Practice in Sex Trafficking Cases', special issue of *International Review of Victimology* on Trafficking, 11(1): 89–110.

Goodey, J. (2004b) Sex Trafficking in Women from Central and East European Countries: Promoting a 'Victim-Centred' and 'Woman-Centred' Approach to Criminal Justice Intervention, *Feminist Review*, special issue on 'Post-Communism: Women's Lives in Transition', 76, pp. 26–45.

Gottfredson, M. (1984) *Victims of Crime: The Dimensions of Risk*, Home Office Research Study 81, London: Home Office.

Grabbe, H. (2001) 'Breaking New Ground in Internal Security' in *Europe After September 11th*, London: Centre for European Reform, pp. 63–75.

Grady, A. (2002) 'Female-on-Male Domestic Abuse: Uncommon or Ignored?' in C. Hoyle and R. Young (eds) *New Visions of Crime Victims*, Oxford: Hart, pp. 71–96.

Greer, D. (ed.) (1996) *Compensating Crime Victims: A European Survey*, Freiburg im Breisgau: IUSCRIM.

Griffin, S. (1971) Rape: The All-American Crime, *Ramparts*, September: 26–35.

Griffiths, D. and Moynihan, F. (1963) Multiple Epiphysical Injuries in Babies ('Battered Baby Syndrome'), *British Medical Journal*, 11(1158).

Hale, C. (1996) Fear of Crime: A Review of the Literature, *International Review of Victimology*, 4: 79–150.

Hamill, H. (2002) 'Victims of Paramilitary Punishment Attacks in Belfast' in C. Hoyle and R. Young (eds) *New Visions of Crime Victims*, Oxford: Hart, pp. 49–69.

Hammar, T. (1990) *Democracy and the Nation State: Aliens, Denizens and Citizens in a World of International Migration*, Aldershot: Avebury.

Hanmer, J. and Saunders, S. (1984) *Well Founded Fear: A Community Study of Violence to Women*, London: Hutchinson.

Harding, J. (1996) 'Whither Restorative Justice in England and Wales? A Probation Perspective' in B. Galway and J. Hudson (eds) *Restorative Justice: International Perspectives*, Monsey, NY: Criminal Justice Press, pp. 261–270.

Herbert, D.T. and Moore, L. (1991) *Street Lighting and Crime: The Cardiff Project*, Cardiff: University of Cardiff.

Hindelang, M.J., Gottfredson, M.R. and Garofalo, J. (1978) *Victims of Personal Crime: An Empirical Foundation for a Theory of Personal Victimization*, Cambridge, Mass.: Ballinger.

Hirsch, A., von Roberts, J., Bottoms, A., Roach, K. and Schiff, M. (eds) (2003) *Restorative Justice and Criminal Justice*, Oxford: Hart Publishing.

Hobbs, D. and Dunnigham, C. (1998) 'Global Organised Crime: Context and Pretext' in V. Ruggiero, N. South and I. Taylor (eds) *The New European Criminology*, London: Routledge, pp. 289–303.

Hollway, W. and Jefferson, T. (1997) The Risk Society in an Age of Anxiety: Situating the Fear of Crime, *British Journal of Sociology*, 48(2): 255–266.

Hollway, W. and Jefferson, T. (2000) *Doing Qualitative Research Differently: Free Association, Narrative and the Interview Method*, London: Sage.

Holsti, K. (1996) *The State, War, and the State of War*, Cambridge: Cambridge University Press.

Home Office (1998) *Speaking Up for Justice*, report of the interdisciplinary working group on the treatment of vulnerable or intimidated witnesses in the criminal justice system, London: Home Office.

Honess, T. and Charman, E. (1992) *Closed Circuit Television in Public Places*, Crime Prevention Unit Paper No. 35, London: Home Office.

Hope, T. (2001) 'Crime Victimisation and Inequality in Risk Society' in R. Matthews and J. Pitts (eds) *Crime, Disorder and Community Safety*, London: Routledge.

Hope, T. and Shaw, M. (eds) (1988) *Communities and Crime Reduction*, London: HMSO.

Hope, T. and Sparks, R. (eds) (2000) *Crime, Risk and Insecurity: Law and Order in Political Discourse and Everyday Life*, London: Routledge.

Hough, M. (1995) *Anxiety About Crime: Findings from the 1994 British Crime Survey*, Research Findings No. 25, London: Home Office.

Hough, M. and Mayhew, P. (1983) *The British Crime Survey: First Report*, Home Office Research Study No. 76, London: HMSO.

Hough, M. and Tilley, N. (1998) *Auditing Crime and Disorder: Guidance for Partnerships*, Police Research Group Detection and Prevention Series No. 91, London: Home Office.

Hoyle, C., Cape, E., Morgan, R. and Sanders, A. (1998) *Evaluation of the 'One-Stop-Shop' and Victim Statement Pilot Projects*, London: Home Office.

Hoyle, C. and Sanders, A. (2000) Police Response to Victim Empowerment: From Victim Choice to Victim Empowerment?, *British Journal of Criminology*, 40: 14–36.

Hughes, R. (1994) *Culture of Complaint: The Fraying of America*, London: Harvill Press.

Ignjatović, D. (2002) Some Problems in Investigation of War Victimisation in the Territory of the Former Socialist Federal Republic of Yugoslavia, *European Journal of Crime, Criminal Law and Criminal Justice*, 10(2–3): 98–108.

International Narcotics Control Board (2004) *Chapter One of 2003 INCB report 'Drug-related crime and violence: the micro-level impact'*, Vienna: INCB.

International Organisation for Migration (1995) *Trafficking and Prostitution: The Growing Exploitation of Migrant Women from Central and Eastern Europe*, Geneva: IOM.

Jackson, John D. (2003) Justice for All: Putting Victims at the Heart of Criminal Justice?, *Journal of Law and Society*, 30(2): 309–326.

Jamieson, R. (1998) 'Towards a Criminology of War in Europe' in V. Ruggiero, N. South and I. Taylor (eds) *The New European Criminology*, London: Routledge, pp. 480–506.

Johnathan, S. (1987) The Emergence of a Risk Society: Insurance, Law and the State, *Socialist Review*, 95: 61–89.

Johnson, J., Kerper, H., Hayes, D. and Killenger, G. (1973) *The Recidivist Victim: A Descriptive Study*, Criminal Justice Monograph Vol. IV, No. 1, Institute of Contemporary Corrections and the Behavoiral Sciences, Sam Houston State University, Texas.

Johnstone, P. (1995) The Victim's Charter and the Release of Long-Term Prisoners, *Probation Journal*, 42(1): 8–12.

Johnstone, P. (1996) Probation Contact with Victims: Challenging Throughcare Practice, *Probation Journal*, 43(1): 26–28.

Jones, T., Maclean, B. and Young, J. (1986) *The Islington Crime Survey: Crime, Victimisation and Policing in Inner-City London*, London: Gower.

Joyce, E. (forthcoming) 'Expanding the International Regime on Money Laundering in Response to Transnational Organized Crime, Terrorism and Corruption' in P. Reichel (ed.) *Handbook of International Crime and Justice*, Newbury Park, Calif.: Sage.

JUSTICE (1998) *Victims in Criminal Justice*, Report of the Committee on the Role of the Victim in Criminal Justice, London: JUSTICE.

Kaiser, G., Kury, H. and Albrecht, H.J. (eds) (1991) *Victims and Criminal Justice*, Vols 50–53, Freiburg: Max-Planck Institut.

Kangaspunta, K., Joutsen, M. and Ollus, N. (1998) *Crime and Criminal Justice in Europe and North America*, Helsinki: HEUNI.

Karmen, A. (1990) *Crime Victims: An Introduction to Victimology*, Pacific Grove, Calif.: Brooks Cole.

Kartusch, A. (2001) *Reference Guide for Anti-Trafficking Legislative Review: With Particular Emphasis on South-Eastern Europe*, Vienna: Ludwig Boltzmann Institute of Human Rights/OSCE.

Kelly, L. (1987) 'The Continuum of Sexual Violence' in J. Hanmer and M. Maynard (eds) *Women, Violence and Social Control*, London: Macmillan, pp. 46–60.

Kelly, L. and Regan, L. (2000) *Stopping Traffic: Exploring the Extent of, and Responses to, Trafficking in Women for Sexual Exploitation in the UK*, Police Research Series No. 125, London: Home Office.

Kennedy, H. (1992) *Eve Was Framed*, London: Vintage.

Kenney, J.S. (2002) Metaphors of Loss: Murder, Bereavement, Gender, and Presentation of the 'Victimized' Self, *International Review of Victimology*, 9: 219–251.

Kilchling, M. and Löschnig-Gspandl, M. (2000) Legal and Practical Perspectives on Victim/Offender Mediation in Austria and Germany, *International Review of Victimology*, 7: 305–332.

Killias, M. (1990) Vulnerability: Towards a Better Understanding of a Key Variable in the Genesis of Fear of Crime, *Violence and Victims*, 5: 97–108.

Killias, M. and Clerici, C. (2000) Different Measures of Vulnerability in their Relation to Different Dimensions of Fear of Crime, *British Journal of Criminology*, 40: 437–450.

King, M. (1981) *The Framework of Criminal Justice*, London: Croom Helm.

Kinsey, R. (1984) *The Merseyside Crime Survey: First Report*, Liverpool: Merseyside County Council.

Kinsey, R. (1985) *The Merseyside Crime and Police Surveys: Final Report*, Liverpool: Merseyside Metropolitan Council.

Kinsey, R. and Anderson, S. (1992) *Crime and the Quality of Life: Public Perceptions and Experiences of Crime in Scotland: Findings from the 1988 British Crime Survey*, Scottish Office Central Research Unit.

Knox, C. (2001) The 'Deserving' Victims of Political Violence: 'Punishment' Attacks in Northern Ireland, *Criminal Justice*, 1(2): 181–199.

Knudten, R. (1992) 'A Dynamic Theory of Victimisation' in S.B. David and G.F. Kirchhoff (eds) *International Faces of Victimology*, Mönchengladbach: WSV Publishing, pp. 52–67.

Lees, S. (1996) *Carnal Knowledge: Rape on Trial*, London: Hamish Hamilton.

Lees, S. (1997) *Ruling Passions: Sexual Violence, Reputation and the Law*, Buckingham: Open University Press.

Levi, M. (1998) Organising Plastic Fraud: Enterprise Criminals and the Side-Stepping of Fraud Prevention, *Howard Journal*, 37(4): 423–438.

Levi, M. (2002) 'The Organisation of Serious Crimes' in M. Maguire, R. Morgan and R. Reiner (eds) *The Oxford Handbook of Criminology*, Oxford: Oxford University Press, pp. 878–913.

Levi, M. (2003) 'Criminal Asset Stripping – Confiscating the Proceeds of Crime in England and Wales' in A. Edwards and P. Gill (eds) *Transnational Organised Crime: Perspectives on Global Security*, London: Routledge, pp. 212–226.

Levi, M. and Sherwin, D. (2000) *Fraud – The Unmanaged Risk: An International Survey of the Effects of Fraud on Business*, London: Ernst & Young.

Levrant, S., Cullen, F.T., Fulton, B. and Wozniak, J.F. (1999) Reconsidering Restorative Justice: The Corruption of Benevolence Revisited?, *Crime and Delinquency*, 45(1): 3–27.

Lewis, R. (1998) 'Drugs, War and Crime in the Post-Soviet Balkans' in V. Ruggiero, N. South and I. Taylor (eds) *The New European Criminology*, London: Routledge, pp. 216–229.

Loader, I. and Sparks, R. (2002) 'Contemporary Landscapes of Crime, Order and Social Control: Governance, Risk and Globalization' in M. Maguire, R. Morgan and R. Reiner (eds) *The Oxford Handbook of Criminology* (third edition), Oxford: Oxford University Press, pp. 83–111.

London Borough of Newham (1987) *Crime in Newham: The Survey*, London Borough of Newham.

Łoś, M. (2002) Post-Communist Fear of Crime and the Commercialization of Security, *Theoretical Criminology*, 6(2): 165–188.

Lurigio, A.J., Skogan, W.G. and Davies, R.C. (eds) (1990) *Victims of Crime: Problems, Policies and Programs*, New York: Sage.

Mac an Ghaill, M. (1994) *The Making of Men*, Buckingham: Open University Press.

MacLeod, M., Prescott, R. and Carson, L. (1996) *Listening to Victims of Crime*, Edinburgh: Scottish Office Central Research Unit.

MacPherson, W. (1999) *The Stephen Lawrence Inquiry*, report of an inquiry by Sir William MacPherson, London: The Stationary Office, Cm 4262–1.

Madigan, L. and Gamble, N. (1991) *The Second Rape: Society's Continued Betrayal of the Victim*, New York: Lexington Books.

Maguire, M. (1980) The Impact of Burglary Upon Victims, *British Journal of Criminology*, 20: 261–275.

Maguire, M. and Corbett, C. (1987) *The Effects of Crime and the Work of Victim Support Schemes*, Aldershot: Gower.

Maguire, M. and Pointing, J. (eds) (1988) *Victims of Crime: A New Deal?*, Milton Keynes: Open University Press.

Maguire, M. and Shapland, J. (1990) 'The "Victims Movement" in Europe' in A.J. Lurigio, W.G. Skogan and R.C. Davies (eds) *Victims of Crime: Problems, Policies and Programs*, London: Sage, pp. 205–225.

Marshall, I.H. (ed.) (1997) *Minorities, Migrants and Crime*, London: Sage.

Marshall, T. (1950) *Citizenship and Social Class*, Cambridge: Cambridge University Press.

Marshall, T. (1984) *Reparation, Conciliation and Mediation: Current Projects in England and Wales*, Home Office Research and Planning Unit Paper 27, London: HMSO.

Marshall, T. (1997) 'Seeking the Whole Justice' in S. Hayman (ed.) *Repairing the Damage: Restorative Justice in Action*, London: ISTD, pp. 10–17.

Marshall, T. and Merry, S. (1990) *Crime and Accountability: Victim/Offender Mediation in Practice*, London: HMSO.

Martens, P.L. (2001) Immigrants as Victims of Crime, *International Review of Victimology*, 8: 199–216.

Mason, A. and Palmer, A. (1996) *Queer Bashing: A National Survey of Hate Crime Against Lesbians and Gays*, London: Stonewall.

Mawby, R.I. and Gill, M.L. (1987) *Crime Victims: Needs, Services and the Voluntary Sector*, London: Tavistock.

Mawby, R.I. and Walklate, S. (1994) *Critical Victimology*, London: Sage.

Maxwell, G. and Morris, A. (1993) *Families, Victims and Culture: Youth Justice in New Zealand*, Wellington: Social Policy Agency and Institute of Criminology, Victoria University of Wellington.

McEvoy, K. and Newburn, T. (eds) (2003) *Criminology, Conflict Resolution and Restorative Justice*, New York: Palgrave Macmillan.

McKeganey, N. and Norrie, J. (2000) Association Between Illegal Drugs and Weapon Carrying in Young People in Scotland: Schools' Survey, *British Medical Journal*, 320: 982–984.

McLaughlin, E., Fergusson, R., Hughes, G. and Westmarland, L. (2003) *Restorative Justice: Critical Issues*, London: Sage.

Mendelsohn, B. (1956) Une Nouvelle Branche de la Science Bio-psycho-sociale: Victimologie, *Revue Internationale de Criminologie et de Police Technique*, 10–31.

Messerschmidt, J. (1993) *Masculinities and Crime: Critique and Reconceptualization of Theory*, Lanham, Md.: Rowman and Littlefield.

Miers, D. (1978) *Responses to Victimisation*, Abingdon: Professional Books.

Mikaelsson, J. and Wergens, A. (2001) *Repairing the Irreparable*, Umeå: Swedish Crime Victim Compensation and Support Authority.

Milivojević, S. (1999) Domestic Violence During NATO Aggression on FRY, 2 *Temida*, 45–48.

Mirrlees-Black, C. (1998) *Domestic Violence: Findings from a New British Crime Survey Self-Completion Questionnaire*, Home Office Research Study No. 192, London: HMSO.

Mirrlees-Black, C. and Allen, J. (1998) *Concern About Crime: Findings from the 1998 British Crime Survey*, Research Findings No. 83, London: Home Office.

Mirrlees-Black, C. and Byron, C. (1999) *Domestic Violence: Findings from the BCS Self-Completion Questionnaire*, Research Findings No. 86, London: Home Office.

Mirrlees-Black, C., Mayhew, P. and Percy, A. (1996) *The British Crime Survey: England and Wales*, Statistical Bulletin 19, London: Home Office.

Mirrlees-Black, C. and Ross, A. (1995) *Crime Against Retail and Manufacturing Premises: Findings from the 1994 Commercial Victimisation Survey*, London: HMSO.

Mitsilegas, V. (2003) 'Countering the Chameleon Threat of Dirty Money: "Hard" and "Soft" Law in the Emergence of a Global Regime Against Money Laundering and Terrorist Finance' in A. Edwards and P. Gill (eds) *Transnational Organised Crime: Perspectives on Global Security*, London: Routledge, pp. 195–211.

Moody, S. (2003) 'What Victims Want to Know: Information Needs and the Right to Information', paper presented at the Eleventh International Symposium on Victimology, 13–18 July, Stellenbosch, South Africa.

Morgan, R. and Sanders, A. (1999) *The Uses of Victim Statements*, London: Home Office.

Morris, A. (1999) 'Key Findings from the New Zealand Women's Safety Survey' in J.J.M. van Dijk, R.G.H. van Kaam and J. Wemmers (eds) *Caring for Victims of Crime*, selected proceedings of the ninth international symposium on victimology, New York: Criminal Justice Press, pp. 71–77.

Morris, A., Maxwell, G. and Shepherd, P. (1997) *Being a Youth Advocate: An Analysis of their Roles and Responsibilities*, Wellington: Institute of Criminology, Victoria University of Wellington.

Morris, A. and Maxwell, G. (2000) 'The Practice of Family Group Conferences in New Zealand: Assessing the Place, Potential and Pitfalls of Restorative Justice' in A. Crawford and J. Goodey (eds) *Integrating a Victim Perspective within Criminal Justice: International Debates*, Aldershot: Ashgate, pp. 207–225.

Morris, T. and Blom-Cooper, L. (1964) *A Calendar of Murder*, London: Michael Joseph.

Morrison, J. (1998) *The Cost of Survival: The Trafficking of Refugees to the UK*, London: Refugee Council.

Mulcahy, L. (2000) The Devil and the Deep Blue Sea? A Critique of the Ability of Community Mediation to Suppress and Facilitate Participation in Civil Life, *Law and Society*, 27(1): 133–150.

Nadar, L. and Todd, H. (eds) (1978) *The Disputing Process: Law in Ten Societies*, New York: Columbia University Press.

Nagel, W.H. (1963) The Notion of Victimology in Criminology, *Excerpta Criminologica*, 3: 245–247.

Nelken, D. (ed.) (1997) *Comparing Legal Cultures*, Aldershot: Dartmouth.

Nelken, D. (2002) 'White-Collar Crime' in M. Maguire, R. Morgan and R. Reiner (eds) *The Oxford Handbook of Criminology*, Oxford: Oxford University Press, pp. 844–877.

Nettleton, H., Walklate, S. and Williams, B. (1997) 'The Politicisation of Work with Victims by the Probation Service in England and Wales, and the Marginalisation of Feminist and Self-Help Victims' Groups', paper presented at the Ninth International Symposium on Victimology, Amsterdam.

Newburn, T. et al. (2001) *The Introduction of Referral Orders into the Youth Justice System: Second Interim Report*, RDS Occasional Paper No. 73, London: Home Office.

Newburn, T. and Stanko, E.A. (1995) 'When Men Are Victims: The Failure of Victimology' in T. Newburn and E.A. Stanko (eds) *Just Boys Doing Business?*, London: Routledge, pp. 153–165.

Newman, O. (1972) *Defensible Space*, New York: Macmillan.

Nikolić-Ristanović, V. (ed.) (2000) *Women, Violence and War*, Budapest: Central European University Press.

Nikolić-Ristanović, V. (2002) War and Post-War Victimization of Women, *European Journal of Crime, Criminal Law and Criminal Justice*, 10(2–3): 138–145.

Norris, F. and Kaniasty, K. (1994) Psychological Distress Following Criminal Victimization in the General Population: Cross-Sectional, Longitudinal, and Prospective Analyses, *Journal of Consulting and Clinical Psychology*, 62: 111–123.

O'Connell, T. (1995) 'Responding to Crime: Practice of Reintegrative Shaming' in C. Martin (ed.) *Resolving Crime in the Community: Mediation in Criminal Justice*, London: ISTD, pp. 15–21.

O'Donnell, I. and Edgar, K. (1996) *Victimisation in Prisons*, RDS No. 37, London: Home Office.

O'Donnell, I. and Edgar, K. (1998) Routine Victimisation in Prisons, *Howard Journal*, 37(3): 266–279.

O'Mahoney, D., Chapman, T. and Doak, J. (2002) *Restorative Cautioning: A Study of Police Based Restorative Cautioning in Northern Ireland*, Research and Statistical Series Report No. 4, Belfast: Northern Ireland Office.

Pain, R. (1991) Space, Sexual Violence and Social Control: Integrating Geographical and Feminist Analyses of Women's Fear of Crime, *Progress in Human Geography*, 15: 415–431.

Pain, R. (1995) Elderly Women and Fear of Violent Crime: The Least Likely Victims?, *British Journal of Criminology*, 35(4): 584–598.

Pain, R. (2001) Gender, Race, Age and Fear of Crime, *Urban Studies* 38(5–6): 899–913.

Painter, K. (1989) *Crime Prevention and Public Lighting with Special Focus on Women and Elderly People*, London: Middlesex Polytechnic.

Painter, K. and Tilley, N. (eds) (1999) *Surveillance of Public Space: CCTV, Street Lighting and Crime Prevention*, Monsey, NY: Criminal Justice Press.

Palmer, D. (1997) When Tolerance is Zero: Is This the Future of Policing and Crime Prevention?, *Alternative Law Journal*, 22(5): 232–236.

Pantazis, C. (2000) 'Fear of Crime', Vulnerability and Poverty, *British Journal of Criminology*, 40: 414–436.

Pawson, R. and Tilley, N. (1994) What Works in Evaluation Research?, *British Journal of Criminology*, 34: 291–306.

Pearce, F. (1990) *Second Islington Crime Survey: Commercial and Conventional Crime in Islington*, Enfield: Centre for Criminology, University of Middlesex.

Pearson, E. (2002) *Human Traffic: Human Rights*, London: Anti-Slavery International.

Pease, K. (1991) The Kirkholt Project: Preventing Burglary on a British Public Housing Estate, *Security Journal*, 2: 73–77.

Pease, K. (1998) *Repeat Victimistion: Taking Stock*, Police Research Group Crime Detection and Prevention Series Paper 90, London: Home Office.

Pease, K. (ed.) (1999) *Uses of Criminal Statistics*, Aldershot: Ashgate.

Pease, K. and Laycock, G. (1999) *Revictimisation: Reducing the Heat on Hot Victims*, Trends and Issues in Crime and Criminal Justice Series No. 128, Canberra: Australian Institute of Criminology.

Phillips, C. and Sampson, A. (1998) Preventing Repeated Racial Victimization, *British Journal of Criminology*, 38(1): 124–144.

Piva, P. (1996) 'Italy' in D. Greer (ed.) *Compensating Crime Victims: A European Survey*, Freiburg im Breisgau: IUSCRIM, pp. 373–399.

Plotnikoff, J. and Woolfson, R. (1998) *Witness Care in Magistrates Courts and the Youth Court*, Research and Statistics Directorate No. 68, London: Home Office.

Police Magazine (2003) 'Minor Crime? Major Problem!', *Police Magazine*, January 2003, www.polfed.org/magazine/02_2003.

Préfontaine, D. (2000) *The Victim in the Parole Process*, Tenth International Symposium on Victimology, Montreal, August 2000.

Presser, L. and Gaarder, E. (2000) Can Restorative Justice Reduce Battering? Some Preliminary Considerations, *Social Justice*, 27(1): 175–195.

Quinney, R. (1972) Who Is the Victim?, *Criminology*, November: 309–329.

Radford, J. and Russell, D. (eds) (1992) *Femicide: The Politics of Women Killing*, Buckingham: Open University Press.

Ready, J., Weisburd, D. and Farrell, G. (2002) The Role of Crime Victims in American Policing: Findings from a National Survey of Police and Victim Organizations, *International Review of Victimology*, 9: 175–195.

Resick, P.A. and Nishith, P. (1997) 'Sexual Assault' in R.C. Davis, A.J. Lurigio and W.G. Skogan (eds) *Victims of Crime*, Thousand Oaks, Calif.: Sage, pp. 27–52.

Rigakos, G. (1999) Risk Society and Actuarial Criminology: Prospects for a Critical Discourse, *Canadian Journal of Criminology*, 41(2): 137–150.

Robinson, M. (1998) Burglary Revictimization, *British Journal of Criminology*, 38(1): 78–87.

Rock, P. (1993) *The Social World of an English Crown Court*, Oxford: Clarendon Press.

Rock, P. (ed.) (1994) *Victimology*, Aldershot: Dartmouth.

Rock, P. (1998a) *After Homicide*, Oxford: Clarendon Press.

Rock, P. (1998b) Murderers, Victims and Survivors, *British Journal of Criminology*, 38(2): 185–200.

Rock, P. (2002) 'On Becoming a Victim' in C. Hoyle and R. Young (eds) *New Visions of Crime Victims*, Oxford: Hart, pp. 1–22.

Ruback, R.B. and Thompson, M.P. (2001) *Social and Psychological Consequences of Violent Victimisation*, Thousand Oaks, Calif.: Sage.

Ruggiero, V. (1992) 'Realist Criminology: A Critique' in R. Matthews and J. Young (eds) *Issues in Realist Criminology*, London: Sage, pp. 123–140.

Salzinger, S., Feldman, R.S. and Stockhammer, T. (2002) An Ecological Framework for Understanding Risk of Exposure to Community Violence and the Effects of Exposure of Children and Adolescents, *Aggression and Violent Behavior*, 7: 423–451.

Sampson, A. and Phillips, C. (1992) *Multiple Victimisation: Racial Attacks on an East London Estate*, Police Research Group Crime Prevention Unit Series No. 36, London: HMSO.

Sanders, A. (2002) 'Victim Participation in an Exclusionary Criminal Justice System', in C. Hoyle and R. Young (eds) *New Visions of Crime Victims*, Oxford: Hart Publishing, pp. 197–222.

Sanders, A. and Young, R. (2001) Discontinuances, The Rights of Victims and the Remedy of Freedom, *New Law Journal*, 19 January 2001.

Sarat, A. (1997) Vengeance, Victims and the Identities of Law, *Social and Legal Studies*, 6(2): 163–189.

Schafer, S. (1968) *The Victim and His Criminal*, New York: Random House.

Schuck, P.H. (2003) 'Some Thoughts on Compensating Victims', paper presented at the National Roundtable on Victim Compensation, 10 June 2003, Washington DC: National Center for Victims of Crime; see: www.ncvc.org.

Schwendinger, H. and Schwendinger, J. (1970) Defenders of Order or Guardians of Human Rights?, *Issues in Criminology*, 123–197.

Sebba, L. (1982) The Victim's Role in the Penal Process, *American Journal of Comparative Law*, 30(2): 217–240.

Sebba, L. (1996) *Third Parties: Victims and the Criminal Justice System*, Columbus: Ohio State University Press.

Sebba, L. (2000) 'The Individualization of the Victim: From Positivism to Postmodernism', in A. Crawford and J. Goodey (eds) *Integrating a Victim Perspective within Criminal Justice*, Aldershot: Ashgate, pp. 55–76.

Sebba, L. (2001) On the Relationship Between Criminological Research and Social Policy: The Case of Crime Victims, *Criminal Justice*, 1(1): 27–58.

Shapland, J. (1984) Victims, the Criminal Justice System and Compensation, *British Journal of Criminology*, 24(2): 131–149.

Shapland, J. (2000) 'Victim and Criminal Justice: Creating Responsible Criminal Justice Agencies', in A. Crawford and J. Goodey (eds) *Integrating a Victim Perspective within Criminal Justice*, Aldershot: Ashgate, pp. 147–164.

Shapland, J., Willmore, J. and Duff, P. (1985) *Victims and the Criminal Justice System*, Aldershot: Gower.

Shearing, C. and Wood, J. (2003) Nodal Governance, Democracy, and the New 'Denizens', *Journal of Law and Society*, 30(3): 400–419.

Shepherd, J. and Lisles, C. (1998) Towards Multi-Agency Violence Protection and Victim Support, *British Journal of Criminology*, 38(3): 351–370.

Sherman, L., Gartin, P. and Buerger, M. (1989) Hot Spots of Predatory Crime: Routine Activities and the Criminology of Place, *Criminology*, 27(1): 27–55.

Sherman, L. and Strang, H. (1997) 'The Right Kind of Shame for Crime Prevention', RISE Working Papers 1, Canberra: Australian National University.

Sim, J. (1994) 'Tougher Than the Rest? Men in Prison' in T. Newburn and E.A. Stanko (eds) *Just Boys Doing Business? Men, Masculinities and Crime*, London: Routledge, pp. 100–117.

Simon, J. (1988) The Ideological Effects of Actuarial Practices, *Law and Society Review*, 22(4): 772–800.

Simon, J. (1997) 'Governing Through Crime' in L. Friedman and G. Fisher (eds) *The Crime Conundrum: Essays on Criminal Justice*, Boulder, Colo.: Westview.

Singh Makkar, S.P. and Friday, P. (eds) (1995) *Global Perspectives in Victimology*, Jalandhar, India: ABS Publications (export edition).

Slapper, G. and Tombs, S. (1999) *Corporate Crime*, Harlow: Longman.

Smart, C. (1990) 'Feminist Approaches to Criminology or Postmodern Woman Meets Atavistic Man' in L. Gelsthorpe and A. Morris (eds) *Feminist Perspectives in Criminology*, Milton Keynes: Open University Press, pp. 70–84.

Smart, C. and Smart, B. (eds) (1978) *Women, Sexuality and Social Control*, London: Routledge.

Smith, D. (1997) 'Ethnic Origins, Crime and Criminal Justice' in M. Maguire, R. Morgan and R. Reiner (eds) *The Oxford Handbook of Criminology* (second edition), Oxford: Clarendon, pp. 703–759.

Smith, R.G. (1999) *Organizations as Victims of Fraud, and How They Deal With It*, Trends and Issues in Crime and Criminal Justice No. 127, Canberra: Australian Institute of Criminology.

Smith, W.R., Torstensson, M. and Johansson, K. (2001) Perceived Risk and Fear of Crime: Gender Differences in Contextual Sensitivity, *International Review of Victimology*, 8: 159–181.

Soothill, K. and Walby, S. (1991) *Sex Crime in the News*, London: Routledge.

South, N. (1998) 'Corporate and State Crimes Against the Environment' in V. Ruggiero, N. South and I. Taylor (eds) *The New European Criminology*, London: Routledge, pp. 443–461.

Sparks, R. (1982) *Research on Victims of Crime: Accomplishments, Issues, and New Directions*, Rockville: US Department of Health and Human Services.

Sparks, R., Genn, H. and Dodd, D. (1977) *Surveying Victims: A Study of the Measurement of Criminal Victimization*, Chichester: John Wiley and Sons.

Spencer, J. and Flin, R. (1993) *The Evidence of Children: The Law and the Psychology*, London: Blackstone.

Spencer, J. and Spencer, M. (2001) *Witness Protection and the Integrity of the Criminal Trial*, Second World Conference on Investigation of Crime, Institute for Human Rights and Criminal Justice Studies, Durban, December.

Stanko, E. (1988) 'Hidden Violence Against Women' in M. Maguire and J. Pointing (eds) *Victims of Crime: A New Deal?*, Buckingham: Open University Press, pp. 40–46.

Stanko, E.A. (1990) *Everyday Violence*, London: Pandora.

Stanko, E.A. and Hobdell, K. (1993) Assault on Men: Masculinity and Male Victimization, *British Journal of Criminology*, 33(3): 400–415.

Stenson, K. and Sullivan, R. (eds) (2001) *Crime, Risk and Justice: The Politics of Crime Control in Liberal Democracies*, Cullompton: Willan Publishing.

Strang, H. and Sherman, L. (1997) 'The Victim's Perspective', RISE Working Papers 2, Canberra: Australian National University.

Taylor, I., Evans, K. and Fraser, P. (1996) *A Tale of Two Cities: A Study in Manchester and Sheffield*, London: Routledge.

Taylor, I., Walton, P. and Young, J. (1973) *The New Criminology*, London: Routledge and Kegan Paul.

Trickett, A., Osborn, D., Seymour, J. and Pease, K. (1992) What is Different About High Crime Areas?, *British Journal of Criminology*, 32(1): 81–89.

Truman, C., Bewley, B., Hayes, C. and Boulton, D. (1994) *Lesbians' and Gay Men's Experiences of Crime and Policing: An Exploratory Study*, Manchester: Manchester Metropolitan University.

Tudor, B. (2000) 'Mediation and the Victims of Violent Crime: A Practitioner's View' in H. Kemshall and J. Pritchard (eds) *Good Practice in Working with Victims of Violence*, London: Jessica Kingsley Publishers, pp. 119–127.

Tulloch, M. (2000) The Meaning of Age Differences in the Fear of Crime, *British Journal of Criminology*, 40: 451–467.

Turnbill, P. (1997) The Fusion of Immigration and Crime in the European Union: Problems of Co-operation and the Fight Against the Trafficking in Women, *Transnational Organized Crime*, 3(4), 189–213.

UNODCCP (United Nations Office for Drug Control and Crime Prevention) (1998) *Financial Havens, Banking Secrecy and Money-Laundering*, Vienna: UNODCCP.

UNODCCP (United Nations Office for Drug Control and Crime Prevention) (1999a) *Handbook on Justice for Victims*, New York: UN.

UNODCCP (United Nations Office for Drug Control and Crime Prevention) (1999b) *Guide for Policymakers*, New York: UN.

UNODCCP (United Nations Office for Drug Control and Crime Prevention) (2002) *A Participatory Handbook for Youth Drug Abuse Prevention Programmes*, Vienna: UNODCCP.

US Department of Justice (1999) *Crime Victim Compensation Program Directory: 1998–1999*, Washington DC: Office for Victims of Crime.

Valentine, G. (1989a) 'Women's Fear of Male Violence in Public Space', unpublished PhD thesis, University of Reading, UK.

Valentine, G. (1989b) The Geography of Women's Fear, *Area*, 21: 385–390.

Valentine, G. (1990) Women's Fear and the Design of Public Space, *Built Environment*, 16: 279–287.

Valentine, G. (1997a) My Son's a Bit Dizzy. My Wife's a Bit Soft. Gender, Children and Cultures of Parenting, *Journal of Gender, Place and Culture*, 4(1): 37–62.

Valentine, G. (1997b) 'Oh yes you can', 'Oh no you can't': Children and Parents' Understanding of Kids' Competence to Negotiate Public Space Safely, *Antipode*, 29(1): 65–89.

Van Dijk, J.J.M. (1985) *Regaining a Sense of Community and Order*, General Report of the Sixteenth Criminological Research Conference of the European Committee on Crime Problems, The Hague: Dutch Ministry of Justice.

Van Dijk, J.J.M. (1988) 'Ideological Trends Within the Victims Movement: An International Perspective' in M. Maguire and J. Pointing (eds) *Victims of Crime: A New Deal?*, Milton Keynes: Open University Press, pp. 115–126.

Van Dijk, J.J.M. (1992) 'Towards a Research-Based Victim Policy: Report of the General Rapporteurs, Part II' in S.B. David and G.F. Kirchhoff (eds) *International Faces of Victimology*, Mönchengladbach: WSV Publishing, pp. 16–29.

Van Dijk, J.J.M. (1999) 'Introducing Victimology' in J.J.M. van Dijk, R.G.H. van Kaam and J. Wemmers (eds) *Caring for Crime Victims*, New York: Criminal Justice Press, pp. 1–12.

Van Dijk, J., Mayhew, P. and Killias, M. (1990) *Experiences of Crime Across the World: Key Findings of the 1989 International Crime Survey*, The Netherlands: Kluwer.

Van Kesteren, J., Mayhew, P. and Nieuwbeerta, P. (2000) *Criminal Victimisation in Seventeen Industrialised Countries: Key Findings from the 2000 International Crime Victims Survey*, The Hague: WODC.

Viano, E. (ed.) (1989) *Crime and Its Victims*, New York: Hemisphere Publishing Corporation.

Victim Support (1993) *Compensating the Victim of Crime*, report of an independent working party, London: Victim Support.

Von Hentig, H. (1948) *The Criminal and His Victim: Studies in the Sociobiology of Crime*, New Haven: Yale University Press.

Walgrave, L. (2000) 'Extending the Victim Perspective Towards a Systematic Restorative Justice' in A. Crawford and J. Goodey (eds) *Integrating a Victim Perspective within Criminal Justice: International Debates*, Aldershot: Ashgate, pp. 253–284.

Walklate, S. (1989) *Victimology: The Victim and the Criminal Justice Process*, London: Unwin and Hyman.

Walklate, S. (1995) *Gender and Crime*, London: Prentice Hall.

Walklate, S. (2000) 'From the Politicization to the Politics of the Crime Victim' in H. Kemshall and J. Pritchard (eds) *Good Practice in Working with Victims of Violent Crime*, London: Jessica Kingsley, pp. 10–19.

Walklate, S. (2002) 'Victim Impact Statements: Voices to be Heard in the Criminal Justice Process?,' in B. Williams (ed.) *Reparation and Victim-Focused Social Work*, Aldershot: Ashgate, pp. 146–159.

Weiss, C.H. (1987) 'The Diffusion of Social Science Research to Policymakers: An Overview' in G.B. Melton (ed.) *Reforming the Law: Impact of Child Development Research*, New York: Guildford Press, pp. 63–85.

Wemmers, J. (1996) *Victims in the Criminal Justice System*, Amsterdam: Kugler.

Wikström, P.O. and Dolmén, L. (2001) Urbanisation, Neighbourhood Social Integration, Informal Social Control, Minor Social Disorder, Victimisation and Fear of Crime, *International Review of Victimology*, 8: 121–140.

Williams, B. (1996) The Probation Service and Victims of Crime: Paradigm Shift or Cop-Out?, *Journal of Social Welfare and Family Law*, 18(4): 461–474.

Williams, B. (1999) *Working with Victims of Crime: Policies, Politics and Practice*, London: Jessica Kingsley Publishers.

Williams, K. (1983) *Community Resources for Victims of Crime*, Research and Planning Unit Paper 14, London: Home Office.

Willis, P. (1977) *Learning to Labour*, Aldershot: Saxon House.

Wilson, J.Q. and Kelling, G. (1982) Broken Windows: The Police and Neighbourhood Safety, *Atlantic Monthly*, March: 29–37.

Winfree, L.T. (2000) 'Peacemaking and Community Harmony: Lessons (and Admonitions) from the Navajo Peacemaking Courts', paper presented at Fourth International Conference on Restorative Justice for Juveniles, Tübingen, Germany, 1–4 October.

Winkel, F.W. (1998) Fear of Crime and Criminal Victimization, *British Journal of Criminology*, 38(3): 473–484.

Wittebrood, K. and Nieuwbeerta, P. (2000) Criminal Victimization During One's Life Course: The Effects of Previous Victimization and Patterns of Routine Activities, *Journal of Research in Crime and Delinquency*, 37(1): 91–122.

Wolfgang, M.E. (1957) Victim-Precipitated Criminal Homicide, *Journal of Criminal Law and Criminology and Police Science*, 48: 1–11.

Wolfgang, M.E. (1958) *Patterns of Criminal Homicide*, Philadelphia: University of Pennsylvania Press.

Woltman, H., Turner, A. and Bushery, J. (1980) A Comparison of Three Mixed-Mode Interviewing Procedures in the National Crime Survey, *Journal of the American Statistical Association*, 75: 534–543.

Woodiwiss, M. (2001) *Organized Crime and American Power: A History*, Toronto: University of Toronto Press.

Wortman, C.B., Battle, E.S., Parr Lemkau, J. (1997) 'Coming to Terms with the Sudden, Traumatic Death of a Spouse or Child' in R.C. Davis, A.J. Lurigio and W.G. Skogan (eds) *Victims of Crime*, Thousand Oaks, Calif.: Sage, pp. 108–133.

Wright, M. (1991) *Justice for Victims and Offenders*, Milton Keynes: Open University Press.

Young, J. (1997) 'Left Realist Criminology: Radical in its Analysis, Realist in its Policy' in M. Maguire, R. Morgan and R. Reiner (eds) *The Oxford Handbook of Criminology* (second edition), Oxford: Clarendon Press, pp. 473–498.

Young, J. (1999) *The Exclusive Society: Social Exclusion, Crime and Difference in Late Modernity*, London: Sage.

Young, J. (2000) 'The Labour Party and Social Exclusion: Crime, Indiscipline and Salvation through Labour', paper presented to the American Society of Criminology Conference, San Francisco, November 2000.

Young, J. (2002) 'Crime and Social Exclusion' in M. Maguire, R. Morgan and R. Reiner (eds) *The Oxford Handbook of Criminology* (third edition), Oxford: Oxford University Press, pp. 457–490.

Young, M. (1999) 'Justice for All – Even the Victims' in J.J.M. van Dijk, R.G.H. van Kaam and J. Wemmers (eds) *Caring for Crime Victims*, New York: Criminal Justice Press, pp. 179–186.

Young, R. (2000) 'Integrating a Multi-Victim Perspective into Criminal Justice Through Restorative Justice Conferences' in A. Crawford and J. Goodey (eds) *Integrating a Victim Perspective within Criminal Justice: International Debates*, Aldershot: Ashgate, pp. 227–251.

Young, R. (2002) 'Testing the Limits of Restorative Justice: The Case of Corporate Victims' in C. Hoyle and R. Young (eds) *New Visions of Crime Victims*, Oxford: Hart, pp. 133–172.

Young, R. and Goold, B. (1999) Restorative Police Cautioning in Aylesbury: From Degrading to Reintegrative Shaming Ceremonies?, *Criminal Law Review*, 126–138.

Zauberman, R. (2000) 'Victims as Consumers of the Criminal Justice System?' in A. Crawford and J. Goodey (eds) *Integrating a Victim Perspective within Criminal Justice*, Aldershot: Ashgate, pp. 37–53.

Zehr, H. (1990) *Changing Lenses*, Scottdale, Pa.: Herald Press.

Ziegenhagen, E. (1976) The Recidivist Victim of Violent Crime, *Victimology: An International Journal*, 1: 538–550.

Zilli, L. (2002) The Crime of Rape in the Case Law of the Strasbourg Institutions, *Criminal Law Forum*, 13: 245–265.

Index